Apple Pro Training Series
Logic Pro X

David Nahmani

D1211355

Apple
Certified

Apple Pro Training Series: Logic Pro X
David Nahmani
Copyright © 2014 by David Nahmani

Peachpit Press
www.peachpit.com

To report errors, please send a note to errata@peachpit.com.
Peachpit Press is a division of Pearson Education.

Apple Series Editor: Lisa McClain
Editor: Bob Lindstrom
Production Coordinator: Kim Elmore, Happenstance Type-O-Rama
Technical Editor: Robert Brock
Apple Project Manager: Shane Ross
Apple Reviewer: Shane Ross
Copy Editor: Darren Meiss
Technical Reviewer: John Moores
Proofreader: Darren Meiss
Compositor: Cody Gates, Happenstance Type-O-Rama
Indexer: Jack Lewis
Cover Illustration: Paul Mavrides
Cover Production: Cody Gates, Happenstance Type-O-Rama

ISBN 13: 978-0-321-96759-6
ISBN 10: 0-321-96759-3
9 8 7 6 5 4 3 2 1
Printed and bound in the United States of America

Acknowledgments My deepest gratitude to the artists and producers who agreed to provide their Logic sessions for this book: Distant Cousins for their songs "Raise It Up" and "BIG," Televisor for their song "Alliance," and Matt McJunkins for helping me write and produce the song "Little Lady."

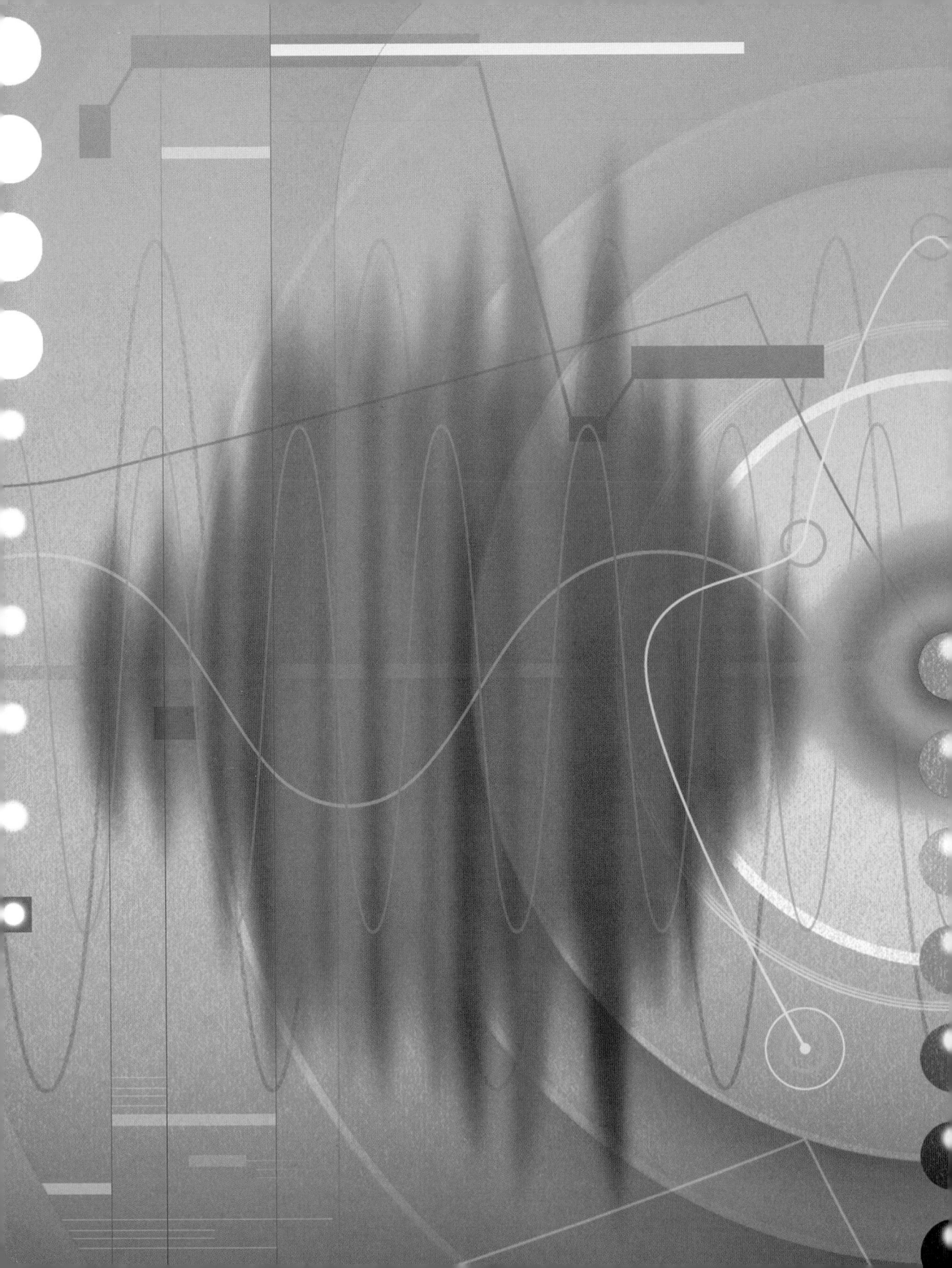

Contents at a Glance

Table of Contents

Working with Virtual Instruments

Building a Song

Mixing and Automating a Song

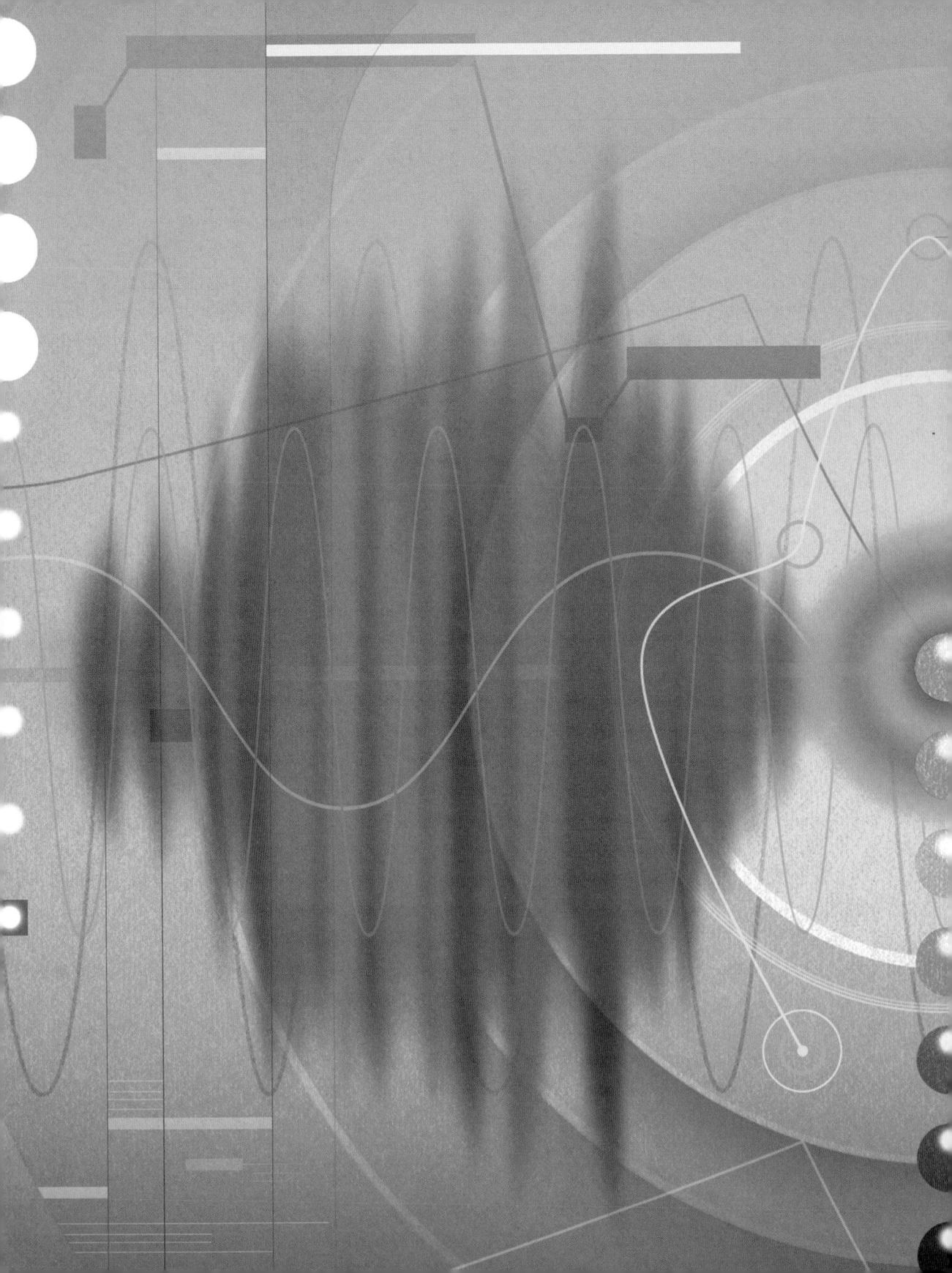

Getting Started

Welcome to the official Apple Pro Training Series course for Logic Pro X. This book is a comprehensive introduction to professional music production with Logic Pro X. It uses real-world music and hands-on exercises to teach you how to record, edit, arrange, mix, produce, and polish audio and MIDI files in a professional workflow. So let's get started!

The Methodology

This book takes a hands-on approach to learning the software, so you'll be working through the project files and media you download from www.peachpit.com. It's divided into lessons that introduce the interface elements and ways of working with them, building progressively until you can comfortably grasp the entire application and its standard workflows.

Each lesson in this book is designed to support the concepts learned in the preceding lesson, and first-time readers should go through the book from start to finish. However each lesson is self-contained, so when you need to review a topic, you can quickly jump to any lesson.

The book is designed to guide you through the music production process as it teaches Logic. The lessons are organized into four sections.

Lessons 1–3: Exploring the Interface and Working with Real Instruments

In this section, you'll explore the fundamentals of Logic Pro X, and learn to record and edit audio.

Lesson 1 starts you out with an overview of the entire process. You'll become familiar with the interface and the various ways to navigate a project; use Apple loops to build a song from scratch; and then arrange, mix, and export the song to an MP3 file.

Lessons 2 and 3 dive deeper into typical situations you may encounter when recording from microphones or other audio sources. You'll edit recordings to select the best portions of multiple takes, remove clicks, align recordings, and even reverse a recording to create a special effect.

Lessons 4–6: Working with Virtual Instruments

Lesson 4 describes how to produce a virtual drummer performance using the new Drummer and Drum Kit Designer features. You will choose the right drummer for the project, swap a drum kit with the kit of another drummer, edit the patterns, change which kit elements the drummer plays, shape an interpretation, and precisely control where fills are placed.

Lessons 5 and 6 immerse you in using software instruments. After choosing virtual instruments and recording MIDI performances, you'll map Smart Controls to various plug-ins and assign them to your MIDI controller. Using the free Logic Remote app, you'll control Logic from your iPad, and then create virtual performances in MIDI editors using your mouse or your MIDI keyboard.

Lessons 7–8: Building a Song

In Lessons 7 and 8, you'll apply Flex editing to precisely adjust the timing and pitch of notes in an audio recording. Varispeed will allow you to work with your project at different tempos. You'll add tempo changes and tempo curves to a project, match the tempos of multiple tracks, and make a track follow the groove of another track. Also covered are tuning a vocal recording, editing a project's regions in the workspace to complete an arrangement, and adding and removing sections of a project.

Lessons 9–10: Mixing and Automating a Song

Lessons 9 and 10 instruct you in mixing audio and MIDI files into a final project: adding audio effects, adjusting levels, panning, EQing, adding delay and reverb, automating the mix by creating automation curves on your screen, and altering parameter values in real time with the mouse or a MIDI controller.

Appendix A describes how to use external MIDI devices, and Appendix B lists a wealth of useful keyboard shortcuts.

System Requirements

Before using *Apple Pro Training Series: Logic Pro X,* you should have a working knowledge of your Mac and the Mac OS X operating system. Make sure that you know how to use the mouse and standard menus and commands; and also how to open, save, and close files. If you need to review these techniques, see the printed or online documentation included with your system.

Logic Pro X and the lessons in this book require the following system resources:

▶   Mac computer with an Intel processor, including:

4 GB of RAM

Display with 1280 x 768 or higher resolution

Mac OS X v10.8.4 or later

Minimum 40 GB of disk space to install Logic Pro X and its default media content

High-speed Internet connection for installation

▶   A USB-connected MIDI keyboard (or compatible MIDI keyboard and interface) to play software instruments

▶   A low-latency multi-I/O audio interface (highly recommended for audio recording)

▶   An iPad (optional, for controlling Logic using the Logic Remote iPad app)

Preparing Your Logic Workstation

The exercises in this book require that you install Logic Pro X along with its default media content. If you have not yet installed Logic, you may purchase it from the App Store. When your purchase is completed, Logic Pro X will automatically be installed on your hard drive.

All the instructions and descriptions in this book assume that you installed Logic Pro X on a Mac without any legacy Logic media, and that you downloaded all the additional media except for the Legacy and Compatibility content.

When you first open Logic Pro X, the app will automatically download and install about 2 GB of essential content. An alert then offers to download additional media content.

Click Download Additional Content to make sure that you install all the Logic Pro X media content. Depending on the speed of your Internet connection, the download process may take several hours.

> **NOTE ▶** If you have already installed Logic Pro X but did not install the additional content, choose Logic Pro X > Download Additional Content, click Select All Uninstalled (make sure the Legacy and Compatibility content is not selected) and click Install.

NOTE ▶ If you have previously installed the Legacy and Compatibility content, or if you have earlier versions of Logic installed on your Mac, you may not always see the same results as those shown in the book, especially when viewing the Library, the Loop Browser, or the plug-in settings menus.

Downloading and Using the Logic Lesson Files

The downloadable content for *Apple Pro Training Series: Logic Pro X* includes the project files you will use for each lesson, as well as media files that contain the audio and MIDI content you will need for each exercise. After you save the files to your hard disk, each lesson will instruct you in their use.

To download these files, you must have your guide's access code—provided on a card in the back of the printed editions of this book or on the "Where Are the Lesson Files?" page in electronic editions of this book. When you have the code:

1   Go to www.peachpit.com/redeem, and enter your access code.

2   Click Redeem Code, and sign in or create a Peachpit.com account.

3   Locate the downloadable files on your Account page under the Lesson & Update Files tab.

4   Click the lesson file link and download the file to your Mac desktop.

     NOTE ▶ If you purchase or redeem a code for the electronic version of this guide directly from Peachpit, the lesson file link will automatically appear on the Lesson & Update Files tab without the need to redeem an additional code.

5   After downloading the file to your Mac desktop, you'll need to unzip the file to access a folder titled Logic Pro X Files, which you will save to your Mac desktop.

     Logic Pro X Files contains two subfolders, Lessons and Media, that contain the working files for this course. Make sure you keep these two folders together in the Logic Pro X Files folder on your hard disk. If you do so, your Mac should be able to maintain the original links between the lessons and media files. Each lesson explains which files to open for that lesson's exercises.

Using Default Preferences and Selecting the Advanced Tools

All the instructions and descriptions in this book assume that you are using the default preferences (unless instructed to change them) and the initialized key command preset for a U.S. keyboard. At the beginning of Lesson 1, you will be instructed how to show advanced tools and select all additional options.

If you have changed some of your Logic Pro X preferences, you may not realize the same results as described in the exercises. To make sure that you can follow along with this book, it's best to revert to the initial set of Logic preferences before you start the lessons. Keep in mind, however, that when you initialize preferences, you lose your custom settings, and later you may want to reset your favorite preferences manually.

1   Choose Logic Pro X > Preferences > Initialize All Except Key Commands.

   A confirmation message appears.

2   Click Initialize.

   Your preferences are initialized to their default states.

   If you're jumping ahead to a lesson other than Lesson 1, make sure that you select all additional options as detailed in the following steps.

3   Choose Logic Pro X > Preferences > Advanced Tools.

4   Under Additional Options, select Audio, Surround, MIDI, Control Surfaces, Score, and Advanced Editing, and then close the preferences window.

Using the U.S. Key Command Preset

This book assumes that you are using the default initialized key command preset for a U.S. keyboard. So, you may find that some of the key commands in your Logic installation do not function as they are described in this book.

If at any point, you find that the key commands don't respond as described (for example, T doesn't open the Toolbox as explained in the first exercise of Lesson 3), then you should perform the following steps to back up your current key command set and replace it with the key command preset included with the lesson files downloaded from www.peachpit.com.

1   Choose Logic Pro X > Key Commands > Edit.

   First, it is important to back up your current key commands, particularly if you've already created a set of custom key commands and want to restore it after you've finished working with this book.

2 In the Key Commands window, choose Options > Export Key Commands.

A Save As dialog opens.

3 In the Save As dialog, keep the default Key Commands location in the Save As field, and name your preset *My shortcuts*.

Your custom shortcuts can now be recalled as any other key command preset.

4 In the Key Commands window, choose Options > Preset to open the menu.

Your new preset appears at the bottom of the Presets sub-menu.

Now let's import the key commands that you downloaded with your lesson files. The next steps assume that you've completed the steps in the Getting Started section, "Downloading and Using the Logic Lesson Files," and that the Logic Pro X folder you downloaded from peachpit.com is on your desktop.

5 In the Key Commands window, choose Options > Import Key Commands.

An Open dialog appears.

6   In the Open dialog, click the Desktop icon in the sidebar (or press Command-D). Open the Logic Pro X Files folder, and inside the Media folder, open US-Defaults.logikcs.

Logic will now respond to the key commands as described in this book.

Screen Resolution

Depending on your display resolution, some of the project files may appear different on your screen than they do in the book. When you open a project, if you can't see the whole Arrange window, move the window until you can see the three window controls at the left of the title bar, and click the Zoom button (the third button from the left) to fit the window to the screen.

When using a low display resolution, you may also have to zoom or scroll more often than instructed in the book when performing some of the exercise steps. In some cases, you may have to temporarily resize or close an area of the Arrange window to complete an action in another area.

About the Apple Pro Training Series

Apple Pro Training Series: Logic Pro X is both a self-paced learning tool and the official curriculum of the Apple Pro Training and Certification Program. Developed by experts in the field and certified by Apple, the series is used by Apple Authorized Training Centers worldwide and offers complete training in all Apple Pro products. The lessons are designed to let you learn at your own pace. Each lesson concludes with review questions and answers summarizing what you've learned, which can be used to help you prepare for the Apple Pro Certification Exam.

For a complete list of Apple Pro Training Series books, see the ad at the back of this book or visit www.peachpit.com/apts.

Apple Pro Certification Program

The Apple Pro Training and Certification Program is designed to keep you at the forefront of Apple digital media technology while giving you a competitive edge in today's ever-changing job market. Whether you're an editor, graphic designer, sound designer, special-effects artist, or teacher, these training tools are meant to help you expand your skills.

Upon completing the course material in this book, you can become a certified Apple Pro by taking the certification exam at an Apple Authorized Training Center. Successful certification as an Apple Pro gives you official recognition of your knowledge of Apple professional applications while allowing you to market yourself to employers and clients as a skilled, pro-level user of Apple products.

For those who prefer to learn in an instructor-led setting, Apple offers training courses at Apple Authorized Training Centers worldwide. These courses, which use the Apple Pro Training Series books as their curriculum, are taught by Apple Certified Trainers and balance concepts and lectures with hands-on labs and exercises. Apple Authorized Training Centers have been carefully selected and have met Apple's highest standards in all areas, including facilities, instructors, course delivery, and infrastructure. The goal of the program is to offer Apple customers, from beginners to the most seasoned professionals, the highest-quality training experience.

For more information, please see the ad at the back of this book, or to find an Authorized Training Center near you, go to training.apple.com.

Resources

Apple Pro Training Series: Logic Pro X is not intended as a comprehensive reference manual, nor does it replace the documentation that comes with the application. For comprehensive information about program features, refer to these resources:

▶ Logic Pro Help, accessed through the Logic Pro X Help menu, contains a description of most features. Other documents available in the Help menu can also be valuable resources.

▶ The Apple websites www.apple.com/logic-pro/ and www.apple.com/support/logicpro/.

▶ The Logic Pro Help website, an online community of Logic users moderated by the author of this book, David Nahmani: www.logicprohelp.com/forum.

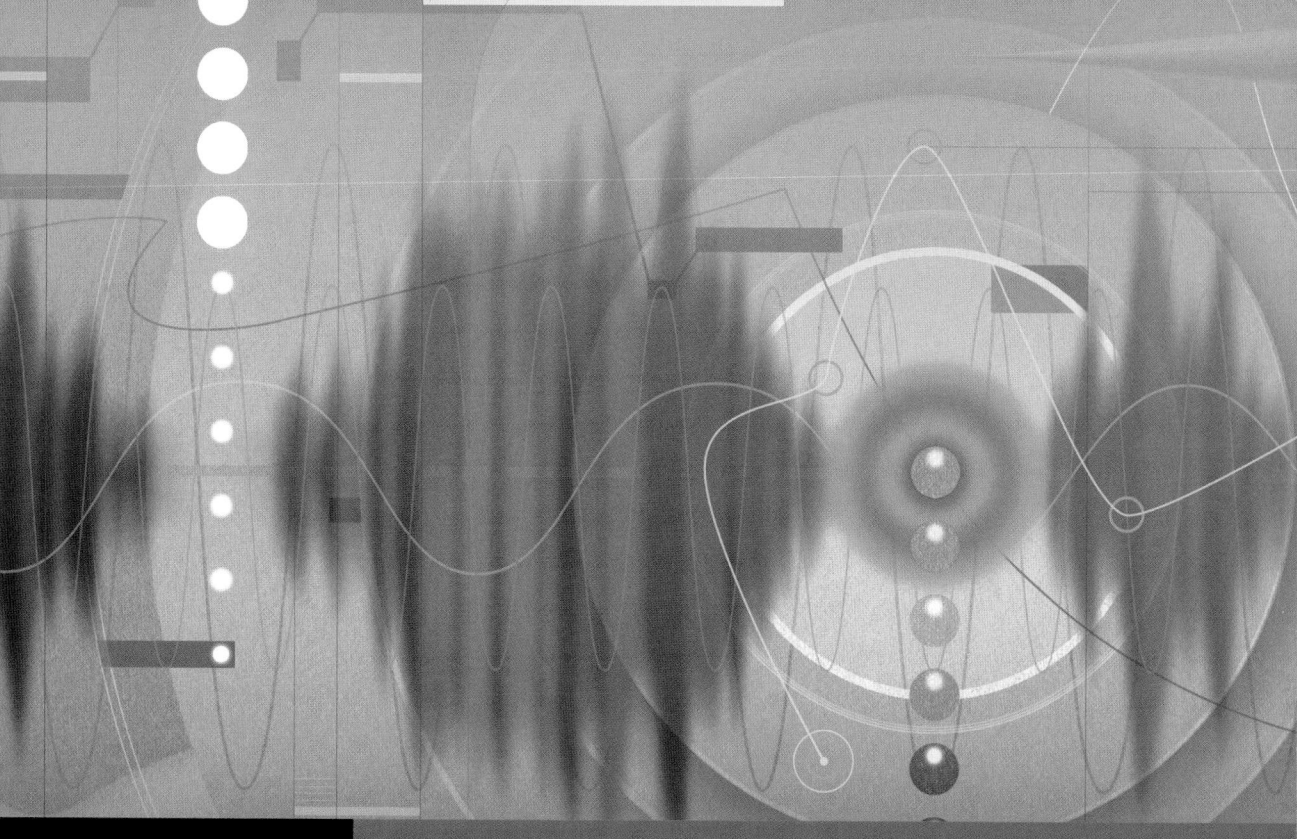

Exploring the Interface and Working with Real Instruments

1

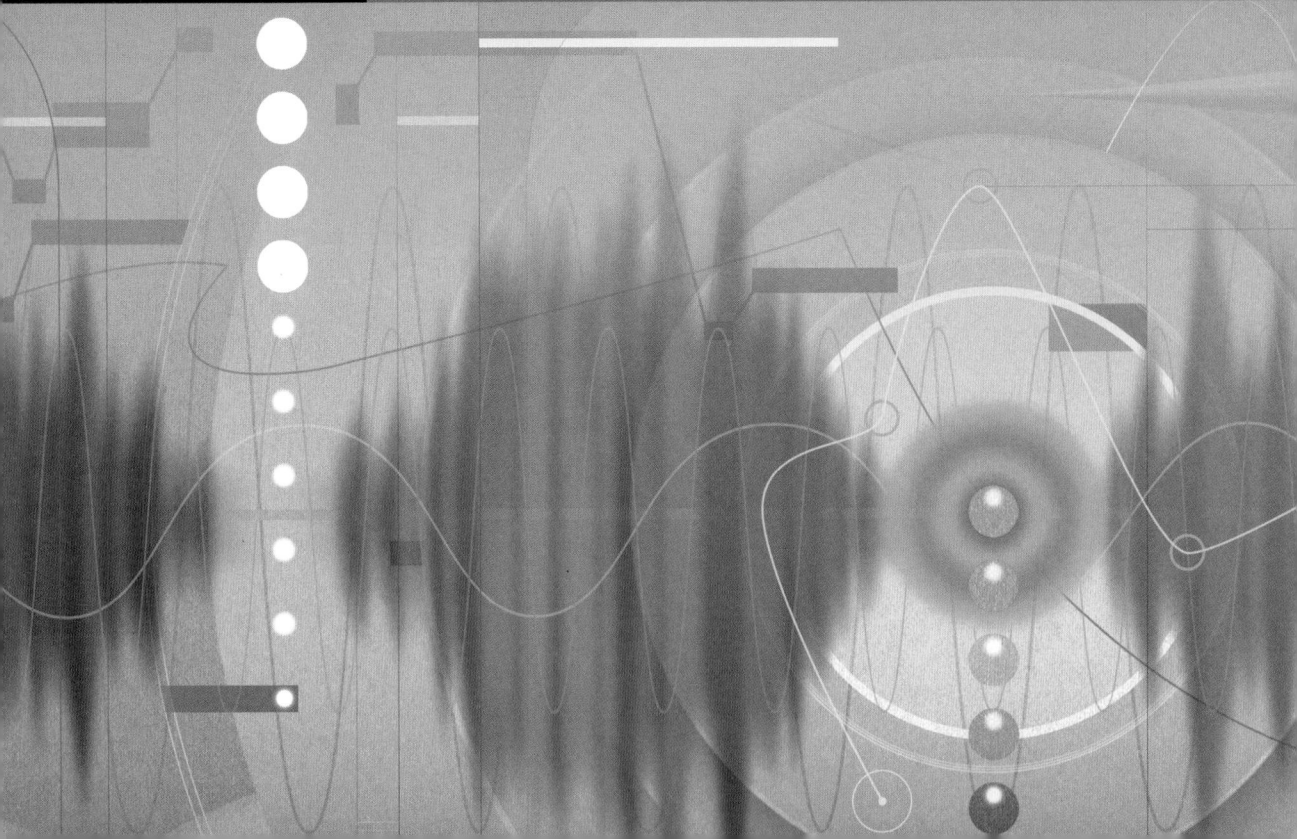

Make Music with Logic Now!

Let's get right to the heart of the matter and start producing music immediately. In this lesson, you will go straight to the fun part of using Logic Pro X. You will create a one-minute hip-hop instrumental while gaining familiarity with Logic Pro X, its main window, and many of its features.

You will take an entire Logic project from start to finish. Using the Loop Browser, you will preview and add loops. You will navigate and zoom the workspace to efficiently move, copy, loop, or trim regions. Finally, you will hone those newly learned skills to build an arrangement, mix down the song, and export it.

Creating a Logic Pro X Project

In most cases, Logic should automatically open after you install it. To open Logic Pro X manually, you can use the Launchpad.

1   In the Dock, click the Launchpad icon.

The Launchpad opens, displaying your applications.

TIP ▶ To search an application by name in the Launchpad, start typing the first few letters of the application's name.

2   Click the Logic Pro X icon.

Logic Pro X opens, and after a moment, the Project Chooser opens.

TIP ▶ To add Logic Pro X to the Dock, drag its icon from the Launchpad into the Dock. The next time you want to open Logic Pro X, you can click its icon in the Dock.

3   In the Project Chooser, double-click the Empty Project template.

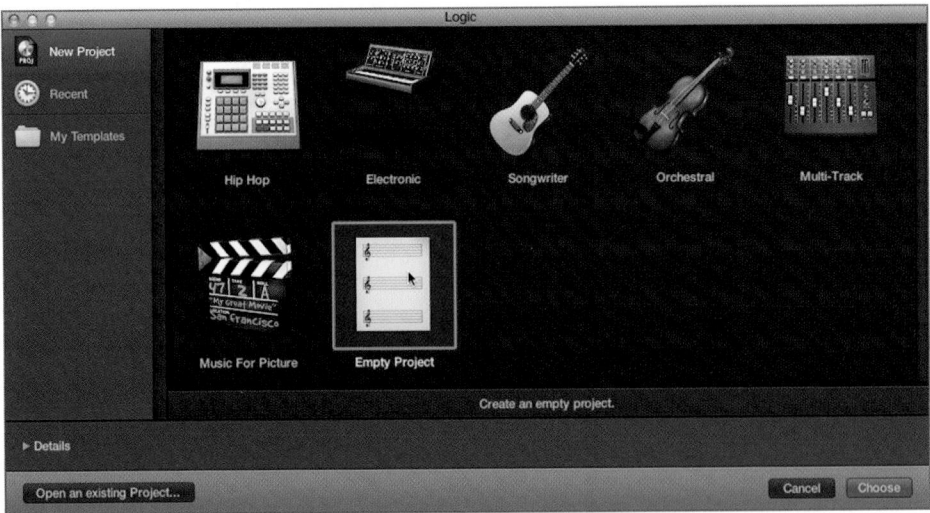

A new empty project is created, and the New Tracks dialog opens.

4   In the New Tracks dialog, select Audio, and click Create (or press Return).

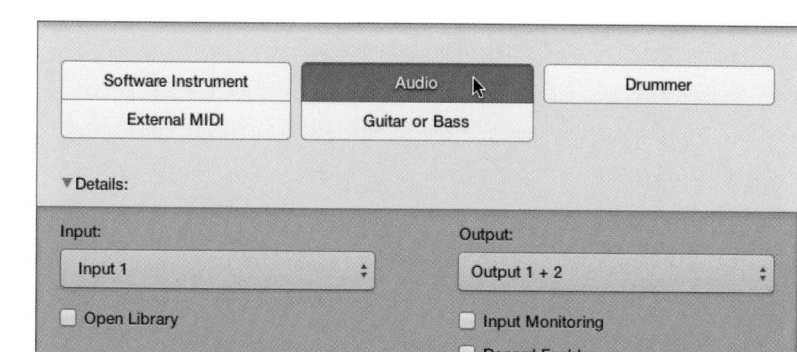

A new Audio track is created in your project.

In Logic Pro X, some advanced tools are not available by default. Before you continue, let's make sure that you select all the advanced tools in your preferences to enable all of Logic Pro X's features.

5   Choose Logic Pro X > Preferences > Advanced Tools.

The Preferences window opens.

6   In the Preferences window, make sure all Additional Options are selected.

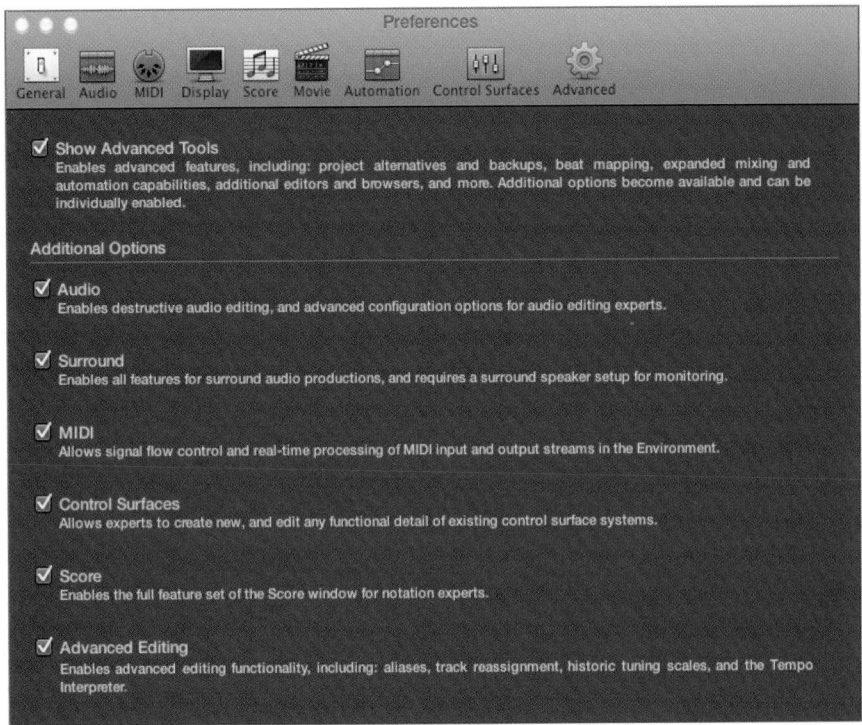

NOTE ▶ Note that you'll have to select all the Additional Options on any Mac you use to work with this book, or you may not be able to access some of the features discussed in this book.

Saving your project before you start working on it is always a good idea. That way you won't have to worry later about picking a name and a location when inspiration strikes.

7   Choose File > Save (or press Command-S).

You're saving this project for the first time, so a Save dialog appears. The first time you save a file, you have to provide:

▶   A filename

▶   A location on the hard drive where you want to save the file

8   In the Save As field, type your project name, *Get Dancing*. From the Where pop-up menu, choose Desktop (or press Command-D).

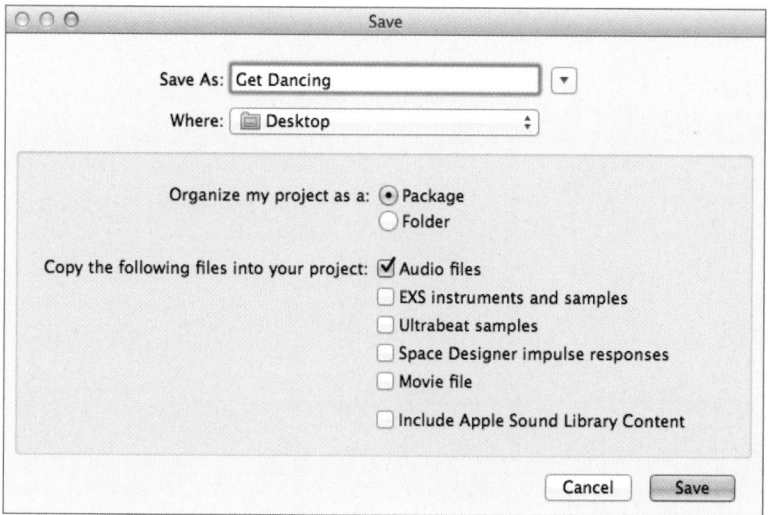

9   Click Save (or press Return).

The project is now saved on your desktop, and its name is displayed at the top of the Logic Pro X window. To avoid losing your work, save your project often.

NOTE ▶ Logic Pro X automatically saves your project at regular intervals while you're working on it. If the application unexpectedly quits, the next time you reopen the project, a dialog prompts you to reopen the most recent manually saved version or the most recent auto-saved version.

You've now set up your new project. With a blank canvas ready, you can start being creative.

Creating a new project in Logic opens the main window, which will be your main work area. In the next exercise, you will examine the panes of the main window.

Exploring the Interface

When working with Logic Pro X, you will spend most of your time in the main window. To customize the main window, you can toggle and resize its various panes to access all the media, tools, and features you need for your project.

Control bar

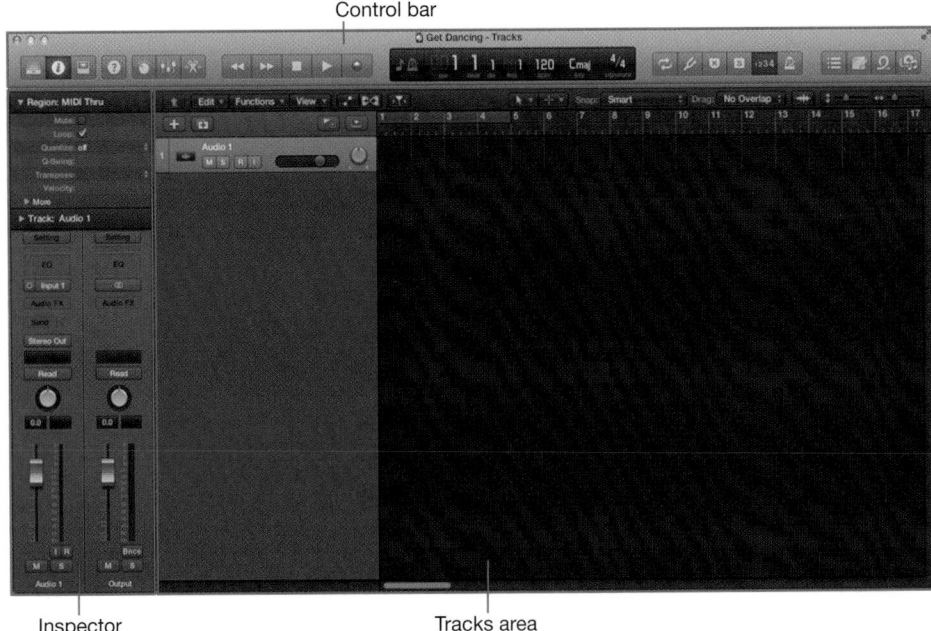

Inspector   Tracks area

In its default configuration, the main window has three areas:

▶   Control bar—The control bar contains buttons to toggle areas on and off; transport
    buttons to control playback operations (such as play, stop, rewind, and forward);
    information displays to indicate the playhead position, project tempo, key, and time
    signatures; and mode buttons such as Count-in and Metronome.

▶   Inspector—The inspector provides access to a contextual set of parameters. The specific
    parameters displayed depend on the selected track or region, or the area in key focus.

▶   Tracks area—The Tracks area is where you build your song by arranging regions on
    tracks located below a ruler.

Customizing your main window layout to display the tools you need allows you to work
faster and more comfortably, thereby giving you more time to focus on your music.

1   In the control bar, click the Inspector button (or press I).

The inspector is hidden, which allows you to see more of the Tracks area.

2   Click the Toolbar button.

The toolbar opens below the control bar. It displays buttons for easy access to the most-used features.

TIP   To customize the control bar, Control-click it, and from the shortcut menu, choose "Customize Control Bar and Display." To customize the Toolbar bar, Control-click it, and choose Customize Toolbar.

3   Click the Quick Help button.

A Quick Help floating window appears. As you hover the mouse pointer over elements of the Logic Pro X interface, the Quick Help window describes that element.

4   In the toolbar, position the mouse pointer over the Auto Zoom button.

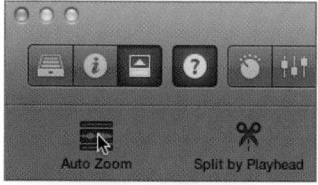

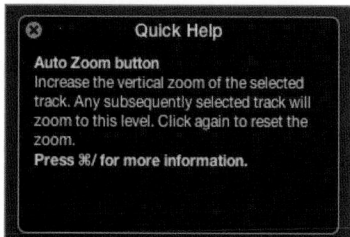

The Quick Help window displays the function's name, defines what it does, and sometimes offers extra information. Whenever you're not sure what an interface element does, use Quick Help.

MORE INFO ▸ To go further, read the Logic Pro Help documentation within the free Logic Remote iPad app. The documentation automatically displays the section relevant to the Logic Pro X area where you place the mouse pointer. You will learn more about Logic Remote in Lesson 5.

5   Click the Quick Help button to close the Quick Help window.

6   Click the Toolbar button to close the toolbar.

7   Click the Mixer button.

The Mixer opens below the Tracks area.

8   After viewing the tools in the Mixer, click the Mixer button again to close it.

9   In the control bar, click the Apple Loops button (or press O).

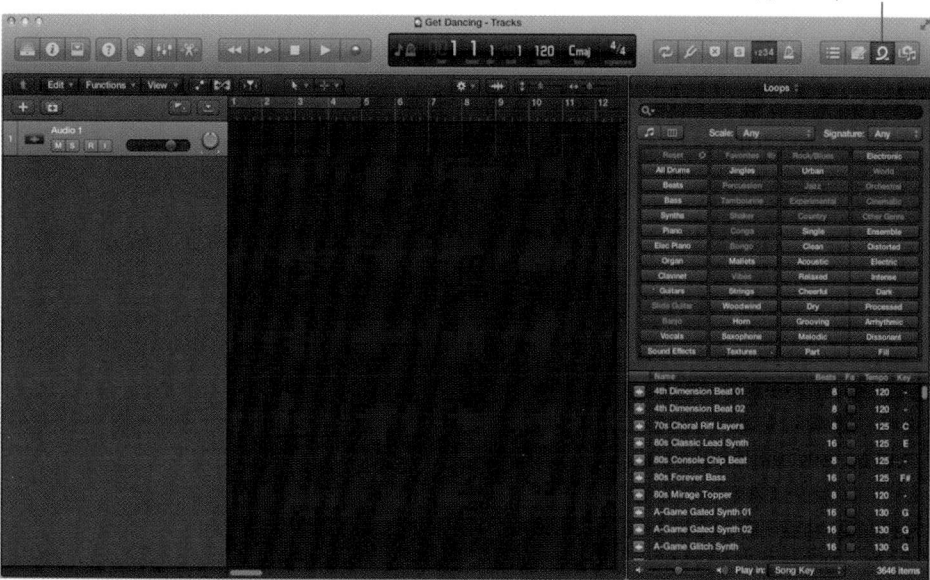

Apple Loops button

The Loop Browser opens to the right of the Tracks area.

NOTE ▸ The first time you open the Loop Browser, you have to wait for Logic to index the loops before you can use it.

You now have the control bar at the top, the Tracks area to the left, and the Loop Browser to the right, which is the perfect layout for the next exercise.

You're already gaining familiarity with the Logic Pro X interface. By showing only those panes needed for the task at hand, you make your work easier and faster, allowing you to focus on the creative side. And talking about creative side, let's start making some music!

Adding Apple Loops

You will now start building your project using Apple Loops, which are prerecorded music snippets that automatically match the tempo of your project and are designed to be repeated seamlessly.

Professional producers use Apple Loops all the time for video soundtracks, to add texture to a beat, to create unexpected effects, and so on. At least one major hit song was produced entirely around a single Apple Loop. The Apple Loops included with Logic Pro X (and earlier versions of Logic) are royalty free, so you can use them in professional projects without worrying about licensing rights.

Browsing and Previewing Loops

To start building this song, you need to preview loops, and choose which ones to use. The Loop Browser is the perfect tool for this job. It allows you to browse loops by instrument, genre, mood, and other attributes.

1 In the Loop Browser, click the All Drums, Acoustic, and Distorted keyword buttons.

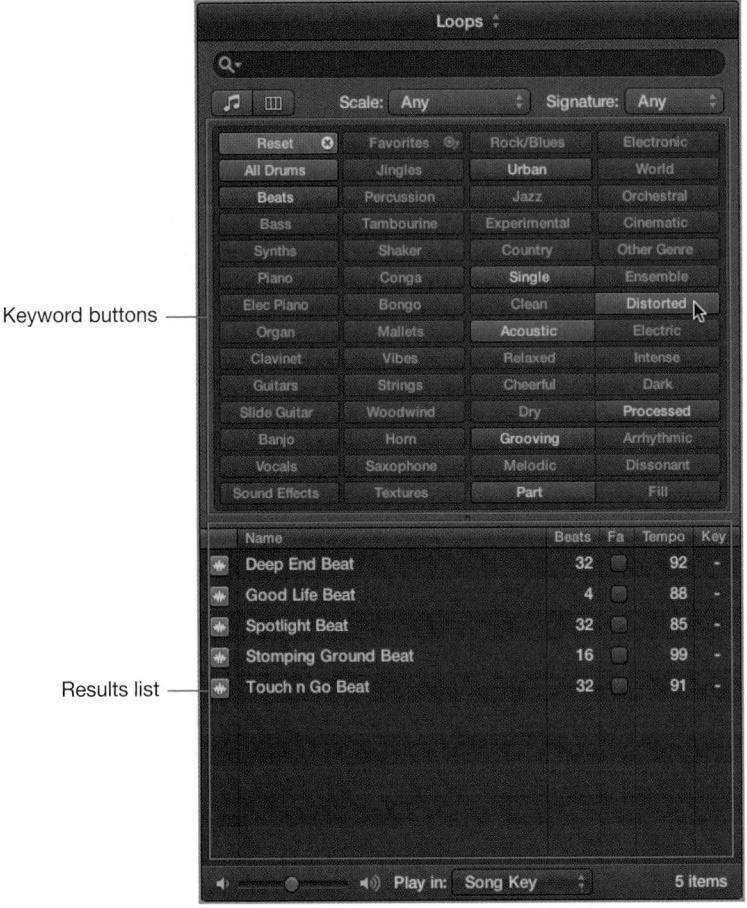

Keyword buttons

Results list

NOTE ▶ The lessons in this book assumes you begin with a default installation of Logic Pro X as described in "Getting Started," along with the additional media provided with the book—but not including the Legacy and Compatibility content. Your Loop Browser and Library may display additional items if you have installed the Legacy and Compatibility content.

Each time you click a keyword button, the results list is shortened because fewer loops match the narrowing keyword search.

You can preview loops by clicking them.

2   In the results list, click the first loop, **Deep End Beat** (or press Control-Spacebar).

The loop is selected, its blue loop icon turns into a speaker and the loop plays. At any time you can click another loop to preview it, or click the currently-playing loop to stop playback.

Apple Loops are previewed at the project's tempo. In the control bar, the LCD display shows the default project tempo of 120 bpm (beats per minute). You are currently previewing the loop at that default tempo.

Project tempo

In the results list, you can see that **Deep End Beat** was produced at a tempo of 92 bpm. Loops usually work best when used at or near their original tempos, so let's change the project tempo.

TIP ▶ You can change numerical values in Logic Pro X two ways: Drag the value up or down to increase or decrease it, or double-click the value and enter the desired number.

3   In the control bar's LCD display, drag the tempo value down to 92 bpm.

As you adjust the project tempo, you can hear the loop slow down and finally settle to the 92 bpm project tempo. The loop does seem to groove better at the slower tempo.

4 Click the next loop, **Good Life Beat**, to preview it at the project tempo of 92 bpm.

This loop has a nice funky feel, and you are going to use it as the beat for your music project.

5 Drag **Good Life Beat** from the results list to track 1 in the workspace, making sure the help tag reads *Position: 1 1 1 1*.

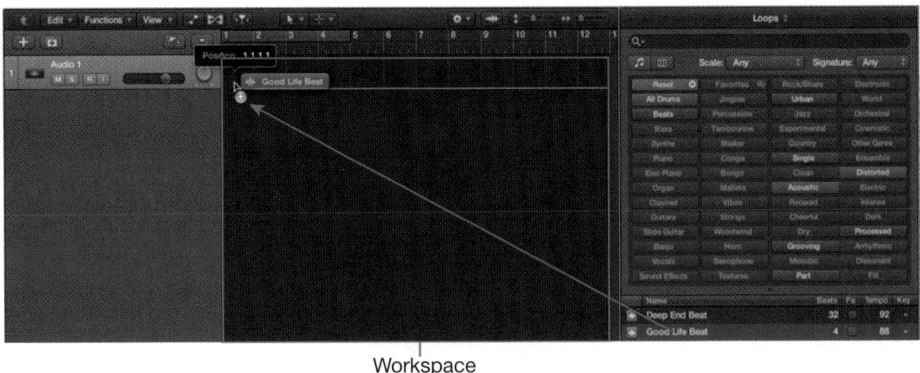

Workspace

The workspace is the area below the ruler and to the right of the track headers, where regions are arranged to build a song.

The loop is imported, and an audio region is placed on the audio track at the very beginning of the project. An alert asks if you would like to use the tempo information embedded in the loop. The Loop Browser shows that the **Good Life Beat** original tempo is 88 bpm, a little slower than your current 92 bpm tempo. You will use that new tempo.

6 Click Import (or press Return).

In the control bar's LCD display, the project tempo changes to 88 bpm.

7 Choose File > Save (or press Command-S).

Your project now contains a single drum loop on a single track that plays only during bar 1. It's the most basic project, just enough for you to dive into the basic tasks of positioning the playhead, and starting and stopping playback. Later you will use those navigation chops to preview bass lines while listening to your new drum region, and add more loops.

Navigating the Project

One of the big advantages to producing music with a computer is that the whole song is laid out right before your eyes. This representation makes it extremely easy to jump to a particular part of the song, start playback, quickly return to the beginning, or continuously repeat a section.

Logic offers many ways to navigate your project. In the following two exercises, you will use the transport buttons and their key commands; and you will learn how to continuously repeat a section of the project, which will allow you to keep playing the drum loop while you preview bass loops.

Using Transport Buttons and Key Commands

When you're producing music, time is of the essence. Because many producing tasks are repetitive, you may find yourself playing, stopping, and positioning the playhead every few seconds. Minimizing the time it takes to perform these basic operations will greatly improve your workflow and save valuable time.

While you may initially find it easier to click transport buttons with the mouse, moving a mouse with your hand while keeping your eyes on the screen is actually a time-consuming task. Using key commands to control playback can significantly reduce that time, increasing your workflow efficiency as your fingers build up muscle memory.

To fully master key commands, you first need to understand *key focus*. To start this next exercise, you will preview an Apple Loop to make sure your Loop Browser has key focus.

1   In the Loop Browser results list, click any loop to preview it.

2   Click that same loop again to stop it.

Notice the blue frame around the Loop Browser. It indicates that the Loop Browser has key focus, and is ready to respond to all Loop Browser key commands. Only one area at a time can have key focus. Right now the Tracks area does not have key focus and may not respond to some Tracks area key commands such as the Spacebar, which you can press to start and stop project playback.

3   Press the Spacebar.

Nothing happens. You first need to give key focus to the Tracks area.

4   Click the background of the workspace (or press Tab).

The blue frame appears around the Tracks area to show that the Tracks area has key focus.

TIP ▶ When multiple panes are open in the main window, you can press Tab and Shift-Tab to cycle the key focus forward and backward through the panes.

5   Press the Spacebar.

In the Tracks area, the playhead starts moving, playback begins, and you can hear the drum region on your track. When the playhead reaches bar 2, the drum region stops. Because the track contains no other regions, there's nothing else to play.

To navigate your project, you can also click the transport buttons in the control bar.

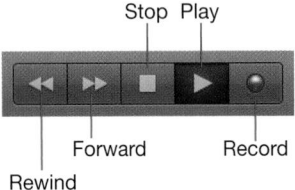

6   In the control bar, click the Stop button (or press the Spacebar).

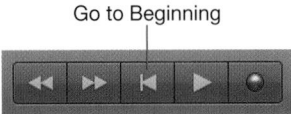

The playhead stops, and the Stop button is replaced with a Go to Beginning button.

7   Click the Go to Beginning button (or press Return) to return the playhead to the beginning of the project.

8 Click the Forward button, (or press . [period]) a few times.

The playhead jumps one bar forward each time.

9 Click the Rewind button (or press , [comma]) a few times.

The playhead jumps one bar backward each time.

TIP ▶ To fast forward or fast rewind eight bars at a time, press Shift-. (period) and Shift-, (comma).

You can also position the playhead precisely where you want it by clicking in the ruler.

10 In the lower half of the ruler, click bar 5 to move the playhead to that location.

To start or stop playback at a specific location, you can double-click the lower half of the ruler.

11 Double-click the lower half of the ruler at bar 3.

Playback starts from bar 3. You can also position the playhead without interrupting playback.

12 Without stopping playback, click the lower half of the ruler at bar 1.

You can again hear your drum loop.

13 Double-click in the lower-half of the ruler.

Playback stops and the playhead moves to the location you clicked.

Continuously Repeating a Section

Sometimes when you are working on a specific section of your project, you may want to repeat a section multiple times without stopping playback. As you're working, the beat keeps going, and you no longer have to manually relocate the playhead.

You will continue building your project by adding a bass track. To determine which bass loop works best with your drums, you will use Cycle mode to continuously repeat bar 1 as you preview bass loops in the Loop Browser.

1   In the control bar, click the Cycle button.

In the ruler, the cycle area turns yellow, indicating that Cycle mode is enabled.

Left locator   Right locator

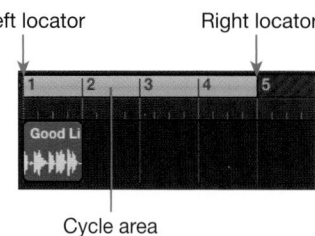

Cycle area

The cycle area shows the section of the song that will repeat. The start and end positions of the cycle area are called left and right locators. Currently the cycle area extends from bar 1 to bar 5, but our drum loop is only one bar long.

You need to adjust the locators so that the cycle area spans the same length as the drum region. To do so, you will first select the drum region, which was deselected in the previous exercise when you clicked the background of the workspace.

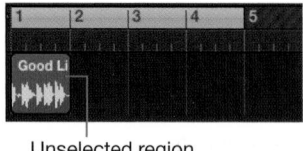

Unselected region

2   Click the drum region.

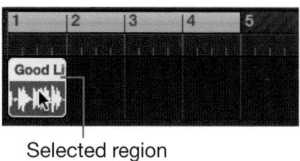

Selected region

The region is highlighted to indicate that it is selected.

3   Choose Navigate > Set Rounded Locators by Selection (or press U).

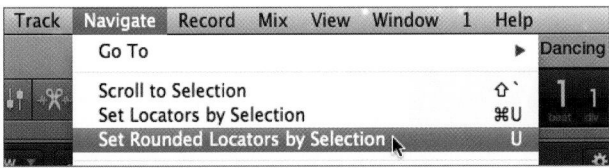

TIP When choosing a menu command, the corresponding key command usually appears to the right.

The cycle area now goes from bar 1 to bar 2 like the drum region. When you choose "Set Rounded Locators by Selection," the locators are always rounded to the nearest bar, so repeating the cycle area keeps the groove going.

TIP To turn on Cycle mode and set locators by selection, you can click the Set Locators button in the toolbar.

4 Press the Spacebar to start playback.

The playhead starts moving and your drums play. When the playhead reaches bar 2, it immediately jumps back to the beginning of bar 1 and continues playback.

While your drums continue playing, you can preview some bass loops.

5 In the Loop Browser, click the Reset button.

All keyword buttons are disabled.

For the bass loops, let's limit the search to a specific musical genre.

6   At the top of the Loop Browser, from the Loops pop-up menu, choose Hip Hop.

Only loops from the Hip Hop collection are displayed in the results list.

7   Below the All Drums keyword button, click the Bass button.

Since we know loops typically work better when played close to their original tempos, let's sort the results list by tempo and look for loops that were produced at or around 88 bpm.

8   At the top of the results list, click the Tempo column name.

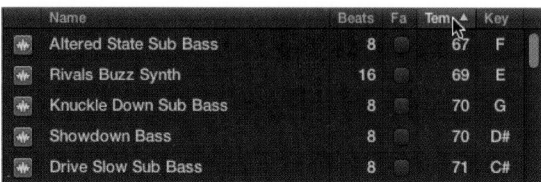

The loops in the results list are sorted by increasing tempo.

9   Scroll down to see loops with a tempo of 88 bpm.

10 Click the first loop.

After a moment, Logic syncs the loop with the project and you can hear it playing, grooving along with the drums in your project.

11 Continue clicking the following loops to preview them one by one.

Most of them are too synthetic for this project, but Skyline Bass seems to have the right sound and it works with your drums. With an original tempo of 90 bpm, it's still very close to your project tempo, which means it should work great.

Skyline Bass is listed in the results list as a 16 beats loop, but right now your cycle area is playing only one bar (at the current 4/4 time signature, 1 bar = 4 beats), so you're hearing only a portion of the bass loop. Let's add it to the project to audition the entire loop.

12 In the Control bar, click the Stop button (or give key focus to the Tracks area and press the Spacebar) to stop playback.

13 Drag Skyline Bass to the workspace below the drum loop, making sure the help tag reads 1 1 1 1.

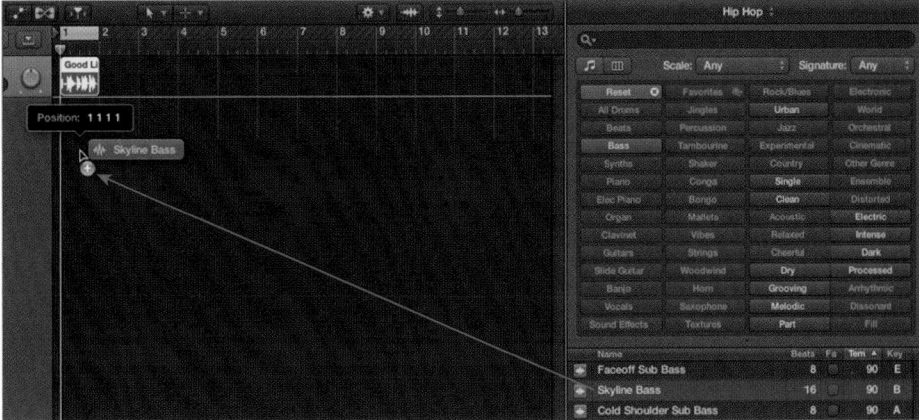

A new track is automatically created for the new Skyline Bass region.

14 In the ruler, click the yellow cycle area (or press C) to turn off Cycle mode.

15 In the control bar, click the Go to Beginning button (or press Return).

16 Press the Spacebar to start playback.

In the first bar, you can hear both the drum loop and the bass loop, then the drums drop off while the bass continues playing for three more bars. You can now hear the entire bass line, which is even more melodic than the limited preview you heard previously.

17 Press the Spacebar again to stop playback.

18 Choose File > Save (or press Command-S).

As you work in Logic, keep saving your project at regular intervals to avoid losing any of your work.

Setting locators to adjust the cycle area is a technique you'll use often throughout your production to focus on part of a project. And if you work with other musicians in your studio, they will love you for not interrupting the playback (and ruining their creative flow) every few bars!

Building Up the Rhythm Section

All the material you use for a project is contained in regions that are on tracks in the workspace. Creating an arrangement is a little like playing with building blocks—moving, copying, or repeating regions as needed to determine at which points specific instruments start and stop playing.

In this exercise, you will start building an arrangement with the drum and bass loops, and later add more loops to complete your project. First, you will loop both regions so they play continuously.

1   In the control bar, click the Inspector button (or press I).

The Inspector appears. Region parameters for the selected region(s) are displayed in the Region inspector near the top.

2   In the workspace, click the Good Life Beat region in track 1 to select it.

The Region inspector shows the parameters of the Good Life Beat region.

3   In the Region inspector, select the Loop checkbox (or press L).

In the workspace, Good Life Beat is now looping until the end of the project.

4   In the workspace, click the bass region in track 2 to select it.

5   In the Region inspector, select the Loop checkbox.

In the workspace, both the drum and the bass regions are now looping.

6   Listen to a few bars of the project.

The drums and bass are grooving together perfectly. You're going to layer the drums with an urban percussion loop that will also help create a nice little intro.

TIP▶ To work more efficiently, remember to hide those areas you don't need to see. For the next few exercises, in the control bar, click the Inspector button (or press I) and click the Apple Loops button (or press O) to turn those two areas on and off as needed.

7   At the top of the Loop Browser, from the View pop-up menu, choose Loops.

All keyword buttons are reset.

8   In the Loop Browser, click the search box and type *fine line*.

9   From the results list, drag **Fine Line Beat** to bar 1 below the two tracks in the workspace.

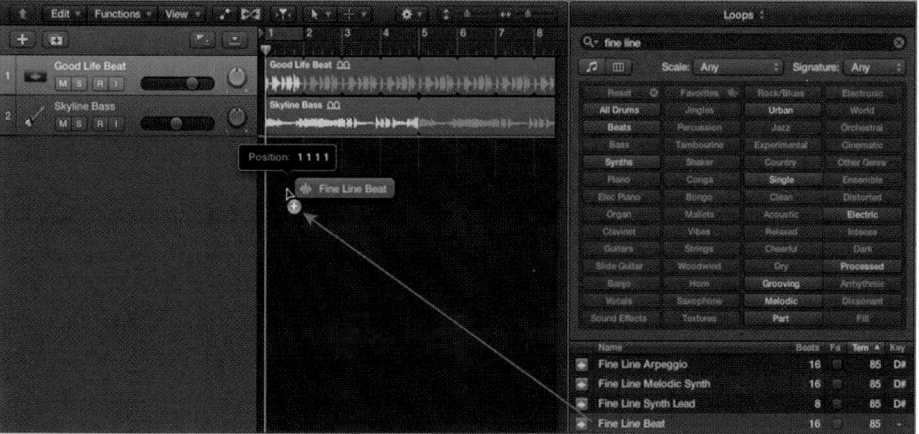

A new track is created for the Fine Line Beat region. Since Fine Line Beat is still selected, you can access its region parameters at the top of the inspector.

10 In the Fine Line Beat region parameters, select the Loop checkbox (or press L).

The Fine Line Beat region is now looping in the workspace. Since Fine Line Beat will be used for the intro, you can move it to the top of the workspace.

11 In the Fine Line Beat track header, click-hold the track icon and drag up until the two other tracks move down.

The tracks are reordered with the new Fine Line Beat track at the top.

To create an intro in which only Fine Line Beat is playing, you'll move the two other regions further to the right. To select multiple regions at once, you can click in the workspace background and drag the pointer over the regions.

12 In the workspace, click the background, and drag up to select both the Good Life Beat and the Skyline Bass regions.

Both regions are highlighted to indicate that they're selected. You can now move them both at the same time.

13 Make sure you click one of the selected regions (don't click one of the loops to their right), and drag to bar 5.

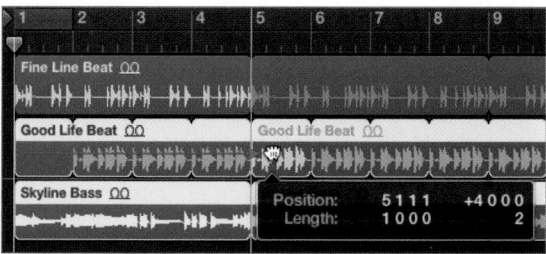

If you clicked Good Life Beat, the help tag shows:

▶ Position: 5 1 1 1—Where the regions are moved

▶ +4 0 0 0—The regions are moved exactly 4 bars later.

▶ Length: 1 0 0 0—Length of the clicked region

▶ 2—Track number of the clicked region

If you clicked Skyline Bass, the second line in the help tag shows:

▶ Length: 4 0 0 0

▶ 3

The help tag displays positions and lengths in bars, beats, divisions, and ticks. You will often refer to a position or a length with those four numbers.

▶ The bar consists of several beats (four beats in the 4/4 time signature here).

▶ The beat is the denominator in the time signature (quarter note here).

▶ The division determines how the grid is subdivided in the ruler when zoomed in horizontally (sixteenth note here).

▶ A clock tick is 1/960 of a quarter note. A sixteenth note contains 240 ticks.

Note that in the control bar, the LCD displays the position of the playhead using the same four units.

14 Listen to your project from the beginning.

It's time to practice your navigation chops! You can click the Play and Stop/Go to Beginning buttons in the control bar, click and double-click the lower half of the ruler, or use the key commands:

▶ Spacebar = Play/Stop

▶ Return = Go to Beginning

▶ . (period) = Forward

▶ , (comma) = Rewind

The intro sounds good, and the layered drum loops work great together. However, Good Life Beat is too loud.

15 In the Good Life Beat track header (track 2), drag the Volume slider to the left to turn down the volume to about –8.0 dB.

Now the two drum loops blend together.

Near the end of this lesson, you will spend more time mixing the song; but for now let's continue editing regions and adding more loops to continue the arrangement.

Zooming In to Edit the Intro

Your project starts with a 4-bar intro in which only the Fine Line Beat region on track 1 plays the beat. It feels sparse, but the beat is original enough to capture attention, which is the role of an intro. Then at bar 5 both the Good Life Beat and Skyline Bass regions on tracks 2 and 3 come in, making the beat sound complete and introducing the melody.

To accentuate the starting impact of the two new regions, you will create a couple of unexpected edits at the end of the intro that are bound to make the listener's head turn. To be able to edit the Fine Line Beat region in the intro without affecting its loops to the right, you first have to copy the region to bar 5.

1   Option-drag the Fine Line Beat region to bar 5.

When Option-dragging to copy regions, always make sure you release the mouse button first and the Option key last. If you try to release both at the same time, you may sometimes release the Option key slightly before the mouse button without noticing, and then the region is moved instead of copied.

If you copied the Fine Line Beat region successfully, your workspace will look like this:

If you don't see a Fine Line Beat region between bars 1 and 5, you've moved the region rather than copying it. To reverse your last action, choose Edit > Undo Drag, and then try again.

The new Fine Line Beat.1 region at bar 5 currently stops the original Fine Line Beat region at bar 1 from looping. However the region's Loop parameter is still on, so its loops reappear if there's room for them on the track. To create a break, you need to stop the region from looping.

2   Click the Fine Line Beat region at bar 1 to select it.

3   In the inspector, deselect the Loop checkbox (or press L).

To create a break in the beat at the end of the intro, you will shorten the Fine Line Beat region so that it doesn't play the last two notes of the region. To resize the region comfortably, you need to zoom in until you can clearly see the individual drum hits on the waveform.

To turn the mouse pointer into a Zoom tool, you hold down Control and Option, and then drag the area you want to magnify. The size of the area you drag determines how far you will zoom in: the smaller the area that you drag, the closer you'll zoom in.

4   Control-Option-drag a small blue highlight rectangle about one bar wide, but straddling the junction of the two regions on track 1 at bar 5.

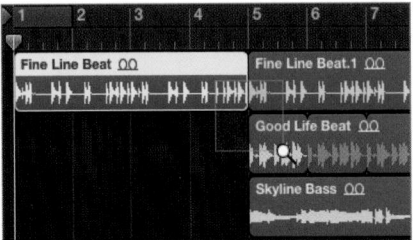

The area you highlighted expands to fill the workspace, and you can clearly see individual drum hits on the waveform.

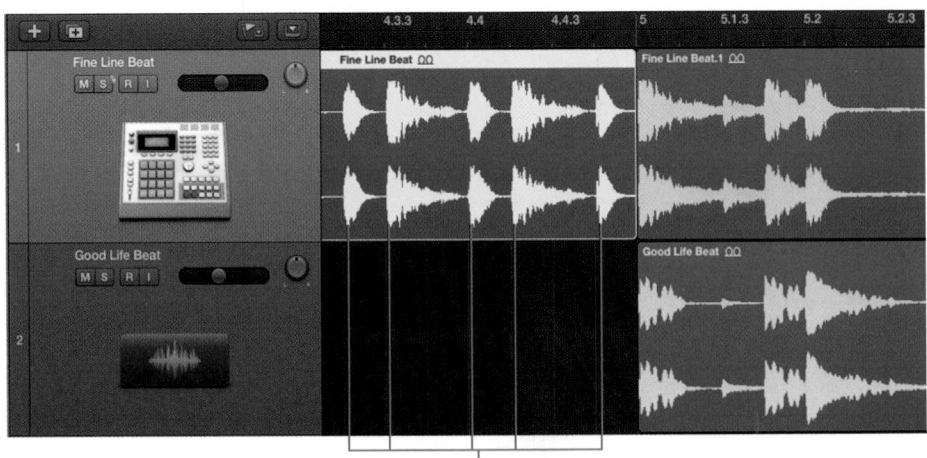

Individual drum hits

Zooming in and out efficiently to see exactly what you need takes practice. If you're not happy with what you're seeing in your workspace, Control-Option-click the workspace to zoom back out, and try again.

TIP ▶ If you're happy with your workspace view but feel that you should zoom in even closer, zoom in again. You can Control-Option-drag to zoom in multiple times and Control-Option-click the workspace multiple times to zoom back out through the same zoom levels.

To create the break at the end of the Fine Line Beat region, you will drag its lower-right corner to the left until the final two drum hits are hidden.

5   Move the mouse pointer over the lower-right corner of the Fine Line Beat region (the mouse pointer should be located just before bar 5).

— Resize pointer

The mouse pointer turns into a Resize pointer you can drag to determine where the region stops playing.

6   Drag the Resize pointer to the left to hide the final two drum hits.

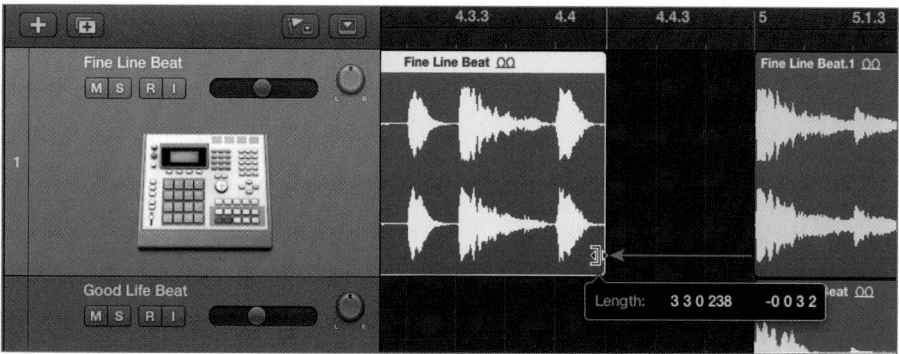

7   Control-Option-click the workspace to zoom out.

8   Listen to the song from the beginning.

The drum break creates a sudden void at the end of the intro, which reinforces the impact of the drums and bass. But a void calls to be filled! That break in the drum loop is the perfect time to capture the attention of the listener by introducing the bass a few notes earlier.

This time you will copy the bass region from bar 5 to bar 1, and resize the bass region in the intro from the left so it plays only the final few notes.

9   On track 3, Option-drag the Skyline Bass region to bar 1.

10   In the new Skyline Bass.1 Region inspector, deselect the Loop checkbox (or press L).

This time you will use the Z key to zoom in and out of the selection.

11   Press Z.

The Skyline Bass expands to fill the workspace.

12   Move the mouse pointer over the lower-left corner of the region, and drag the Resize pointer to the right, leaving only the last group of five notes.

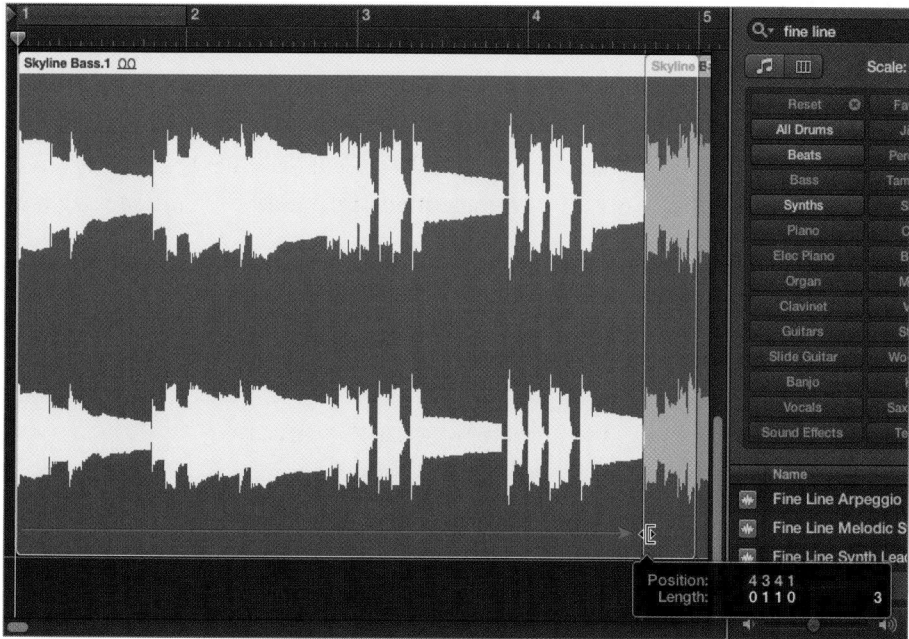

13 Click the background of the workspace to deselect all regions.

When there's no selection, pressing the Z key shows you all the regions in your workspace.

14 Press Z.

The workspace zooms out to display all the regions. It doesn't allow for the region's loops. You can use zoom sliders or key commands to fine-tune the zoom level.

15 At the top of the workspace, drag the horizontal zoom slider to the left (or press Command-Left Arrow).

Horizontal zoom slider

Vertical zoom slider

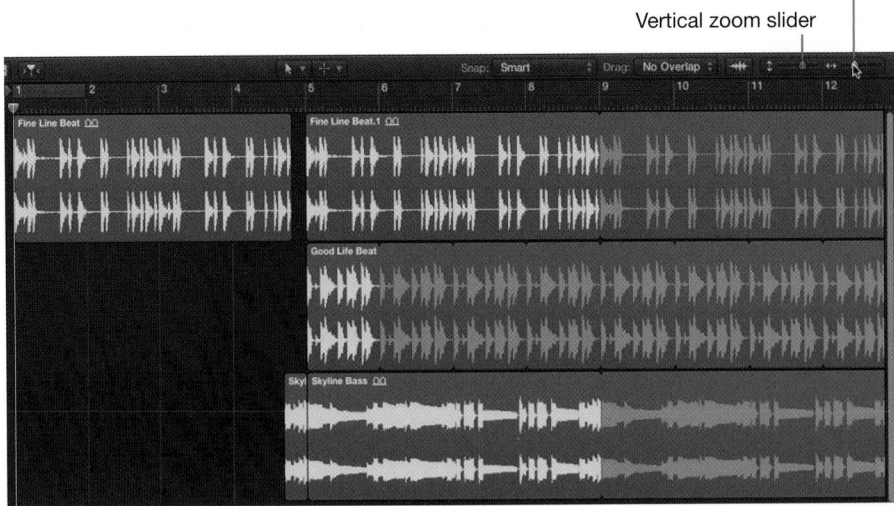

The workspace zooms out horizontally, and you can see a few more bars in your ruler.

NOTE ▶ When zooming horizontally using the zoom sliders or Command-Arrow key combinations, the playhead stays at the same position on your screen, unless a region is selected and the playhead is not within that region's borders. In that case the left edge of the region stays at the same position on your screen.

When zooming vertically with the zoom sliders or Command-Arrow keys, the selected track stays at the same position on your screen.

16 Play your new intro.

It works! You start with an original but commanding beat with kicks and hand claps, then all of a sudden, the bass announces the melody with a few pickup notes while the beat stops. On the first beat of the next bar, all three tracks play the entire groove together. That little break at the end of the intro really helps call attention to the layered drum and bass groove that starts after the intro.

Remember your newly acquired navigation and zooming skills. You will continue using them to finish this arrangement, and throughout the rest of this book (and long after).

Build Up the Arrangement

Now that you have the rhythmic foundation of your project (the drums and bass), you can continue building up the arrangement and avoid monotony by adding melodic elements.

Adding Lead Synths

In the next exercise, you will add a couple of synth arpeggio loops. And rather than let them loop throughout the song, you will keep things moving by alternating between the two synth melodies.

1   In the Loop Browser, click the X symbol in the search field to clear the previous search.

You already have a solid rhythmic section with bass and low kick drums, so now you are looking for rather clean and high-pitched sounds.

2   Click the Synths and Clean keyword buttons.

3   In the search field, type *Arpeggio*, and press Return.

4   In the results list, click the Name column title to reorder the results by loop name.

5   In the results list, click the first six or seven loops to preview them.

Two loops fit the bill perfectly: **Barricade Arpeggio** and **Deal Breaker Arpeggio**. If necessary, adjust the zoom level in the workspace so you can comfortably drag both loops to two new tracks.

6   Drag the **Barricade Arpeggio** loop to the bottom of the workspace at bar 9.

7   Drag the **Deal Breaker Arpeggio** loop to the bottom of the workspace at bar 10.

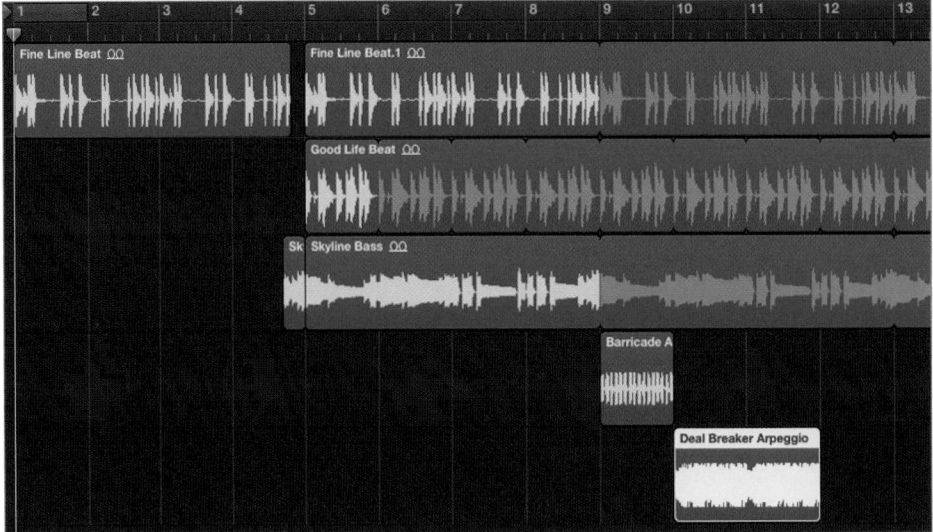

You will resize the Deal Breaker Arpeggio region to make it one bar long, the same length as the Barricade Arpeggio region.

8   Drag the lower-right corner of the Deal Breaker Arpeggio region to make it one bar long.

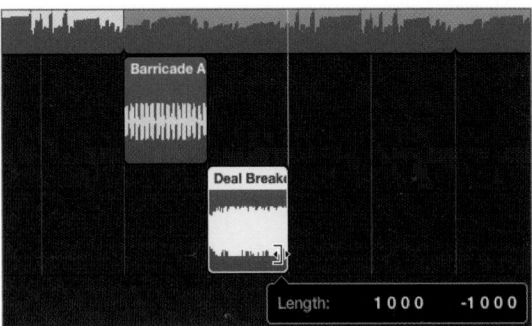

You will now copy both regions so they play alternately.

9   Click the background, and drag a rectangle around both regions to select them.

10 Option-drag the selected regions so that the copy of the Barricade Arpeggio region starts where the Deal Breaker Arpeggio region ends.

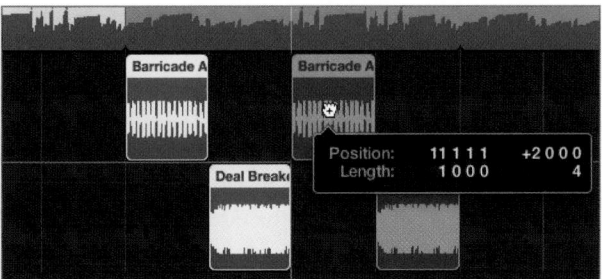

11 Play the new synth section.

The two synths bring much-needed melody and movement to the song, and they work well in answering each other, each one successively playing its melody.

Currently, both synths sound as if they are coming from the center of the stereo field. To give them a little space, you can spread them apart acoustically by positioning them to either side of the stereo field.

12 On the Barricade Arpeggio track header, click the Balance knob and drag down to turn the knob to the left.

NOTE ► When working with stereo audio content, the rotary knob in the track header (and the rotary knob to the top of the Volume fader on the channel strip) is a Balance knob. When working with mono audio content, that knob is a Pan knob.

13 On the Deal Breaker Arpeggio track, click the Balance knob and drag up to turn it to the right.

14 Play the synth section again.

You can now hear the two synths playing from opposite sides of the stereo field, which adds dimension to the music and helps to separate the two instruments.

Creating a Break

Until now, you have kept your project interesting by introducing new elements on a regular basis: the bass at the end of the intro, the drums at bar 5, a synth at bar 9, and another synth at bar 10. But if you keep building your song by adding more elements, at some point those additions may backfire. The song can become bloated with the arrangement losing focus, the mix becoming muddy, and the listeners tuning out. Who wants that?

So if you can't add any more to your song, subtract! By the end of the new synth section, the listeners are so used to hearing the drums and the bass that they may no longer pay attention to them. If you remove them, you can create a big impact. So let's add a piano loop after the synth section, and then delete the drums and bass while the piano plays.

At the top of the Tracks area, look at the tool menus:

The menu to the left corresponds to the tool assigned to the mouse pointer.

The menu to the right corresponds to the tool assigned to the mouse pointer when holding down Command.

Currently the Left-click tool is assigned to the Pointer tool (arrow icon) and the Command-click tool is assigned to the Marquee tool (crosshair icon). You don't need to change those assignments, but if you're curious, feel free to click one of the tool menus to open it and see what's available. Click it again to close it.

The Loop Browser sometimes shows multiple loops with similar names, and that usually means that the loops all follow the same groove, the same chord progression, or are otherwise meant to work together. Let's see if we have any other Skyline Apple Loops meant to work with our **Skyline Bass** loop.

1   In the Loop Browser, click the Reset button to clear all keyword buttons.

2   In the search field, type *Skyline*.

The results list shows four loops containing *Skyline* in their names.

3   Preview the four loops.

The loops sound like they would all work great together because they all follow the same harmony and rhythm.

4   Drag the Skyline Piano loop to the bottom of the workspace at bar 13.

You will now create the break by deleting the drums in track 2 and the bass in track 3 for the entire time the piano is playing.

5   Hold down the Command key to turn the mouse pointer into a Marquee tool.

6   Command-drag around tracks 2 and 3 from bar 13 to bar 17.

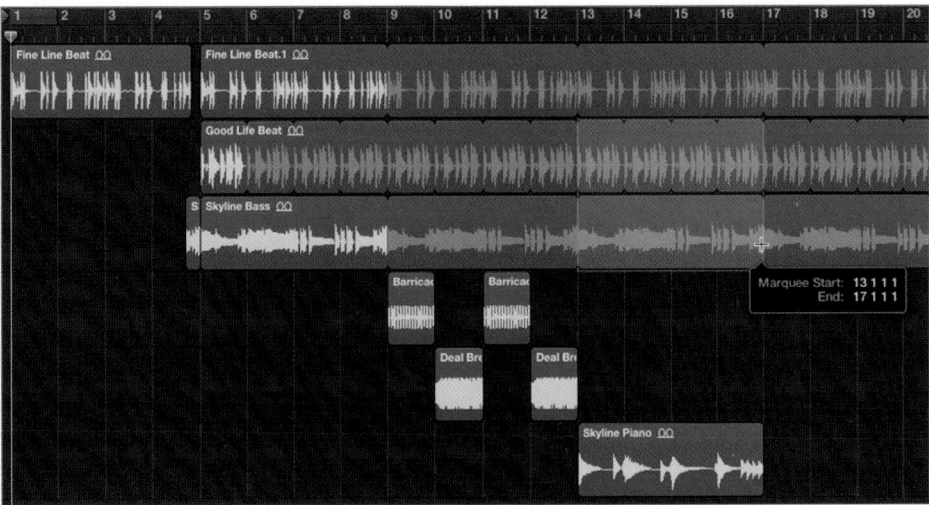

The Marquee tool places a white highlight rectangle around the selected section of the loops.

7   Choose Edit > Delete (or press Delete).

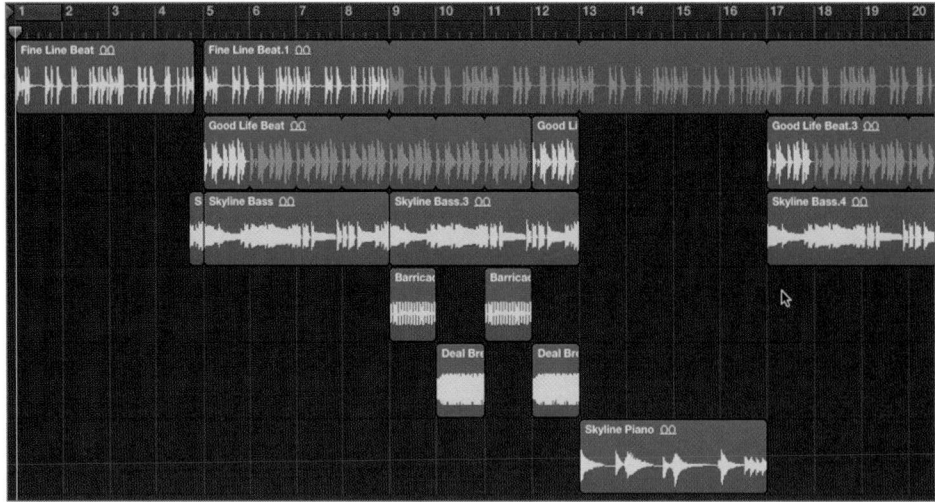

The section of the loops selected by the Marquee tool is deleted. Some loops are turned into regions before and after the empty space so the tracks stop and resume playing at the beginning and end of the removed section.

Let's finish the song. You will let the rhythm section play four bars after the piano stops, and you'll end the song at bar 21.

8   Move the mouse pointer to the upper part of the loops on track 1.

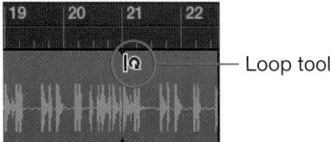

Loop tool

The mouse pointer turns into a Loop tool. You can click or drag the Loop tool where you want a region's loops to end. Dragging offers the advantage of seeing the exact position in a help tag.

9   Drag the Loop tool to bar 21.

The Fine Line Beat.1 region stops looping at bar 21.

10 Repeat the same process to stop the drums on track 2 and the bass on track 3 at bar 21.

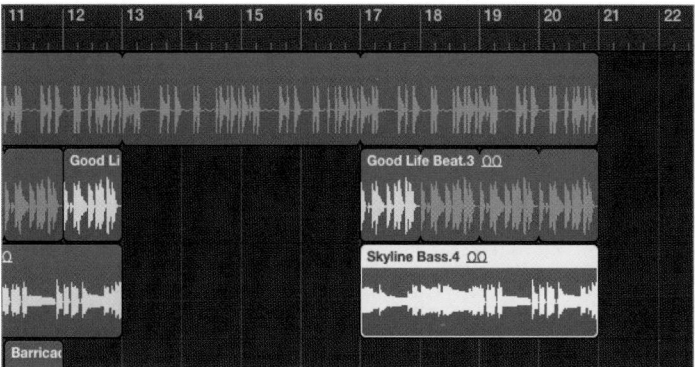

11 Move the playhead to bar 11 and press Spacebar to play through the break and ending.

The break brings much needed space and silences, interrupts the flow of the rhythmic section, and automatically shines a light on the two remaining elements: the drum loop and the piano. After the break, the rhythmic section resumes, but the ending at bar 21 is too abrupt. Let's bring back the piano by itself to create a quick outro.

12 On track 6, Option-drag the Skyline Piano region to bar 21.

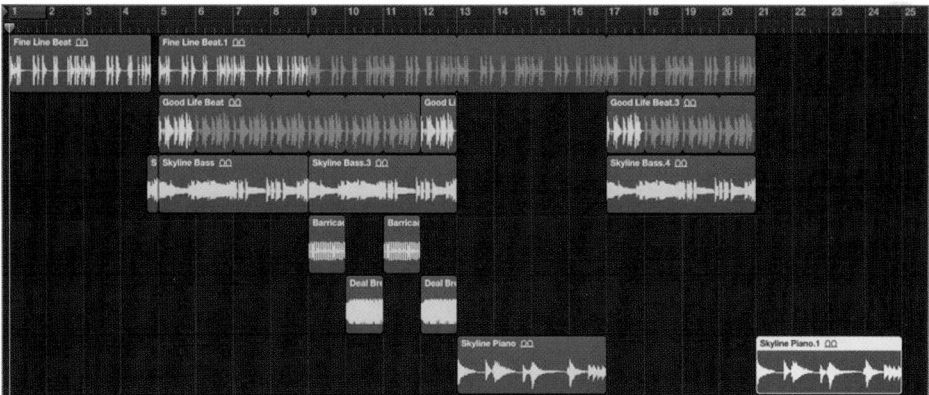

You will finally shorten the new copy of the piano region so it ends with a sustaining note, which will work better for an ending.

13 Control-Option-drag around the Skyline Piano.1 region to zoom in on it.

14 Drag the lower-right corner of the Skyline Piano.1 region to the left so that it ends with the long sustaining note in bar 23.

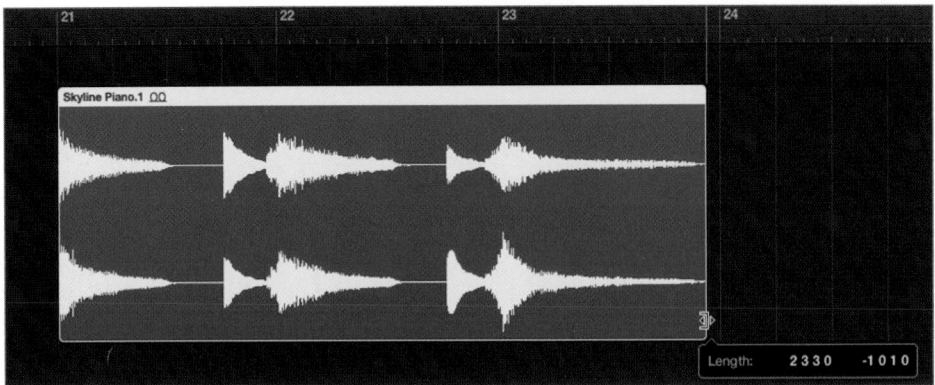

15 Control-Option-click the workspace to zoom out.

16 Play the entire project.

You have arranged your first song. Using only six Apple Loops, you've built a simple one-minute song that evolves from an original intro into a solid bass and drums groove. Then two synths share the lead melody for a few bars before the bass and drums abruptly stop to leave room for a piano break. Finally, the bass and drums groove returns, and the song finishes with a few sustained piano notes. Really nice! You will now quickly mix the song and later export it to share it.

Mixing the Song

Now that you have arranged your regions in the workspace, you can focus on the sound of each instrument, and how they sound as an ensemble. You can adjust each instrument's loudness and its position in the stereo field, and even modify its timbre so all the instruments blend harmoniously.

You will open the Mixer, and name your channel strips so you can easily determine which instrument they control. You will then adjust the Volume faders and Balance knobs to change levels and stereo positions, and apply patches and plug-ins to process some of the instruments.

Choosing Names and Icons for Tracks and Channel Strips

1 In the control bar, click the Mixer button (or press X).

At the bottom of the main window, the Mixer opens.

The channel strips are named after the Apple Loops you previously dragged to the workplace. To more quickly locate instruments, you can assign the channel strips more descriptive names.

To edit the name on a track header and on its corresponding channel strip, you can double-click either, and type the new name.

2 At the bottom of the first channel strip, double-click the Fine Line Beat name.

A text entry box appears, and the previous name—Fine Line Beat—is selected.

3   Type *Beat Loop*, and press Return.

Both the first channel strip in the Mixer and track 1 in the Tracks area are renamed Beat Loop. Renaming tracks in the track header is often easier because you can quickly identify instruments by looking at the regions you've been arranging.

4   In the control bar, click the Mixer button again (or press X) to close the Mixer.

5   In track 2's track header, double-click the Good Life Beat name.

A text entry box pops up. This time you will enter a name and pop up the text entry box of the next track with a single key command.

6   Type *Drums*, and press Tab.

Track 2 is renamed Drums. A text entry box appears on track 3's name, ready to be edited.

7   Type *Bass*, and press Tab.

Track 3 is renamed Bass, and track 4 is ready to be renamed. Continue this process to change the name of the three remaining tracks as follows:

▶   Track 4 to *Synth 1*

▶   Track 5 to *Synth 2*

▶   Track 6 to *Piano*

TIP ▶ In the Mixer, you can also press Tab to enter a name and open the text entry box of the next channel strip. Should you enter a name incorrectly, press Shift-Tab to open the text entry box of the previous track or channel strip.

Notice that track 2 has only a generic audio waveform icon. That's because the track was created before you dragged the **Good Life Beat** loop to it at the very beginning of this lesson.

8   In the Tracks area, Control-click the icon in track 2's track header.

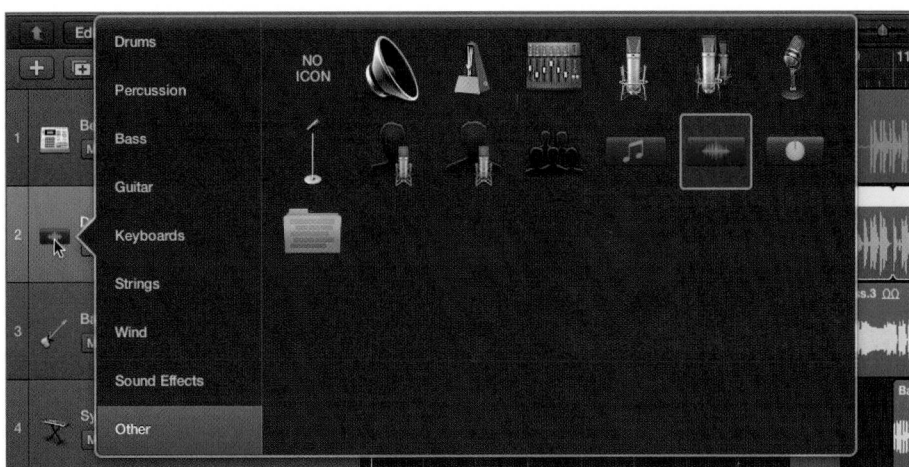

A shortcut menu displays icons organized in categories.

9   In the shortcut menu, click the Drums category.

A collection of various drum icons appears.

10   Click an icon representing a drum kit.

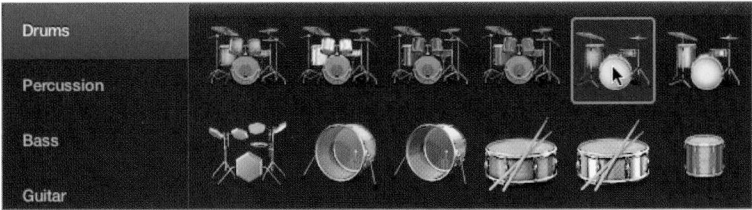

The icon is now visible in the track header. The same icon is also assigned to the corresponding channel strip in the Mixer, as you will see in a moment.

When your creative juices are flowing, and you just want to make a quick adjustment to the sound of an instrument, wasting time looking for the correct track or channel strip can be frustrating. Or worse, you could become a victim of the classic mistake: turning knobs and faders but not hearing the sound reacting to your adjustments, until you realize you were adjusting the wrong instrument!

Taking a minute to assign your tracks and channel strips descriptive names and appropriate icons can accelerate your workflow and avoid potentially costly mistakes.

Adjusting Volume and Stereo Position

With new names and icons assigned, your Mixer is ready. You will now open it and adjust some of the instruments' volume levels and stereo positions.

1 In the control bar, click the Mixer button (or press X) to open the Mixer.

You can see your new names at the bottom of the channel strips. You can resize the Mixer area to see more of the channel strips.

2 Place the mouse pointer between the Tracks area and the Mixer area.

A Resize pointer appears.

3 Drag the Resize pointer up as far up as it will go.

The Mixer is now taller, and you can see more options above the channel strips. There are a lot of options, but don't worry. Just because you have many tools available doesn't mean you have to use them all. You will learn about those options as needed.

NOTE ▶ Depending on the size of your display, you may not be able to open up the Mixer all the way. In that case, you can drag the vertical scrollbar to the right of the Mixer to scroll up and see all the options.

4   Play your song.

With the Mixer open and occupying most of the main window, the workspace is much smaller. Depending on your display resolution, navigating your song efficiently may prove challenging (or nearly impossible). To remedy that, you will now adjust the locators in the Tracks area ruler, and use Cycle mode to continuously repeat a part of the song that contains all the instruments.

5   Click the Mixer button (or press X) to close the Mixer.

If necessary, scroll or zoom out in the workspace so you can see your entire arrangement. Remember: To see all your regions, click the background of the workspace, and press Z.

6   Drag the upper half of the ruler from bar 9 to bar 13.

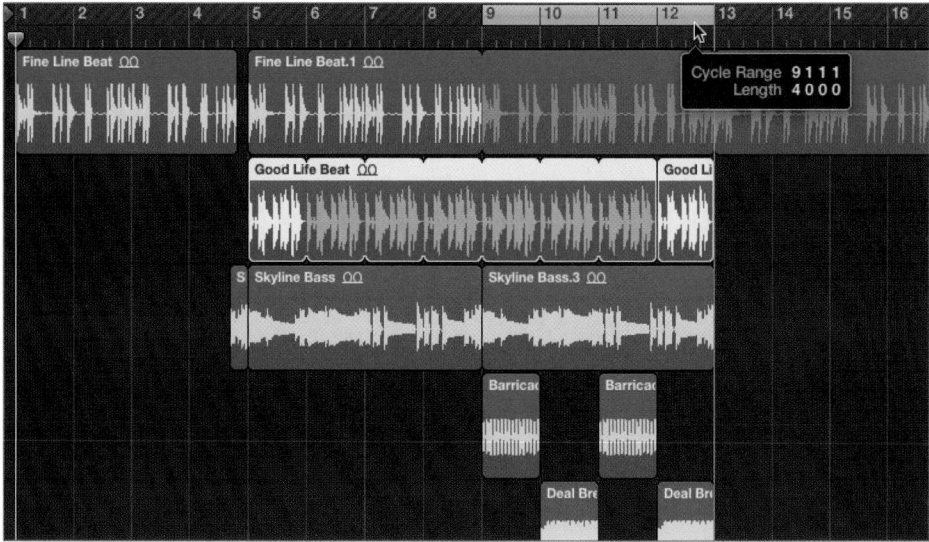

Cycle mode is turned on, and a cycle area appears where you dragged. The cycle area spans the part of the song in which the two synths, the drums, and the bass play, so you can focus on adjusting the sounds of those instruments. Later, when you're ready to work with the piano, you will just drag the cycle area to the following four bars where the piano plays.

7   Press the Spacebar.

Playback starts at the beginning of the cycle area, and the playhead keeps repeating bars 9 through 13, where the two synths are playing.

8   Click the Mixer button (or press X) to open the Mixer.

Synth 2 is significantly louder than Synth 1. Let's bring its level down so that both synths are equally loud.

9   On the Synth 2 channel strip, drag down the Volume fader.

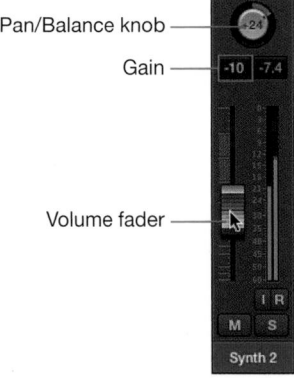

Continue adjusting the Volume fader until the Gain display reads –*10*. The Volume fader affects how much gain is applied to the audio signal at the output of the channel strip, and therefore, controls how loudly that instrument plays. Synth 2 is now quieter and closer to the level of Synth 1.

You will now adjust the Balance knobs on the two synth tracks to spread them a little farther apart in the stereo image.

10   On the Synth 1 channel strip, drag the Balance knob all the way down to –64.

11 On the Synth 2 channel strip, drag the Balance knob all the way up to +63.

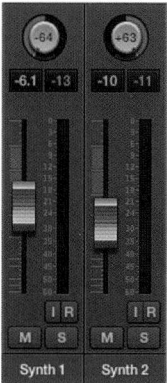

The synths sound too far apart now and seem disconnected from the rhythm section. The effect is even more pronounced if you listen to the song through headphones.

Let's bring the two synths back toward the center of the mix.

12 Adjust the Synth 1 and Synth 2 pan knobs to values of about −35 and +35, respectively.

The two synths come back closer to the center of the stereo field. Now they sound like they belong in the mix.

13 Press the spacebar to stop playback.

Processing Instruments with Plug-Ins

There's more to mixing than adjusting each instrument's volume and stereo position. Now you will apply effect plug-ins to process the audio signal flowing through the channel strip, thereby changing the tone of your instruments.

In this exercise you will use a bass amp plug-in to add an edgier character to the bass, and a reverberation plug-in to bring warmth and dimension to the piano.

1 On the Bass channel strip, click the Audio FX slot to open the plug-in menu.

2 From the menu, choose Amps and Pedals > Bass Amp Designer.

TIP When choosing a plug-in from a pop-up menu, you need to navigate to the name of the plug-in, but you don't have to select a plug-in format such as stereo or mono. When multiple formats are available in the menu, if you navigate to only the name of the plug-in, the most likely plug-in format is automatically used.

Bass Amp Designer

The Bass Amp Designer plug-in is inserted in the Audio FX slot on the channel strip, and its interface opens. Let's compare the sound of the bass with and without the plug-in applied.

3   Click the Power button.

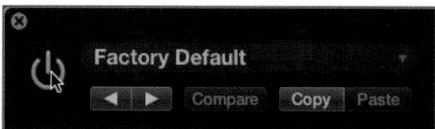

The Power button dims to indicate that the plug-in is off. You can hear what the bass sounds like without the plug-in. It sounds a bit muffled and vaguely distant.

4   Click the Power button again.

The attacks of the bass notes sound brighter, and have a little grit to them, giving the bass character. You could experiment with different amp models, but right now the Factory Default setting works great, so let's move on.

The bass amp also made the bass a bit louder. In fact, it is a little too loud now.

5   Close the plug-in windows by clicking the close button.

6   In the Mixer, drag down the Bass Volume fader until the Gain display reads about –*11.0*.

You will now add a plug-in to the Piano channel strip. But first you need to move the cycle area so you can hear the piano.

7   In the Tracks area, in the ruler, drag the cycle area 4 bars to the right, so it goes from bar 13 to 17.

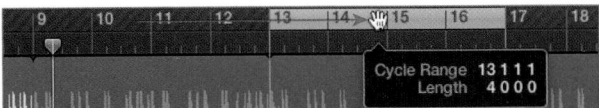

8   Start playback.

9   In the Mixer, click the Audio FX slot on the Piano channel strip.

10   From the pop-up menu, choose Reverb > Space Designer.

Now change the plug-in setting.

11   At the top of the plug-in interface, from the Setting pop-up menu, choose Medium Spaces > Rooms > 1.5s Piano Warmth.

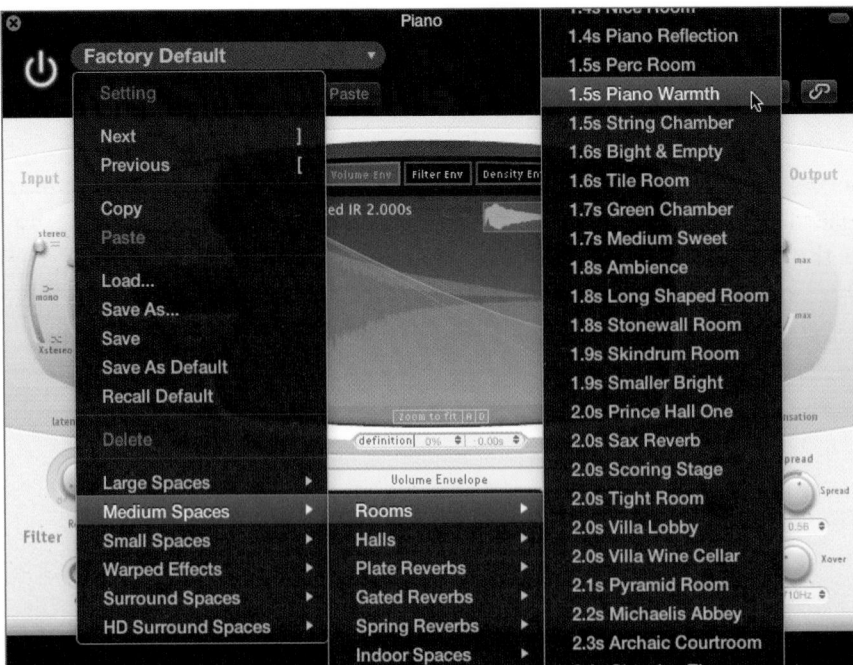

The piano immediately occupies more space and has more body. And in your arrangement, whenever the piano plays, not many other instruments are playing, so this setting works great.

12 Click the close button to close the Space Designer plug-in window.

13 Click the Mixer button (or press X) to close it.

14 In the ruler, click the cycle area (or press C) to turn off Cycle mode.

15 Play the entire song.

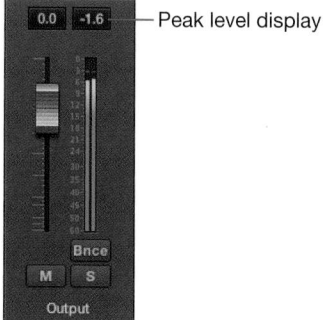 —Peak level display

In the Inspector, look at the peak level display on the Output channel strip. When a part of the song is too loud, the Output channel strip peak level display shows a positive value and turns red, indicating that the audio signal is distorted. In this project, the highest peak in the song is under 0 dB FS, and no distortion is created.

In a relatively short time, you have produced a one-minute instrumental song with six tracks, edited the regions in the workspace to build an arrangement, mixed the instruments in the Mixer, and added plug-ins to process their sounds. You now have a piece of music that would work fine, for example, during the credits of a radio or TV show, or as a music bed for a TV ad.

Mixing Down to a Stereo File

The last step is to mix down the music to a single stereo audio file so that anyone can play it on consumer-level audio software or hardware. In this exercise, you will bounce the project to a stereo audio file. By first selecting all your regions, you can avoid the need to manually adjust the bounce start and end positions.

1   In the Tracks area, choose Edit > Select > All (or press Command-A) to select all regions.

2   In the main menu bar, choose File > Bounce > Project or Section (or press Command-B) to open the Bounce dialog.

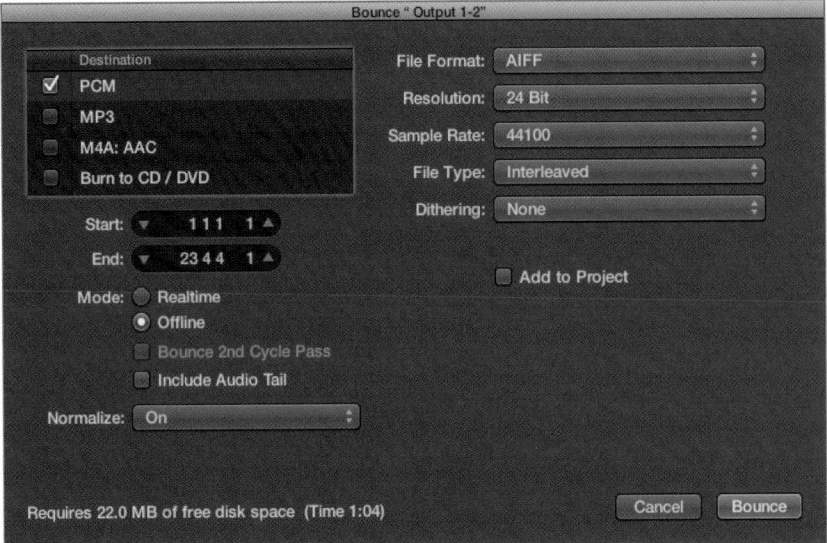

You can choose one or more Destination formats and adjust parameters for each format. You will learn more about the available file types in Lesson 10.

You will bounce an MP3 format file that you can easily email or upload to a website.

3   Deselect the PCM checkbox.

4   Select the MP3 checkbox.

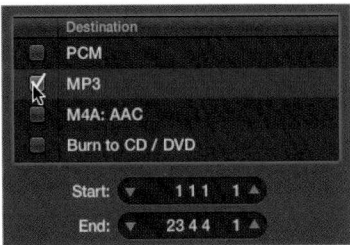

Below the Destination box, notice that the End position is correctly adjusted to the end of bar 23, when the last piano note finishes sustaining. That's because you selected all the regions in your workspace at the beginning of this exercise.

5 In the Bounce dialog, click the Bounce button (or press Return).

A Bounce Output 1-2 dialog opens. Bouncing creates a new stereo audio file on your hard drive, and you can now choose a filename and a location for the new file. The Save As field is already selected.

6 Type *Get Dancing*.

You will save the new MP3 file to your desktop.

7 From the Where pop-up menu, choose Desktop (or press Command-D).

8 Click Bounce (or press Return).

A Bouncing progress bar opens, and toward the end of the operation, an additional progress bar indicates the preparation of the MP3 file.

When the progress bars disappear, your MP3 file is ready on your desktop.

9 Choose Logic Pro X > Hide Logic Pro X (or press Command-H).

Logic Pro X is hidden, and you can see your desktop.

TIP ▶ If you have multiple apps open and you want to hide them all in order to see your desktop, first click the Finder icon in the Dock (or press Command-Tab to select the Finder) and choose Finder > Hide Others (or press Command-Option-H).

10 On your desktop, click **Get Dancing.mp3** to select it.

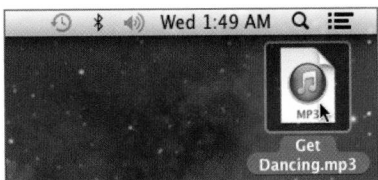

11 Press the Spacebar to play your song.

A quick look window opens, and your file starts playing. You can now share that MP3 file with all your friends and family!

Lesson Review

1. Where is the inspector and what are its uses?

2. Where is the Tracks area and what does it contain?

3. Where is the control bar and what does it contain?

4. Where is the workspace and what does it contain?

5. When multiple panes are open, how do you make sure the desired pane reacts to key commands?

6. Describe two ways to adjust a numerical value in Logic.

7. How do you copy a region?

8. How do you resize a region?

9. How do you loop a region?

10. In the Mixer, where do you add effect plug-ins?

11. In the help tag, what are the units of the four numeric values used to determine the length and position of a region?

12. How many ticks are there in a sixteenth note?

13. How do you mix down your project to a stereo audio file?

Answers

1. The inspector opens to the left of the Tracks area. Its contextual parameters adapt depending on which area has key focus, and what is selected.

2. The Tracks area is in the center of the main window. It contains the Track headers to the left, the ruler at the top, and the workspace where you edit regions.

3. The control bar is the row of buttons and displays at the top of your display. It contains transport buttons, information LCD displays, and mode buttons.

4. The workspace is in the Tracks area, to the right of the track headers, below the ruler, and contains the regions used in your project.

5. Click the area's background to give it key focus.

6. Drag the value vertically, or double-click it and enter a new value.

7. Option-drag the region and always release the mouse button first, followed by the Option key.

8. Place the mouse pointer over one of the two lower corners so it changes to a Resize tool, and then drag horizontally.

9. Select the region and press L, or select the Loop checkbox in the inspector.

10. In the Audio FX slots of the channel strips.

11. Bars, beats, divisions, and ticks

12. There are 240 ticks in a sixteenth note.

13. Choose File > Bounce > Project or Section (or press Command-B) to open the Bounce dialog.

Keyboard Shortcuts

Panels and Windows

I	Opens and closes the inspector
X	Opens and closes the Mixer
O	Opens the Loop Browser

Navigation

Spacebar	Plays or stops project
Control-Spacebar	Plays or stops selection (in browsers and editors)
, (comma)	Rewinds one bar
. (period)	Forwards one bar
Return	Returns to beginning of project
U	Sets rounded locators by selection
C	Toggles Cycle mode on and off

Zooming

Control-Option-drag	Expands the dragged area to fill the workspace
Z	Expands the selection to fill workspace, or goes back to previous zoom level, and shows all regions when no regions are selected
Command-Left Arrow	Zooms out horizontally
Command-Right Arrow	Zooms in horizontally
Command-Up Arrow	Zooms out vertically
Command-Down Arrow	Zooms in vertically

Keyboard Shortcuts

General

Command-Z	Undoes the last action
Command-Shift-Z	Redoes the last action
L	Toggles Loop parameter on and off for the selected region(s)
Command-A	Selects all
Command-B	Bounces the project
Command-S	Saves the project
Tab	Cycles key focus forward through open panes
Shift-Tab	Cycles key focus backward through open panes

Mac OS X

Command-D	Selects Desktop from "Where" pop-up menu in Save dialog
Command-H	Hides current application
Command-Option-H	Hides all other applications
Command-Tab	Cycles forward through open applications
Shift-Command-Tab	Cycles backward through open applications

2

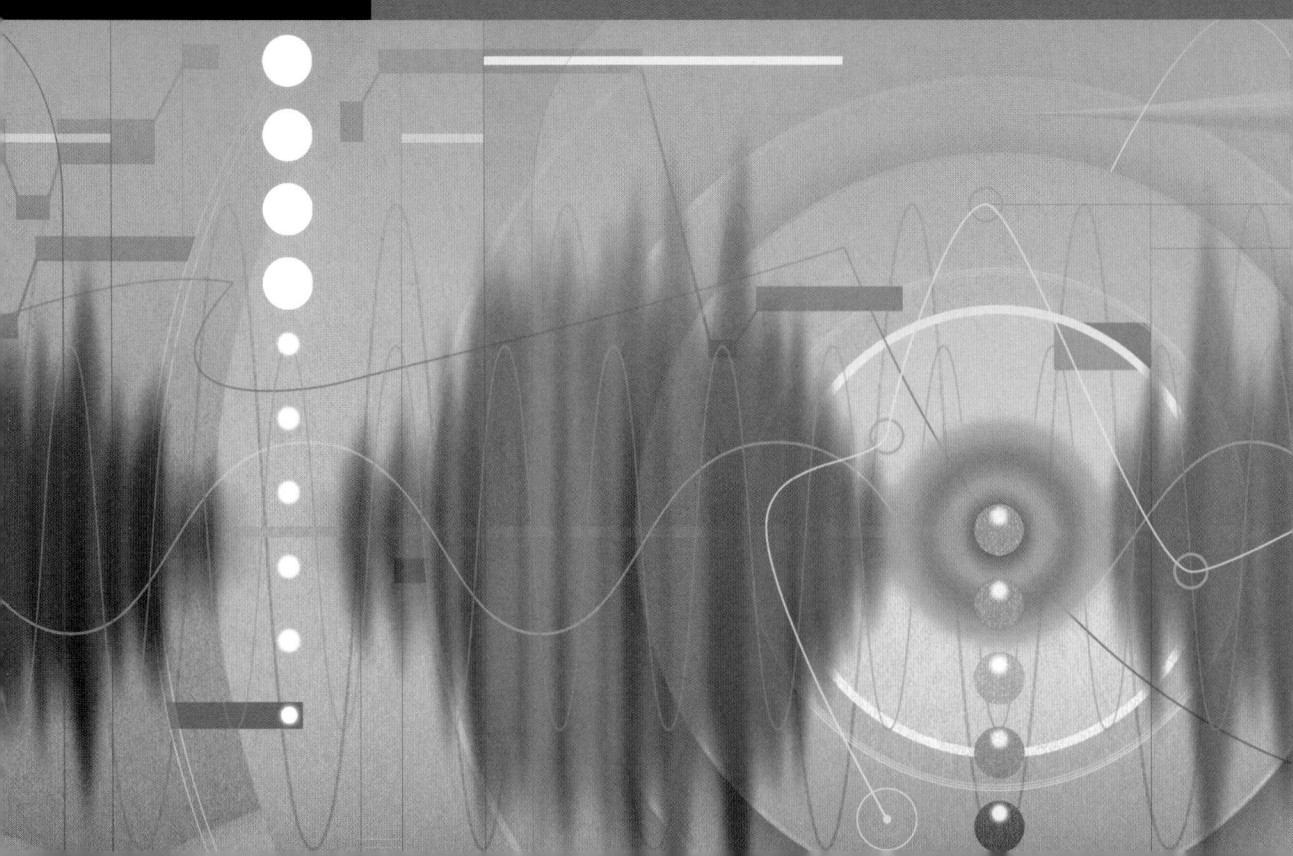

Recording Audio

To build a song, you need to come up with the raw material you will later arrange and mix. You might start with an idea you have in your head, a part you rehearsed on an instrument, or a prerecorded sample or loop, or you may just start experimenting until inspiration strikes. To sustain and develop that initial inspiration, you need to master the techniques that Logic offers to record, create, and edit the audio and MIDI regions that constitute the building blocks of your project.

In this lesson, you will configure Logic for audio recording and study activities you will typically perform when working with live musicians: recording a single instrument, recording additional takes of the same instrument, cycle recording, multitrack recording, punching on the fly, and automatic punching.

Setting Up Digital Audio Recording

Before you record audio in Logic, you have to connect a sound source (such as a microphone, an electric guitar, or a synthesizer) to your Mac. You then choose the desired recording settings, and adjust the recording level of your sound source to avoid distortion.

In the following exercises, you will set up Logic to prepare for a music recording.

▶ **Digital Recording, Sample Rate, and Bit Depth**

When audio is recorded in Logic Pro, sound pressure waves are turned into a digital audio file, as follows:

1.   The microphone transforms sound pressure waves into an analog electrical signal.

2.   The microphone preamp amplifies the analog electrical signal. A gain knob lets you set a proper recording level and avoid distortion.

3.   The analog-to-digital (A/D) converter transforms the analog electrical signal into a digital data stream.

4.   The audio interface sends the digital data stream from the converter to the computer.

5.   Logic Pro saves the incoming data as an audio file displayed on the screen by a waveform representing the sound pressure waves.

To convert the analog signal into a digital data stream, the digital converters sample the analog signal at a very fast time interval, or *sample rate*. The sample rate identifies how many times per second the audio is digitally sampled. The *bit depth* identifies the number of data bits used to encode the value of each sample. The sample rate and bit depth settings determine the quality of a digital audio recording.

During recording, the only role for Logic is to save the digital data generated by the A/D converter to an audio file. Assuming that you have the correct sample rate and bit depth settings, Logic does not exert any influence over the quality of your recordings.

NOTE ▶ Most audio interfaces include analog-to-digital converters, and many include microphone preamps. Also, most modern Mac computers include a built-in audio interface. Many Mac notebook computers and iMac computers even have internal microphones. Although those microphones are generally not intended to produce professional-quality recording, you can use the internal microphones to perform the exercises in this lesson in the absence of an external microphone.

Setting the Sample Rate

By setting your project's sample rate before starting your first recording, you help to insure that all the audio files used in that project will be recorded and played at the same sample rate. Playing an audio file at the wrong sample rate will result in the wrong pitch and tempo, much like playing an audiotape or vinyl record at the wrong transport speed.

> **NOTE** ▶ Be sure to read "Installing the Logic Lesson Files" in "Getting Started" before you continue.

1 Choose Logic Pro X Files > Lessons, and open **02 Get Dancing** (the song you created in Lesson 1).

2 Choose File > Project Settings > Audio.

The Project Settings window opens and you can see your Audio settings.

By default, the sample rate is set to 44.1 kHz.

To determine which sample rate to choose, consider the sample rate of any prerecorded material you will use (such as samples), and the sample rate of the target delivery medium. Some producers who make intensive use of 44.1 kHz samples choose to work at that sample rate. Traditionally, music is recorded at 44.1 kHz (which is the sample rate of compact discs), whereas audio for video is recorded at 48 kHz (which is the sample rate used on DVDs).

Note that Apple Loops (such as the ones used on the six existing tracks in this project) always play at the pitch and tempo determined by the project's key and tempo settings, independent of the project sample rate.

> **NOTE** ▶ The Audio Engineering Society recommends a 48 kHz sample rate for most applications, but recognizes the use of 44.1 kHz for compact disc and other consumer uses.

Let's keep the default 44.1 kHz sample rate.

3   Press Command-W to close the Project Settings window.

> **NOTE** ▶ In Logic, settings fall into two categories: Project settings, such as the sample rate, can be set individually for each project, so that each project can have unique project settings; Logic preferences, such as the bit depth, are the same in all projects.

Choosing the Bit Depth

The more bits you use to encode a sample, the more accurate the encoding, and the lower the level of noise in the digital audio file. Logic handles audio files of various bit depths in the same project without causing problems during playback, so you can choose a new bit depth when recording new content even if your project is already using files recorded with other bit depths.

Let's choose an audio interface and set the bit depth.

1   Choose Logic Pro X > Preferences > Audio.

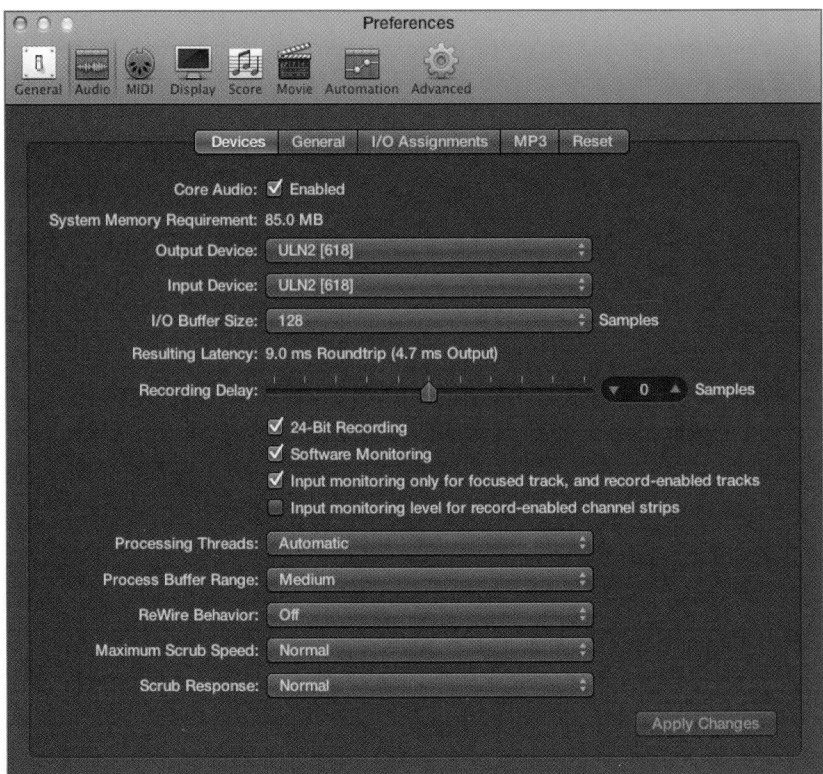

The Audio preferences appear.

2   From the Output Device and Input Device menus, choose the desired audio interfaces.

> ▶ The Output Device is the device connected to your monitors or headphones.

> ▶ The Input Device is the device into which you plug your microphones or
> instruments.

NOTE ▶ Using the same audio interface for both audio output and input is very common.

If you do not have an audio interface connected to your Mac, choose from the built-in output and input devices.

When the 24-Bit Recording option is not selected, Logic records at 16-bit resolution. A 24-bit recording has a significantly greater dynamic range than a 16-bit recording. The extended dynamic range lets you record at lower levels without having to worry about digital noise, thereby decreasing the chances of clipping your recording.

3   Make sure the 24-Bit Recording option is selected.

4   Press Command-W to close the Preferences window.

If you choose a new output or input device, Logic automatically reinitializes the Core Audio engine when you close the window.

MORE INFO ▶ Some options seldom need to be changed from the default settings. For more information on these, see "Changing Recording Settings" later in this lesson.

Recording a Single Track

In this example, you will record a single instrument. The exercise describes recording an electric guitar plugged directly into an instrument input on your audio interface, but feel free to record your voice or any instrument you have.

Preparing a Track for Recording

To record audio, you first have to create a new audio track, select the correct input (the input number on your audio interface where the guitar is plugged in), and enable that new track for recording.

When adding tracks, the new tracks are inserted below the selected track. To create a new track at the bottom of the Tracks area, you first need to select the bottom track.

1   At the bottom of the track headers, click the Piano track header (track 6) to select it.

2   Above the track headers, click the Add Tracks button (+) (or press Command-Option-N).

The New Tracks dialog appears.

3   Make sure the Audio track type is selected.

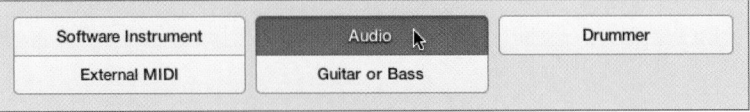

4   From the Input menu, choose the audio interface input number to which you've con-nected your instrument or microphone. If you are using your Mac computer's built-in audio interface or your notebook's microphone, leave the option set to Input 1.

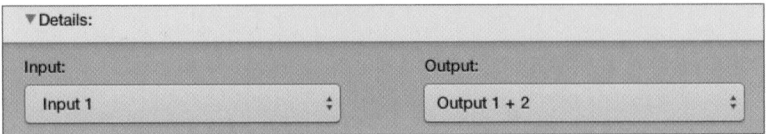

NOTE ▶ Below the Input and Output menus, the input and output devices selected earlier in your Audio preferences are displayed. Should you need to change the input and/or output device, click one of the arrow buttons to the right of the device names to open the Audio preferences.

You can record-enable the track by selecting the Record Enable option below the Output menu; however, in some situations creating a record-enabled track may produce feedback. You will later take precautions to avoid feedback and then record-enable the track from the track header.

5   Ensure that "Number of tracks" is set to 1.

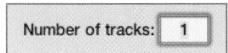

6   Click Create (or press Return).

A new audio track set to Input 1 is created. Logic automatically assigns the new track to the next available channel. Since six audio tracks were created when you dragged Apple Loops in Lesson 1, the new track is assigned to the Audio 7 channel and is automatically named Audio 7. For clarity, let's rename it.

TIP ▶ Logic automatically assigns the name of a track to the audio files recorded on that track, so naming a track before recording on it is always a good idea. If you don't name the track, Logic assigns the name of the project to the audio files. More-descriptive names will help you identify files in the future.

7   In the Audio 7 track header, double-click the name, and type *Guitar*.

The new track has a generic audio waveform icon. You will now choose a more appropriate icon.

8   In the Guitar track header, Control-click the icon, and from the shortcut menu, choose the desired icon.

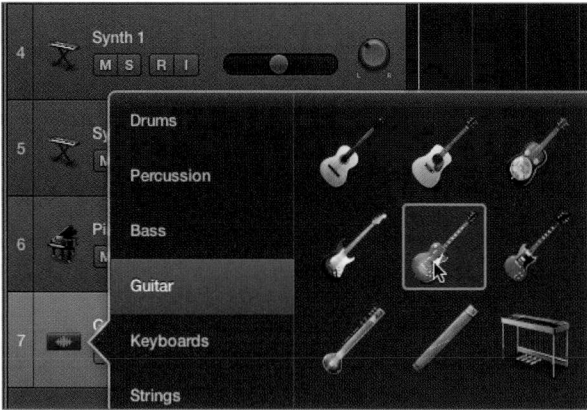

NOTE ▶ To avoid feedback when recording with a microphone, monitor your recording using headphones, and make sure your speakers are off.

9   In the Guitar track header, click the R (Record Enable) button.

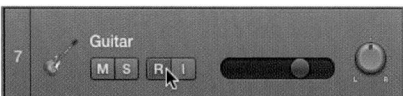

You can now hear your guitar and see its input level on the Guitar channel strip meter in the Inspector.

NOTE ▶ You may hear a small delay between the time you play a note and when you hear it. This delay is called *latency*. You will learn how to reduce latency at the end of this lesson, in the section "Choosing the I/O Buffer Size."

Because your new audio track is record-enabled (the R button on the track header is red), the next recording will create an audio region on that track. You can monitor the audio routed to record-enabled tracks while Logic is stopped, playing, or recording.

NOTE ▶ If you are already using a hardware mixer or your audio interface's software to monitor the audio signal routed to record-enabled tracks, turn off Software Monitoring in the Logic Audio preferences. Otherwise, you will be monitoring the signal twice, resulting in a flangy or robotic sound.

Monitoring Effects During Recording

When a guitar or bass is plugged directly into an audio interface's instrument preamp, the sound is clean and raw. To emulate the character a guitar amp can give to a guitar sound, you can use Amp Designer, a guitar amplifier modeling plug-in.

Note that you are still recording a dry guitar sound. The effect plug-in processes the dry audio signal in real-time during the recording and playback. Recording a *dry signal* means that you can continue fine-tuning the effect plug-ins (or exchange them for other plug-ins) after the recording is completed.

1   In the Inspector, click the Audio FX insert, and choose Amps and Pedals > Amp Designer.

Amp Designer opens. Here, you can dial in a sound, or choose a preset.

2   In the Amp Designer window, click the settings menu and choose a setting that inspires you.

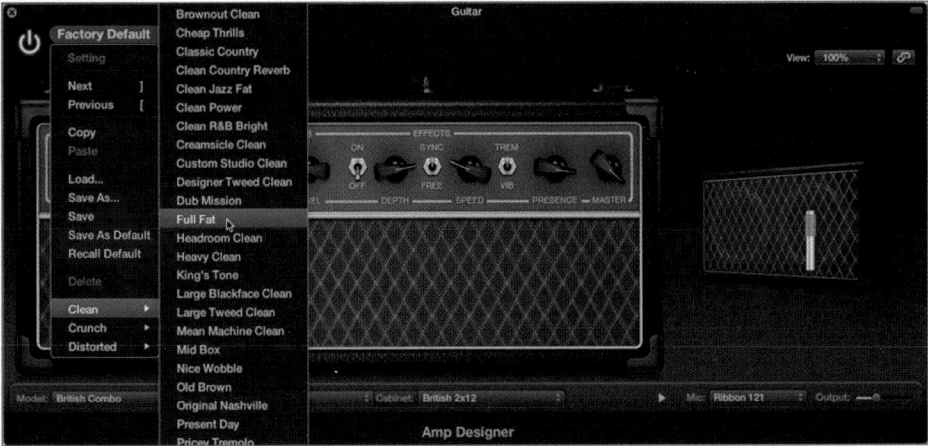

You can now hear your guitar processed through Amp Designer. It sounds like a guitar plugged into a guitar amp, and recorded by a microphone in front of the amp's speaker cabinet. Feel free to spend a few minutes exploring various settings and tweaking the amp's knobs until you're happy with your sound.

3   Press Command-W to close the Amp Designer window.

Adjusting the Recording Level

Before recording, make sure you can monitor the sound through Logic, and then adjust the source audio level to avoid overloading the converters. On the channel strip, look at the peak level meter, and make sure it always stays below 0 dBFS (decibels full scale, the unit used to measure levels in digital audio), which would indicate that you are clipping the input of your converter. Keep in mind that you need to adjust the audio level before the converter input by using your microphone preamp gain knob. Allow some headroom, especially if you know that the artist might play or sing louder during the actual recording. Working with a low-level recording is better than clipping the input.

> **NOTE** ▶ If you are using the built-in Mac line input or microphone, you can adjust the input level in the Sound pane's Input tab in System Preferences.

Let's adjust the recording and monitoring levels, tune the guitar, and find a cool acoustic guitar sound.

1   Play the loudest part of the performance you are about to record, and as you watch the peak level meter on the channel strip adjust the level on the instrument preamp.

2   If the peak level meter turns yellow, lower the gain on the preamp, and click the peak level meter to reset it.

Make sure the peak sits comfortably below 0 dBFS: The wider the dynamic range of the source, the more headroom it needs to avoid clipping.

 Peak level meter

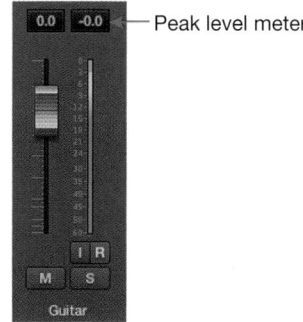 Peak level meter

Audio not clipping   Audio clipping

When your signal peaks below –2.0 dBFS, the peak level meter value is green. When it peaks between –2.0 and 0 dBFS, the peak level meter value is yellow to indicate that you are within 2 dB of clipping. (That is, you have less than 2 dB of headroom.)

Tuning the Instrument

Making sure an instrument is in tune before recording is always a good idea. The control bar's Tuner button gives you quick access to Logic's Tuner plug-in.

1   In the control bar, click the Tuner button.

The Tuner opens.

NOTE ▶ The Tuner is only available in the control bar when an audio track is selected and an input is selected in the input slot of the corresponding channel strip. You can also insert the Tuner as a plug-in on a channel strip: Click an Audio FX slot, and choose Metering > Tuner.

2   One by one, tune the guitar strings, trying to get each string as close as possible to a 0 cents deviation of the target pitch.

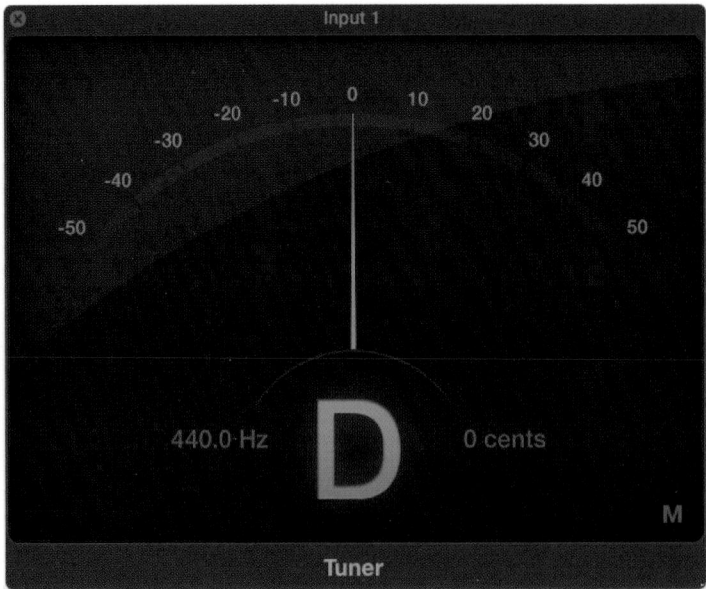

3   Close the Tuner window.

Checking the Balance

Now that the guitar is tuned, you can practice the performance and make sure you can hear yourself and the other instruments comfortably.

1   Press the Spacebar to start playback, and play along with the song. If the guitar is now too loud or too soft in comparison to the other tracks, use the volume slider in the Guitar track header to adjust the monitoring level, or drag the volume fader on the Guitar channel strip in the Inspector.

The track header's volume slider and the channel strip's volume fader adjust the monitoring and playback level, but they do not alter the recording level.

2   Press the Spacebar to stop playback.

Recording Audio

You have set the desired sample rate and bit depth, adjusted the recording and monitoring levels, inserted a plug-in to emulate the sound of a guitar amp, and tuned the instrument. You are now ready to start recording.

Let's record a guitar part from bar 13 to bar 17.

1   In the lower half of the ruler, click at bar 13.

The playhead is positioned at bar 13. In the control bar's LCD display, make sure the playhead position is exactly bar 13, beat 1, div 1, tick 1. If you need to adjust the position of the playhead, drag it left or right.

2   In the control bar, click the Record button (or press R).

The playhead and the LCD display in the control bar both turn red to indicate that Logic is recording. The playhead jumps one bar earlier and gives you a four-beat count-in with an audible metronome click before the recording starts. A new red region is created behind the playhead on the record-enabled track, and you can see the recording's waveform drawn in as you play or sing.

NOTE ► By default, the metronome automatically turns on during recording, and you get a four-beat count-in (in the control bar, the Count-in and Metronome buttons are enabled). You will learn how to alter both the metronome and the count-in settings later in this lesson.

Count-in

Metronome

3   After you've recorded a few bars, in the control bar, click the Stop button (or press the Spacebar).

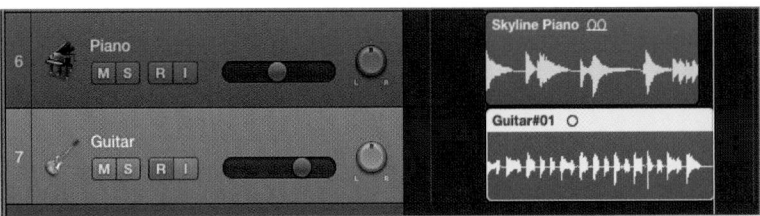

The new recording, Guitar#01, appears as a blue-shaded audio region. To the name of the track, Logic appends the number of the recording. Note that this new region is selected, which makes listening to it easy using the "Play from Selection" key command.

4   Press Shift-Spacebar.

The playhead jumps to the beginning of the selected region and playback starts.

5   Stop playback.

If you are not happy with your new recording, you can delete it and start over.

6   Press Delete.

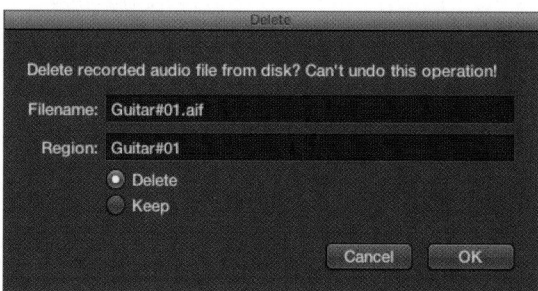

A Delete alert appears with two choices:

▶   Delete—The audio region is removed from the Tracks area, and the audio file is removed from the Project Audio Browser. In the Finder, the audio file is moved from inside the project package to the Trash.

▶   Keep—The audio region is removed from the Tracks area. The audio file stays in the All Files Browser and is still present inside the project package, allowing you to later drag it back to the workspace if necessary.

NOTE ▶ To find the audio files inside a project package, Control-click the project package in the Finder, choose Show Package Contents, and then navigate to Media > Audio Files.

This alert appears only when you try to delete a recording made since you most recently opened the project. When deleting an audio region that was previously recorded, the behavior corresponding to the Keep option is automatically applied and an alert does not appear.

TIP ▶ Despite what the alert says, if you chose Delete and clicked OK by mistake, you can still choose Edit > Undo (or press Command-Z) to undo the operation (as long as you don't empty the Trash).

You will keep your recording so you can experiment with recording additional takes in the next exercise.

7   In the Delete pop-up window, click Cancel.

Recording Additional Takes

When recording a live performance, musicians can make mistakes. Rather than deleting the previous recording and repeatedly recording until you get a flawless performance, you can record several takes (repeat performances of the same musical part), and later choose the best take, or even combine the best parts of each take to create a *comp* (composite take).

To preserve multiple takes in Logic, you can record new performances over previous ones. All the takes (including the original recording) will be placed into a take folder.

1   Make sure the Guitar track is still record-enabled.

2   Position the playhead on bar 13.

3   In the control bar, click the Record button (or press R) to record a second take slightly longer than the first.

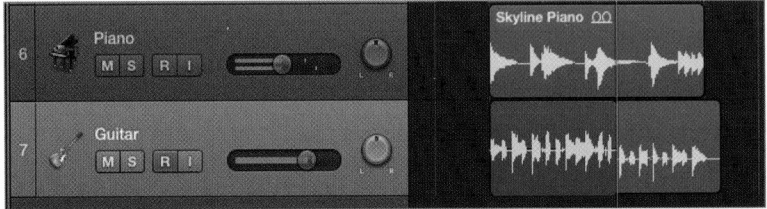

The new recording (in red) appears to be recorded over the previous blue audio region.

4 Stop the recording.

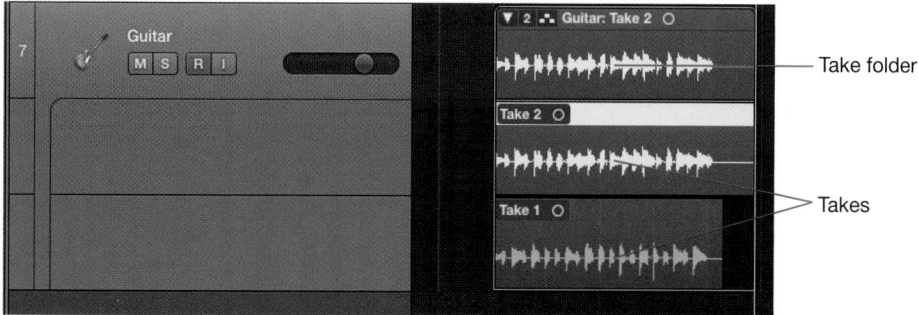

Take folder

Takes

Both the original recording (Take 1) and the new recording (Take 2) have been saved into a take folder. The take folder is on the Guitar track. It is currently open, so the two takes you recorded are displayed on subtracks below.

The take folder is named Guitar: Take 2, the name of the track appended with the name of the take it's playing. By default, the take folder plays the most recent take you recorded, Take 2, in this case. The previous take, Take 1, is dimmed and muted.

NOTE ▶ If the recent take that you recorded is shorter than a take you recorded earlier, the take folder is named Guitar: Comp A, and plays a comp made of the recent take and the end of the previous take.

5 Record a third take.

6 In the Guitar track header, click the R (Record Enable) button to disable it.

The track is disarmed, and you can no longer hear the sound coming from input 1 on your audio interface.

The take folder now contains three takes. It plays back the most recent one, Take 3, while the two previous ones, Take 1 and Take 2, are muted.

MORE INFO ▸ You will examine take folders in more detail and learn to comp takes in Lesson 3.

7 At the top left of the Guitar take folder, click the disclosure triangle to close the folder.

TIP ▸ You can also double-click a take folder to open or close it.

Recording Takes in Cycle Mode

Recording multiple takes can be very useful when you are both the engineer and the musician because switching from playing your instrument to operating Logic between each take isn't always practical (and it can really destroy your creative vibe). Recording in Cycle mode allows you to repeatedly record a single section, thereby creating a new take for each pass of the cycle. When you stop recording, all the takes are saved inside a take folder.

1 In the lower-half of the ruler, drag a cycle area from bar 5 to bar 9.

TIP ▸ You don't have to position the playhead when recording in Cycle mode; recording automatically starts at the beginning of the cycle, after the count-in.

2 Make sure the Guitar track is selected, and click Record (or press R).

The Guitar track is automatically record-enabled. The playhead jumps a bar ahead of the cycle for a one-measure count-in, and starts recording the first take. When it reaches bar 9, the end of the cycle area, it jumps back to bar 5 and starts recording a new take.

NOTE ► If no track is record-enabled, Logic automatically record-enables the selected track during recording.

Logic keeps looping the cycle area, recording new takes until you stop recording. Record two or three takes.

3 Click Stop (or press the Spacebar).

All the takes recorded in Cycle mode are packed into a take folder. The Guitar track is automatically disabled for recording.

NOTE ► When you stop recording, if the recent take is shorter than a bar, Logic automatically discards it. To keep the last take of a cycle recording, make sure you stop the recording more than one bar after the beginning of the cycle area.

4 At the top left of the take folder, click the disclosure triangle.

The take folder closes.

5 In the ruler, click the cycle area (or press C) to turn it off.

Recording Multiple Tracks

You can use the same single-track techniques you've learned to record multiple tracks simultaneously. Doing so allows you to record several instruments at once, placing each instrument on a separate track, so that you can later adjust their volumes and stereo positions, or process them individually.

You first create the desired number of tracks, making sure that each track is assigned to a different input number that corresponds to the input number on your audio interface where the microphone is plugged in.

> **NOTE ▸** Logic does not let you record-enable multiple tracks set to the same input number because you would record the same input on different tracks, and end up with redundant audio files.

In the following exercise, you will record two mono tracks at the same time, which you can do using the built-in Mac audio interface. To record more than two tracks at once, you need an audio interface with more than two inputs. The exercise describes recording an acoustic guitar on Input 1 and a vocal microphone on Input 2.

> **NOTE ▸** To avoid the sound of the guitar bleeding into the vocal microphone or the sound of the vocals bleeding into the guitar microphone, the guitar player and the singer should be located in different rooms.

1   At the bottom of the Tracks area, click the Guitar track header to ensure that the tracks you are about to create will be added below the Guitar track.

2   Above the track headers, click the Add Tracks button (+) (or press Command-Option-N) to open the New Tracks dialog.

3   At the top of the New Tracks dialog, make sure the Audio track type is selected.

4   From the Input menu, choose Ascending.

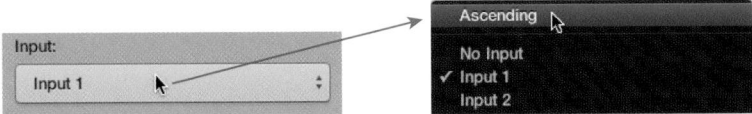

When creating multiple tracks, choosing Ascending automatically sets the inputs (or outputs) to ascending settings. In this case, you will create two tracks, so the first will be assigned to Input 1 and the second to Input 2.

Make sure you took precautions to avoid feedback as explained at the beginning of this lesson; this time you will create record-enabled tracks.

5   Below the Output menu, select Record Enable.

6   At the bottom of the New Tracks dialog, set "Number of tracks" to 2.

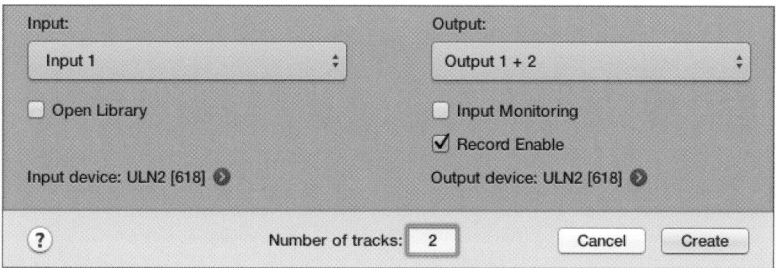

7   Click Create (or press Return).

Two new tracks are added at the bottom of the Tracks area, and automatically assigned to the next available audio channels (Audio 8 and Audio 9). Their inputs are set to Input 1 and Input 2, and both are record-enabled.

TIP ▶ If you need to reassign a track's input, click the Input slot on the track's channel strip and choose the new input.

NOTE ▶ The number of inputs available in the Input menu depends on the audio interface selected as an input device in the Logic Audio preferences.

8 Rename the tracks *Acoustic Gtr* and *Vocals*.

9 In the control bar, click the Go to Beginning button (or press Return).

10 Start recording.

The multitrack recording starts, and after a one-measure count-in, you see the red playhead appear to the left of the workspace, creating two red regions, one on each record-enabled track.

11 After a few bars, stop recording.

You now have a new blue-shaded audio region on each track.

12 In the Acoustic Gtr and Vocals track headers, click the R (Record Enable) buttons to disable recording for both tracks.

You can use the same procedure to simultaneously record as many tracks as needed. If the tracks already exist in the Tracks area, make sure you assign them the correct inputs, record-enable them, and start recording.

> **NOTE ▶** You can record multiple takes on multiple tracks the same way you previously recorded to a single track: Either return the playhead to the beginning of the first take and record a new take, or record multiple takes in Cycle mode.

Punching In and Out

When you want to correct a specific section of a recording—usually to fix a performance mistake—you can restart playback before the mistake, punch in to engage recording just before the section you wish to fix, and then punch out to stop recording immediately after the section while playback continues. A take folder is created, containing a comp that combines the old recording outside the punch-in/punch-out range with the new recording inside that range. This technique allows you to fix smaller mistakes in a recording while still listening to the continuity of the performance.

> **TIP** ▶ Punching is nondestructive. At any time, you can open the take folder and select the original recording.

There are two punching methods: on the fly and automatic. Punching on the fly allows you to press a key to punch in and out while Logic plays, whereas automatic punching requires you to identify the autopunch area in the ruler before recording. Punching on the fly is fast but usually requires an engineer to perform the punch in and punch out while the musician is performing. Automatic punching is ideal for the musician-producer who is working alone.

Assigning Key Commands

To punch on the fly, you will use the Record Toggle command, which is unassigned by default. First, you'll open the Key Commands window and assign Record Toggle to a key combination.

1   Choose Logic Pro X > Key Commands > Edit (or press Option-K) to open the Key Commands window. Click the disclosure triangle next to Global Commands.

The Key Commands window lists all available Logic commands and the keyboard shortcuts they are assigned to, if any.

TIP ▶ Many commands are unassigned by default. When looking for a specific functionality in Logic Pro X, open the Key Commands window, and try to locate the function using the search field. A command likely exists for that functionality that may or may not be assigned.

2   In the Command list, click the Record Toggle command.

3   Click Learn by Key Label.

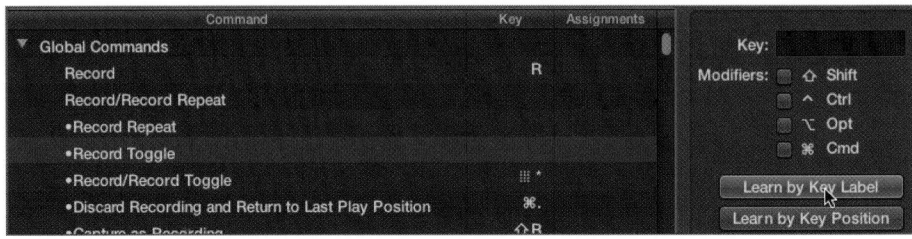

When Learn by Key Label is selected, you can press a key, or a key plus a combination of modifiers (Command, Control, Shift, Option), to create a keyboard command for the selected function.

4   Press R.

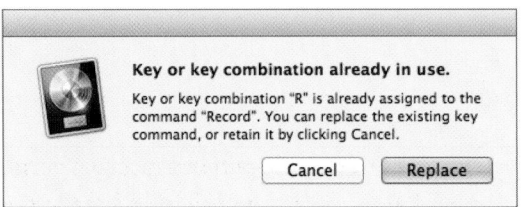

An alert indicates that the R key is already assigned to the Record command. You could click Replace to assign R to Record Toggle, but then Record would no longer be assigned to a keyboard shortcut. Instead, let's use another key combination.

5   Click Cancel (or press Esc).

6   Press Control-J.

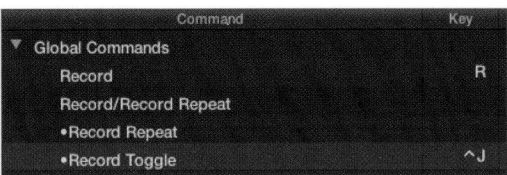

Control-J is now listed in the Key column next to Record Toggle, indicating that the command was successfully assigned.

TIP ▶ To unassign a key command, select the command, make sure Learn by Key Label is selected, and press Delete.

7   Close the Key Commands window.

TIP ▶ To reset all key commands to their defaults, choose Logic Pro X > Key Commands > Presets > U.S. (or the language of your choice).

Punching on the Fly

You will now use the Record Toggle key command you assigned in the previous exercise to punch on the Vocals track (the bottom track in your Tracks area).

1   In the Vocals track header, click the R button to record-enable the track.

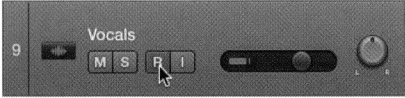

When punching on the fly, you may first want to play the performance to determine which section needs to be re-recorded, and to be ready to punch in and out at the desired locations.

2   Listen to the Vocals track and determine where you're going to punch in and out.

3   In the control bar, click the Go to Beginning button (or press Return).

4   Click Play (or press the Spacebar) to start playback.

Position your fingers on the keyboard to be ready to press your Record Toggle key command when you reach the point where you want to punch in.

NOTE ▸ To be able to punch on the fly, in the control bar, Control-click the Record button and make sure Allow Quick Punch-In is selected.

5   Press Control-J (Record Toggle).

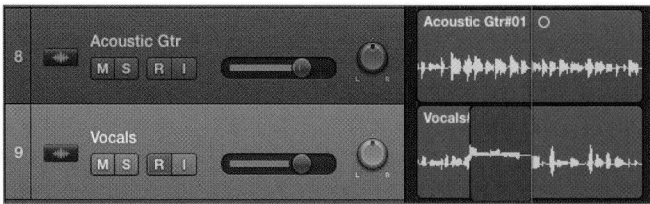

The playhead continues moving, but Logic is now recording a new take on top of the previous recording. Keep your fingers in position to be ready to punch out.

6   Press Control-J again.

The recording stops while the playhead continues playing the project.

7   Stop the playback.

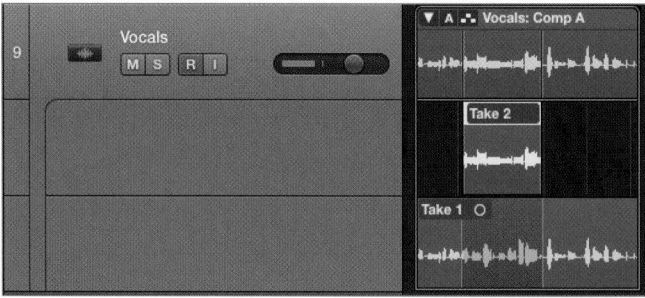

On the Vocals track, a take folder was created. It contains your original recording (Take 1) and the new take (Take 2). A comp is automatically created (Comp A) that combines the original recording up to the punch-in point, the new take between the punch-in and punch-out points, and the original recording after the punch-out point.

8   Listen to your Vocals track.

In the next exercise you will examine another punching technique, so let's undo this recording.

9   Choose Edit > Undo Recording (or press Command-Z).

The take folder disappears and you once again see the Vocals#01 region on the Vocals track.

Punching on the fly is a great technique to use when the musician can focus on his performance while the engineer takes care of punching in and out at the right times. On the other hand, if you worked alone through this exercise and tried to punch in and punch out while playing your instrument or singing, you realize how challenging it can be. When working alone, punching automatically is recommended.

Punching Automatically

To prepare for automatic punching, you enable the Autopunch mode and set the autopunch area. Setting the punch-in and punch-out points in advance allows you to focus entirely on your performance during recording.

First, you will customize the control bar to add the Autopunch button.

1   Control-click the control bar, and choose Customize Control Bar and Display.

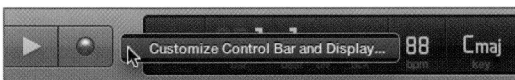

A dialog opens in which you can choose the buttons you would like to see in the control bar, and the information you'd like to see in its LCD display.

2   In the dialog's Modes and Functions column, choose Autopunch to add the Autopunch button to the control bar.

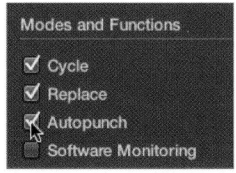

NOTE ▶ The control bar is customized independently for each Logic project file, which allows you to show different buttons and displays depending on the specific needs of each project.

3   Click the Autopunch button (or press Command-Control-Option-P).

NOTE ▸ When the main window is not wide enough for the control bar to display all the buttons selected in the control bar customization dialog, you can click the chevron (>>) to the right of the mode buttons to access the hidden functions in a shortcut menu.

The ruler becomes taller to accommodate for the red autopunch area.

The autopunch area defines the section to be re-recorded. You can define the auto-punch area with more precision when you can clearly see where the mistakes are on the audio waveform.

TIP ▸ To toggle the Autopunch mode on and off, Command-click the lower half of the ruler.

4   Click the background of the workspace to deselect every region.

5   On the Vocals track, click the Vocals#01 region to select it.

6   Press Z.

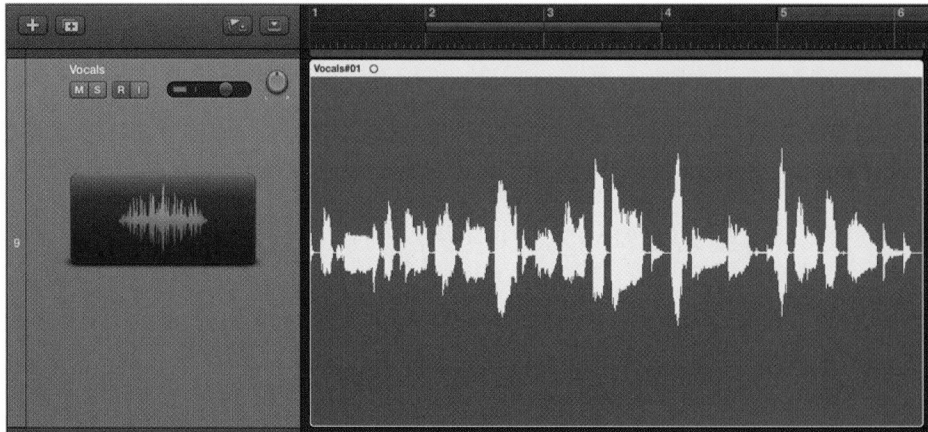

Logic zooms in, and the selected region fills the workspace.

7 Listen to the vocal recording and determine which section you're going to fix.

Here we have a vocal recording in which the two first words of measure 2 need to be re-recorded. Listen while watching the playhead move over the waveform to determine which part of the waveform corresponds to the words you need to replace.

8 Adjust the autopunch area so that it encompasses the area you want to re-record.

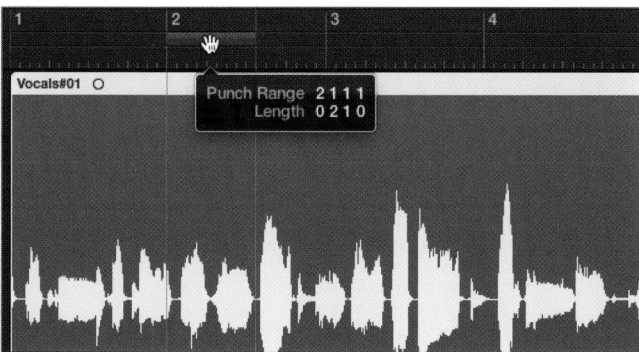

You can drag the edges of the autopunch area to resize it, or drag the entire area to move it. Red vertical guidelines help you align the punch-in and punch-out points with the waveform. You may need to zoom in closer to make sure you're re-recording exactly what you want.

9 Control-Option-drag around the waveform below the autopunch area.

10 Fine-tune the position of the autopunch area.

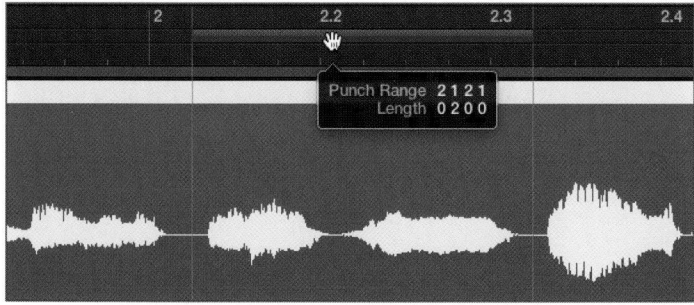

11 Click Go to Beginning (or press Return).

12 Click Record (or press R).

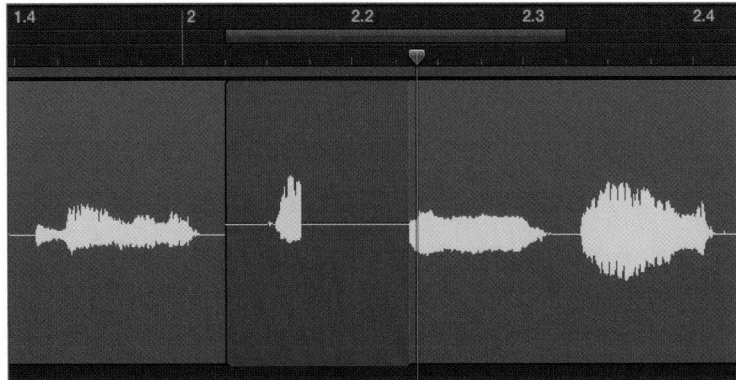

Playback starts. In the control bar, the Record button blinks; Logic isn't yet recording.

When the playhead reaches the punch-in point (the left edge of the autopunch area), the Record button turns solid red, and Logic starts recording a new take.

When the playhead reaches the punch-out point (the right edge of the autopunch area), the recording stops but the playback continues.

13 Stop playback.

A take folder Vocals: Comp A is created on the track.

14 Click the take folder to select it.

15 Press Z.

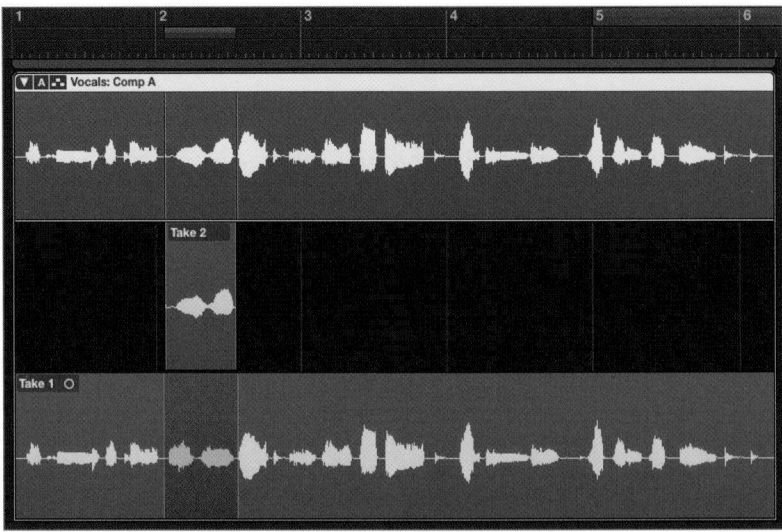

Logic zooms out so you can see the entire take folder filling the workspace.

Just as when you punched on the fly in the previous exercise, a comp is automatically created that plays the original recording up to the punch-in point, inserts the new take between the punch-in and punch-out points, and continues with the original recording after the punch-out point.

16 In the control bar, click the Autopunch button (or press Command-Control-Option-P) to disable Autopunch mode.

17 At the top left of the take folder, click the disclosure triangle to close the take folder.

> **TIP** ▸ You can speed up the Autopunch recording process by using the Marquee tool described in Lesson 3. When a marquee selection is present, starting a recording automatically turns on the Autopunch mode, and the autopunch area matches the marquee selection.

Changing Recording Settings

Although you can immediately record audio with Logic Pro X, sometimes you'll want to change its default recording settings. Some settings do not affect the quality of the audio recording, but can alter the behavior of your project during recording, or change the audio file format used for recordings. The next few exercises will show you how those settings affect the audio recording process, and how to modify them.

Setting the Count-In

The count-in is the time you have to prepare yourself and get in the groove before the actual recording begins.

1 On the Vocals track at the bottom of the workspace, click the take folder to select it, and press Delete.

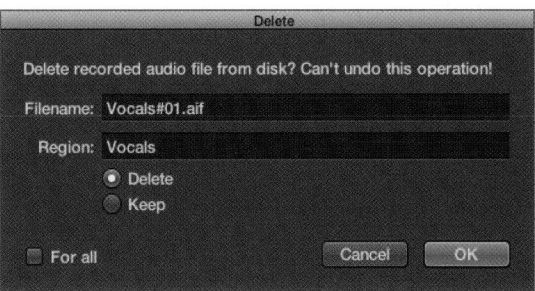

An alert asks you to confirm the operation. If you were only experimenting and wanted to remove the files you recorded during the two previous punching exercises, you could delete them now. Selecting the "For all" option allows you to apply the Delete operation to all the selected files (meaning all the recordings inside the selected take folder), which expedites the process when you want to delete multiple files.

2   Select the "For all" option, and click OK (or press Return).

The take folder is deleted, and all the audio files it contained are moved to the Trash.

3   Go to the beginning of the project.

Until now, every time you pressed Record, the playhead jumped to the beginning of the previous measure so you could have a four-beat count-in. However, sometimes you may want to start recording without a count-in.

4   In the control bar, click the Count-in button to turn off count-in.

5   Start recording, and stop after a couple of bars.

The playhead starts from its current position, and Logic starts recording right away.

At other times, you may need a longer count-in, or you may want Logic to count-in for a specific number of beats.

6   Press Command-Z to undo the recording.

The audio region is removed from the workspace, but the audio file is still in the project folder.

See the "Deleting Unused Audio Files" section later in this chapter to learn how to delete all unused recordings by using the Project Audio Browser.

7   From the main menu, choose Record > Count-in > 2 Bars.

8   Position the playhead at bar 5, and start recording.

The playhead jumps two bars ahead to bar 3, and playback starts. When the playhead reaches bar 5, Logic starts recording.

NOTE ▸ In Logic a count-in always starts at the beginning of a bar, even when you start recording in the middle of a bar.

9 Press Command-Z to undo the recording.

Setting the Metronome

By default, the metronome is turned off during playback and automatically plays during recording. In this exercise, you will change the default behaviors using the Metronome button and later go into the Metronome settings to adjust its sounds.

1 In the control bar, click the Metronome button to turn it on.

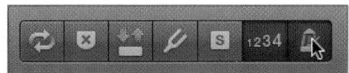

2 Start playback.

The metronome is on.

3 Stop playback and start recording.

The metronome is on.

4 While Logic is still recording, turn off the metronome.

The metronome is off.

5 Stop recording.

The metronome is back on. You now have inverted the default behavior: The metronome is on during playback and is automatically turned off during recording.

6 In the control bar, Control-click the Metronome button, and deselect Click While Playing.

The metronome is now off regardless of whether you're playing or recording.

7 Click the Metronome button to turn it back on.

8 Control-click the Metronome button, and choose Metronome Settings.

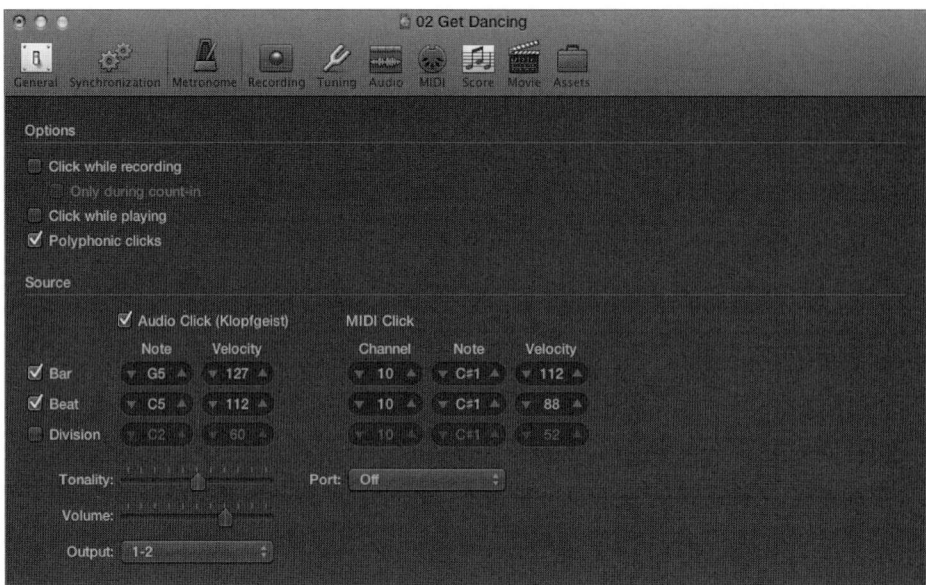

The Metronome Settings window opens. There are settings for two metronomes: Audio Click (originally named Klopfgeist, which is German for *Knocking Ghost*, in earlier Logic versions), which you are using, and MIDI Click, which is now off.

NOTE ▶ If you want your metronome to play a specific sound on an external hardware MIDI synthesizer, sampler, or drum machine, use the MIDI Click. From the Port menu, choose a MIDI Out port, and connect a MIDI cable from that MIDI Out port on the MIDI Interface to the MIDI In port on your hardware sampler/synthesizer.

Under the name of each metronome you can adjust the pitch and velocity of the notes playing on each bar and beat. You can play a sound on every division, which can be useful when working with very slow tempos.

9 Go to the beginning of the song, start playback, and listen to the metronome.

The metronome sounds a little low compared to the drum loop on track 1. In fact, you can hear it only when no drum hit occurs on that beat. At the bottom of the Metronome Settings window, you can drag a couple of sliders to adjust the sound of the metronome.

10 Drag the Volume slider all the way to the right.

Even with the volume turned all the way up, it's challenging for a dry metronome sound to cut through a busy mix, and you still have to strain to hear it, especially starting at bar 5, where the bass and drums come in.

11 Drag the Tonality slider slowly toward the right.

The metronome sound changes, and you can start hearing a pitch. Adjusting the tonality of the metronome is important: A pitched sound (slider to the right) will better cut through a busy mix, but it will also bleed through the musician's headphones into the microphone. A more muted sound (slider to the left) is more suitable for quiet mixes in which you can't tolerate any metronome bleed.

12 Adjust the metronome so that it is loud and clear.

When a project already contains a drum track, you may need the metronome only during the count-in to get into the groove before the song starts.

13 At the top of the Metronome Settings window, under Options, select "Click while recording" and "Only during count-in."

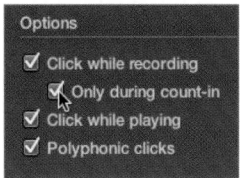

14 Close the Settings window, go to the beginning of the project, and start recording.

You hear the metronome for two measures, and then it stops playing as the song and the recording start at bar 1.

15 Stop and undo the recording.

16 Click the Metronome button to turn it off.

Choosing the I/O Buffer Size

When communicating with the audio interface, Logic does not receive or transmit just one sample at a time. It places a number of samples in an input buffer for recording, and an output buffer for monitoring. When a buffer is full, Logic processes or transmits the entire buffer. The larger the buffers, the less computing power is required from the CPU. The advantage of using larger input and output buffers is that the CPU has more time to calculate other processes such as instrument and effects plug-ins. The drawback to using a larger buffer is that you may have to wait a bit for the buffer to fill before you can monitor your signal. That means a longer delay between the original sound and the one you hear through Logic, a delay called *roundtrip latency*.

Usually, you want the shortest possible latency when recording and the most available CPU processing power when mixing, so that you can use more plug-ins. You can adjust the I/O buffer size depending on your situation.

1 Choose Logic Pro X > Preferences > Audio.

The Audio preferences pane opens. The default I/O Buffer Size is 128 Samples, which should have a latency below 10 ms (milliseconds) for most devices.

NOTE ▶ The driver used by your audio interface also influences the roundtrip latency. Depending on the audio device selected in your Audio preferences, you may see different latencies for the same I/O buffer size. When choosing a different audio device, make sure you click Apply Changes to update the Resulting Latency value displayed.

2 From the I/O Buffer Size pop-up menu, choose 32.

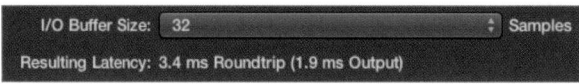

The latency is now shorter.

NOTE ▶ Sound travels at roughly one foot per millisecond, so a guitar player whose ear is five feet from his guitar amp's speaker will also hear notes five milliseconds after playing them.

3   Close the Preferences window.

The Core Audio engine is initialized with a 32-samples I/O buffer.

To monitor the impact of the I/O buffer size on the CPU, you need to customize the control bar to display the CPU meter.

4   In the control bar, click the note and metronome icons to the left of the LCD display, and choose Custom.

The LCD display now displays more information, including CPU and HD meters to the right.

5   Double-click the CPU or HD meter.

The CPU/HD window appears with more detailed meters. If your Mac has a multi-core CPU, you can see a meter for each core.

6   Start playback at bar 13.

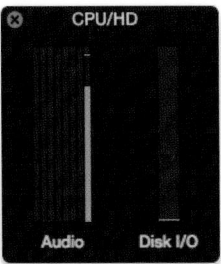

NOTE ▸ Depending on your Mac computer's CPU, you may not see the same number of cores or the same amount of activity on the meters.

One of the cores is working quite hard. As the CPU works harder, you might hear pops and crackles while the song plays. When playing the project becomes too much work for the CPU, playback stops and you will see a System Overload alert.

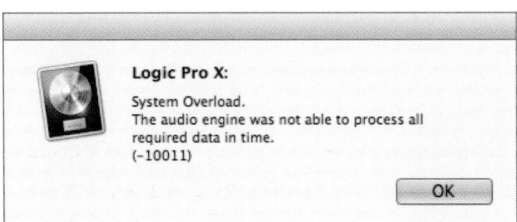

7   In the Audio preferences, set the I/O Buffer Size to 1024.

Note that a longer resulting latency is displayed below the menu.

8   Click Apply Changes.

The Core Audio engine is initialized with a 1024-samples I/O buffer.

9   Start playback at bar 13.

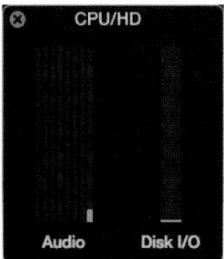

The CPU meter hits much lower. It doesn't have to work as hard with the larger buffer size. However, if you try to record audio with that setting, you will hear a delay between the notes you play and the notes you hear. That's latency. If you intend to do more audio recordings, find the lowest I/O buffer size setting that still allows clean monitoring.

NOTE ▸ Some audio effect plug-ins can also introduce latency. Choose Record > Low Latency Mode to automatically bypass those plug-ins.

Choosing the Recording File Type

Logic can record in three digital audio file formats: AIFF (the most commonly used audio file format on Mac computers), Broadcast Wave File (BWF or WAVE), and Core Audio Format (CAF). All three formats record the same audio data, so the sound quality is the same between them; but each format has its own features. For example, Apple Loops can be CAF or AIFF files; CAF is practically unlimited in file size so it can be used for very large audio files; and BWF can contain timestamps.

The Audio Engineering Society recommends using BWF for most applications.

1   In the Audio preferences, click the General tab.

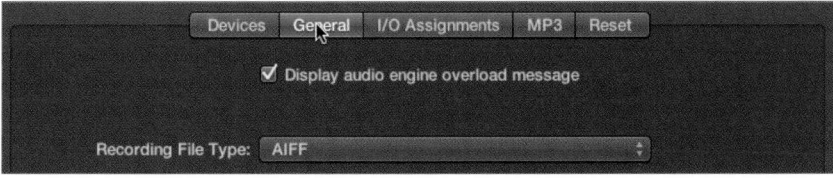

2   Set the Recording File Type to WAVE (BWF).

3   Close the Preferences window.

From now on, any new audio recorded in Logic will create BWF files.

Deleting Unused Audio Files

The Project Audio Browser shows all the audio files and audio regions that have been imported or recorded in your project. During a recording session, the focus is on capturing the best possible performance, and you may want to avoid burdening yourself with the decision making that comes with deleting bad takes. You may also have several unused audio files in the Project Audio Browser that make the project package (or folder) bigger than it needs to be.

In this next exercise, you will select and delete all unused audio files from your hard drive.

1   In the control bar, click the Browsers button (or press F) and ensure that the Project tab is selected.

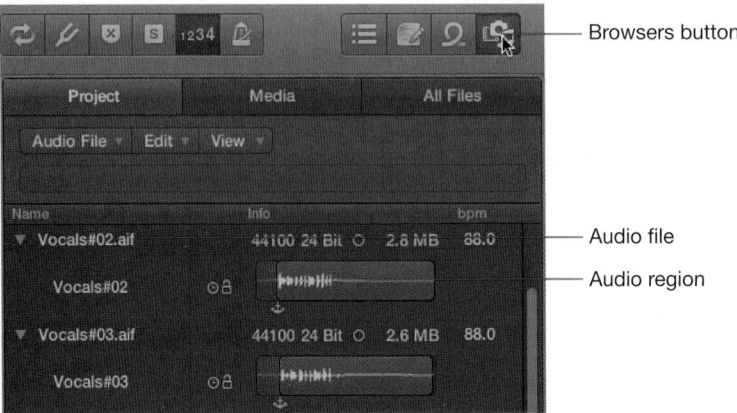

The Project Audio Browser opens, listing all the Apple Loops used on tracks 1 through 6, and all the audio files you've recorded during this lesson.

For each audio file, the Info column shows:

► Sample rate (44,100 Hz)

► Bit depth (24 bits)

► Format icon (a single circle indicates a mono audio file)

► File size

Clicking the disclosure triangle in front of the audio filename toggles the display of audio regions referring to that audio file.

NOTE ► Resizing, cutting, or copying regions in the workspace is called nondestructive editing. The audio data in the audio file stays intact, and the regions merely point to different sections of the audio file. You will learn more about nondestructive editing in Lesson 3.

2   In the workspace, select any audio regions you don't want to keep, and press Delete.

The regions are removed from the workspace, but their parent audio files are still present in the Project Audio Browser.

3   From the Project Audio Browser menu, choose Edit > Select Unused (or press Shift-U).

All the audio files that do not have an associated region in the workspace are selected. If you're not sure about deleting the files, you can first preview their associated regions.

4   At the lower left of the Browser, click the Prelisten button.

All selected regions play in sequence (from top to bottom), and you can see a small white playhead that travels through the regions.

TIP ► In the Project Audio Browser, to play a region from a specific point, click and hold down the mouse button over its waveform at the desired location.

Once you feel satisfied that the selected audio files do not contain any useful material, you can delete them.

5   From the Project Audio Browser menu bar, choose Audio File > Delete Audio File(s).

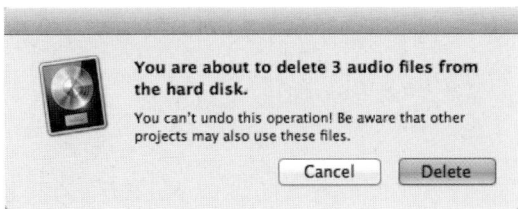

An alert asks your confirmation.

6   Click Delete.

The audio files are removed from the Project Audio Browser. In the Finder, the files are moved to the Trash.

You are now ready to tackle many recording situations: You can record a single track or multiple tracks, add new takes in a take folder, and fix mistakes by punching on the fly or automatically. You know where to adjust the sample rate and bit depth, as well as understanding which settings affect the behavior of the software during a recording session. And you can trim the fat off your projects by deleting unused audio files—which will save disk space, and download and upload time should you wish to collaborate with other Logic users over the Internet.

Lesson Review

1.   What two fundamental settings affect the quality of a digital audio recording?

2.   In Logic, where can you find those two settings?

3.   What precaution must you take before record-enabling multiple tracks simultaneously?

4.   In Autopunch mode, how do you set the punch-in and punch-out points?

5.   Describe an easy way to access your Metronome settings.

6.   Describe an easy way to access your count-in settings.

7.   What happens when you raise the I/O buffer size?

8.   In the Project Audio Browser, when selecting unused files, what determines whether a file is used or unused?

Answers

1. The sample rate and the bit depth

2. The sample rate is found under File > Project Settings > Audio. The bit depth is found under Logic Pro X > Preferences > Audio, in the Devices tab.

3. Make sure the tracks are assigned different inputs.

4. Adjust the left and right edge of the autopunch area in the middle of the ruler.

5. Control-click the Metronome button, and choose Metronome settings.

6. In the main menu, choose Record > Count-in > and choose the appropriate setting.

7. The CPU works less hard so you can use more plug-ins, but the roundtrip latency is longer.

8. An audio file is considered unused when no regions present in the workspace refer to that file.

Keyboard Shortcuts

Recording

R	Starts recording
Command-Control-Option-P	Toggles Autopunch mode
Command-click **lower half of ruler**	Toggles Autopunch mode

Tracks

Command-Option-N	Opens New Tracks dialog

Key Commands

Option-K	Opens Key Commands window

Project Audio Browser

F	Opens or closes the Browser pane
Shift-U	Selects unused audio files

3

Lesson Files	Logic Pro X Files > Lessons > 03 Get Dancing
	Logic Pro X Files > Media > Additional Media > wave.aif
Time	This lesson takes approximately 90 minutes to complete.
Goals	Assign Left-click and Command-click tools
	Edit audio regions nondestructively in the workspace
	Add fades and crossfades
	Create a composite take from multiple takes
	Import audio files
	Edit audio regions nondestructively in the Audio Track Editor
	Edit audio files destructively in the Audio File Editor
	Align audio using the anchor and the Flex tool

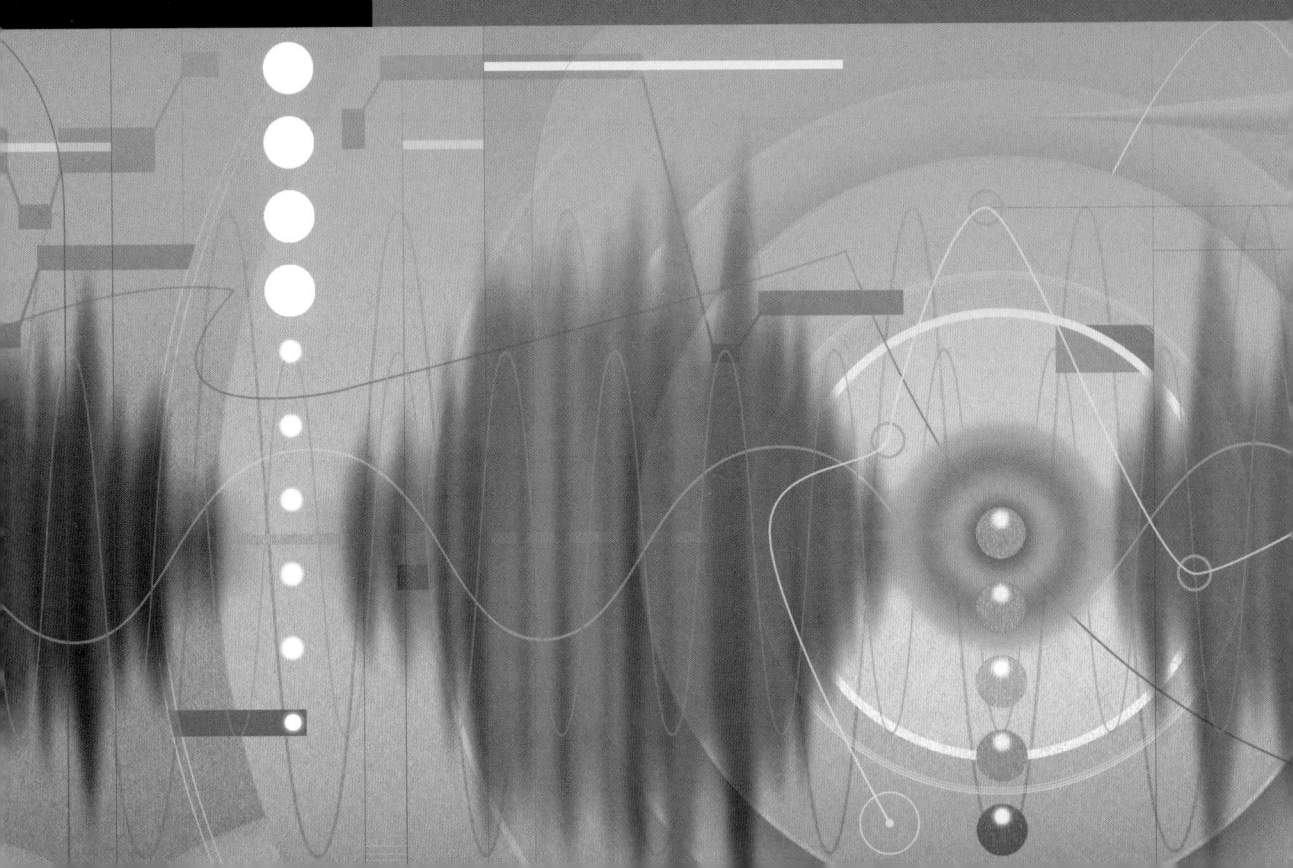

Lesson 3
Editing Audio

Audio engineers have always looked for new ways to edit recordings. In the days of magnetic recording, they used razor blades to cut pieces of a recording tape, and then connected those pieces with special adhesive tape. They could create a smooth transition (or crossfade) between two pieces of magnetic tape by cutting at an angle.

Digital audio workstations revolutionized audio. The waveform displayed on the screen is a visual representation of the digital audio recordings stored on the hard disk. The ability to read that waveform and manipulate it using the Logic editing tools is the key to precise and flexible audio editing.

In this lesson, you will edit audio regions nondestructively in the workspace and the Audio Track Editor, and add fades and crossfades. You will open a take folder and use Quick Swipe Comping to create a single composite take. Finally, you'll apply destructive audio editing in the Sample Editor to reverse a guitar recording.

Even as your ability to read waveforms and use the Logic editing tools develops, never forget to use your ears and trust them as the final judge of your work.

Assigning Mouse Tools

Until now, you have exclusively worked with the default tools. You have also used keyboard modifiers such as Control-Option to choose the Zoom tool, and changed the pointer to tools such as the Resize or Loop tools. When editing audio in the workspace, you will need to access even more tools.

In the Tracks area (and in various editors), two menus are available to assign the Left-click tool and the Command-click tool.

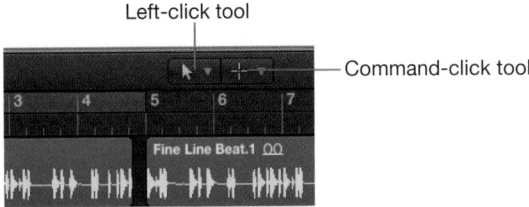

Previewing and Naming Regions

During recording sessions, helping the talent produce the best possible performance often takes priority over secondary tasks such as naming regions. In the aftermath of such sessions, when you don't know what musical material is contained in the regions on a track, taking the time to preview those tracks and give them descriptive names will help prepare for an efficient editing session.

In this exercise, you will assign tools to the mouse pointer. You will use the Solo tool to preview the audio regions on the new Guitar track, and apply the Text tool to rename them.

1   In the Tracks area title bar, click the Left-click Tool menu, and choose the Solo tool.

When placed over a region, the mouse pointer has a little S next to it indicating that it's a Solo tool. You can hear a region play back in solo mode by placing the Solo tool over the region and holding down the mouse button.

2   With the Solo tool over the Guitar track (track 7), hold down the mouse button at the beginning of the Guitar #10.4 region.

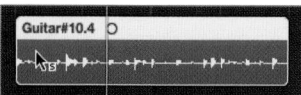

In the control bar, the Solo button comes on, and the LCD display and the playhead both turn yellow. The region is soloed, and you can play back starting from the location where you placed the Solo tool.

TIP ▶ You can also drag the Solo tool to scrub the region. You can change the playback speed or direction by dragging the Solo tool to the right or to the left. This technique can be useful when you're trying to locate a specific piece of audio material within a region.

You can hear that the guitar is playing single, muted notes, so you will give it a descriptive name based on those notes.

3   Click the Command-click Tool menu, and choose the Text tool.

Your Left-click Tool menu now displays the Solo tool, and the Command-click Tool menu displays the Text tool. If you hold down Command when your pointer is over a region, it changes to the Text tool.

4   Command-click the Guitar#10.4 region.

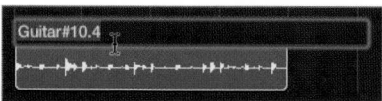

A text field appears, in which you can enter a new name for the region.

5   Type *Muted Single Notes*, and press Return to rename that region.

6 Farther to the right on the same Guitar track, using the Solo tool, hold down the mouse button in the Guitar take folder at bar 13.

You can hear some dead notes at the beginning of this take folder, and about a bar of funk rhythm guitar (in bar 14). You will edit this take folder later in this lesson.

7 Command-click the take folder, and rename it *Funk Rhythm.*

8 Using the Solo tool, listen to each one of the three small regions at the end of the Guitar track.

> **TIP** ▶ To make sure you start playback from the beginning of each region, Option-click the region with the Solo tool.

In those regions, the guitar sustains chords, so you will name the regions after the chord names. When naming multiple regions, you may find it cumbersome to repeatedly hold down Command, so let's assign the Text tool to the Left-click tool.

Instead of moving back and forth from the workspace to the tool menus in the Tracks area menu bar, you can press T to open the Tool menu at the current pointer position.

9 Press T (Show Tool Menu).

> **NOTE** ▶ If you press T and the Tool menu does not open at your pointer position, read "Using the U.S. Key Command Preset" in "Getting Started" before you continue. This section of "Getting Started" will teach you how to make your key commands consistent with those used throughout this book.

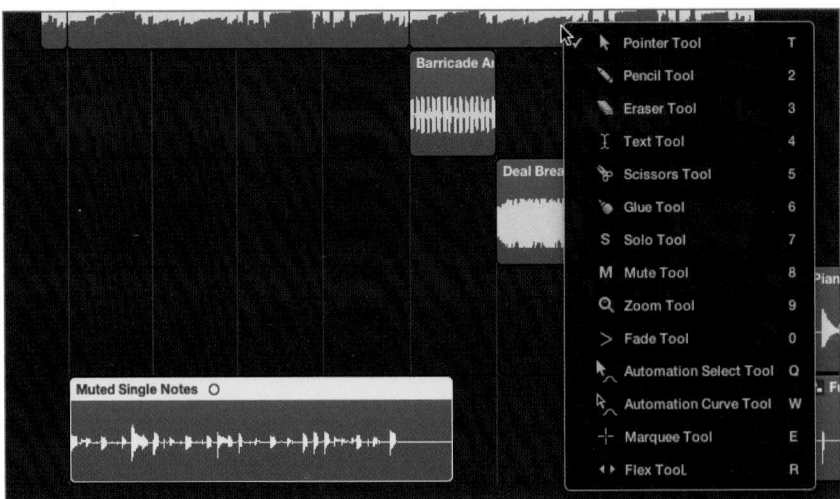

A Tool menu appears at the pointer position. This key command will save you a lot of trips to the title bar.

NOTE ▶ Different areas of the main window (such as the Tracks area or the Mixer) have their own sets of tools. You can change an area's tools in the Tool menus in its title bar, or by positioning the pointer over that area and pressing T.

10 In the Tool menu, choose the Text tool.

TIP ▶ When the Tool menu is open, you can press the key command listed to the right of a tool to assign that tool to the Left-click tool.

11 Rename the last three regions on the Guitar track *Ab chord, Bb chord*, and *Cm chord*.

You can also Command-click a tool in the pop-up Tool menu to assign it to the Command-click tool.

12 Press T to reopen the Tool menu, and Command-click the Marquee tool.

Now, let's return the Left-click tool to the Pointer tool.

13 Press T twice.

The Tool menu opens and closes, and the Left-click tool reverts to the Pointer tool.

Both tools are back to their default assignments: the Pointer tool for the Left-click tool and the Marquee tool for the Command-click tool.

TIP ▶ If you have a two-button mouse, you can assign a third tool to the right mouse button by choosing Logic Pro X > Preferences > General and clicking the Editing tab. From the Right Mouse Button pop-up menu, choose "Is Assignable to a Tool." The Right-click Tool menu will appear to the right of the two existing Tool menus.

Now that you know how to choose the best tool for the job, you're ready to start editing the audio regions on the Guitar track.

Editing Regions in the Workspace

Editing audio regions in the workspace is nondestructive. Regions are merely pointers that identify parts of an audio file. When you cut and resize regions in the workspace, only those pointers are altered. No processing is applied to the original audio files, which remain untouched on your hard disk. As a result, editing in the workspace provides a lot of flexibility and room for experimentation because you can always adjust your edits at a later date.

In this next exercise, you will edit the Muted Single Notes region on the Guitar track. You will first resize the region to make it exactly four-measures long, and then you'll use the Marquee tool to select some of the audio material in the region and copy it later in the track.

Since you'll be working with whole bars, you'll first choose snap modes to make the mouse pointer snap to bar lines on the grid, making the editing session easier and faster.

1   At the top of the Tracks area, from the Snap menu, choose Bar.

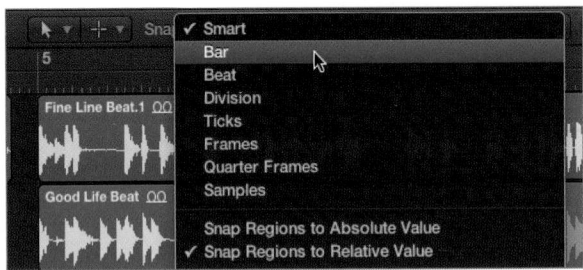

NOTE ▶ If the Tracks area is not wide enough to display the Snap menu in its menu bar, click the action pop-up menu that appears, and choose Snap > Bar.

In the Snap menu, a checkmark appears in front of the modes you choose.

2   From the Snap menu, choose Snap Regions to Absolute Value.

3   On the Guitar track (track 7), resize the Muted Single Notes region to exactly 4 0 0 0.

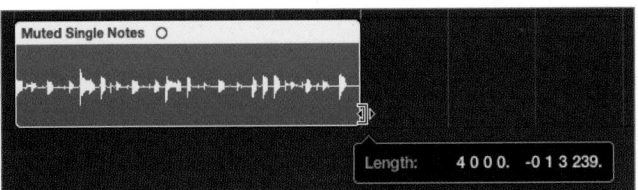

As soon as you start dragging the Resize tool toward the left, it snaps to bar 4.

TIP ▶ To disable snapping when using various tools in the workspace, hold down Control or (for even greater precision) Control-Shift.

4 Listen from the beginning of the song to the end of the Muted Single Notes region.

You will now repeat the simple motif in the last two bars of the Muted Single Notes region a couple more times, from bars 9 to 13 where the synthesizers play.

The Command-click tool is now the Marquee tool, and the Left-click tool is the Pointer tool. This is a very powerful tool combination when editing audio in the workspace. You can select a section of an audio region with the Marquee tool, and move or copy that selection using the Pointer tool.

5 Command-drag the waveform in the Muted Single Notes region from bar 7 to bar 9.

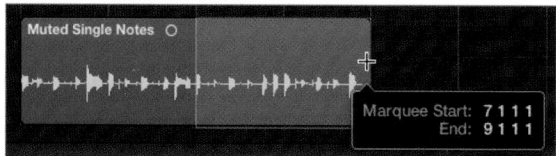

The section you selected with the Marquee tool is highlighted.

6 Press the Spacebar to play the selection.

TIP ▶ When a marquee selection is present, playback starts at the beginning and stops at the end of that marquee selection, even when Cycle mode is turned on.

The playhead jumps to bar 7 and plays the selection. It corresponds exactly to the two-bar pattern of the guitar you are going to copy.

7 Option-drag the marquee selection to bar 9, releasing the mouse button first followed by the Option key.

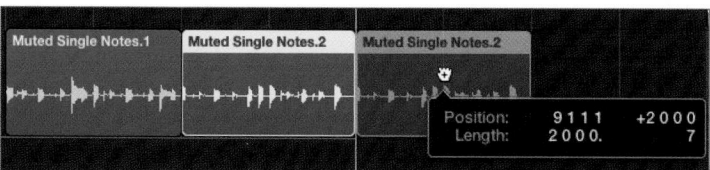

Option-dragging a marquee selection automatically divides, copies, and pastes the selection to a new location regardless of region boundaries. In this example, the two-bar guitar pattern is copied and pasted at bar 9.

Remember to release the mouse button first and the Option key second. When the mouse button is released, the original region is automatically restored.

8   Option-drag the new two-bar Muted Single Notes.3 region to bar 11.

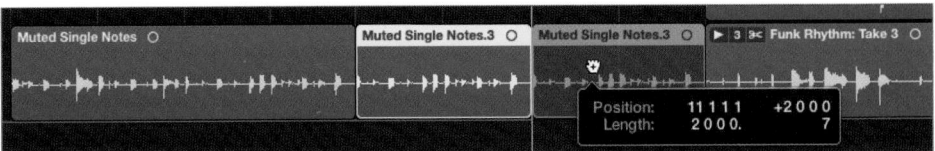

9   Listen from the beginning of the song to the Funk Rhythm take folder at bar 13.

The guitar plays a melodic riff with high notes when it first comes in, and then it plays more discretely throughout the following sections leaving room for the two synths to shine.

Still, you can bring back a little bit of the excitement just before the breakdown at bar 13.

10   In the first Muted Single Notes region, Command-drag from bar 6 to bar 7.

11   Option-drag the marquee selection to bar 12.

As you copy the new region to bar 12, the two-bar region that existed at bar 11 is trimmed down to a one-bar region to make space for the new region.

12   From the Snap menu, choose Smart.

13 Listen to this new edit.

This last region brings back a welcome variation to the monotonous pattern that the guitar has been playing for the past five bars, returning in time to lead to the break in the next section.

Now you know how to select the desired material within a region and move or copy that material anywhere on the track. You could, for example, move or copy a single drum hit, or a single word in a vocal performance, to replace another one that doesn't sound as good.

Comping Takes

In the previous lesson, you recorded several takes of a guitar performance and packed them into a take folder. Now you will learn how to preview those individual takes and assemble a composite take by choosing sections from multiple takes, a process called *comping*.

Comping techniques are useful when you have recorded several takes of the same musical phrase, each with its good and bad qualities. In the first take, the musician may have messed up the beginning but played the ending perfectly; and in the following take, he nailed the beginning and made a mistake at the end. You can create a perfectly played comp using the beginning of the second take and the ending of the first take.

You can use the same comping techniques to create a single musical passage from multiple musical ideas. As they improvise in the studio, musicians will often record a few takes and later comp the best ideas of each performance into a new, virtual performance.

Previewing the Takes

Before you start comping, you need to get familiar with the takes you are going to comp. While doing so, you will assign the takes different colors to help distinguish between them, and then decide which part of which take you will use.

1 At bar 13 on the Guitar track, double-click the take folder to open it.

2 Press Z to zoom in on the selection.

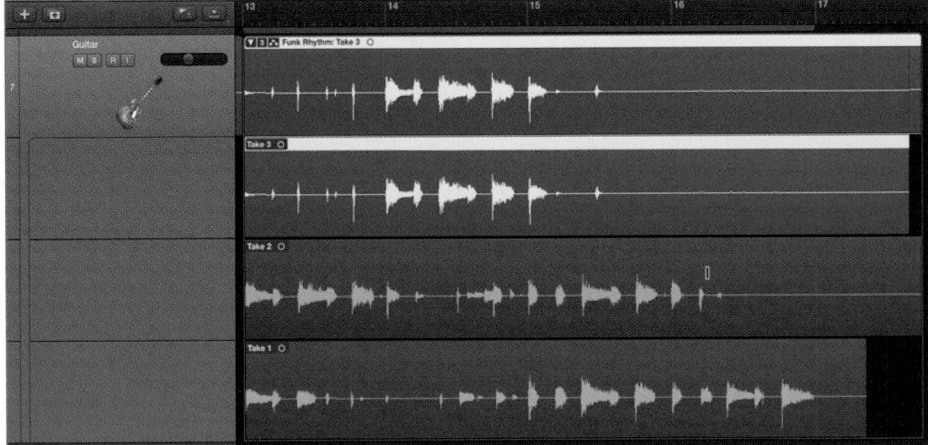

The selected take folder and its takes fill the workspace. The take folder is on the Guitar track, and the three takes it contains are on lanes below the Guitar track. Take 3 at the top is selected and is the take currently playing. The other takes are dimmed to indicate that they are muted.

Take folder pop-up menu ⌐ ⌐ Quick Swipe Comping button

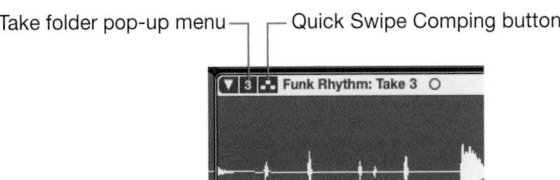

You'll see three buttons at the upper left of a take folder:

▶ The disclosure button allows you to open or close the take folder.

▶ The Take Folder pop-up menu displays the current take number (or the current comp letter) and contains options to manage your takes and comps.

▶ The Quick Swipe Comping button allows you to toggle Quick Swipe Comping on and off to edit the individual takes in the same way you would edit regions on a track.

After those three buttons, you'll see the name you previously gave your take folder (Funk Rhythm) followed by the comp name (Take 3).

Let's assign each take a unique color.

3 Press Option-C to open the Color palette.

TIP ▶ The Color palette displays a white frame around the color(s) of the selected region(s). This is useful when you need to assign other regions the same color.

4 Click Take 1 to select it.

5 In the Color palette, click a purple color square.

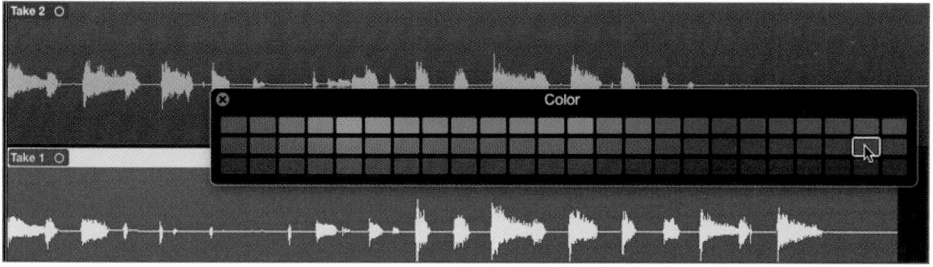

Take 1 is purple.

You will keep the blue color for Take 2, and choose a new color for Take 3.

6 Click Take 3, and in the Color palette, click a green square.

7 Close the Color palette.

8 Press C to turn on Cycle mode, and press Command-U to make the locators match the selected take folder.

9 In the Guitar track header, click the S (Solo) button, or make sure the Guitar track is selected and press S.

10 Press the Spacebar.

The selected take, Take 3, plays. There's really only one useable bar in this whole take, the second bar (between bars 14 and bar 15).

11 Stop playback, and listen to Take 2.

This time the first bar sounds good, but the second bar is rather messy; the third bar sounds good, and then the guitar player plays the wrong chord and stops. So far, between Take 2 and Take 3, you have just enough material to cover the first three bars of the breakdown, and you're missing the fourth bar.

NOTE ▶ Logic can also continue playing in Cycle mode as you select different takes. When you do so, a brief delay will occur as Logic switches playback between takes.

12 Listen to Take 1.

This time the guitarist misses the entire beginning, but gives a good performance in the fourth bar of the breakdown.

Although each take is a very poor performance, you have all the material you need to create a comp take that will sound good. You will use the following sections of each take:

▶ Take 1: The fourth bar

▶ Take 2: The first and third bars

▶ Take 3: The second bar

Comping the Takes

Now you'll assemble the best sections of each take to create a single, flawless composite take using the Quick Swipe Comping feature. You will swipe your mouse across the parts of the takes you want to hear in your comp.

1 Click Take 2 to select it.

The entire take is selected, and its color and name are displayed in the take folder.

2 Click Take 3 at bar 14, and drag to the right to select one measure.

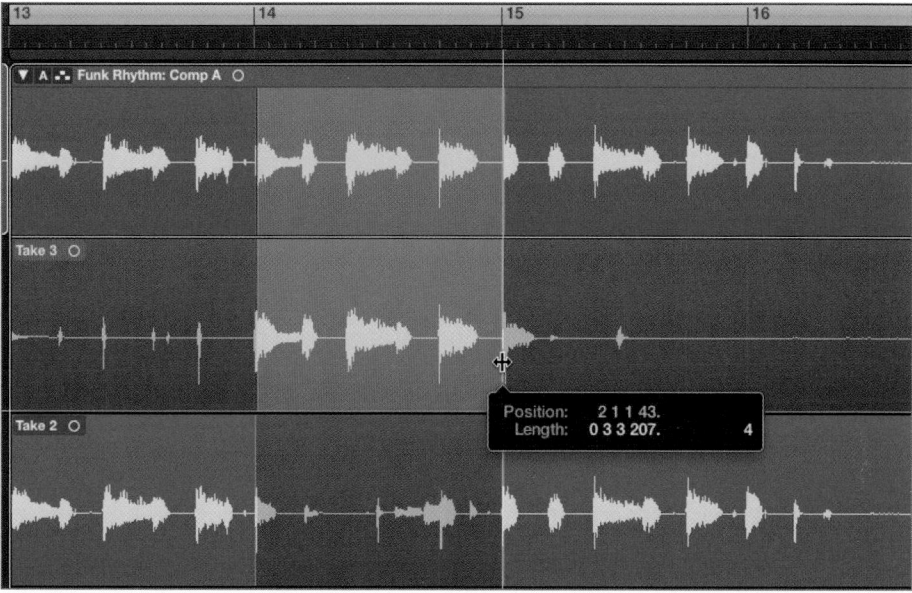

The mouse pointer does not automatically snap to the grid when Quick Swipe Comping, but snapping would really help you edit this kind of rhythmic material.

3   At the top of the Tracks area, from the Snap menu, choose "Snap Quick Swipe Comping to Absolute Values."

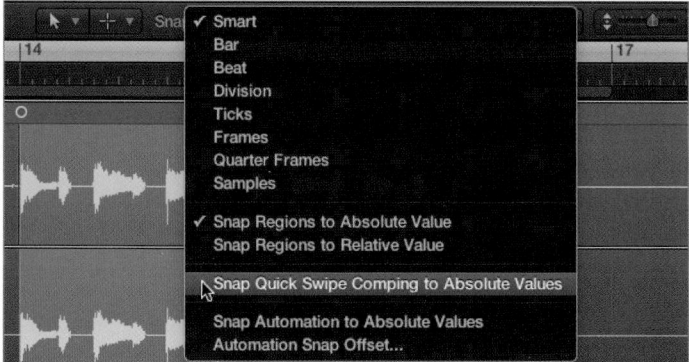

Let's undo the previous selection and try repeating that operation with snapping turned on.

4   Choose Edit > Undo Edit Comp (or press Command-Z).

5   Click Take 3 at bar 14 and drag right to select one measure.

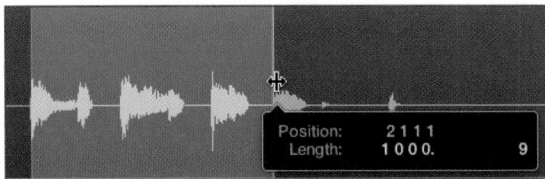

This time the mouse pointer snaps, making it easier to select exactly one measure.

6   Click Take 1 at bar 16 and drag to select one measure.

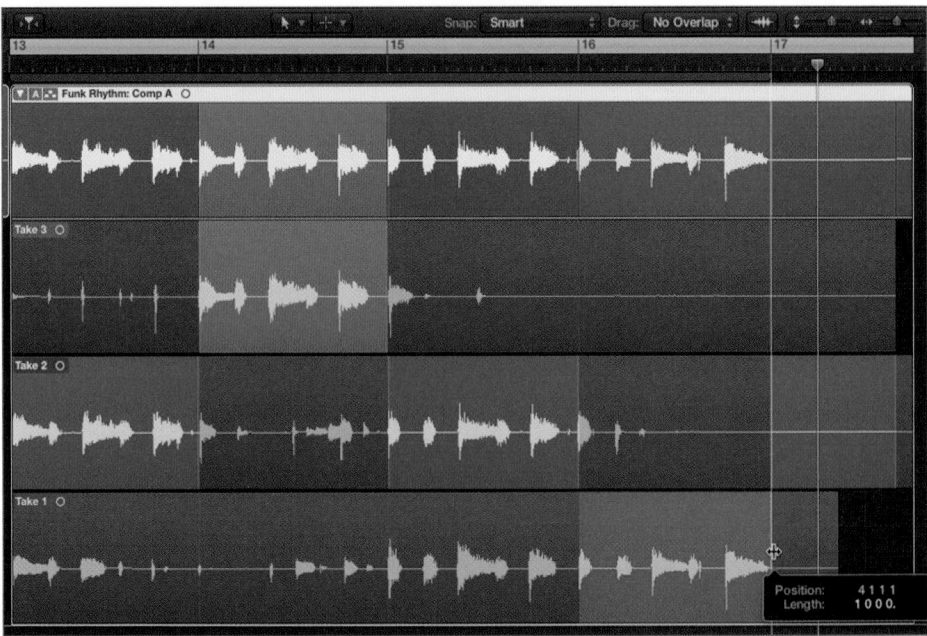

Notice that in the take folder on the Guitar track, the waveform and its background color match the sections of the selected takes. Your comp name, Comp A, now appears next to the take folder name, and the letter A is displayed in the Take Folder pop-up menu (to the right of the disclosure triangle).

NOTE ▶ A take folder can contain multiple comps you can choose from the Take Folder pop-up menu. An easy way to start a new comp is to Option-click a take to select it, and start comping again.

7 Listen to your comp.

While each individual guitar take was pretty poor, you've edited them together into a good sounding guitar part. There is, however, a lingering noise present at the end of Take 2 you can delete.

8 At the end of Take 2, click the last section highlighted in blue.

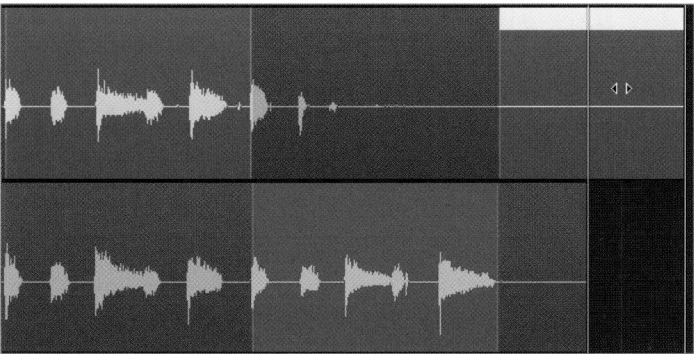

The upper part of the clicked section is white, indicating that the section is selected.

9 Press Delete to remove the selected section.

10 From the Take Folder pop-up menu, choose Flatten.

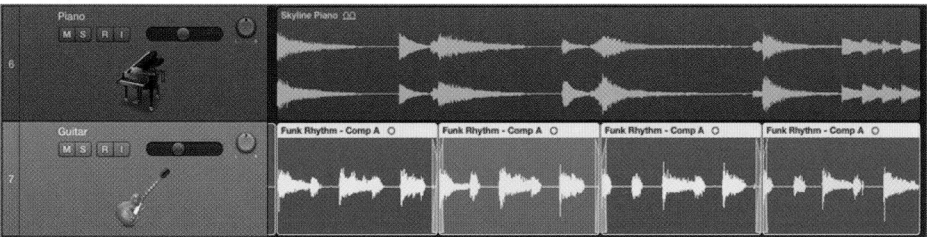

The take folder is replaced by the current comp. The selected sections of the takes in the folder are now replaced by audio regions, and crossfades are displayed at the junctions between regions.

11 Click the Guitar track's Solo button (or press S) to unsolo the track and listen to the result.

12 Turn off Cycle mode.

You now have a flawless funk rhythm guitar performance during the break. The cross-fades, automatically added between edit points during the comping, ensure smooth transitions between the regions. You will learn how to apply and adjust your own fades and crossfades in the following two exercises.

Adding Fades and Crossfades

When editing audio, you usually want to avoid abrupt transitions on edit points: the region boundaries and the junctions between regions. You can use nondestructive fades in the workspace to create smooth transitions.

Adding a Fade-Out

The very last region on the Guitar track ends abruptly, before the guitar chord has finished its natural decay. You will now add a fade-out to make that last chord end more naturally.

1 Solo the Guitar track (track 7).

2 At the end of the Guitar track (at bar 21), listen to the three regions containing guitar chords.

You can hear odd blip sounds at the edit points: the beginning of the first region, the junction between the regions, and the end of the last region. The clicks are exacerbated by the reverb in the Amp Designer plug-in on the channel strip. Let's turn off that plug-in.

3 In the inspector, on the Guitar channel strip, place the mouse pointer over the Amp Designer plug-in, then click the power button that appears to the left of the plug-in slot.

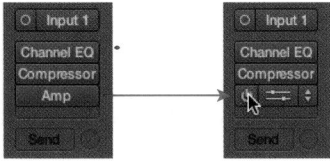

The plug-in is dimmed to indicate that it's turned off.

4 Just above the Amp Designer plug-in, turn off the Compressor plug-in.

5 Listen again to the three guitar regions at bar 21.

You can now clearly hear the clicks. The third region, a C minor chord, ends abruptly and the sustain tail of that chord does not sound natural.

6 Press T to open the Tool menu at the mouse pointer position.

7 Click the Fade tool, or press 0 (zero), to assign it as the Left-click tool.

8 Drag the Fade tool over the end part of the Cm chord region, starting about halfway into the region.

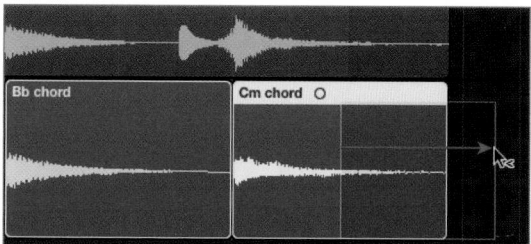

To apply a fade, always ensure that you drag over a region's boundary, or nothing will happen. You can create fades only over region boundaries. Here, the shaded rectangle should cover the end of the region.

A fade-out is created. The position where you started dragging determines the length of the fade-out.

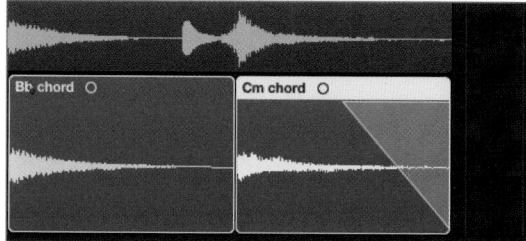

9 Listen to the fade-out.

The level of the guitar chord progressively decreases until it's silent at the end, effectively removing the click at the end of the Cm chord region.

You can now adjust the fade's length and curve to fine-tune its sound.

10 Place the Fade tool on the left side of the fade, and drag toward the left to start the fade-out at the beginning of the Cm chord region.

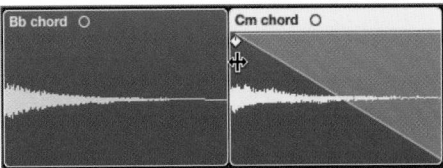

11 Place the Fade tool in the middle of the fade, and drag to the right to curve the fade.

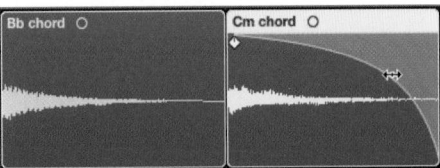

The fade is curved in the direction you drag.

12 Unsolo the Guitar track, and in the inspector, turn on the Compressor and the Amp Designer.

13 Listen to the entire outro section starting at bar 21.

The guitar and the piano fade out simultaneously at the end of the song, which now sounds cleaner and smoother.

14 Press T twice.

The Left-click tool is reassigned as the Pointer tool.

Adding Fades to Remove Clicks

In this exercise, you will add very short fades and crossfades to eliminate click sounds that occur at edit points on the final three regions on the Guitar track.

1 Solo the Guitar track, and in the Inspector, turn off the Compressor and Amp Designer.

2 Listen to the Ab chord region at bar 21, starting playback slightly before the beginning of that region.

You can hear a click at the beginning of the region. Let's zoom in to take a closer look at the waveform.

3   Control-Option-drag around the left edge of the Ab chord region.

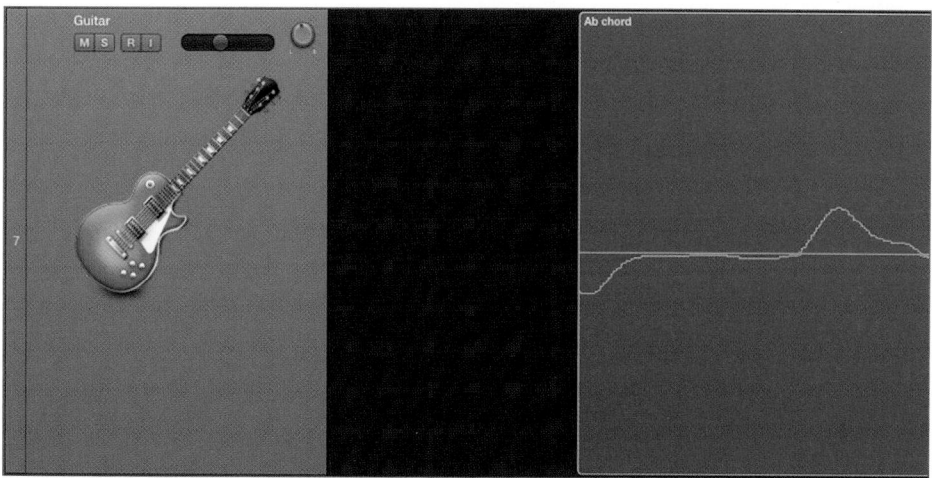

You may need to zoom in a few more times to clearly see the shape of the waveform.

To add fades using the Pointer tool, you can Control-Shift-drag over the region boundary.

4   Control-Shift-click inside the region, and drag toward the left over the region start.

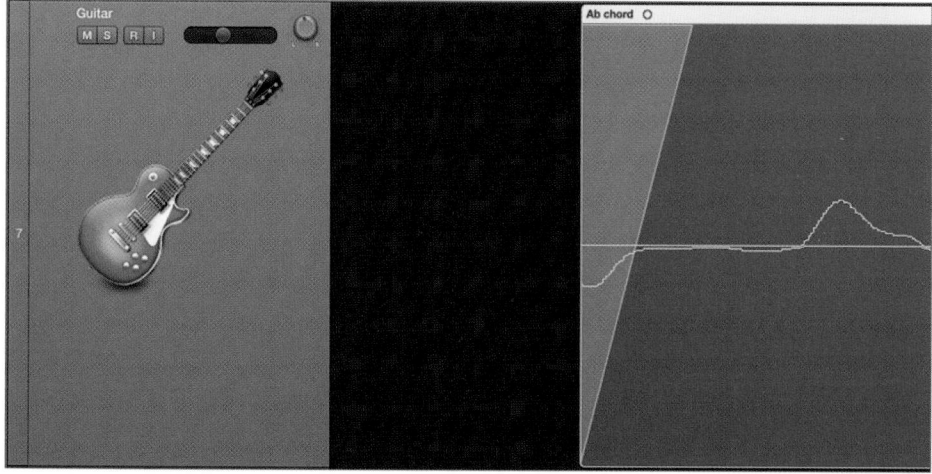

A fade-in is added.

5   Zoom out and listen to the fade-in.

The click sound at the beginning of the Ab chord region disappeared.

TIP ▸ To compare the sound before and after the edit, choose Edit > Undo Crossfade Edit (or press Command-Z) to undo the previous edit, and choose Edit > Redo Crossfade Edit (or press Command-Shift-Z) to reapply that edit.

6   Listen to the junction between the first two regions of the outro, Ab chord and Bb chord. You can hear a click sound at the edit point.

7   Zoom in closer to the junction between the two regions, and Control-Shift-drag over the junction.

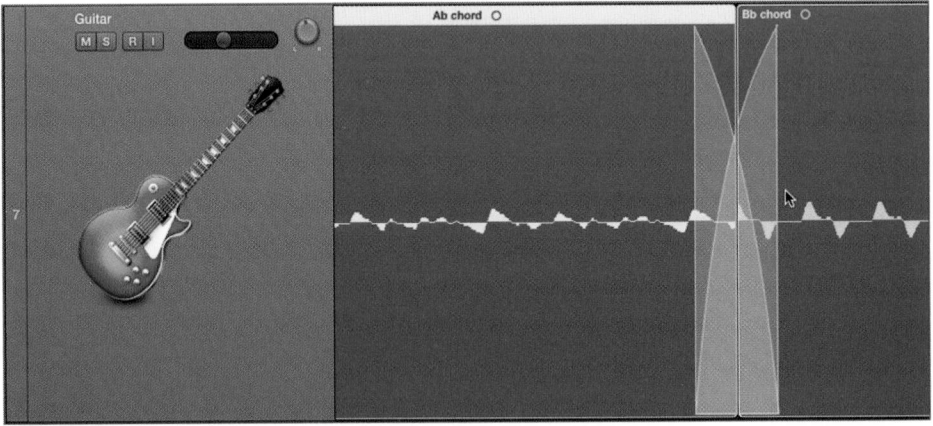

A crossfade is added at the junction between the two regions.

TIP ▸ You can change the curve of a crossfade by placing the mouse pointer on the crossfade and dragging toward the left or right.

8   Zoom out and listen to the crossfade.

The click sound at the junction between the regions disappeared.

When adding short fades or crossfades to avoid clicks, you don't really need to zoom in and look at the waveform. All you need is a very short fade at the edit point to smooth the transition.

There's one click left to remove, at the junction between the two final regions on the track, a Bb chord and a Cm chord. This time you will add the crossfade using the parameters in the Region inspector to avoid zooming in and out.

9 Click the Bb chord region.

10 At the top of the inspector, in the Region inspector, select the More option to display the fade parameters.

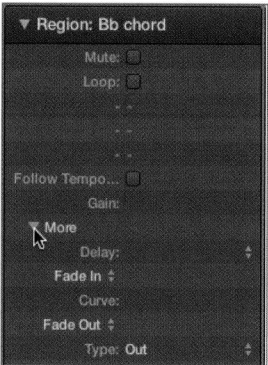

11 Double-click to the right of the Fade Out parameter to activate the data field, and enter 5.

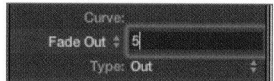

A five-millisecond fade-out is added at the end of the selected region.

12 Click the Type parameter value, and choose EqP (Equal Power Crossfade).

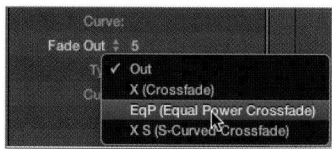

In the workspace you can see that the fade-out at the end of the selected region is replaced by a crossfade.

NOTE ▶ While X, EqP, and X S crossfades offer different shapes, the shape of EqP crossfades keeps the volume of the sound constant throughout the fade, which makes EqP the best choice for most situations.

13 Unsolo the Guitar track, turn the Compressor and Amp Designer back on, and listen to the outro.

After editing a section, you may have many small regions with fades between them. You can choose to keep those small regions with the fades, so you can readjust the edits later. However, if you're ready to commit and would rather deal with a single audio region for the entire section, you can join the regions to render your edits into a new audio file.

14 Select the A flat, B flat, and C minor chord regions.

15 Choose Edit > Join > Regions (or press Command-J).

An alert asks you to confirm the creation of a new audio file.

16 Click Create.

A new audio region is created in place of the selected regions and their fades.

17 Using the Text tool, rename the new region *Gtr chords*, then revert to the Pointer tool.

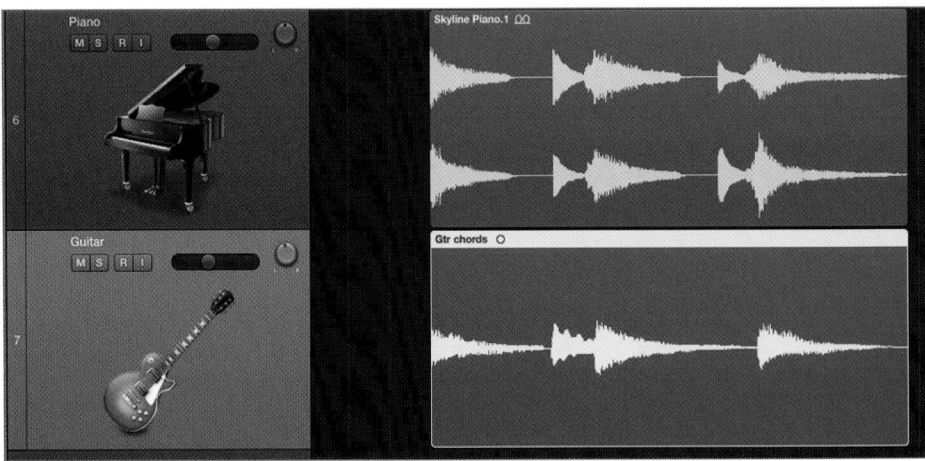

Editing Regions in the Audio Track Editor

For some editing, you need to clearly see the grid behind the regions, or have the bar ruler displayed directly on top of the regions you're editing. Zooming and scrolling in the work-space can help to an extent; however, when you want to edit the regions of a single track, you can use the Audio Track Editor to focus on that track without changing the zoom level of the Tracks area.

Importing Audio Files Using the All Files Browser

You will now import a new audio file to the project: a white noise sound effect you will use later to accentuate the transition between song sections at bar 17.

1   In the control bar, click the Browsers button (or press F).

2   At the top of the browsers, click the All Files tab.

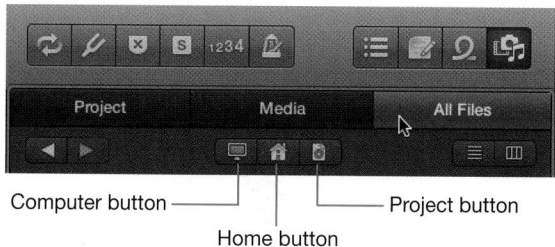

The All Files Browser opens. At the top, three buttons allow you to access all the vol-umes connected to your computer, your home folder, or the current project folder.

3   Click the Home button.

The contents of your home folder appear in the browser.

4   Double-click Desktop, and continue double-clicking folders to navigate to Logic Pro X Files > Media > Additional Media.

5   In the All Files Browser, select **wave.aif**.

6   At the lower left of the All Files Browser, click the Play button (or press Control-Spacebar).

The **wave.aif** file plays. It's a sound effect of white noise rising and falling in level, similar to the sound of an ocean wave.

7   Drag **wave.aif** to the bottom of the workspace at bar 13.

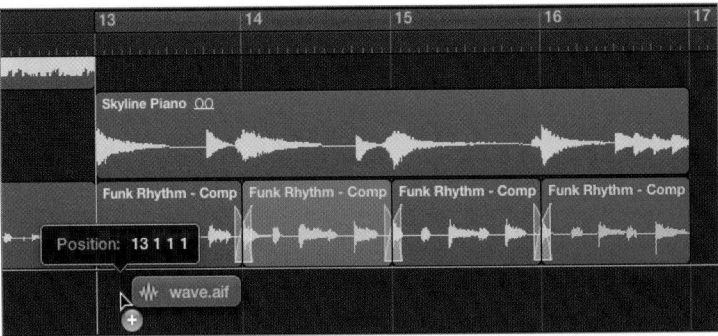

A new track is created, and the wave audio region is added at bar 13. The audio file was recorded at a low level, and its waveform is rather flat. Depending on your zoom level, you may not even see a waveform at all. In the next exercise, you will zoom into the waveform so you can see it clearly.

8   In the control bar, click the Browsers button (or press F) to close the browser.

9   Play the song from bar 13 to bar 18.

The white noise effect sounds like it will work in that section. However, for maximum effect, it must be moved so that the climax of the wave sound occurs at bar 17.

Using the Audio Track Editor

You will now continue editing the wave region nondestructively, but this time in the Audio Track Editor, which allows you to clearly see the grid and the ruler above the regions without having to change the zoom level of the Tracks area.

1   In the workspace, double-click the wave region to open the editors area.

2   At the top of the editors area, click Track.

The Audio Track Editor opens, displaying the wave track and its single region.

TIP ▶ To make the Audio Track Editor taller, place the mouse pointer between the Tracks area and the Audio Track Editor and drag up.

3   Press Z.

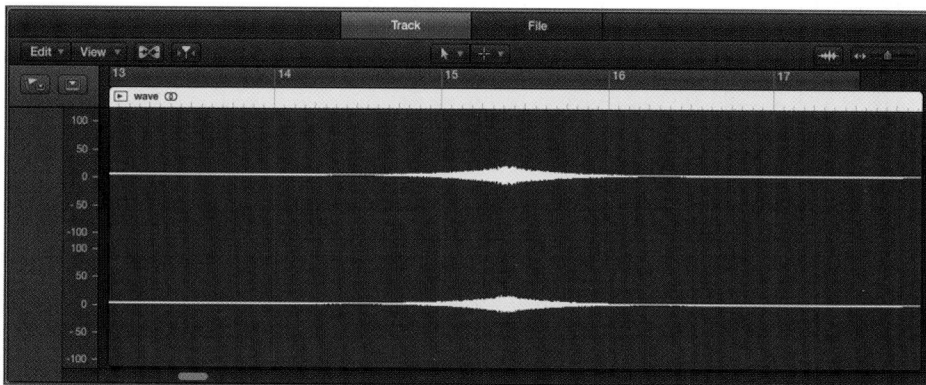

The wave region fills the Audio Track Editor. You can clearly see the ruler just above the waveform, with vertical grid lines displayed under the waveform.

You can see that the wave region is a stereo audio region because it has two interleaved circles next to its name, and two waveforms are displayed in the Audio Track Editor.

NOTE ▶ In the workspace, when zoomed out vertically, stereo audio regions appear as a single waveform. A rectified waveform above the center line represents the left channel while another rectified waveform under the center line represents the right channel. As you reach a certain vertical zoom level, two waveforms are displayed, one for each channel.

Let's zoom in on the waveform.

4   At the top right of the Audio Track Editor, click the Waveform Zoom button.

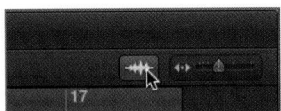

The waveform is a little taller. Let's zoom in even closer.

5   Click and hold down the Waveform Zoom button until the vertical zoom slider appears, and then drag up until you can clearly see the waveform.

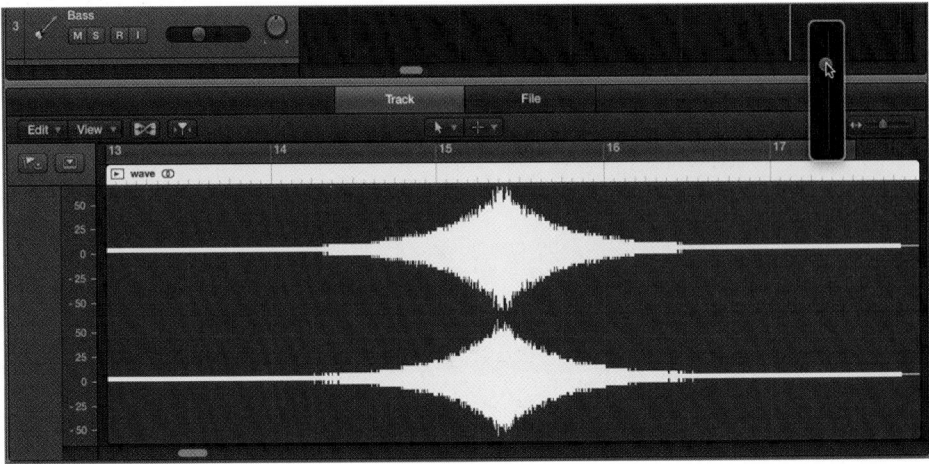

NOTE ▶ Another Waveform Zoom button at the upper right of the Tracks area allows you to adjust the vertical zoom level of audio region waveforms in the workspace.

6 In the Audio Track Editor, drag the wave region to the right until the highest point on the waveform is aligned with bar 17.

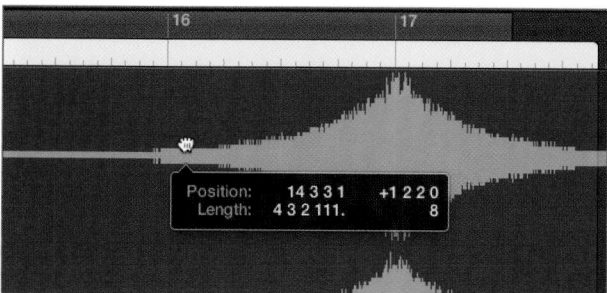

In the workspace, the wave audio region is moved accordingly.

7 In the Tracks area, position the playhead before the wave region, and press the Spacebar to play the results.

The climax of the wave sound is now perfectly aligned with the transition between song sections at bar 17. The effect would sound even better if the rise before bar 17 were shorter.

8 Stop playback.

9 In the Audio Track Editor, place the mouse pointer at the lower left of the wave region until it turns into the Resize tool. Then drag to the right so the region starts at bar 16.

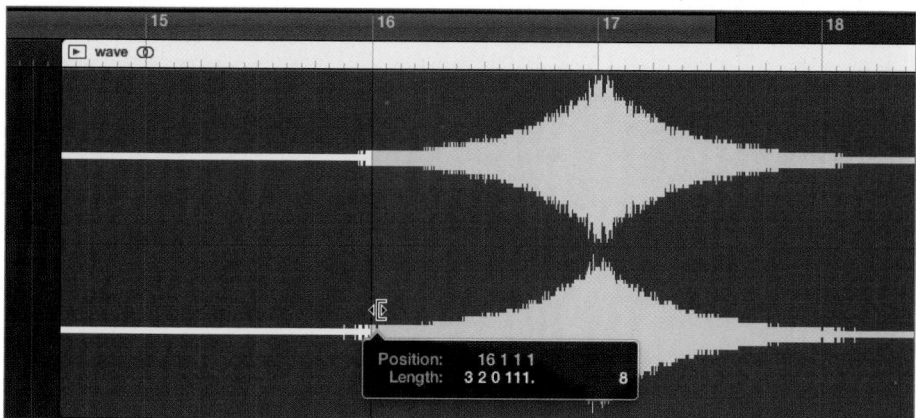

The region is now trimmed. Let's add a fade-in.

10 In the Audio Track Editor, Control-Shift-click the waveform at bar 17 and drag toward the left over the region start.

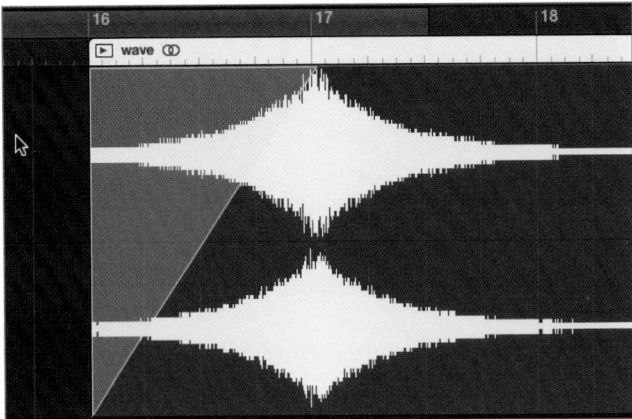

A fade-in is added. All the edits you perform in the Audio Track Editor are reflected in the workspace.

11 In the control bar, click the Editors button (or press E) to close the Audio Track Editor.

12 Listen to the song from the beginning of the breakdown at bar 11.

The wave sound now rises rapidly in the last bar of the breakdown, and decays slowly in the next section, which works better for this transition.

Editing Files in the Audio File Editor

The Audio File Editor allows you to perform destructive audio editing. Although nondestructively editing audio regions in the workspace and Audio Track Editor keeps the parent audio file intact, processing an audio file in the Audio File Editor actually modifies the data contained in the audio file.

Playing an Audio Region Backward

You will now create a new region from the last chord of the Gtr chords region at the end of the Guitar track and convert it into a new audio file. You will then reverse the new audio file in the Audio File Editor to create a swelling sound you will use for the introduction of this song.

1   On the Guitar track, Command-drag the last bar of the Gtr chords region to select it with the Marquee tool.

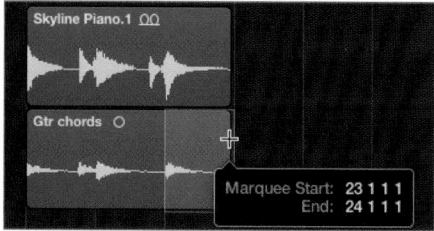

You will now copy that region to bar 4, the last bar of the introduction.

If bar 4 is not visible in the Tracks area, drag the region to the left edge of the workspace, and continue holding down the mouse button without dragging as the workspace starts to scroll toward the left. Do not continue dragging the mouse pointer into the track header section, or the workspace will stop scrolling.

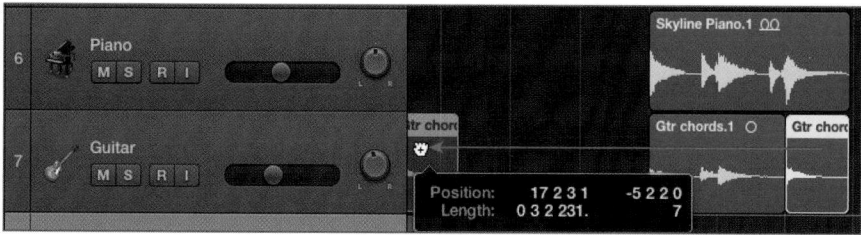

2   Release the mouse when the help tag displays Position: 4 1 1 1.

You have a new Gtr chord.3 region in the introduction you will reverse destructively in the Audio File Editor. However, this new region references the same audio file as the last region on the track, Gtr chords. If you destructively reverse the audio in this new region's parent audio file, all regions referencing that parent file will have that audio reversed, including the Gtr chords region.

To avoid modifying the Gtr chords region at the end of the Guitar track, you will convert this new Gtr chords.3 region into a new audio file.

3   At bar 4, ensure that the new Gtr chords.3 region is still selected, and choose Edit > Convert > Audio Region to New Audio File (or press Command-Option-F).

In the Save As dialog, you can choose a filename and location for the new audio file. You will name the file but keep the default location (the audio files folder in the project folder).

4   Name the file *Reversed Gtr*, and click Save (or press Return).

A new Reversed Gtr region replaces the old Gtr chord.3 region. The new region references the audio file you just saved, so editing it destructively will not affect the Gtr chords region at the end of the Guitar track.

5   Double-click the Reversed Gtr region to open it in the Audio Track Editor.

6   At the top of the Audio Track Editor, click File to open the Audio File Editor.

Play button

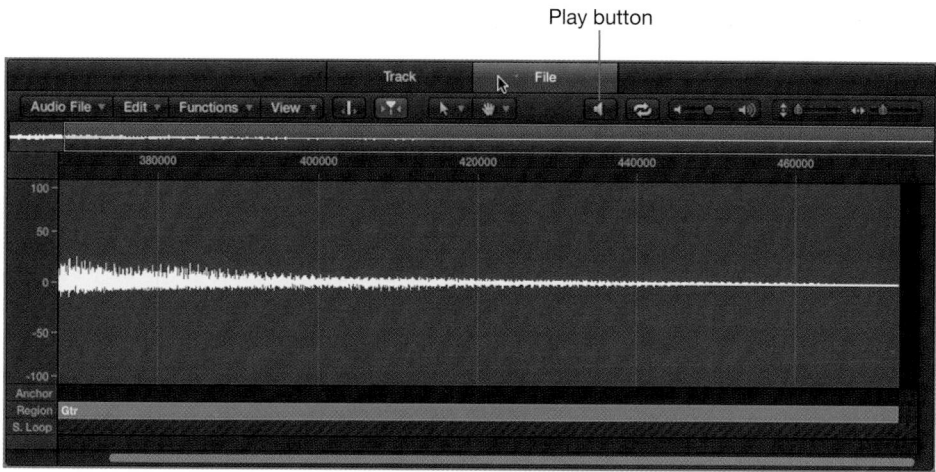

7 At the top of the Audio File Editor, click the Play button (or press Control-Spacebar).

You hear the single sustained chord. Let's reverse it!

8 Choose Functions > Reverse (or press Control-Shift-R) to reverse the file.

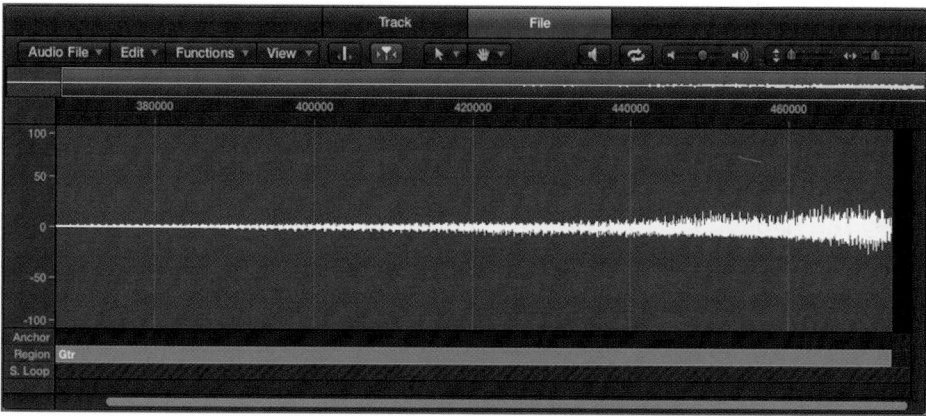

NOTE ▶ Some or all of an audio file open in the Audio File Editor has to be selected for the operations in the Functions menu to be available. By default, the section of the file corresponding to the region you opened is selected. To apply an operation to only a section of the audio file, drag over that section with the Pointer tool to select it, and then choose the desired operation from the Audio File Editor menus.

9   Click the Play button (or press Control-Spacebar) to hear the results.

The guitar chord now slowly rises up from silence and ends at its peak level, which was formerly the attack of the original chord.

10   Click the Editors button (or press E) to close the Audio File Editor.

11   Press the Spacebar to listen to the introduction.

The swelling guitar chord sounds about right. However it's still not in the perfect position because it overlaps the first notes of the bass. To get the full impact of the break at the end of the intro, the Reversed Gtr region should end exactly where the first Skyline Bass region starts. You will move the region to its correct position in the next exercise.

Aligning Audio

Accurately aligning audio material to the grid, or to other instruments in the song, is crucial to realizing a professional sounding song. No amounts of plug-ins, mixing, or mastering techniques can fix a sloppy arrangement, so getting a tight sounding arrangement before moving on is important.

In the next two exercises, you will use two techniques to align audio in the workspace. First, you'll use the anchor in the Audio File Editor to align the Reversed Gtr region you edited in the previous exercise. Second, you'll use the Flex tool in the workspace to move individual notes within a region.

Using the Anchor

Audio regions have an anchor, which positions the region in the workspace. When you drag a region in the workspace, the anchor position is the position displayed in the help tag, and the anchor is used to snap the region to the grid.

By default, the anchor is located at the start point of an audio region. While this makes sense for most audio regions, sometimes the part of the audio region you want to align with the grid is not at the beginning of a region. To line up the attack of a reversed sound with the grid, you need to position the anchor on the attack (the loudest part, or *amplitude peak*) near the end of the region.

In this exercise, you will position the region so that its anchor lines up with the beginning of the first region on the bass track.

1   Zoom in so you can comfortably see all tracks from bar 3 to bar 7.

You will now see how alignment guides can help you align a region with other regions on other tracks. In the next step, don't worry about dragging the region to the wrong place, as you'll be undoing the move later.

2   On the Guitar track (track 3), slowly drag the Reversed Gtr region to the right.

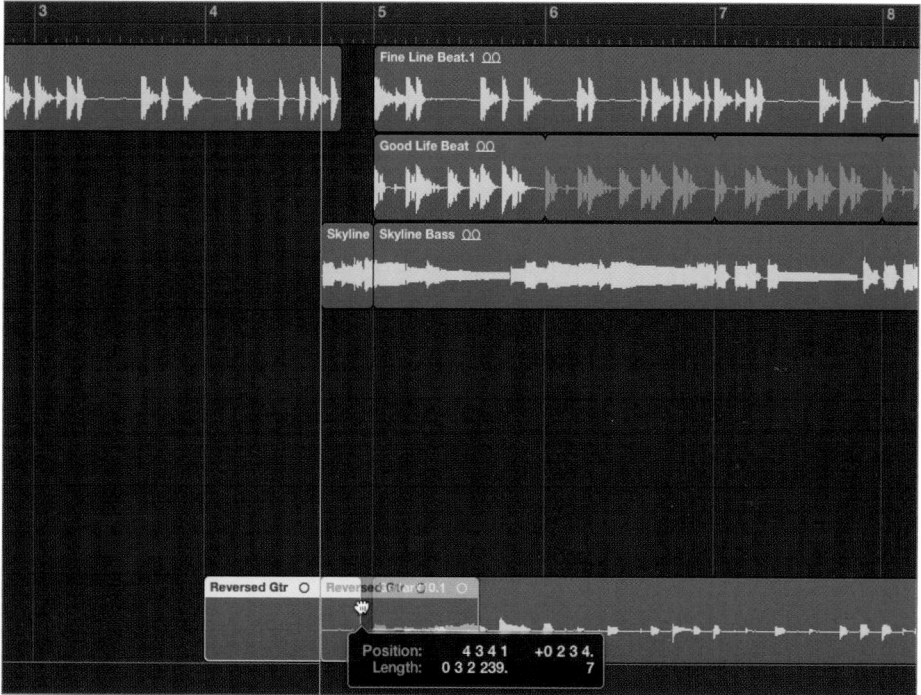

As you drag the Reversed Gtr region, a yellow alignment guide helps you align the region you're dragging with the beginnings or ends of regions on other tracks. However, the current line appears at the beginning of the region you're dragging when you want to align the end.

TIP ▶ To toggle the alignment guides on and off, choose View > Alignment Guides.

3   Choose Edit > Undo Drag (or press Command-Z) to return the Reversed Gtr region to bar 4.

4 Click the Editors button (or press E) to open the Audio File Editor.

The anchor is located at the bottom of the Audio File Editor, on the Anchor lane below the waveform. It is completely to the left, at the beginning of the region.

5 In the Audio File Editor, drag the anchor to the maximum amplitude on the waveform, almost at the end of the file.

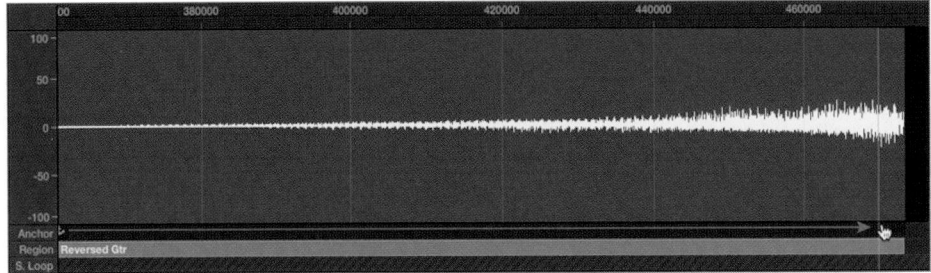

6 Click the Editors button (or press E) to close the Audio File Editor.

7 On the Guitar track (track 7), slowly drag the Reversed Gtr region to the left until you see a yellow alignment guide at the beginning of the first region on the bass track.

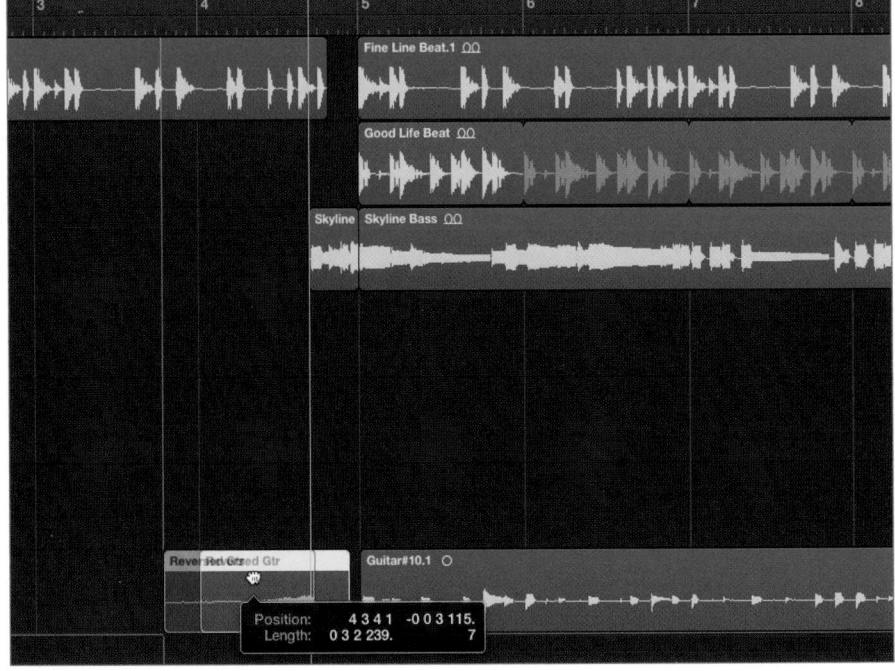

This time the anchor of the Reversed Gtr region lines up with the alignment guides and snaps to the beginning of the first bass region.

8 Play the introduction.

You can hear a click at the beginning of the Reversed Gtr region.

9 Add a long fade-in to the Reversed Gtr region.

10 Listen to the newly improved intro.

Now the swelling guitar chord sounds smooth. It catches the listener's attention just before the bass first comes in, accentuating the effect of the break at the end of the introduction.

Using the Flex Tool

You will now import a guitar recording that was removed from the workspace, but kept in the Project Audio Browser. That guitar was removed because of timing issues, which you can now fix using the Flex tool.

1 In the control bar, click the Browsers button (or press F).

2 At the top of the browser, click the Project tab.

3 In the Project Audio Browser, scroll all the way down, and then drag the Guitar Intro region to the Guitar track at bar 1.

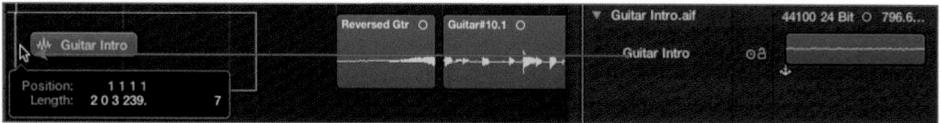

4 Click the Browsers button (or press F) to close the Project Audio Browser.

5 Play the introduction that includes your new Guitar Intro region.

The guitarist is playing four dead notes (unpitched percussive sounds when the string wasn't ringing), that cause a ringing in the vintage spring reverb in the guitar amp modeling plug-in.

The third note, at bar 2, sounds out of place, while the other notes play at the second and fourth beat of each bar, much as a snare would be heard in a drum pattern. You will move that third dead note to the second beat of bar 2.

6   Press T, and choose the Flex tool.

7   Using the Flex tool, click anywhere on the Guitar Intro region.

The audio files used on the Guitar track are analyzed for transients. You may see a progress window very briefly.

NOTE ▸ When clicking an audio region using the Flex tool, Logic automatically chooses a flex mode and analyzes all audio files on the same track to detect their transients. You will learn more about flex modes and flex editing in Lesson 7.

8   Zoom in closer on the Guitar Intro so that you can see the ruler above the waveform (or press Z).

9   Place the Flex tool over the attack of the third note (at bar 2).

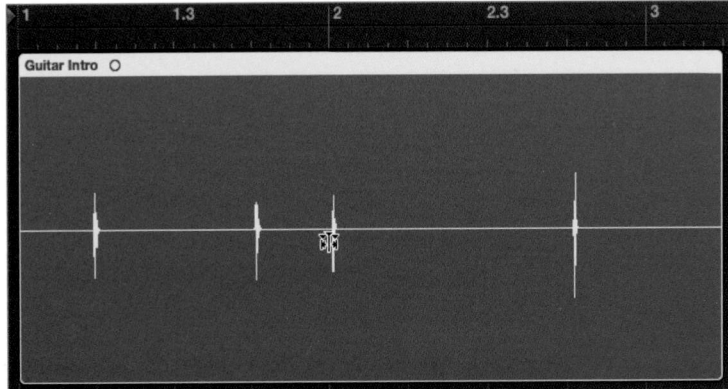

Depending on its position over the waveform, the Flex tool can perform different functions, indicated by different tool icons; so make sure that the tool is located precisely over the note's attack and looks like the pointer icon in the preceding figure.

10 Drag the Flex tool to the right to move the third guitar note to measure 2, beat 2.

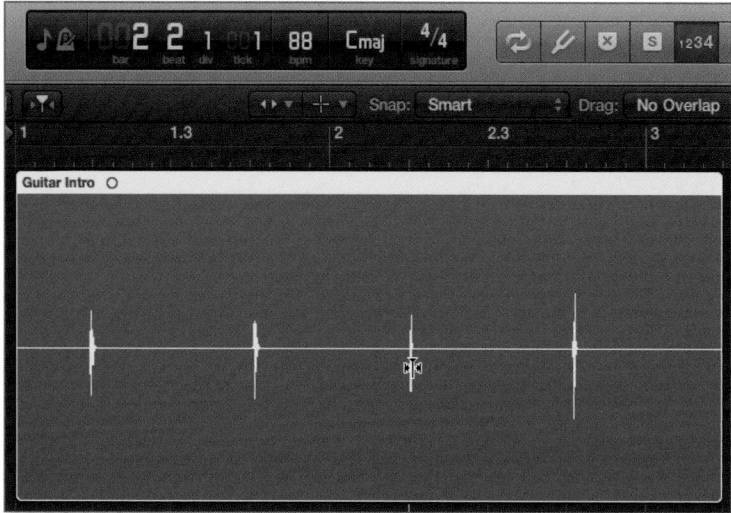

No help tag appears, but the LCD display shows the position of the Flex tool while you are holding down the mouse button. Make sure it shows 2 2 1 1 before you release the mouse button.

11 Play the introduction.

The dead notes in the first two bars now sound consistent.

The dead notes in this guitar region are still not located perfectly on the grid. If you wanted to take this a little further, you could set your snap mode to Beat, zoom in closer on the first guitar note, and use the Flex tool to drag it exactly on the beat. Then you'd repeat this operation on the second and fourth notes.

You now know how to read a waveform, identifying notes and their attacks to perform precise and clean edits. You acquired skills with a number of editing tools—such as the Marquee tool, Fade tool, Resize tool, Flex tool, take folders, and snap modes—that you will continue to use as you edit recordings and arrange projects.

Further, you can now accelerate your workflow by choosing the appropriate Left-click and Command-click tools for each job. As you produce more music in Logic, you will continue sharpening those skills in the course of becoming an increasingly proficient audio engineer.

Lesson Review

1. What is nondestructive audio editing?
2. Where can you perform nondestructive editing?
3. Where can you perform destructive editing?
4. How do you comp takes?
5. How do you prepare to edit the takes inside a take folder?
6. How can you see the result of your comp as regions?
7. How do you add a fade-in or fade-out to a region?
8. How do you add a crossfade between two regions?
9. How do you select a section of an audio region?
10. Which tool allows you to move an individual note inside an audio region, without dividing the region?
11. What is the anchor?
12. What is the purpose of alignment guides?

Answers

1. Audio region editing that does not alter the audio data in the referenced audio file
2. In the workspace or in the Audio Track Editor
3. In the Audio File Editor
4. Open the take folder, and drag over each take to highlight the desired sections. The take folder assembles a comp including all the highlighted sections.
5. Click the Quick Swipe Comping button at the top left of the take folder to disable Quick Swipe Comping mode.
6. From the Take Folder pop-up menu, choose Flatten.
7. Drag the Fade tool over the boundaries of a region (or Control-Shift-drag the Pointer tool), or adjust the Fade In parameter in the Region inspector.
8. Drag the Fade tool over the junction of the regions (or Control-Shift-drag the Pointer tool), or adjust the Fade Out parameter in the Region inspector.
9. Use the Marquee tool.
10. The Flex tool

11. The anchor is a point in an audio region used to position the region to the grid in the workspace.

12. To help line up the anchor in a region with the beginnings or ends of other regions on other tracks

Keyboard Shortcuts

Workspace

Control-Shift-drag with the Pointer tool	Adds a fade
Option-click with the Fade tool	Removes a fade
While dragging press and hold down Control	Disables snapping
While dragging press and hold down Control-Shift	Disables snapping with increased placement precision
Command-J	Renders the selected regions and their fades into a single new audio region

Tools

T	Opens the Tool menu at the mouse pointer position
Press T twice	Changes the Left-click tool to a pointer

Audio File Editor

Control-Shift-R	Reverses an audio file (or the selected section of an audio file)

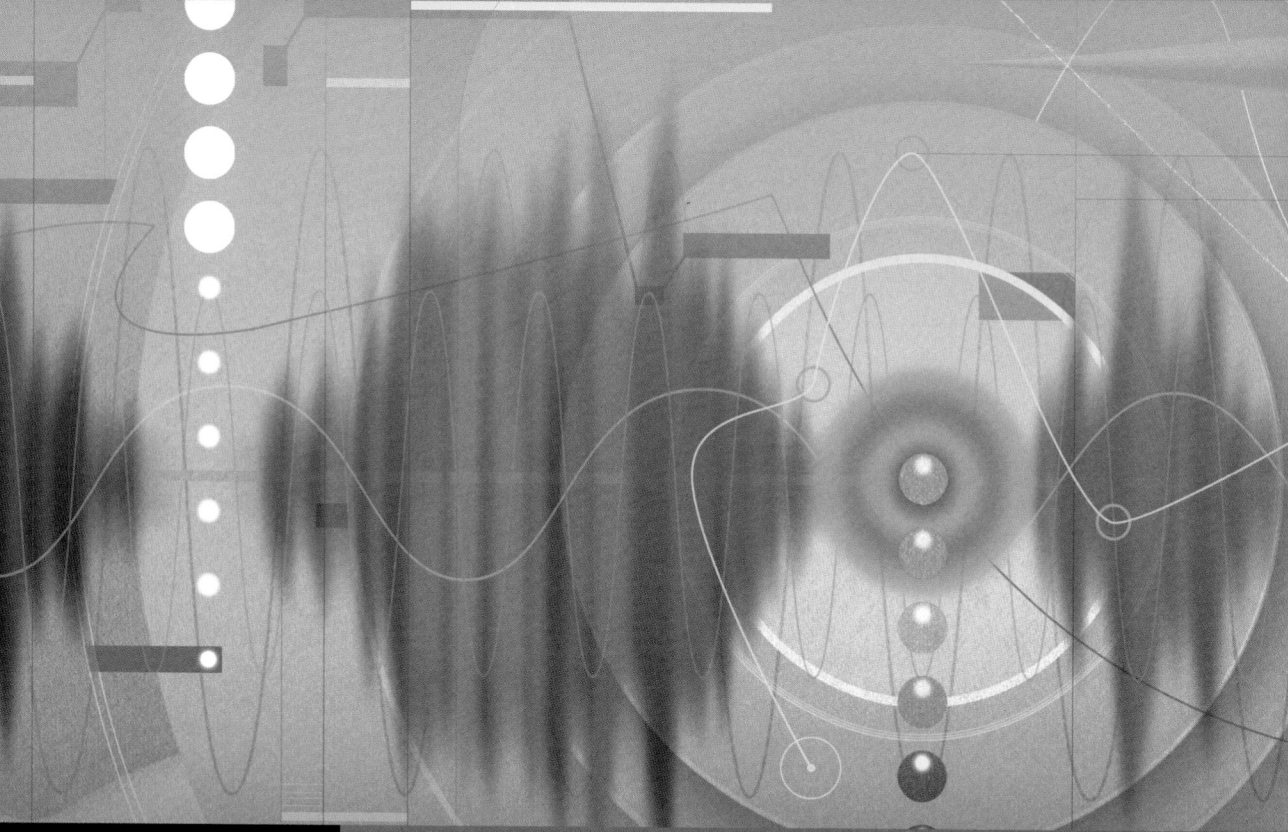

Working with
Virtual Instruments

4

Time

This lesson takes approximately 75 minutes to complete.

Goals

Create a new project with a Drummer track

Choose a drummer and drum kit

Edit the drummer performance

Arrange the song structure

Edit performances in the new sections

Make the drummer play behind or ahead of the beat

Customize the drum kit

Tune and dampen individual kit pieces

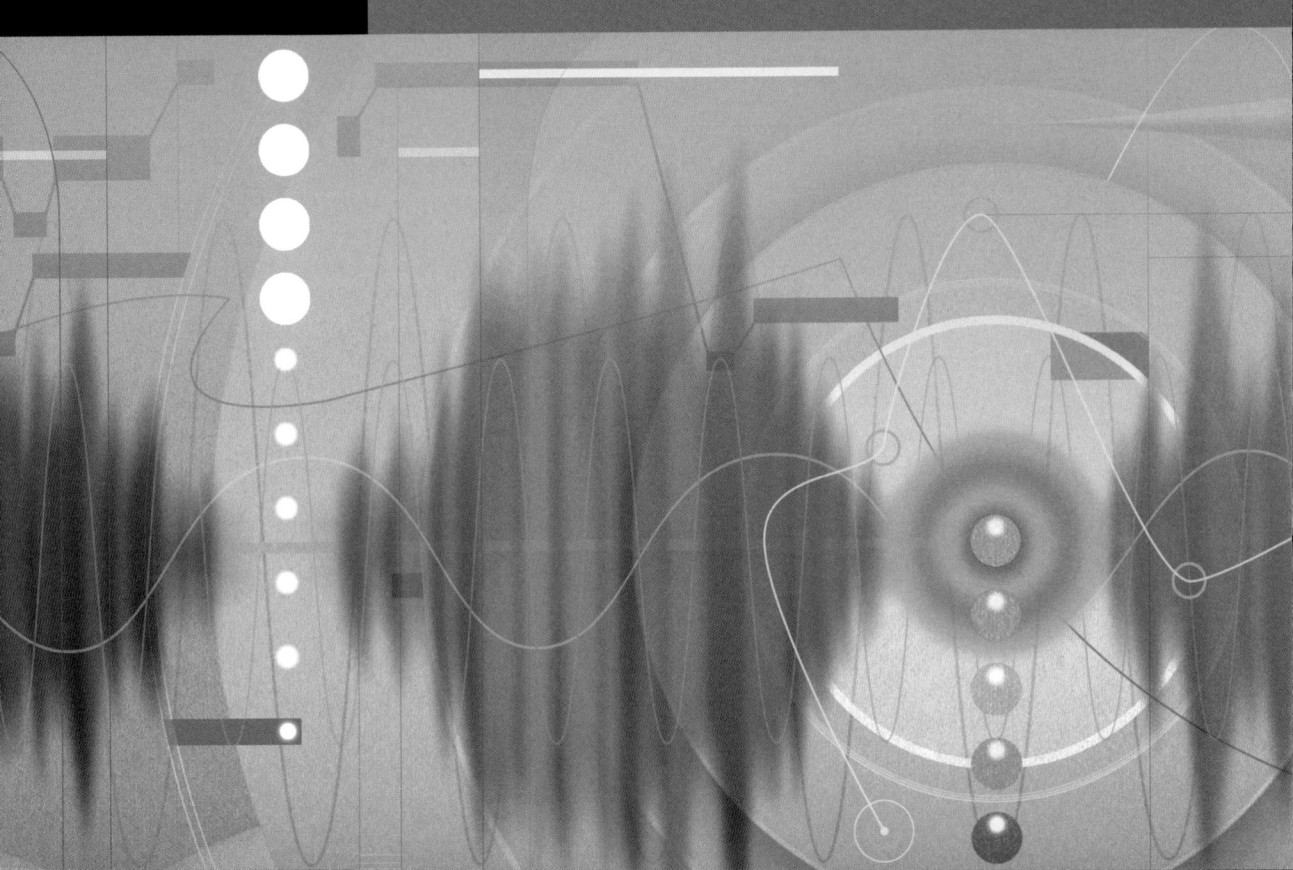

Lesson 4

Produce a Virtual Drum Track

In most popular modern music genres, drums are the backbone of the instrumentation. They provide the foundation for the tempo and the groove of the piece. For recording sessions in which the instruments are not tracked at the same time, drums are usually recorded or programmed first, so that the other musicians can record while listening to their rhythmic reference.

To meet today's high production standards, producing drum tracks usually involves using several techniques, including live recording, programming, sampling, audio quantizing, and sound replacement. In Logic Pro X, you can speed up the process by taking advantage of the new Drummer feature along with its companion software instrument, Drum Kit Designer.

In this lesson, you will produce a virtual drum track to start producing a new imaginary indie-rock song. After selecting a genre and choosing the best drummer for your project, you will adjust the drummer's performance, making him play busier patterns or simpler ones, louder or softer, and changing his feel, almost like a producer would communicate with a real drummer in a recording session.

Creating a Drummer Track

Drummer is a new Logic Pro X feature that allows you to produce drum tracks using a virtual drummer with his own playing style. His performance is placed in Drummer regions on a Drummer track. You edit the performance data in the regions using the Drummer Editor. The virtual drummer also has his own drum kit loaded in a software instrument plug-in called Drum Kit Designer.

First, let's open a new project, add a Drummer track, and examine the display of the drum performance in the Drummer region.

1   Choose File > New (or press Command-Shift-N).

A new project opens along with the New Tracks dialog.

2   In the New Tracks dialog, select Drummer, and click Create.

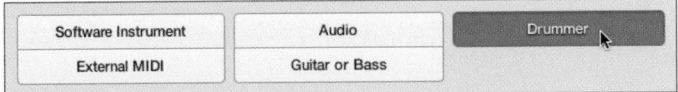

A Drummer track is created along with two eight-bar Drummer regions. At the bottom of the main window, the Drummer Editor opens, allowing you to choose a drummer and his drum kit, and to edit the performance in the Drummer region(s) that are selected in the workspace. The track is named SoCal, which is the name of the drum kit used by the default virtual drummer, Kyle.

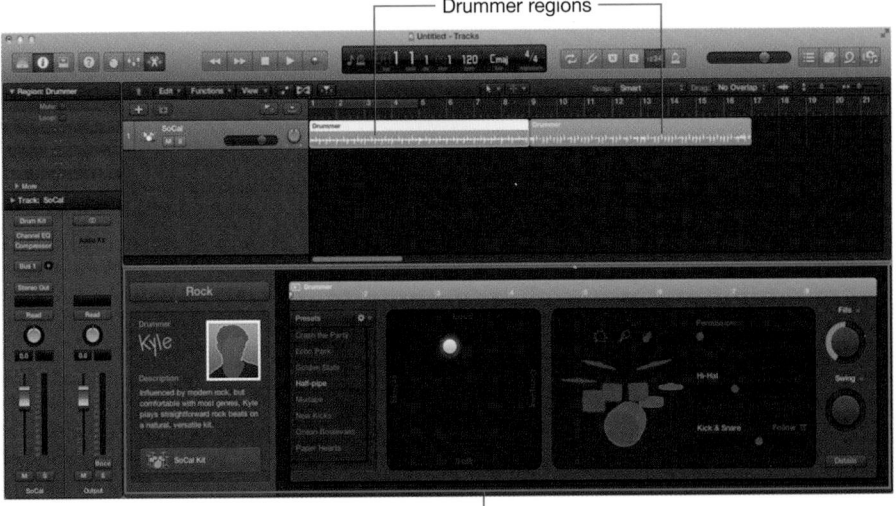

Drummer Editor

3 Press the Spacebar to listen to the two Drummer regions.

In the first region, the drummer starts with a crash cymbal, and plays a straightforward rock pattern. At the end of the first four measures, he plays the simplest of fills (a single tom hit), followed by a crash cymbal that accentuates the first downbeat of bar 5. At the end of the first Drummer region, a drum fill leads into the next section.

In the second region, the drummer switches from the hi-hat to the ride cymbal, and plays a more complex pattern: The kick is busier, and the snare adds ghost notes (very quiet hits) between beats. As in the first region, the drummer plays a fill at the end of the first four measures, followed by a crash. He plays another fill at the end of the region.

Let's take a closer look at that Drummer region.

4 Control-Option-drag over the first bar of the first Drummer region. If necessary, continue zooming vertically by dragging the vertical zoom slider (or pressing Command-Down Arrow) until you can see two lanes in the Drummer region.

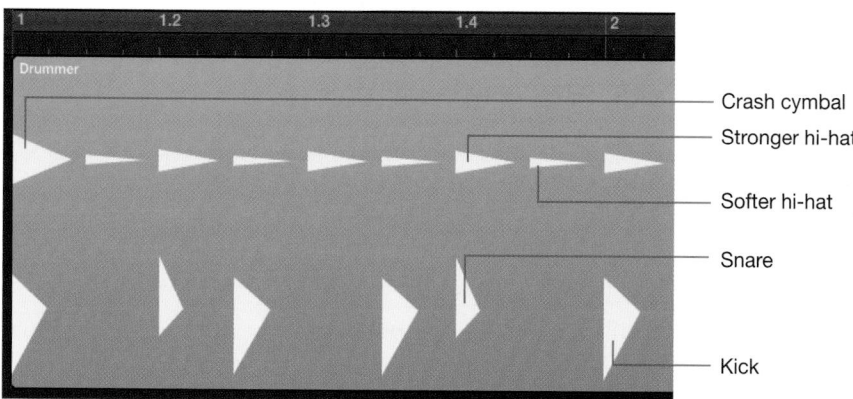

The Drummer region displays drum hits as triangles on lanes, roughly emulating the look of drum hits on an audio waveform. Kicks and snares are shown on the bottom lane; cymbals, toms, and hand percussions are on the top lane.

5   In the top half of the ruler, drag a one-measure cycle area at bar 1.

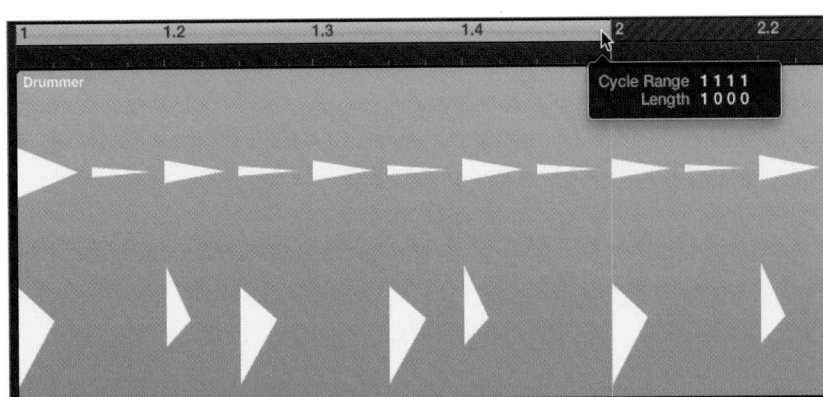

6   Listen to the first bar a few times while looking at the drum hits in the Drummer region.

Although you cannot edit individual drum hits in the Drummer region, the region display gives you a quick glance at the drummer's performance.

MORE INFO ▸ At the end of this lesson you will convert Drummer regions to MIDI regions. In Lesson 6, you will learn how to edit MIDI regions.

7   Turn off Cycle mode.

8   In the workspace, click the background and press Z to zoom out and see both drummer regions.

Now you can read the Drummer regions. In the next exercise, you will listen to multiple drummers and several performance presets. Later, you will zoom in again to see the Drummer regions update as you adjust their settings in the Drummer Editor.

Choosing a Drummer and a Style

Each drummer has his own playing style and drum kit, and those combine to create a unique drum sound. Before you start fine-tuning the drummer's performance, you need to choose the right drummer for the song.

In the Drummer Editor, drummers are categorized by music genres. By default, choosing a new drummer means loading a new virtual drum kit, and updating Drummer region settings; but sometimes you may want to keep the same drum kit while changing the drummer, which you will do in this exercise.

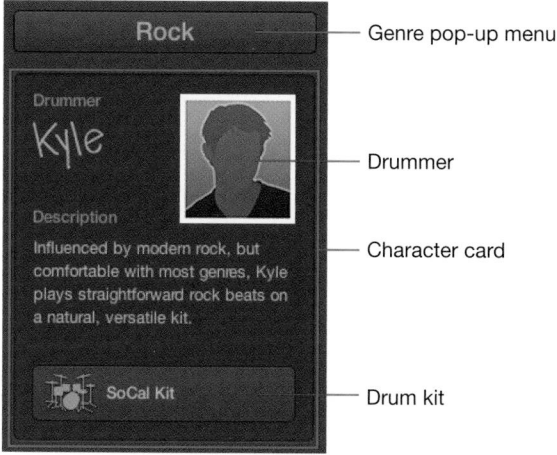

Genre pop-up menu

Drummer

Character card

Drum kit

1   In the character card, click the drummer.

All the drummers from the Rock category are displayed.

2   Place the mouse pointer over Anders (the first drummer in the second row).

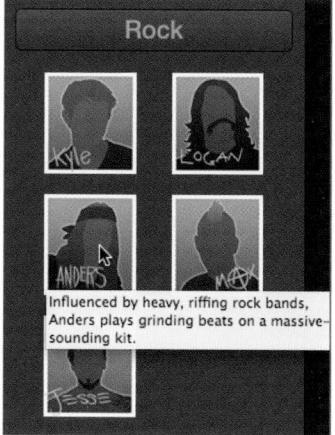

A help tag describes that drummer's playing style and the sound of his drum kit. It mentions straightforward rock beats, which would work for this song; but for now, let's get to know the other drummers.

3 Continue by placing the pointer over other rock drummers to read their descriptions. When you're through, click the last drummer, Jesse.

A dialog explains how to retain region settings when changing the drummer.

4 In the dialog, select "Do not show this message again," and click Change Drummer.

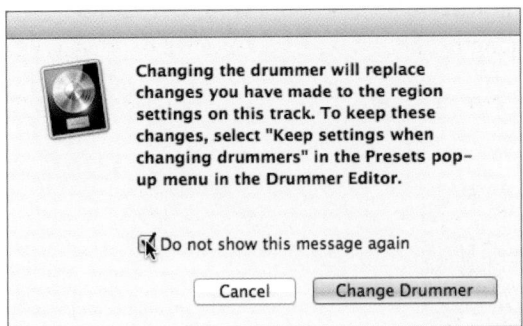

In the workspace, the two Drummer regions update to display Jesse's performance.

5 In the workspace, click the first Drummer region (at bar 1) to select it.

The Drummer Editor shows you the settings for the selected Drummer region. A yellow ruler allows you to position the playhead anywhere within the region, and you can click the Play button to the left of the ruler to preview the Drummer region. As in the Tracks area, you can also double-click the ruler to start and stop playback.

6 In the Drummer Editor, click the Play button.

The selected region plays in Cycle mode, and the cycle area automatically matches the region position and length. The selected region is soloed—indicated by a thin yellow frame—and the other region is dimmed. Soloing the region helps you focus on the drums when you have other tracks in the project.

Although you will later fine-tune the drummer's performance, Jesse's busy, syncopated drum patterns are not a good fit for this indie rock song. You are looking for a drummer with a simple, straightforward style that more appropriately serves the song.

7   Stop playback.

In the Tracks area, Cycle mode is automatically turned off, the dimmed cycle area returns to its original position and length, and the selected region is no longer soloed.

8   In the Drummer Editor, click the Genre menu at the top of the character card, and choose Alternative.

Drummers from the Alternative category are shown.

9   Click the first drummer, Aidan.

10   In the Drummer Editor, click the Play button.

While the region is playing back in Cycle mode, you can try selecting other region settings presets to explore Aidan's full range of playing style.

11   In the Presets column, click a few different presets while the region plays back.

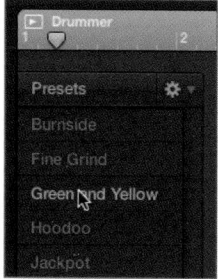

When you click a preset, the region settings update and you can hear another performance from the same drummer.

12 Without stopping playback, from the Genre menu, choose Rock.

13 Click the fourth drummer, Max, and listen to a few of his presets.

Although Max's hyperactive performance is not what you're looking for, his drum kit sounds punchy. Let's assign the first drummer, Kyle, to play on Max's drum set, East Bay Kit.

14 In the character card, click the drummer to display the drummers.

You can Option-click a new drummer to select that drummer while keeping the current drum kit.

15 Option-click Kyle.

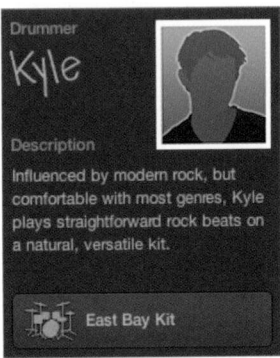

Kyle is now playing Max's East Bay Kit. Let's make him play a bit faster.

16 In the control bar, set the tempo to 142 bpm.

17 Stop playback.

You have found a drummer that plays the straightforward style you're seeking for this project, paired him with a punchy sounding drum kit, and set a tempo that will drive your indie rock song. You are now ready to customize the performance.

Editing the Drum Performance

In a recording session with a live drummer, the artist, the producer, or the musical director must communicate their vision of the completed song. They may ask the drummer to play behind or ahead of the beat to change the feel of the groove, or to switch from the hi-hat to the ride cymbal during the chorus, or to play a drum fill in a specific location.

In Logic Pro X, editing a drummer performance is almost like giving instructions to a real drummer. In this exercise, you will play a drum region in Cycle mode as you adjust the drummer settings.

1   In the workspace, make sure the first Drummer region is still selected, and in the Drummer Editor, click the Play button.

Next to the presets, an XY pad with a yellow puck lets you adjust both the loudness and complexity of the drum pattern.

2   As the region plays, drag the puck, or click different locations inside the pad to reposition it.

TIP To undo your most recent Drummer Editor adjustment, press Command-Z.

After positioning the puck, you must wait for the region to update (update time varies depending on your computer). If you drag the puck constantly, the region will not update.

As you position the puck farther to the right, the drum pattern becomes more complex; and as you move the puck toward the top of the pad, the drummer plays louder. Try placing the puck in the pad's corners for extreme settings, such as soft and simple, or loud and complex.

As the drummer plays softer, he closes the hi-hat and switches from hitting the snare drum on the skin to playing rim clicks (hitting only the rim of the drum). As he plays louder, he opens the hi-hat and start playing rim shots (hitting the skin and the rim simultaneously for accent).

Let's make the drummer play a solid, straightforward beat in this first Drummer region, which will be used for the first verse of the song.

3   Settle for a puck position where the drummer plays a rather simple and fairly loud pattern.

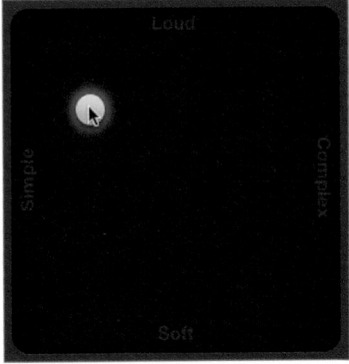

You can still hear a lot of syncopation on the kick drums. To the right of the XY pad, you can choose from several Kick & Snare pattern variations.

4   Drag the Kick & Snare slider to position 2 (or click the second increment on the slider).

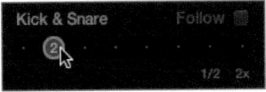

The drummer now simply alternates kick and snare on every beat. If you don't hear the drummer play the snare on beats 2 and 4, slightly readjust the horizontal position of the puck in the XY pad so it's in the same position as in the figure following step 3.

Listen to the hi-hat: It is currently playing eighth notes.

5   Click the first increment on the Hi-Hat slider.

The hi-hat now plays only on the beat (quarter notes), which works well for up-tempo songs.

The drummer is playing a fill in the middle of the region (before bar 5) and another at the end (before bar 9). Let's get rid of the first fill and keep only one at the end.

6   Look at the region in the workspace, and drag the Fills knob down until you see the fill before bar 5 disappear. You should still see a fill at the end of the region.

NOTE ▸ Clicking the small lock icon next to the Fills and Swing knobs locks the knob into position as you preview presets or drummers.

TIP ▸ Each time you adjust a setting in the Drummer Editor, the selected region is refreshed and the drummer plays a new subtle variation. Dragging the Fills knob by a tiny amount is a quick way to refresh a region. You can also click the Action pop-up menu next to the Presets menu, and choose Refresh Region; or Control-click the region in the workspace, and from the shortcut menu, choose Edit > Refresh Region.

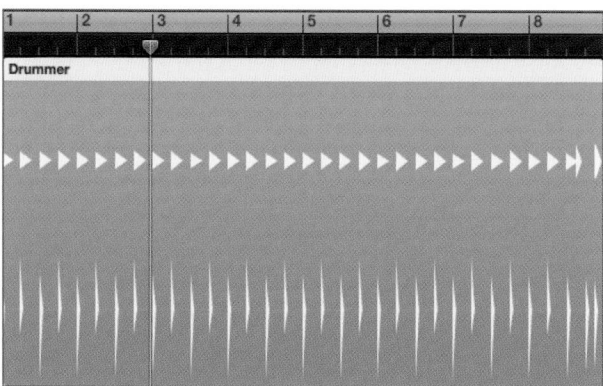

You now have a very straightforward beat. Because the drummer plays less now, he can make the hi-hat ring a bit more.

7   In the Drummer Editor, click the Details button to display three knobs.

8   Below the Hi-Hat knob, deselect the Automatic option.

9   Drag the Hi-Hat knob up to open it a little bit.

This verse drum pattern now sounds great, so let's move on to the second Drummer region, which you'll use for the chorus.

10   In the Drummer Editor, click the Details button to hide the three buttons.

11   Stop playback.

12   In the workspace, select the second Drummer region.

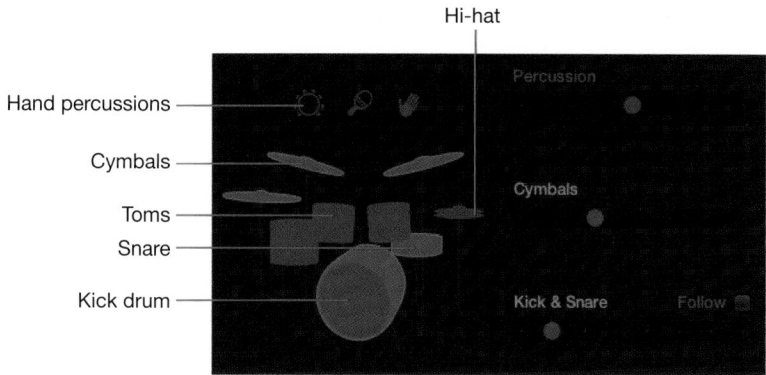

The Drummer Editor updates to show the second region's settings. On the drum kit, the hi-hat is now dimmed, while the cymbals are highlighted in yellow. The drummer no longer plays the hi-hat, but instead plays a ride or crash cymbal in that region.

13 In the Drummer Editor, click the Play button.

You can hear the second region in Cycle mode. The drummer is playing the ride cymbal on every eighth note. For a more powerful chorus, you instead want him to play crash cymbals on every beat.

14 Click the first increment of the Cymbals slider.

You now hear crash cymbals on every beat. Even for a chorus, the beat is a little too busy.

15 On the XY pad, drag the puck toward the left to create a simpler beat, while the kick drum still plays some eighth notes.

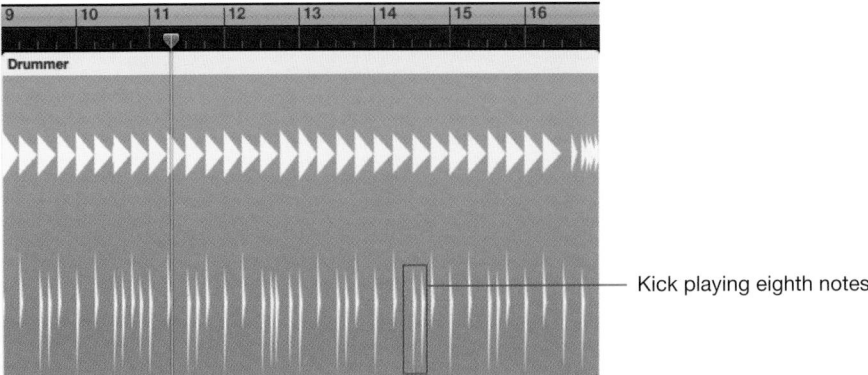

Kick playing eighth notes

Let's listen to the verse going into the chorus.

16 Stop playback.

17 Go to the beginning of the song and listen to both Drummer regions.

You now have a simple, straightforward beat for the verse, and then the drummer switches to the crash cymbal for the busier chorus pattern.

You have carefully crafted two eight-measure drum grooves: one for the verse and one for the chorus. They are the two most important building blocks of the song that you will now start arranging.

Arranging the Drum Track

In this exercise, you will lay out the whole song structure and continue editing drum regions for each section, still using the two Drummer regions you edited for the verses and choruses.

Using Markers in the Arrangement Track

Using the Arrangement track, you will now create arrangement markers for all the sections of your song. You'll adjust their lengths, positions, and order, and fill all the new sections with Drummer regions.

1   At the top of the track headers, click the Global Tracks button (or press G).

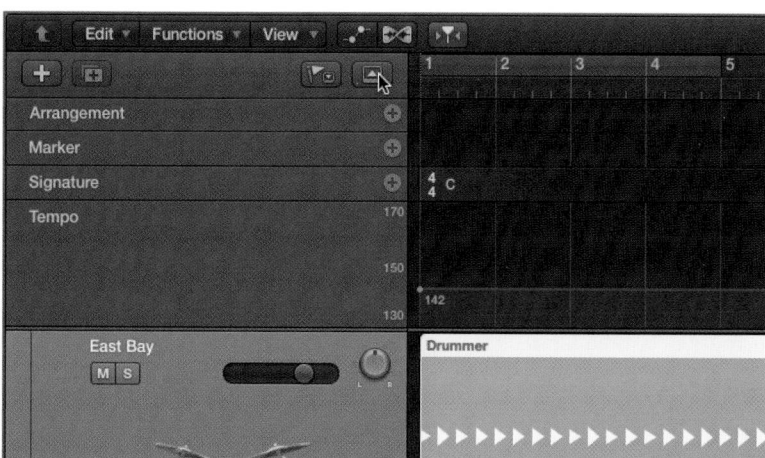

The global tracks open, with the Arrangement track at the top. You won't need the other global tracks, so you can hide them.

2   Control-click a global track header, and choose Hide Marker. Also Control-click the Signature and Tempo tracks, and hide them.

The Arrangement track is now closer to the regions in the workspace, making it easier to see their relationships.

3   In the Arrangement track header, click the Add Marker button (+).

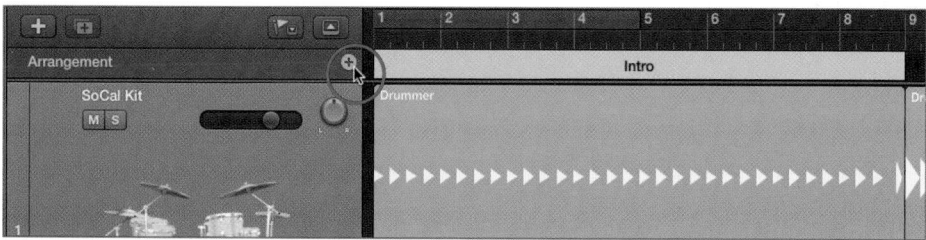

An eight-measure arrangement marker named Intro is created at the beginning of the song. By default, arrangement markers are eight bars long and are placed one after the other, starting from the beginning of the song. Let's rename the marker.

4 Click the name of the marker, and from the menu, choose Verse.

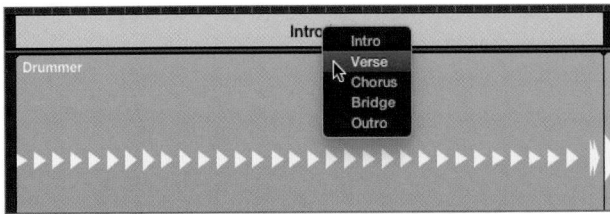

5 Click the Add Marker button (+) to create a marker for the chorus.

An eight-bar marker named Chorus is created.

You will now create a marker for a new intro section and insert it before the Verse and Chorus markers.

6 In the Arrangement track header, click the Add Marker (+) button.

An eight-bar marker named Chorus is created.

7 Click the name of the new marker, and from the pop-up menu, choose Intro.

A four-measure intro will be long enough, so you can resize the Intro marker before moving it.

8 Drag the right edge of the Intro marker toward the left to shorten it to four bars.

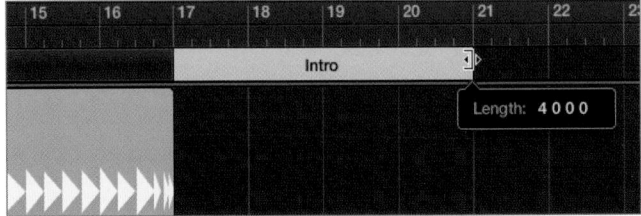

9 Click the marker away from its name (to avoid opening the Name pop-up menu), and drag the Intro marker to bar 1.

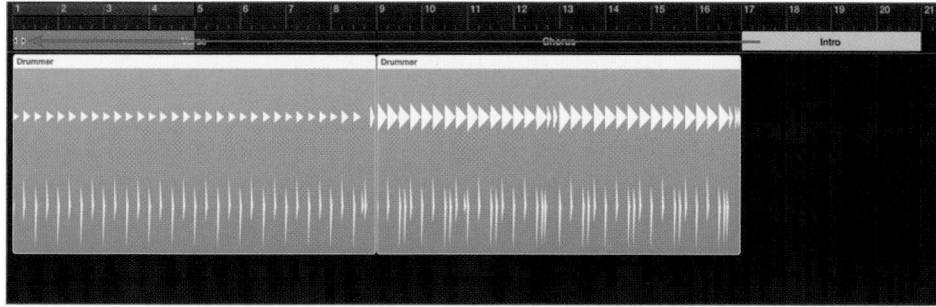

The Intro marker is inserted at bar 1, and the Verse and Chorus markers move to the right of the new Intro section. In the workspace, the Drummer regions move along with their respective arrangement markers.

As with regions in the workspace, you can Option-drag a marker to copy it.

10 Press Command-Left Arrow to zoom out horizontally and make space to the right of the existing song sections. Option-drag the Verse marker to bar 21, right after the chorus.

The Verse marker and the Drummer region are copied together.

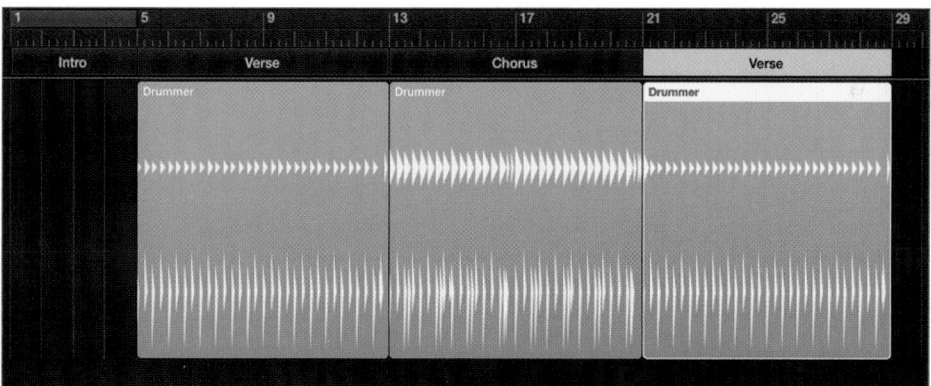

11 Option-drag the Chorus marker to bar 29, after the second verse.

The Chorus and the Drummer region are copied together.

The song is taking shape. You will now finish arranging the song structure with a bridge, a chorus, and an outro section. As you place the last three markers, continue zooming out horizontally as necessary.

12 In the Arrangement track header, click the Add Marker (+) button.

A Verse marker is created after the last chorus.

13 Click the name of the new marker, and from the pop-up menu, choose Bridge.

14 In the Arrangement track header, click the Add Marker (+) button two more times to create markers for the Chorus and Outro sections.

15 Click each one of the last two marker names and choose the correct names, Chorus and Outro.

Let's shorten the outro section a bit.

16 Resize the Outro marker to make it four bars long.

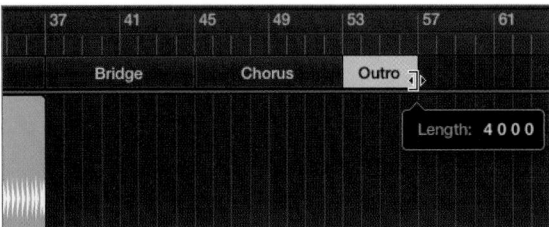

The song structure is now complete, and you can add Drummer regions to fill out the empty sections.

17 On the Drummer track, Control-click the background, and choose "Populate with Drummer Regions."

New Drummer regions are created for all the empty arrangement markers.

18 Listen to the drum track, focusing on the new sections.

New patterns were automatically created for each new Drummer region.

Amazing as his playing is, Kyle (the drummer) might not have guessed what you had in mind for each section. You will now edit the new regions to finish adjusting the drummer's performance.

Editing the Intro Drum Performance

In this exercise, you will make the drummer play the snare instead of the toms. Later, you'll cut the Intro region in two and make the drummer play the snare only during the first half. Then you'll add the kick and hi-hat in the second half.

1   In the workspace, click the background to deselect all regions, and click the Intro region to select it.

The Drummer Editor shows its settings.

Throughout this exercise you can click the Play button in the Drummer Editor to start and stop playback, or you can navigate the workspace by pressing the Spacebar (Play or Stop) and the Return key (Go to Beginning).

2   Listen to the Intro.

Let's mute the toms.

3   In the Drummer Editor, click one of the toms.

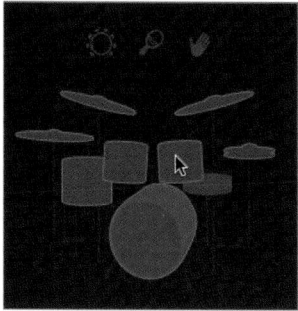

The toms are dimmed to indicate that they are muted. In the Intro region, the toms disappear from the top lane.

4   Click the snare to unmute it.

In the Intro region, snare hits appear next to the kick hits on the bottom lane.

To play the kick in only the first half of the intro, followed by the kick and snare in the second half, you will cut the Intro region in two.

5 Stop playback.

6 Hold down Command to use the Marquee tool, and double-click the Intro region at bar 3.

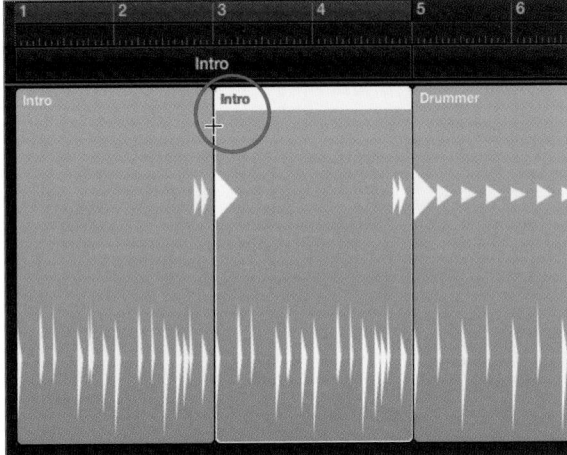

The region is divided into two two-measure regions. When a region is divided, the drummer automatically adapts his performance, and plays a fill at the end of each new region.

7 Select the first Intro region.

8 In the Drummer Editor, drag the Fills knob all the way down.

Notice how the crash disappears from the first beat of the following region. Even though it is in another region, the crash is actually a part of the fill.

9 On the drum kit, click the kick drum to mute it.

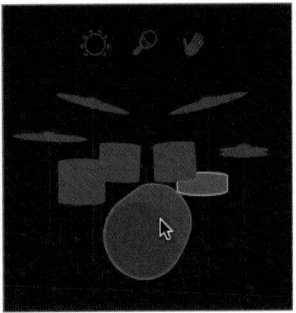

In the first two measures, the drummer will be playing only the snare. Let's have him play the snare very softly on every beat, as if he's counting in the band.

10 In the Kick & Snare slider, click the sixth increment.

The snare plays every beat.

TIP In multi-track projects, when you click the Follow checkbox, a pop-up menu appears instead of the Kick & Snare slider that lets you choose a track to influence what the drummer plays on the kick and snare.

11 In the XY pad, drag the puck all the way down and to the left.

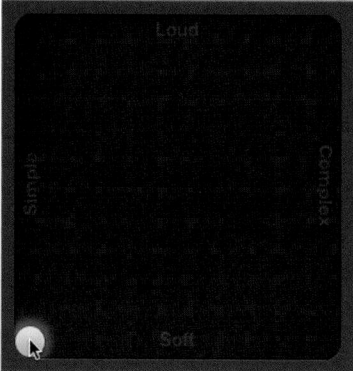

Now the drummer plays rim clicks at the beginning of the first Intro region, and hits the snare a few times at the end.

12 In the workspace, select the second Intro region.

13 In the Kick & Snare slider, click the second increment.

14 On the XY pad, drag the puck toward the upper left.

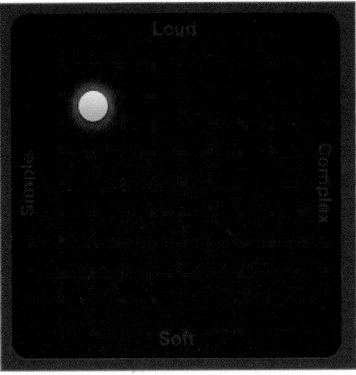

The drums play a straightforward beat with a fill at the end. Let's add an open hi-hat to inject some energy.

15 On the drum kit, click the hi-hat to unmute it.

16 In the Hi-Hat slider, click the first increment.

Now you will open the hi-hat to add energy to the end of the intro.

17 In the Drummer Editor, click the Details button.

18 Below the Hi-Hat knob, deselect Automatic.

19 Drag the Hi-Hat knob up nearly all the way until the hi-hat sounds really open, but you can still clearly hear the individual hits.

20 Click the Details buttons to display the drum kit again.

21 Listen to the whole intro going into the first verse.

Your have a short two-part intro. The drummer plays the snare on the first eight beats, and then a basic rock pattern with a very open hi-hat adds energy. At bar 5, a crash punctuates the fill at the end of the intro. The straightforward groove continues in the Verse section with the hi-hat a little less open to leave space to later add a singer.

Editing the Bridge Drum Performance

In a song, the bridge serves to break the sequence of alternating verses and choruses. Often, the main idea of the song is exposed in the choruses, and verses help support or develop that statement. The bridge can present an alternate idea, a different point of view. Departing from the main idea of the song increases the listener's appreciation for returning to the chorus at the end of the song—almost like taking a vacation can increase your appreciation for going back home.

For this fast, high-energy indie-rock song, a quieter bridge in which the instruments play softer will offer a refreshing dynamic contrast. Playing softer does not mean the instruments have to play less, however. In fact, you will make the drums play a busier pattern during this bridge.

1   Listen to the Bridge region.

> **TIP** ▸ When pressing the Spacebar to play a section, you can use Cycle mode to ensure that playback always starts at the beginning of the section. Drag a section's arrangement marker into the ruler to turn on Cycle mode and create a cycle area that matches the section.

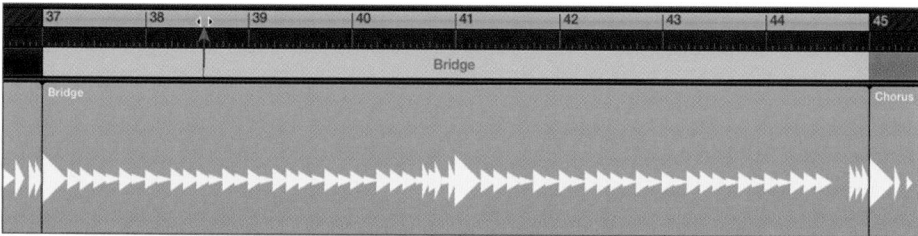

The drummer plays at the same level as in the previous sections, but he plays more here. You need to bring down his energy level.

2   Select the Bridge Drummer region.

3   In the XY pad, position the puck all the way down and to the right.

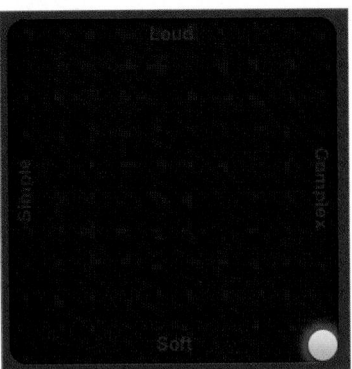

The drummer is still playing a lot, but he's much quieter. He no longer hits the snare's skin but plays rim clicks instead. However, rim clicks are not the type of sound you're going for; you want Kyle to play toms.

4   On the drum kit, mute the snare, and unmute the toms.

When you click the toms, the hi-hat is automatically muted. Aside from the kick and snare, the drummer can focus on the toms, the hi-hat, or the cymbals (ride and crash).

Let's choose a busier pattern for the toms.

5   On the Toms slider, click increment 3.

Kyle is now playing sixteenth notes on the toms, which create a mysterious vibe similar to tribal percussions. You will make him switch from the toms to the ride cymbal in the second half of the bridge to brighten things up.

6   Command-double-click the Bridge region at bar 41 to cut it into two four bar regions.

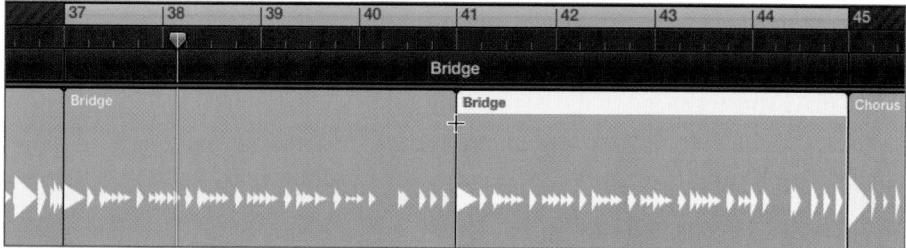

The drummer now plays a different fill at the end of the first Bridge region.

While the second Bridge region is still selected, you can adjust the cycle area.

7 Control-click the cycle area, and choose "Set Locators by Regions/Events/Marquee" (or press Command-U).

8 Unmute the cymbals.

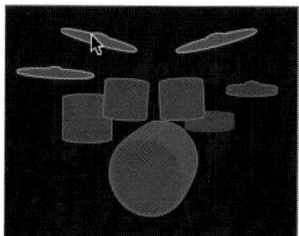

The toms are muted, and the drummer now plays the ride cymbal. However, the groove still seems to be missing something.

9 Unmute the snare.

You can hear rim clicks.

10 In the XY pad, drag the puck up just until Kyle switches from hitting the rim to hitting the head of the snare (about a quarter of the way up).

11 On the Cymbals slider, click the third increment.

The drummer hits the ride cymbal differently, giving it more of a bell-like sound. He plays a crescendo, thereby building up energy to lead into the next chorus.

Kyle plays slightly ahead of the beat during the bridge. However, the timing nuance is subtle, and difficult to hear without any other instruments to compare with Kyle's timing. Let's turn on the metronome and experiment with the feel of his performance.

12 In the control bar, click the Metronome button (or press K).

You will be editing the feel of both Bridge regions simultaneously.

13 In the workspace, select both Bridge regions, and press Command-U to set the locators.

At the top of the Drummer Editor, the ruler, Play button, and playhead are replaced by the message *Multiple regions selected*. You can now adjust the settings of all the selected regions at once.

NOTE ▶ When adjusting a setting that is set to different values in multiple regions, the value offset between the regions stays the same (wherever possible).

14 In the Drummer Editor, click the Details button to display the three setting knobs.

15 Try setting different positions of the Feel knob and then listen to the results.

Both regions change their "feel."

As you experiment with different feels, listen to the way the drums play compared to the steady, precise beat of the metronome. Don't be afraid to drag the Feel knob all the way up or down to hear the effect of extreme Feel settings.

▶ Dragging the Feel knob toward Push makes the drummer play ahead of the beat. He sounds as if he's rushing, thereby creating a sense of urgency.

▶ Dragging the Feel knob toward Pull makes him play behind the beat. He sounds as if he's lazy or late, and the groove is more relaxed.

Settle on a Feel knob position more toward Pull to realize a reasonably relaxed groove.

16 Click the Details button to hide the three setting knobs.

17 Turn off Cycle mode.

18 In the control bar, click the Metronome button (or press K) to turn it off.

You have radically changed the drummer's performance in that region. Kyle now starts the bridge with a busy pattern on the toms, and then moves on to a bell sound on the ride. He uses restraint, hitting softly and behind the beat, with a slight crescendo toward the end. The quiet and laid-back yet complex drum groove brings a welcome pause to an otherwise high-energy drum performance, and builds up tension leading into the last two sections.

Editing the Chorus and Outro Sections

You will now finish editing the drummer's performance by adjusting the settings of the last two Chorus and Outro Drummer regions in your workspace.

1 Select the Chorus region after the bridge and listen to it.

That Chorus region was created when you populated the track with Drummer regions earlier in this lesson. It doesn't have the same settings as the previous two choruses and sounds busier, except for Kyle playing the ride cymbal instead of the crash.

2 On the Cymbals slider, click the first increment.

The drummer now plays the crash, and this last chorus is more consistent with the previous two choruses.

3 Select the Outro region at the end of the track and listen to it.

The drummer plays a loud beat, heavy on the crash, which could work for an outro. You will, however, make him play double-time (twice as fast) to end the song in a big way.

4 On the Kick & Snare slider, click the last increment (8).

Now it sounds like you've unleashed Kyle! Playing double-time at that fast tempo makes the sixteenth notes on the kick drum sound ridiculously fast.

5 On the XY pad, drag the puck toward the left until the drummer stops playing sixteenth notes on the kick drum.

The performance now sounds more realistic while retaining the driving effect of its double-time groove.

Let's finish the song with a longer drum fill.

6 Drag the Fills knob all the way up.

The drum fill at the end of the outro is now longer. However, raising the number of fills has the undesirable effect of adding a new fill in the middle of the outro. To remove that fill, you will cut the Outro region in two.

7 With the Marquee tool, double-click the Outro region at bar 55.

You now have two two-bar Outro regions.

8 Select the first Outro region.

9 Drag the Fills knob all the way down to remove the fill in the middle of the Outro section.

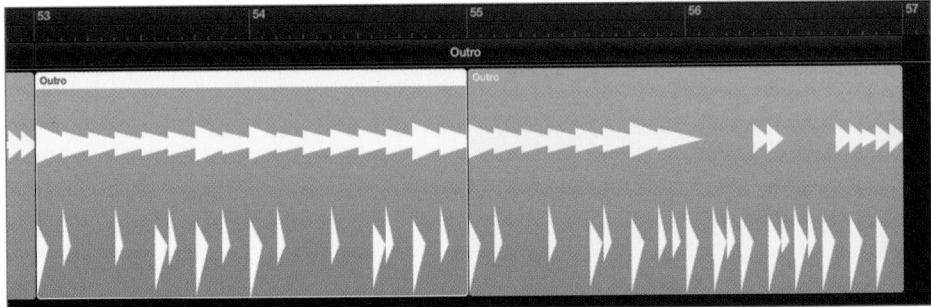

10 Listen to the last chorus and the outro.

The outro has the required power to drive the last four measures; however, it seems like the drummer stops abruptly before he can finish his fill. Usually drummers end a song by playing the last note on the first beat of a new bar, but here a crash cymbal is missing on the downbeat at bar 57. You will resize the last Outro region in the workspace to accommodate that last drum hit.

11 Resize the last Outro region to lengthen it by one beat (until the help tag reads *Length: 2 1 0 0   +0 1 0 0*).

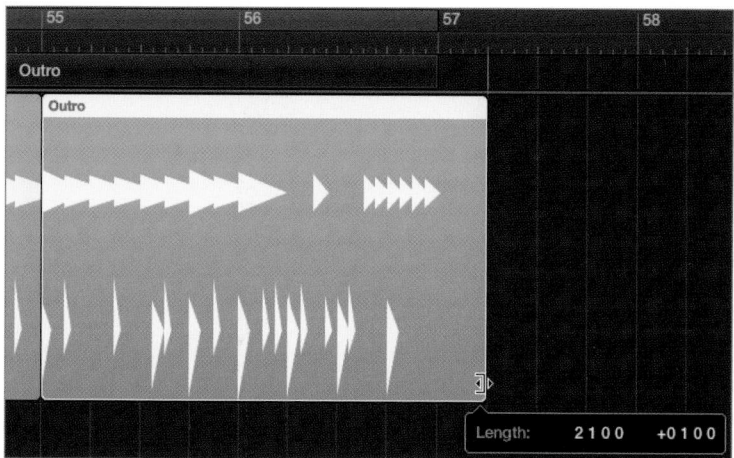

A moment after you release the mouse button, the Drummer region updates, and you can see a kick and a crash on the downbeat at bar 57.

12 Listen to the outro. The drummer finishes his fill, punctuating it with the last hit at bar 57.

> **NOTE** ▶ The final crash cymbal continues ringing until its natural sustain fades out, well after the playhead has passed the end of the last Outro region.

You've laid out the entire song structure by creating section markers in the arrangement track, populated each section with Drummer regions, and edited each region's settings to customize its drum pattern. You are now done editing the drum performance and can focus on the sound of the drums.

Customizing the Drum Kit

When recording a live drummer in a studio, the engineer often positions microphones on each drum. This allows control over the sound of each drum, so he can individually equalize or compress the sound of each kit piece. The producer may also want the drummer to try different kicks or snares, or to experiment with hitting the cymbals softer before he begins recording.

In Logic, when using Drummer, the sounds of each drum are already recorded. However, you can still use several tools to customize the drum kit and adjust the sound of each drum.

Adjusting the Drum Levels Using Smart Controls

Smart Controls are a set of knobs and switches that are premapped to the most important parameters of the plug-ins on the channel strip of the selected track. You will study Smart Controls in more detail in Lesson 5.

In this exercise, you will use Smart Controls to quickly adjust the levels and tones of different drums. Then you'll open Drum Kit Designer to swap one snare for another, and fine-tune the crash cymbal sound.

1 In the control bar, click the Smart Controls button (or press B).

The Smart Controls pane opens at the bottom of the main window, replacing the Drummer Editor. It is divided into three sections: Mix, Compression, and Effects.

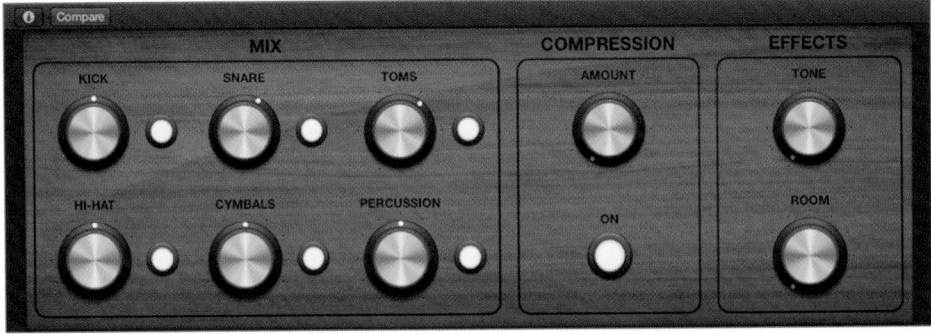

In the Mix section, six knobs allow you to balance the levels of the drum. To the right of each knob, a button lets you mute the corresponding drum or group of drums.

2 Position the playhead before the first chorus and start playback.

3 Turn the cymbals down a bit by dragging the Cymbals knob.

Even with the Amount knob turned all the way down in the Compression section, the compressor is still slightly processing the drum sound. Let's turn it off.

4 In the Compression section, click the On button.

On the left channel strip in the inspector, the Compressor plug-in is dimmed, indicating that it is turned off.

5 In the Effects section, drag the Tone knob up.

As you drag up the knob, the drums' sound changes timbre and becomes brighter. On the left channel strip in the inspector, the EQ curve on the channel strip's EQ display reflects the changes made to the Channel EQ plug-in.

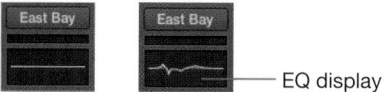

EQ display

MORE INFO ▶ You will further examine the Channel EQ plug-in in Lesson 9.

6 Drag up the Room knob.

As you drag up the knob, you will start hearing the subtle reverberation of a drum booth. In the inspector, you can see the Bus 1 Send knob move along with the Tone knob.

MORE INFO ▶ You will learn how to use bus sends to route an audio signal to a reverb and to change the character of the reverb in Lesson 9.

7 In the control bar, click the Editors button (or press E) to open the Drummer Editor.

TIP You can also double-click a Drummer region to open the Drummer Editor.

You have adjusted the levels and timbres of the drums, and you're now ready to fine-tune the sound of the individual drum kit pieces.

Customizing the Kit with Drum Kit Designer

Drum Kit Designer is the software instrument plug-in that plays drum samples triggered by Drummer. It allows you to customize the drum kit by choosing from a collection of drums and cymbals and tuning and dampening them.

1   At the bottom of the character card, click East Bay Kit to open the Drum Kit Designer.

TIP ▶ To have the Drummer regions play a different instrument, you can choose another patch from the Library or insert another software instrument plug-in on the channel strip. You can also drag Drummer regions to another software instrument track, and they are automatically converted to MIDI regions. (You will learn more about MIDI in Lesson 5.)

2   In Drum Kit Designer, click the snare.

You can hear the snare sample. The snare stays lit while the rest of the drum kit is in shadow. To the left, a Snares panel contains your choice of three snare drums, and to the right, an Edit panel includes three setting knobs.

The left panel shows only a limited selection of snares. To gain access to the entire collection of drum samples included with Logic Pro X, you need to choose a Producer Kit in the Library.

3   In the control bar, click the Library button (or press Y).

To the left of the inspector, the Library opens, listing patches for the selected track. The current patch, East Bay, is selected.

4 In the Library, select Producer Kits, and then select East Bay+.

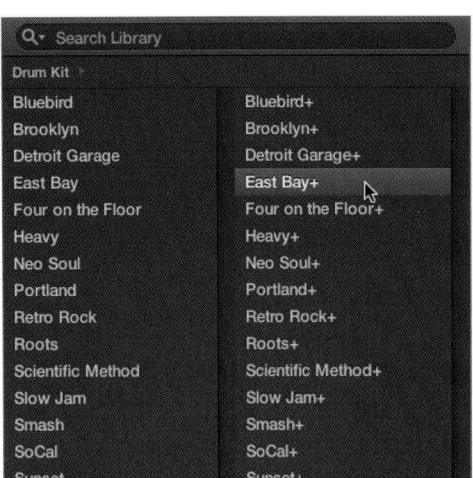

The Drum Kit Designer window is reset. The East Bay+ kit sounds the same as East Bay while allowing a wide array of options to customize the drum kit and its mix.

MORE INFO ▸ In the track header, you may have noticed that the drum icon is now framed in a darker rectangle with a disclosure triangle: The track is now a *Track Stack* that contains one track for each microphone used to record the drum kit. Clicking the disclosure triangle displays the individual tracks and their channel strips. You will use Track Stacks in Lesson 5.

5 Click the Library button (or press Y) to close the library.

6 In Drum Kit Designer, click the snare.

This time the left pane displays a choice of 15 snare drums (use your mouse to scroll down the list). The current snare, Black Brass, is selected.

7 Click another snare, and then click the Info button next to it.

A description of the selected snare opens.

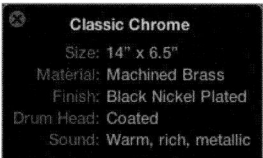

Continue previewing different snares and try listening to a verse or a chorus to hear your customized drum kit in action.

8   At the top of the left pane, click the Bell Brass snare.

9   In Drum Kit Designer, click the kick drum.

The info pop-up window updates to show you information on the selected kick drum.

Listen to the kick drum. This kick is the right choice for your song, but it has a long resonance. Typically, the faster the tempo of the song, the less resonance you want on the kick; otherwise low frequencies build up and could become a problem during the mix. You may have seen drummers stuff an old blanket in their kick drum to dampen them. In Drum Kit Designer, you only have to raise the dampening level.

10 In the right pane, drag the Dampen knob up to about 75%, and click the kick to listen to it.

The kick's resonance is shortened.

You will now tune the toms, which are mainly used in the bridge section.

11 In the workspace, select the first Bridge region.

12 In the Drummer Editor, click the Play button and mute the kick.

You can hear only the low and mid toms.

13 In Drum Kit Designer, click one of the toms.

The Edit panel opens with four tabs: All (for adjusting settings of all three toms in the kit together); and Low, Mid, and High (for adjusting settings of each individual tom).

14 Click the Mid tab and raise the Tune knob to around +156 cent.

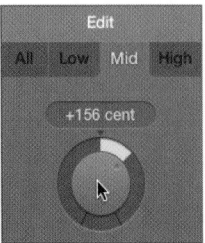

You can hear the mid tom being pitched up as Kyle continues repeating the first half of the bridge.

If you want, feel free to continue exploring Drum Kit Designer and adjusting the sound of the hi-hat, ride, and crash cymbals.

15 Stop playback and close the Drum Kit Designer window.

You have exchanged the snare for another one that sounds a little clearer, dampened the kick drum to tame its resonance, and tuned the mid tom to pitch it a bit higher. You have now fully customized both the drum performance and the drum kit.

Converting the Drummer Performance to MIDI

Now that you're happy with the bulk of the drummer's performance, you will go further and gain complete control over each individual drum hit by converting the Drummer regions to MIDI regions.

1   Click the background of the workspace and press Z to see all the regions.

TIP ▶ To select all regions on a track, make sure Cycle mode is off, and click the track header. If Cycle mode is on, only the regions within the cycle area are selected.

2   Make sure Cycle mode is off, and click the East Bay+ track header to select all the regions on the track.

3   Control-click a region, and from the shortcut menu, choose Convert > Convert to MIDI Region.

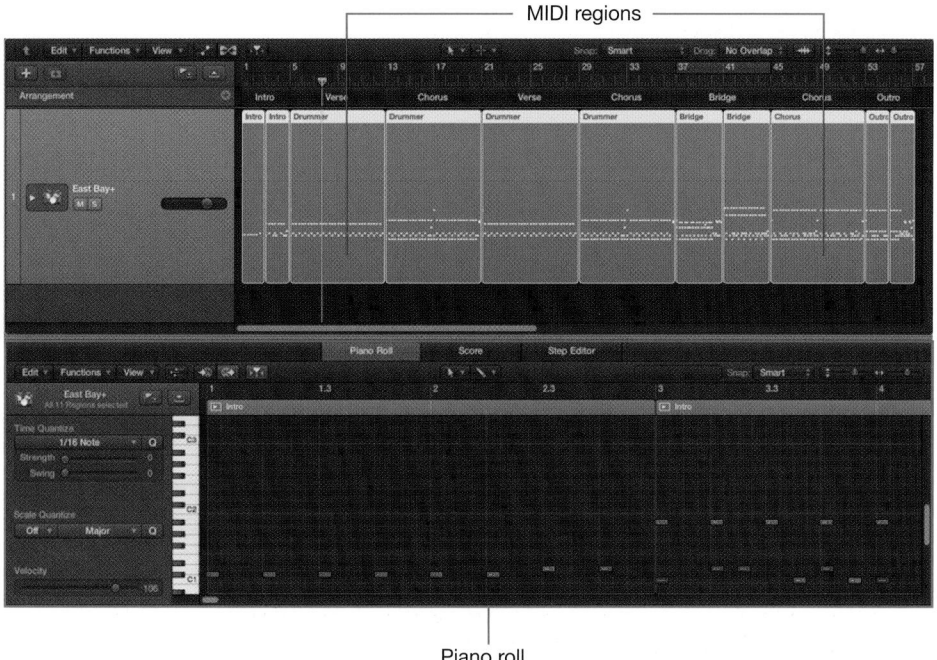

Piano roll

The Drummer regions are converted to MIDI regions. At the bottom of the main window, the Piano Roll opens, showing the contents of the selected regions, ready to be edited. Individual drum hit are represented by note beams on a grid, making it easy to select, move, or delete any of them.

You have produced drums for a whole song, and learned many ways to edit the drummer's performance and change his feel. You also customized the drum kit to get your desired sound. With Drummer and Drum Kit Designer, Logic Pro X allows you to quickly lay down a rhythmic foundation for any new song.

Lesson Review

1. How do you choose a drummer?
2. How do you choose a new drummer while keeping the current drum kit?
3. Where do you edit Drummer regions?
4. How do you mute or unmute drum parts?
5. How do you make the drummer play softer or louder, simpler or more complex?
6. How do you access the Feel knob to make the drummer play behind or ahead of the beat?
7. How do you open Smart Controls?
8. How do you open Drum Kit Designer?
9. When customizing a drum kit, how can you access all the available drum kit pieces?
10. How do you dampen or tune an individual drum?
11. How do you convert Drummer regions to MIDI regions?

Answers

1. Click the drummer in the character card, or from the Genre pop-up menu, choose a genre, and then click the desired drummer.
2. Option-click the desired drummer.
3. In the Drummer Editor at the bottom of the main window
4. Click the drum parts in the drum kit that is displayed in the Drummer Editor.
5. Move the puck on the XY pad.
6. Click the Details button at the bottom right of the Drummer Editor.
7. Click the Smart Controls button in the control bar, or press B.
8. Click the drum kit at the bottom of the character card.
9. Select the appropriate Producer Kit in the Library.
10. In Drum Kit Designer, click a drum and adjust the settings in the Edit panel.
11. Select the regions, Control-click one of them, and choose Convert > Convert to MIDI Region.

Keyboard Shortcuts

Main Window

B	Opens the Smart Controls
G	Opens the global tracks
Command-Shift-N	Opens a new file without opening the Templates dialog
Y	Opens the Library

5

Lesson Files	Logic Pro X Files > Lessons > 05 Dub Beat
Time	This lesson takes approximately 120 minutes to complete.
Goals	Record MIDI performances
	Quantize MIDI recordings
	Merge a MIDI recording with an existing MIDI region
	Record MIDI in take folders
	Punch record a MIDI recording
	Create Track Stacks
	Save layered synthesizer patches
	Map and assign Smart Controls
	Control Logic from the iPad using Logic Remote
	Use MIDI effects
	Record MIDI in step input mode

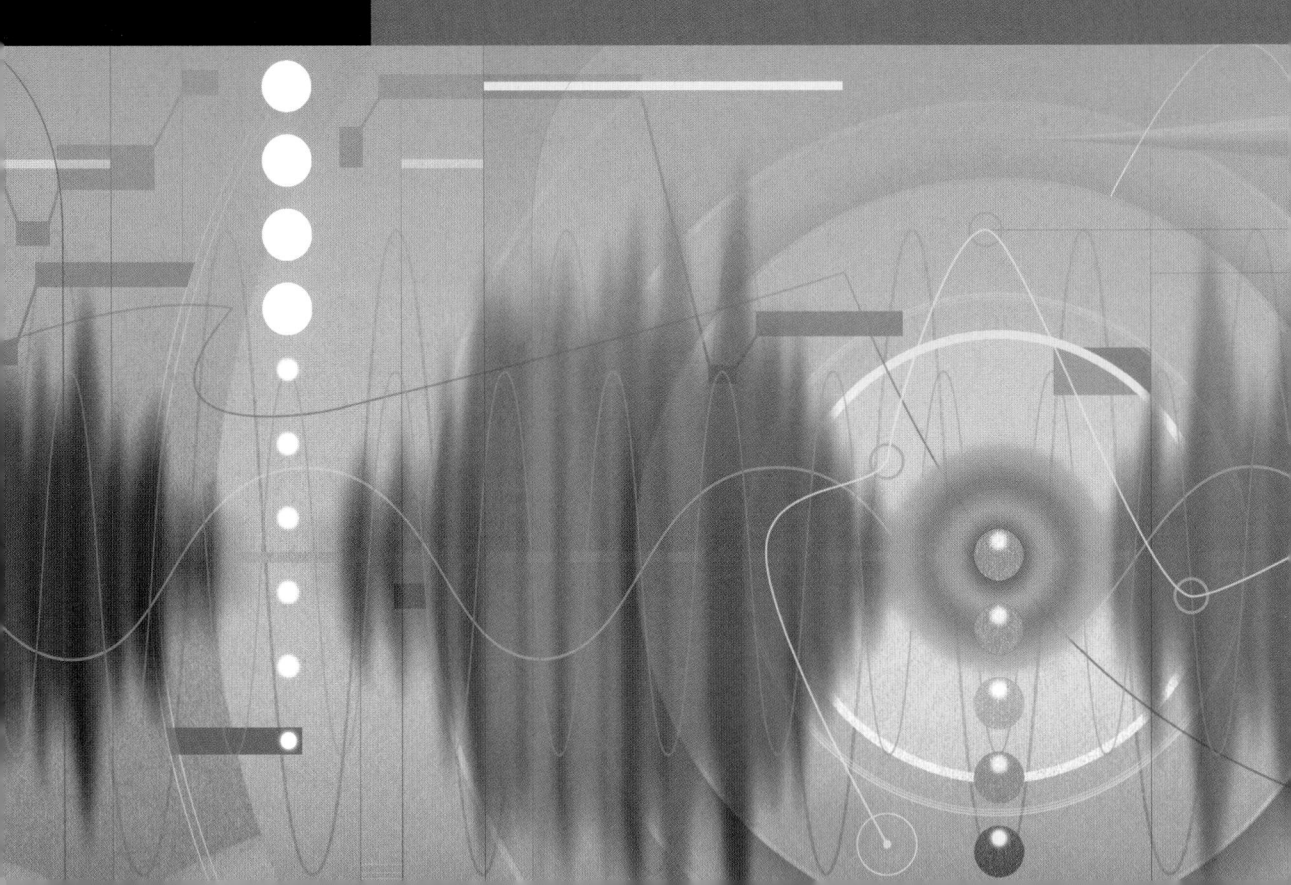

Recording MIDI and Using Controllers

MIDI (Musical Instrument Digital Interface) was created in 1983 to standardize the way electronic musical instruments communicate. Today, MIDI is extensively used throughout the music industry to record and program synthesizers and samplers. Many TV and film composers use MIDI to sequence large software sound libraries getting ever closer to realizing the sound of a real orchestra.

MIDI sequences can be compared to piano rolls, the perforated paper rolls once used by mechanical player pianos. Like the punched holes in piano rolls, MIDI events do not contain audio. They contain note information such as pitch and velocity. To turn MIDI data into sound, MIDI events are routed to a software instrument or to an external MIDI instrument.

There are two basic types of MIDI events: MIDI note events that trigger musical notes, and MIDI continuous controller (MIDI CC) events that control parameters such as volume, pan, or pitch bend.

For example, when you press C3 on a MIDI controller keyboard, the keyboard sends a note on MIDI event. The note on event contains the pitch of the note (C3) and the velocity of the note (which indicates how fast the key was struck, thereby showing how hard the musician pressed the key).

By connecting a MIDI controller keyboard to Logic, you can use Logic to route the MIDI events to a virtual software instrument or to an external MIDI instrument. The instrument reacts to the note on event by producing a C3 note, and the velocity typically determines how loud the note sounds.

When a MIDI controller keyboard is connected to your computer, and its driver is properly installed (some devices are class-compliant and don't require a driver installation), you can use that keyboard to record MIDI in Logic. Logic automatically routes all incoming MIDI events to the record-enabled software instrument or external MIDI track.

MORE INFO ▶ To learn more about the MIDI specification, visit the MIDI Manufacturers Association website at www.midi.org.

TIP ▶ If you don't have a MIDI controller keyboard, choose Window > Show Musical Typing (or press Command-K) to turn your Mac keyboard into a polyphonic MIDI controller. Pressing the Z and X keys allows you to choose the octave range, while pressing C and V lets you adjust the note velocities. Keep in mind that you may need to close the Musical Typing window (or press Command-K) to access some of the Logic key commands.

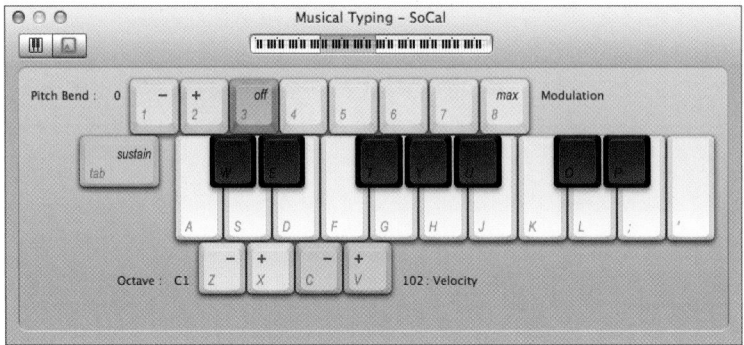

Using a Patch from the Library

When working with software instruments in Logic, the MIDI events can be recorded, created, and edited inside MIDI regions placed on the track. The MIDI events generated by playing your MIDI keyboard are routed to the record-enabled track in the Tracks area. From the track, those real-time events from your keyboard, or the events played back from MIDI regions on the tracks, are routed to the top of the channel strip. They can be preprocessed by MIDI effect plug-ins before the MIDI data is passed to the instrument plug-in. The instrument produces an audio signal that can be further processed using audio effect plug-ins. The audio can then be adjusted with the Volume fader and Pan knob before being routed to the output destination.

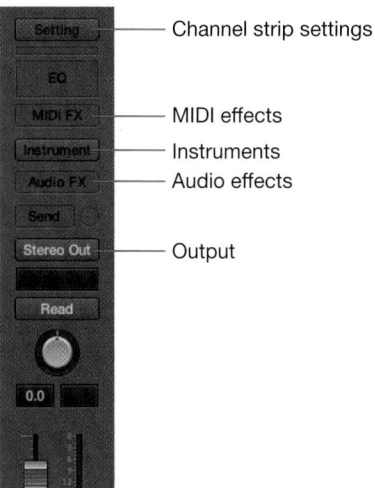

The Setting button at the top of a channel strip allows you to load or save channel strip settings, which contain all the plug-ins inserted on a channel strip and their individual settings.

The Library lets you load or save patches, channel strip settings, or plug-in settings. A patch can be a single channel strip setting, or multiple channel strips and their channel strip settings.

> **TIP** ▸ To see a plug-in's settings in the Library, click to the left of the plug-in on the channel strip in the Inspector. A blue triangle and a white frame indicate which plug-in's settings the Library is currently displaying.

In this exercise, you will create a software instrument track, choose a patch from the Library, and examine the channel strips created in the Mixer.

1   Choose File > New (or press Command-Shift-N).

If a project was already open, an alert asks if you want to close the current project. Click Close (a Save dialog then prompts you to save it).

TIP ▶ When Open Library is selected in the New Tracks dialog, a default electric piano patch is loaded. To load an empty software instrument channel strip, deselect Open Library.

2   In the New Tracks dialog, click Software Instrument, and deselect Open Library. Click Create.

An empty new software instrument track is created.

3   In the control bar, click the Mixer button (or press X).

The Mixer opens and shows three channel strips that are, from left to right:

▶ The software instrument channel strip you just created

▶ The Output channel strip

▶ The Master channel strip

You will now load a patch for the selected software instrument track while watching what happens in the Mixer.

4 In the control bar, click the Library button (or press Y).

The Library opens to the left of the inspector.

5 In the Library, choose Piano > Steinway Grand Piano.

TIP ▶ In the Library, you can press the Up or Down Arrow keys to select categories or patches in a list, and press the Left and Right Arrow keys to navigate to the left or right columns.

6 Play a few keys on your MIDI keyboard to hear the piano sound.

7 In the Mixer, look at the channel strips.

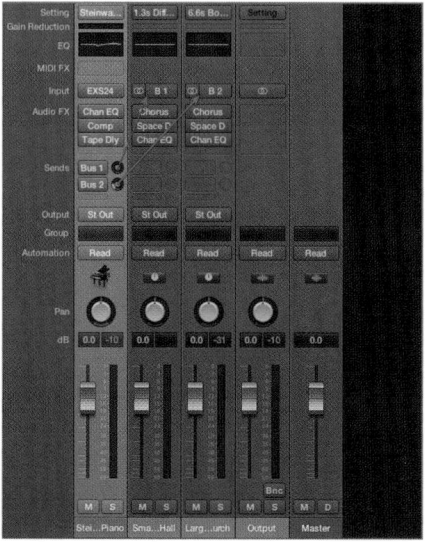

On the software instrument channel strip (Steinway Grand Piano), a channel strip setting is loaded, containing an EXS24 (the Logic sampler) instrument plug-in, and three audio effect plug-ins: a Channel EQ, a Compressor, and a Tape Delay.

Two new auxiliary channel strips are also created (Small Hall/1.3s Diffuse Hall, and Large Hall/6.6s Botta Church), each one with its own channel strip setting. The software instrument channel strip has two bus sends that route the audio signal to the inputs of the two auxiliaries, set to bus 1 (B 1) and bus 2 (B 2). Together, the software instrument channel strip setting, along with the two auxiliaries and their channel strip settings, make up the Steinway Grand Piano patch.

In a mixer, a bus transports the audio signal from one channel strip to another. Here, Bus 1 and Bus 2 route the stereo audio signal of the piano to two different reverberation effects on the two auxiliaries.

NOTE ▶ In Logic, a single bus can transport a mono, stereo, or surround audio signal.

8 On the Steinway Piano channel strip, next to the Bus 1 send, drag the bus Send Level knob all the way up.

Play the piano with your MIDI keyboard. You can hear the reverberation sound of a smaller room.

9 Next to the Bus 1 send, lower the Send Level knob all the way down.

The piano now has a small amount of reverb that comes from the Bus 2 send.

10 Next to the Bus 2 send, lower the send level all the way down.

The piano now sounds completely dry with no reverberation.

11 Next to the Bus 2 send, raise the send level all the way up.

You can hear the reverb of the second auxiliary, which sounds like a much bigger room. Notice how this reverb sustains for a longer time than the first one.

12 Continue adjusting the bus send levels to compare the sound of the two reverbs, and
then set them to a level that sounds good to you.

> **TIP ▶** To load a patch without its bus sends and auxiliary channel strips, start with
> an empty software instrument channel strip. At the lower left of the Library, from the
> Action menu, choose Enable Patch Merging. Then deselect the Sends button.

13 Close the Mixer.

Now that you know how to choose a patch from the library, and how to adjust the amount of
reverb using the bus Send Level knobs, you will explore several MIDI recording techniques.
You will save your own custom patches later in this lesson.

Recording MIDI

In Logic, the basic techniques used to record MIDI are similar to the techniques you used
to record audio in Lesson 2. You will now observe the MIDI In display in the control bar
as you send MIDI events to Logic, and record a simple piano part.

1 Play a few notes on your MIDI keyboard while observing the LCD display.

MIDI input activity

A small dot appears at the upper right of the LCD display to indicate that Logic is
receiving MIDI events.

NOTE ▶ When Logic sends MIDI events to external MIDI devices, a small dot
appears at the lower right of the LCD display.

These small dots can be useful to quickly troubleshoot MIDI connections. Logic can,
however, provide a more detailed view of the incoming MIDI events.

2 Click the note and metronome icons to the left of the LCD display, and choose Custom.

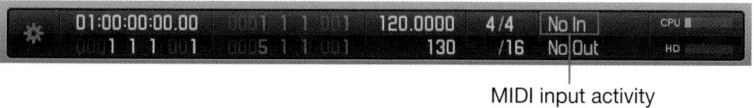

MIDI input activity

The Custom LCD display appears. It includes a MIDI input activity monitor that shows incoming MIDI events in more detail.

3 Hold down a key on your MIDI keyboard.

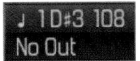

A note icon indicates that the event received is a MIDI note on event. You can also see the MIDI channel number of the MIDI event, the note's pitch, and its velocity. In the previous image, the event's MIDI channel is 1, its pitch is D#3, and its velocity is 108.

NOTE ► MIDI events can be sent on up to 16 different MIDI channels, which allows you to control different timbres on different channels when using multi-timbral instruments.

4 Release the key on your MIDI keyboard.

Depending on your controller, in the LCD display, you may see a note on event with a velocity of zero, or you may see a note with a strike through it, which represents a note off event.

NOTE ► Pressing and releasing a key on a MIDI keyboard sends two events: a note on and a note off event. However, most MIDI editors represent the two events as a single note event with a length attribute.

5 Play a chord on your MIDI keyboard.

The MIDI input activity monitor displays the chord name.

You could start recording a piano part now, but first you'll open the Piano Roll so you can watch the MIDI notes appear on the grid as they are recorded.

6 In the control bar, click the Editors button, and at the top of the Editors pane, ensure that Piano Roll is selected (or press P).

The Piano Roll opens at the bottom of the main window.

7 Make sure the playhead is at the beginning of the project, and click the Record button (or press R).

The LCD display and the playhead turn red to indicate that Logic is recording. The playhead jumps back one bar, giving you a four-beat count-in, and you can hear the metronome.

8   When the playhead appears, play quarter notes for a couple of bars to record a very simple bass line.

When you play the first note, a red MIDI region, temporarily named *recording*, appears on the record-enabled track. The region's length constantly updates to include the most recent MIDI event received.

The MIDI notes appear in the Piano Roll and on the region in the workspace as you record them.

NOTE ▶ If the pitch of the notes you record is outside the range of pitches displayed in the Piano Roll, you will not see the notes as they are recorded.

9   Stop recording.

The region is renamed *Steinway Grand Piano* and is now shaded green. You can see the recorded notes in the Piano Roll.

TIP ▶ To see all the notes in the Piano Roll, make sure that all the notes are deselected, and press Z.

10 In the Piano Roll, click the Play button at the top left of the region.

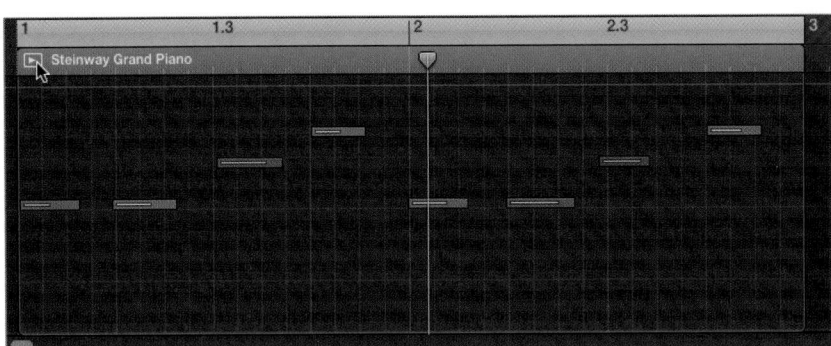

The region starts playback in Cycle mode. If you are not happy with your performance, you can undo it (Command-Z) and try again.

If you are mostly happy, but one or two notes need correction, you can quickly fix them in the Piano Roll:

▶ Drag a note vertically to change its pitch.

▶ Drag a note horizontally to change its timing.

▶ Click a note, and press Delete to remove it.

You will learn how to edit MIDI events in more detail in Lesson 6.

11 Click the region's Play button again (or press the Spacebar) to stop playback.

Correcting the Timing of a MIDI Recording

If you are not happy with the timing of your MIDI performance, you can correct the timing of the notes using a time-correction method called *quantization*. To quantize a MIDI region, you choose a note value from the Quantize menu in the Region inspector, and inside the region, the notes snap to the nearest absolute value.

Quantizing MIDI Regions

In this exercise, you will quantize the piano passage you recorded in the previous exercise, so that the notes are in sync with the metronome.

> **NOTE** ▶ If you were quite happy with the timing of your performance, you may want to undo your previous recording and record again with a less accurate timing so that you can more clearly hear the benefits of quantization.

1   In the workspace, make sure the piano region is still selected.

2   In the Region inspector, click the Quantize value (currently set to off) and choose 1/4 Note while looking at the notes in the Piano Roll.

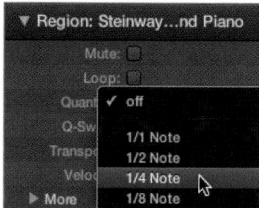

All the MIDI notes in the piano region snap to the nearest quarter note.

3   In the control bar, click the Metronome button (or press K) to turn it on.

4   Play the piano region. The notes are now perfectly in sync with the metronome.

In Logic, quantizing is a nondestructive operation. You can always revert the notes to their original position.

5   In the Region inspector, set Quantize to off.

In the Piano Roll, the notes return to their original recording positions.

6   In the Region inspector, set Quantize back to 1/4 Note.

The notes are once more in sync with the metronome.

7   Turn off the metronome, and stop playback.

Choosing Default Quantization Settings

You can choose a default quantization setting, so that any new recording will automatically be quantized to that value. This is very useful when you are not completely confident of your timing chops. Because the Quantize setting is nondestructive, you can always adjust it or turn it off for that region after you're finished recording.

1   In the workspace, click the background.

All regions are deselected, and the Region inspector now displays the MIDI Thru parameters. The MIDI Thru settings will be automatically applied to any new MIDI region you record.

2   In the MIDI Thru parameters, set Quantize to 1/8 Note.

3   In the workspace, click the piano region, and press Delete to delete the region.

4   Move the playhead to the beginning of the project, and click the Record button (or press R).

    Record another simple bass line as you did in the previous exercise. Feel free to play eighth notes this time since that's the Quantize value you selected.

5   Stop recording.

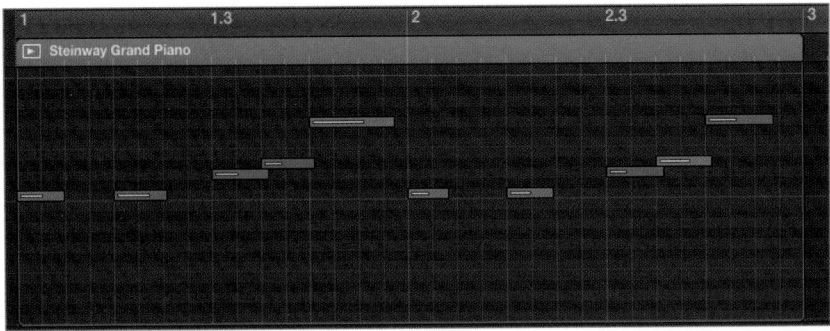

    In the Piano Roll, the notes immediately snap to the nearest eighth note on the grid. In the Region inspector, the Quantize parameter for the new piano region is set to 1/8 Note. Remember that the Quantize setting is nondestructive, which means that you can still turn it off.

6   In the Region inspector, set Quantize to off. In the Piano Roll, the notes move to their original recorded positions.

7   Set Quantize back to 1/8 Note.

Joining Recordings into a MIDI Region

Sometimes you may want to record a MIDI performance in several passes. For example, when recording piano, you want to record just the left hand, and then record the right hand in a second pass. Or you could record drums in multiple passes, recording the kick drum first, then the snare drum, then the hi-hat, then the crash cymbal, building up a drum beat by focusing on a single piece of the drum kit at a time.

In Logic, when recording MIDI events on top of an existing MIDI region, you can choose to join the new recording with the existing MIDI region.

Recording into a Selected MIDI Region

In the previous exercise, you recorded a simple bass line onto a piano track. Now you will record chords as you listen to your bass line, merging the new chords with that bass line inside the same MIDI region. First, you will choose the correct recording setting to merge your new recording with the selected region.

1   Choose File > Project Settings > Recording.

2   Under MIDI, set Overlapping Recordings to "Join with Selected Regions."

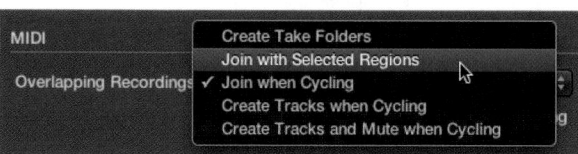

Now you just have to select the existing MIDI region before recording, and the new recording will be joined with the existing region when you stop recording.

3   Close the Project Settings window.

4   Make sure the piano region you recorded in the previous exercise is still selected.

5   Move the playhead to the beginning and start recording.

This time, play only a couple of chords that complement the bass line you previously recorded.

When you play your first note(s), the contents of the existing MIDI region disappear while the Piano Roll displays the contents of the new recording. You can, however, still hear the existing notes while you record the new ones. The new recording is merged with the existing region as soon as you stop recording.

6   Stop recording.

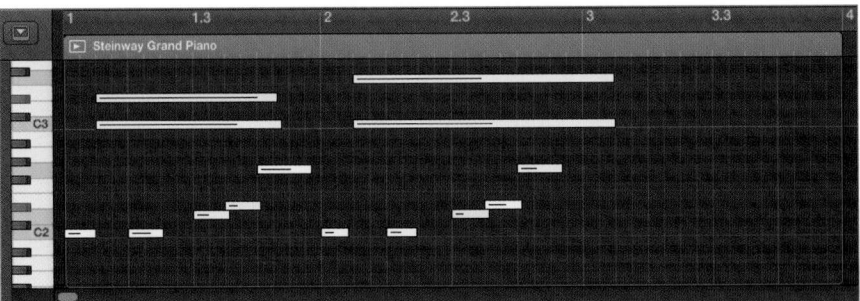

The new notes immediately snap to the nearest eighth note on the grid. The new recording is joined with the existing region, and you can see all the notes in the Piano Roll editor. (You may need to zoom or scroll.) On the track, a single MIDI region contains all the notes recorded in this exercise and the previous one.

TIP You can also use this technique to add MIDI controller events such as pitch bend or modulation to a region after you have recorded the MIDI notes.

Joining Recordings in Cycle Mode

Recording MIDI in Cycle mode allows you to continuously repeat the same section and record new events only when you are ready. This can be very useful when recording a drum pattern. You can loop over a section, building up the drum groove by adding new elements during each pass of the cycle while listening to the drums you have already recorded.

When recording MIDI in Cycle mode, notes recorded in all consecutive passes of the cycle are joined into a single MIDI region. In this exercise, you will record drums in Cycle mode, first recording the kick, then the snare, and finally the hi-hat.

First, let's close the current project and create a new one.

1   Choose File > Close Project (or press Command-Option-W), and when prompted, close but don't save the existing project.

> **TIP** ▶ When only one window is open in Logic, you can close the project by choosing File > Close (or pressing Command-W).

2   Choose File > New. In the New Tracks dialog, select Software Instrument and click Create.

In a new project, "Join when Cycling" is selected by default in the Overlapping Recordings pop-up menu (File > Project Settings > Recording). Recording in Cycle mode will place all recorded notes in the same region, which is the desired behavior for this exercise.

3   In the control bar, click the Library button (or press Y).

4   In the Library, select Drum Kit > Brooklyn.

The Brooklyn patch is loaded, including a channel strip setting that is loaded for the software instrument channel strip in the inspector. It comprises the Drum Kit Designer instrument plug-in, and the Channel EQ, Compressor, and Multipressor audio effect plug-ins. The channel strip sends to bus 1, and if you open the Mixer, you can see a new auxiliary—and its plug-ins—with its input set to bus 1.

Let's customize the LCD display so that you can see the detailed MIDI input activity monitor.

5   To the left of the LCD display, click the note and metronome icons, and choose Custom.

Before you start recording, you need to locate the keys that trigger the kick, snare, and hi-hat on your MIDI controller. You will use:

▶ C1: kick

▶ D1: snare

▶ F#1: closed hi-hat

▶ A#1: open hi-hat

6   Play the lowest C key on your MIDI keyboard while watching the MIDI activity in the LCD display.

If the display doesn't show a C1, you can use the Octave –/+ buttons on your keyboard to offset the pitch range. Once you've found C1, locate D1 (the next white key to the right), F#1, and A#1 (respectively the first and the last keys of the next group of three black keys to the right).

7   In the upper half of the ruler, click the cycle area to turn on Cycle mode.

Since you don't have a region in the workspace, the Region inspector displays the MIDI Thru settings.

8   In the Region inspector, set Quantize to 1/16 Note.

You will now record the drums one at a time. Let's open the Piano Roll to see the notes appear on the grid as you record them.

9   In the control bar, click the Editors button (or press P) to open the Piano Roll.

10   Start recording. You hear a four-beat count-in before the playhead reaches the beginning of the cycle area.

11   Play C1 notes on the first and third beat of every bar.

When the playhead reaches the end of the cycle, it jumps back and starts a new pass. You can hear the kick drum notes you just recorded. Notice that the notes snap to the nearest sixteenth note because you chose that value as your MIDI Thru Quantize setting.

You have all the time in the world before you continue to record. As long as you don't play anything, Logic continues cycling over the existing region, playing back your kick drums. And if you forgot to play one or two kick drum notes, you can record them during one of the subsequent cycle passes.

12 Play D1 notes on the second and fourth beat of every bar. The kick and the snare should alternate on every beat.

As you record new notes in a new cycle pass, the previously recorded notes temporarily disappear. When the playhead starts a new pass, you can see all the notes you've recorded.

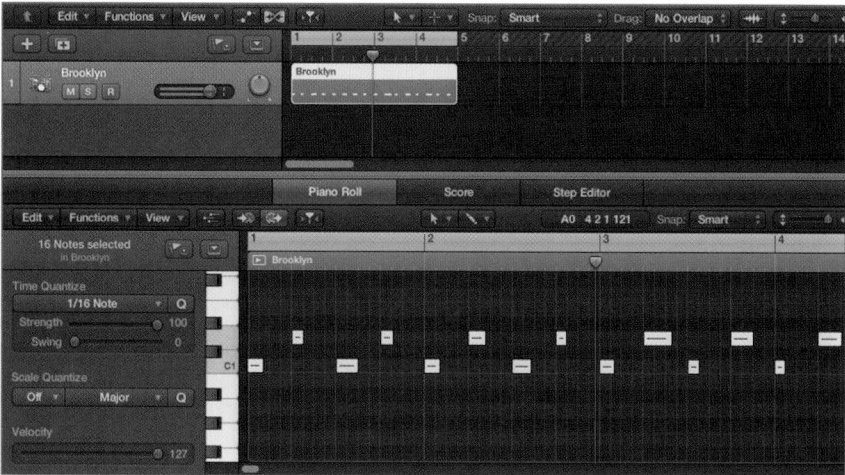

13 Play hi-hats on every eighth note using the F#1 (close hi-hat) and A#1 (open hi-hat) keys, playing the open hi-hat only as the last eighth note of some of the bars.

14 Stop recording, and click the background of the Piano Roll to deselect the notes.

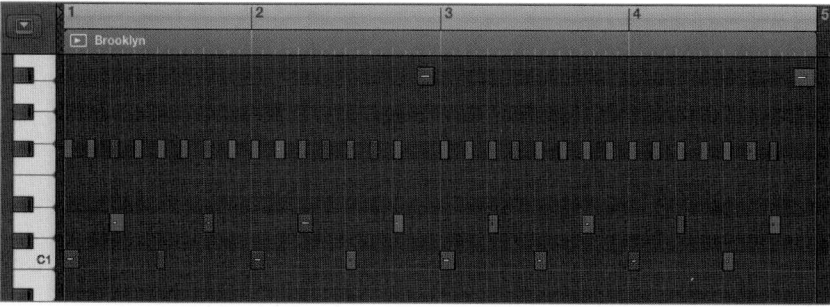

You can see your drum pattern. Now that the notes are not selected, you can see their colors, which vary depending on the note's velocity.

Joining MIDI recordings as you did in the two previous exercises provides a lot of flexibility and allows you to take your time, recording a single part of a performance at a time. These techniques will help in many situations. For example, consider first recording the notes of a cello melody, then later recording the movements of the pitch bend wheel to add cello-like vibrato toward the end of sustained notes.

Recording MIDI Takes

When you want to nail a performance or experiment with several musical ideas, you can record multiple takes and later choose the best one. The techniques for recording MIDI takes are similar to the techniques you used to record audio takes in Lesson 2. You can record new takes over an existing region or take folder, or you can record multiple takes in Cycle mode.

Cycle mode should still be turned on from the previous exercise. Let's record takes in Cycle mode and experiment with using different melodies for a bass line.

1   Choose File > Project Settings > Recording.

2   Under MIDI, from Overlapping Recordings, choose Create Take Folders.

3   Close the Project Settings window.

4   Choose Track > New Software Instrument Track (or press Command-Option-S).

5   Open the Library, and choose Bass > Stinger Bass.

6   Start playback and play a few notes on your MIDI keyboard.

You can hear your bass, and you can practice until you find an idea for a simple bass line that will work with the drums you recorded on track 1.

▶ **About Live Mode**

Selecting a software instrument track automatically record-enables it, but the instrument is not always in Live mode (for example when selecting a software instrument track during playback). An instrument in Live mode requires more CPU resources. When an instrument is not in Live mode, the first note you play will take about 100 ms (milliseconds) to trigger the instrument, which is then placed in Live mode.

You can put an instrument in Live mode by sending any MIDI event to it (playing a dummy note, moving the modulation wheel, and so on), by clicking the R button in the track header to make it solid red, or by starting playback.

Record-enabled instrument not in Live mode   Record-enabled instrument in Live mode

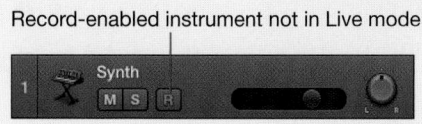 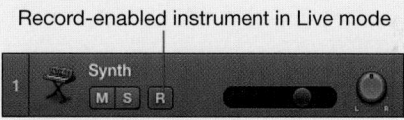

7 While playback continues, click the Record button (or press R). Logic continues repeating the cycle area, so you don't lose your groove.

8 When the playhead starts a new pass of the cycle, play a bass melody on the MIDI keyboard.

When you're done recording the four-bar bass melody, the playhead jumps back to the beginning of the cycle and you cannot hear the take you just recorded. You can continue recording new takes while staying in Cycle mode, or stop recording and start recording again to record new takes.

9 Record two more takes of the bass.

10 Start playback. You can hear the last take of the bass.

11 In the workspace, from the take folder pop-up menu, choose take 2.

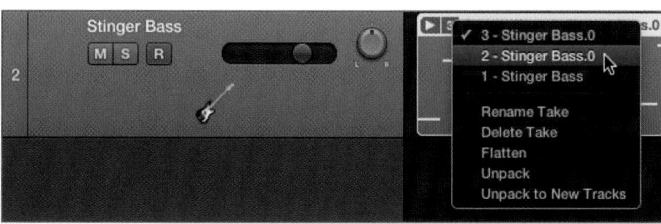

You can hear take 2.

NOTE ▶ Note that there's no Quick Swipe Comping button next to the take folder pop-up menu. Unlike audio take folders, you cannot comp sections of takes in a MIDI take folder.

12 Double-click the take folder to open it and click the first take, at the bottom of the list, to play it.

13 Choose your favorite take, and from the take folder pop-up menu, choose Flatten.

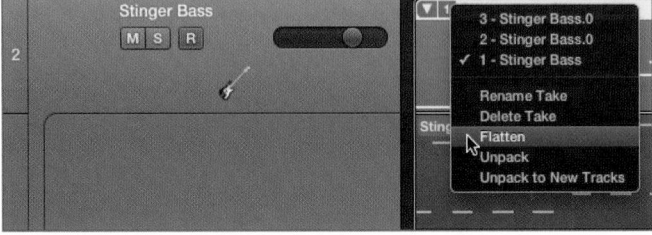

The take folder is flattened and only the selected bass take remains in a MIDI region. You will punch in on that bass MIDI region in the next exercise.

14 Stop playback.

TIP ▶ If you want to keep a performance you played while Logic was in playback mode, click Stop and press Shift-R (Capture as Recording). A MIDI region containing your last performance is created on the track.

Punching In and Out

You can use the punch on the fly and autopunch techniques you learned for audio recording to punch on MIDI recordings. The only difference is that you'll have to enable Replace mode.

In the next exercise, you will use the Replace and Autopunch modes to re-record a section of the bass line you recorded in the previous exercise.

1   Command-click the lower half of the ruler (or press Command-Control-Option-P) to turn on Autopunch mode.

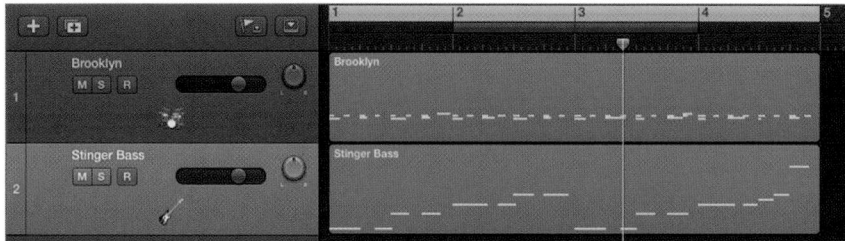

The autopunch area appears in the middle of the ruler.

2   Drag the edges of the autopunch area and adjust it so that it encompasses the section you want to replace.

When recording MIDI in Autopunch mode, Logic records only within the autopunch area. However it does not delete existing notes in that area unless you have enabled Replace mode.

3   In the control bar, click the Replace button.

Replace mode is turned on, and the existing notes within the autopunch section will be deleted when you record.

4   Choose File > Project Settings > Recording.

You will try to punch in with two different recording settings to observe their different behaviors.

5   Under MIDI, set Overlapping Recordings to "Join when Cycling" (the default setting), and close the Project Settings window.

6   Go to the beginning and start recording.

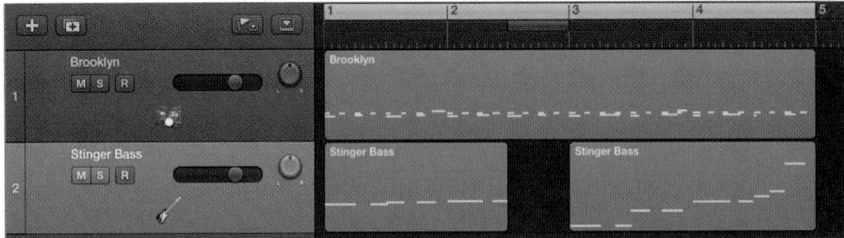

The playhead jumps ahead one bar so you can hear the count-in, and the section of the bass region in the autopunch area is deleted.

You can start playing the bass line from the beginning, but only the notes within the autopunch area will be recorded. This gives you a chance to get into the groove before re-recording the notes that need to be replaced.

NOTE ▶ To successfully punch in and out of MIDI regions, make sure you hit the first note after the punch-in point or it will not be recorded. And make sure you release the last note before the punch-out point or the MIDI note off event will not be recorded, and the last note will sustain until the end of the new region.

When you play notes within the autopunch area, a new region is created that starts at the beginning of the bar. You now have three MIDI regions on the track, and some of them may overlap. Let's join the three regions into a single region to clean this up.

7   In the workspace, drag a rectangle around the three bass regions to select them.

8   Choose Edit > Join > Regions (or press Command-J).

Using the region joining techniques you learned at the beginning of this lesson, you will now "punch and join" in one operation.

9   Choose File > Project Settings > Recording. Set Overlapping Recordings to "Join with Selected Regions," and close the Project Settings window.

10   Go to the beginning, make sure the Stinger Bass region is still selected, and start recording.

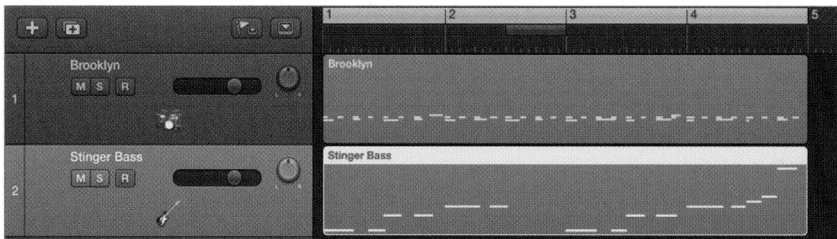

This time the region stays intact. Inside the bass region, the notes within the auto-punch area are deleted. Play the bass line so that new notes are recorded in the auto-punch area. The notes will become visible on the region only after you stop recording.

11   Stop recording.

The notes you recorded in the autopunch area appear in the region.

12 Command-click the lower half of the ruler (or press Command-Control-Option-P) to turn off Autopunch mode.

13 In the control bar, click the Replace button to turn off Replace mode.

Creating a Layered Sound Patch

Well before recording was invented, composers used sound layering to thicken sounds. In a classical orchestra, you often hear multiple musicians playing the same part at the same time. When all the violins play a melody together, you hear a rich warm tone and the emotional level is raised.

Sound layering is a common technique used by music producers to make just about any instrument sound thicker, or to mix the timbres of different sounds. For example, many vocals on commercial songs are doubled (the singer records two identical performances that are played simultaneously), and dance music producers often layer multiple kick drum samples, such as combining a kick drum with a strong percussive attack and another that has a boomy sustain.

In Logic, Track Stacks allow you to combine a group of tracks and control them as a single track. Track Stacks can be used to organize tracks you want to group together (such as drum tracks or backup vocal tracks). They can also be used to group software instrument tracks, so that the MIDI notes on a single track can trigger all the instruments in the Track Stack.

In this exercise, you will create a Track Stack for two different synthesizer patches, and save the Track Stack as a new patch.

1 Choose File > New (or press Command-Shift-N), and when prompted, close but don't save the existing project.

2 In the New Tracks dialog, select Software Instrument, and set "Number of tracks" to 2.

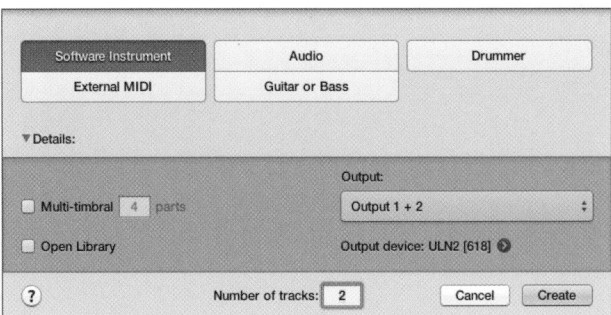

Two empty software instrument tracks are created.

3   Click the Library button (or press Y) to open the Library.

4   In the Tracks area, select the first track, and in the Library, choose Synthesizer >
     Lead > Nightlife Lead.

5   Play your MIDI keyboard.

     The synth sounds modern; it is quite edgy and buzzy. Try playing a bass line in the
     C1–C2 range. This modern bass has a lot of character, but it lacks the body and thick-
     ness of an older analog synth.

6   In the Tracks area, select track 2, and in the Library, choose Synthesizer > Lead > 70s
     Analog Lead.

     That synth is more rounded and warm. Plus, it has more low frequencies, which will bring
     body to the layered sound. Let's select both tracks and create a Track Stack for them.

     TIP ▶ To hear both sounds layered before you create the Track Stack, record-enable
     both track headers and play your MIDI keyboard.

7   Shift-click the unselected track header to select both track headers.

8   Choose Track > Create Track Stack (or press Command-Shift-D).

     A dialog lets you choose between a folder stack or a summing stack. To group soft-
     ware instruments and work with the MIDI data on the main track of a Track Stack,
     you need to use a summing stack.

9   Select Summing Stack, and click Create.

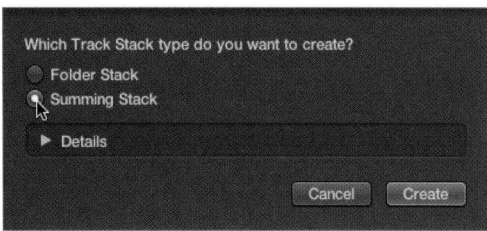

In the Tracks area, the main track of the new summing stack appears at the top, while the two original software instrument tracks become subtracks of the Track Stack.

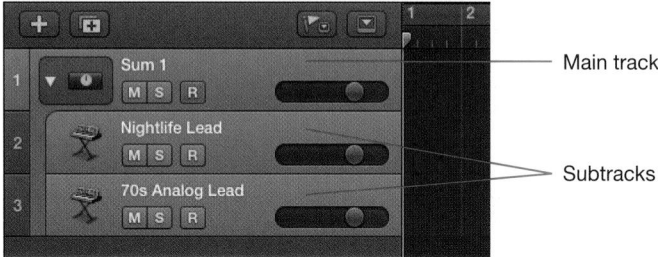

10 Make sure the main track of the Track Stack is record-enabled, and play your MIDI keyboard.

You can now hear the layered sound combining both the Nightlife Lead and the 70s Analog Lead patches.

11 Try muting either subtrack inside the Track Stack.

Muting a subtrack allows you to determine exactly what that subtrack adds to the layered sound. When you mute Nightlife Lead, the sound loses its edge and buzzy quality. When you mute 70s Analog Lead, the sound loses body and warmth.

12 Unmute both subtracks.

Let's give the main track an icon that will be saved along with the patch.

13 On the main track, Control-click the icon, and choose a keyboard icon.

14 In the Library, click Save.

15 In the Save dialog, type a filename for the patch, and save it to the default location.

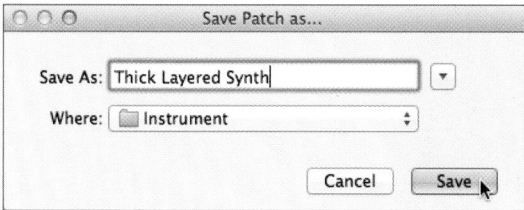

In the Library, a new User Patches category is created in the left column and your new patch is selected inside it.

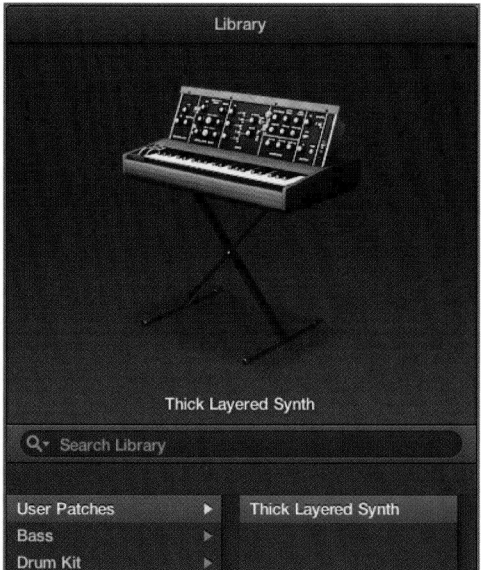

In the workspace, the main track in the Track Stack is renamed after the patch you saved. The main track and the subtracks have a green background to indicate that they all belong to a summing stack.

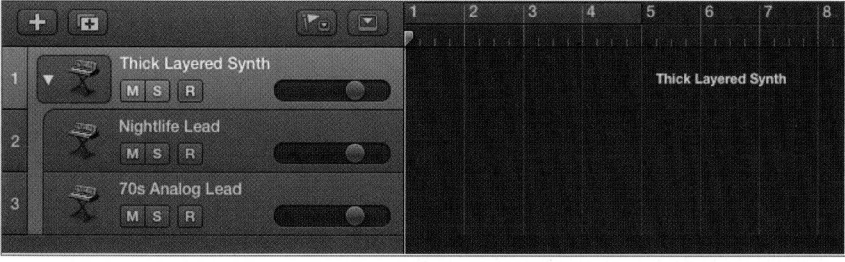

16 On the Track Stack's main track header, click the disclosure triangle next to the icon.

The Track Stack is now closed and appears as a single track. It retains all functionality, and as long as the Track Stack is record-enabled, you can continue playing or recording the layered patch from your MIDI keyboard.

Now that you saved your own custom patch in the library, it will be available in any project you open in Logic when a track of the same type (a software instrument track) is selected. Choosing the Thick Layered Synth patch from the Library will replace the selected software instrument track by the Summing stack and its two subtracks.

Creating a Split Keyboard Patch

In this exercise, you will combine two existing patches into a new patch, but specify a range of notes on the keyboard for each of the two patches. This allows you to effectively split your MIDI keyboard into two or more note ranges, each with a different sound.

You will create a patch that plays a bass sound below the C3 key, and a piano sound above it. First, you can delete the Track Stack you created in the previous exercise as you will no longer need it.

1 Drag the Thick Layered Synth track header toward the left, outside the Tracks area.

When the Pointer tool goes outside the Tracks area, it turns into an Eraser tool, and when you release the mouse button the Track Stack is deleted in a puff of smoke. Because your Tracks area no longer has any tracks, the New Tracks dialog opens.

2 In the New Tracks dialog, make sure Software Instrument is selected and set "Number of tracks" to 2.

Two empty software instrument tracks are created.

3 Select the first track, and in the Library, choose Bass > Upright Studio Bass.

4 Play your MIDI keyboard to hear the sound of an upright bass.

5 Select the second track, and in the Library, choose Vintage Electric Piano > Bright Mk II Blackface.

6 Play your MIDI keyboard to hear the sound of an electric piano with a rhythmic automatic panning effect.

7 In the Tracks area, Shift-click the unselected track to select both tracks.

8 Choose Track > Create Track Stack (or press Command-Shift-D), and create a summing stack.

9 Play your MIDI keyboard.

   You now hear the upright bass and the electric piano sounds layered, as in the previous exercise. You will now limit the pitch ranges each instrument will respond to.

10 Select the Upright Studio Bass subtrack.

11 Below the Region inspector, click the disclosure triangle to open the Track inspector.

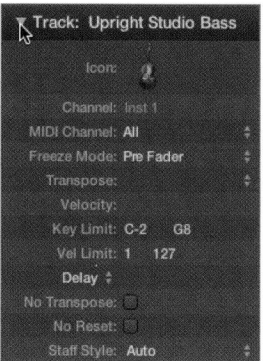

The Track inspector displays the track parameters. The Key Limit parameter values, C-2 and G8, define the key range that this track responds to. Let's limit its key range to notes below C3 so that the new range spans C-2 to B2.

12 Drag G8 down until its value is B2.

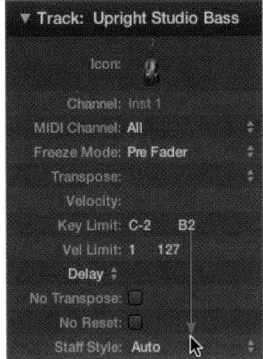

13 Try playing notes over the entire range of the keyboard.

The lower keys up to B2 play the upright bass sound, while the higher keys from C3 don't play any sound.

14 In the Tracks area, select the Bright Mk II Blackface subtrack.

15 In the Track inspector, drag the lower key limit (C-2) up to C3.

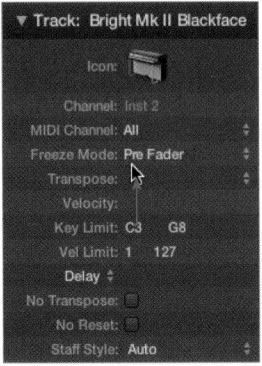

16 In the Tracks area, click the main track of the Track Stack, and play your MIDI keyboard.

All the keys below C3 play the upright bass whereas the keys from C3 and up play the electric piano. Try playing a bass melody with your left hand while sustaining some chords with your right hand.

17 In the Library, click Save, name the patch *Split Bass and E-Piano*, and save it.

Mapping Smart Controls to Patch Parameters

In Lesson 4, you used Smart Controls. You were able to use the Smart Controls as a one-stop shop for adjusting multiple parameters such as a bus send level, parameters of the instrument plug-in, and parameters of the channel EQ plug-in.

This time you will use Smart Controls to adjust parameters of the individual software instrument channel strips on the subtracks of the layered synth patch you previously created in this lesson. You will map the screen controls to plug-in parameters, and assign them knobs on your MIDI controller. Finally, you'll save your Smart Control layout within the patch.

Opening the Plug-Ins for Mapping

In this exercise, you will access the subtracks within the Thick Layered Sound Track Stack to open some of their plug-ins. You will later map one parameter of each plug-in to a screen control in the Smart Controls pane.

1   Ensure that the main track of the Track Stack is still selected, and in the Library, choose User Patches > Thick Layered Synth.

   You will first open the plug-in windows that have parameters you want to map to screen controls.

2   In the Tracks area, select the Nightlife Lead subtrack. The Nightlife Lead channel strip is visible at the bottom left of the inspector.

3   In the inspector, click in the middle of the ES2 instrument plug-in slot to open the plug-in.

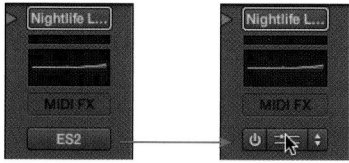

   The ES2 plug-in window opens.

   TIP If the presence of plug-in windows hinders your ability to interact with the main window, press V to toggle all plug-in windows on and off.

4   In the Tracks area, click the 70s Analog Lead subtrack.

5   In the inspector, click in the middle of the Tape Delay plug-in slot to open the Tape Delay plug-in window.

6   In the Tracks area, select the main track of the Track Stack.

You will insert a new audio effect plug-in on the summing channel strip.

7   On the left-channel strip in the inspector, click the empty space below the Channel EQ in the Audio FX section, and choose Modulation > Ring Shifter.

The Ringshifter plug-in opens.

Mapping Screen Controls to Parameters

Now that you have all three plug-ins open, you will use the Smart Controls pane to map the screen controls to some of the plug-in parameters.

1 In the control bar, click the Smart Controls button (or press B).

The Smart Controls pane opens at the bottom of the main window, displaying a collection of screen control knobs and buttons. By default, the screen controls are assigned to parameters on the main track's channel strip.

2 At the upper left of the Smart Controls pane, click the Inspector button.

The Smart Controls inspector opens. It shows the parameter assignments for the selected screen control. First, let's choose a different layout.

3 At the top of the Smart Controls inspector, click the layout name, and choose Factory Layouts > Modern Synth 6.

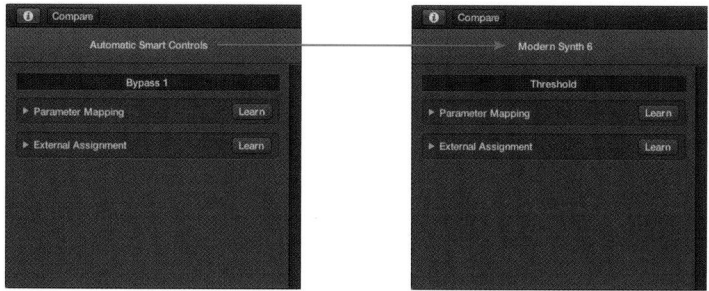

The simpler Modern Synth 6 layout appears. It has only six knobs. The first screen control is highlighted in blue to indicate that it is selected. Let's open the Parameter Mapping area to see the selected screen control's mapping(s).

4   In the Smart Controls inspector, click the disclosure triangle to open the Parameter Mapping area.

By default, the first screen control is mapped to two parameters. You will first delete one mapping, and then learn a new parameter for the remaining mapping.

5   In the Parameter Mapping area, click one of the mappings, and from the Parameter Mapping pop-up menu, choose Delete Mapping.

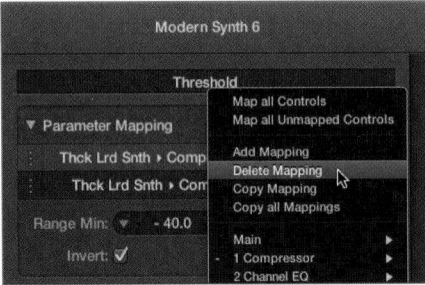

The mapping is deleted. You will now reassign the remaining mapping.

6   In the Parameter Mapping area, click the Learn button.

7   In the ES2, in the Filter section, click the right Cutoff knob (Cut).

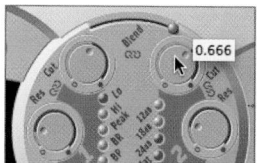

In the Parameter Mapping area, you can see that the selected Smart Controls knob is now mapped to Nightlife Lead > ES2 > LPF Cutoff.

Let's rename this screen control's label.

8   Above Parameter Mapping, double-click the screen control's label, type *Filter*, and press Return. In the Smart Controls pane, the label on top of the first screen control now reads *Filter*.

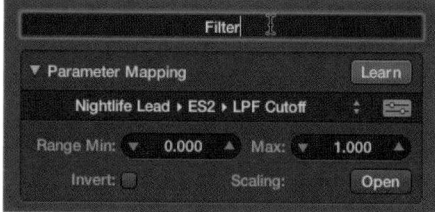

9   In the Smart Controls pane, click the second screen control (Ratio) to select it.

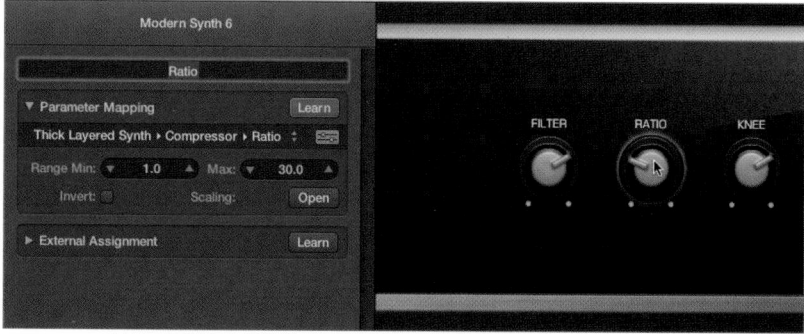

This time the halo around the knob is red because you're in Learn mode.

10 In the Tape Delay plug-in to the left, click the Feedback slider.

In the Parameter Mapping area, make sure the selected screen control is mapped to 70s Analog Lead > Tape Delay > Feedback.

11 In the Smart Controls pane, select the third screen control (Knee) and in the Ringshifter plug-in, click the round Frequency knob.

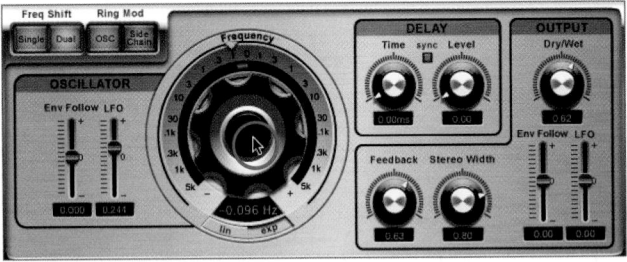

In the Parameter Mapping area, make sure the selected screen control is mapped to Thick Layered Synth > Ringshifter > Frequency.

12 Try turning the first three screen controls. In the plug-in windows, the three parameters you mapped to the screen controls move accordingly.

13 Close all three plug-in windows (or press V to hide them).

You don't need the three remaining screen controls so you will delete their mappings now.

14 In the Smart Controls pane, click the fourth screen control. In the Mapping area, click the mapping, and from the Parameter Mapping pop-up menu, choose Delete Mapping.

The button is disabled and labeled *UNMAPPED*. Repeat this last step for the fifth and sixth screen controls.

15 In the Parameter Mapping area, click the Learn button to turn off Learn mode.

TIP ▶ When closing the Smart Controls inspector, the Parameter Mapping area's Learn button is automatically turned off.

Assign MIDI Controller Knobs to Screen Controls

Most recent MIDI keyboards and MIDI control surfaces have knobs or faders that send MIDI Continuous Controller data, so let's assign hardware knobs to screen controls in the Smart Controls pane.

1 In the Smart Controls pane, click the first screen control (Filter) to select it.

2 In the Smart Controls inspector, in the External Assignment area, click the Learn button.

3 On your MIDI keyboard, turn a knob.

Don't be timid. Move the knob all the way down and all the way up, if necessary. When the knob is assigned, it adjusts the Filter screen control in the Smart Controls pane.

4   In the Smart Controls, click the second screen control (Feedback), and on your MIDI keyboard, turn a knob.

Repeat that procedure one more time to assign another knob to the third screen controller.

5   In the External Assignment area, click the Learn button to turn it off.

6   At the upper left of the Smart Controls pane, click the Inspector button to close the Smart Controls inspector.

The three unmapped screen controls are hidden, leaving you only the three screen controls you mapped to plug-in parameters and assigned to hardware knobs.

7   On your MIDI keyboard, play keys while turning the three assigned knobs.

As you move the knobs on your keyboard, the corresponding screen controls move in the Smart Controls pane. Be careful when adjusting the Feedback parameter. If you leave that knob turned up, a feedback loop is created and the sound sustains and builds up indefinitely, so bring Feedback down after a while.

You can now save this Smart Control layout to the patch.

8   On the main track of the Track Stack, click the disclosure triangle next to the icon to close the Track Stack.

9   At the bottom of the Library, click the Save button.

10 In the Save dialog, keep the same filename and location, and click Save.

An alert asks you to confirm that you want to replace the existing patch of the same name.

11 Click Replace.

You have created and saved your own patch. The patch contains two layered instruments in a Track Stack. It also includes its own Smart Control layout, with screen controls mapped to plug-in parameters, and MIDI controller knobs assigned to those screen controls. Smart Controls allow you to unite all the controls you need in a single pane, making it easy to control multiple parameters in multiple plug-ins without opening the plug-in windows.

Controlling Logic from an iPad Using Logic Remote

Logic Remote is a free iPad app you can download and install from the App Store. Logic Remote lets you choose patches and play Logic software instruments using various multi-touch controllers such as a keyboard, a fretboard, or drum pads. It lets you control Smart Controls and the Mixer, navigate your project, and tap buttons corresponding to Logic key commands. Plus, Logic Remote Smart Help automatically shows the section of Logic Pro Help related to the area where the Mac mouse pointer is located.

1 On the iPad, from the App Store, download and install Logic Remote.

2 On the iPad, tap the Logic Remote icon to open Logic Remote.

3   Make sure the iPad is on the same Wi-Fi network as your Mac. To choose a Wi-Fi network on the iPad, tap the Settings icon. In the Settings column, tap Wi-Fi, and choose from the list of Wi-Fi networks displayed to the right.

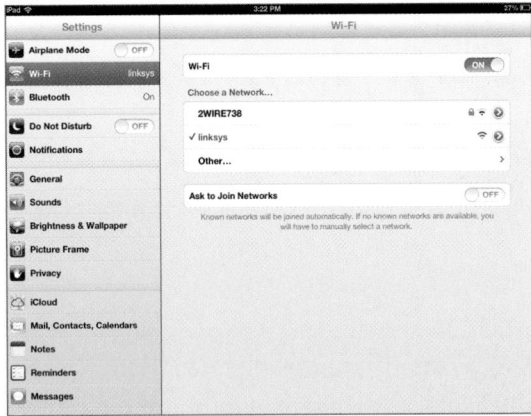

NOTE ▶ On the iPad, you are prompted to choose the Mac you want the iPad to control.

In Logic, an alert appears, asking you to confirm that you want to connect Logic Remote to Logic on that Mac.

4   In Logic, click OK to confirm the alert; and on the iPad, choose your Mac.

5   In the Logic Remote control bar, tap the View button, and choose Smart Controls & Keyboard.

View button —

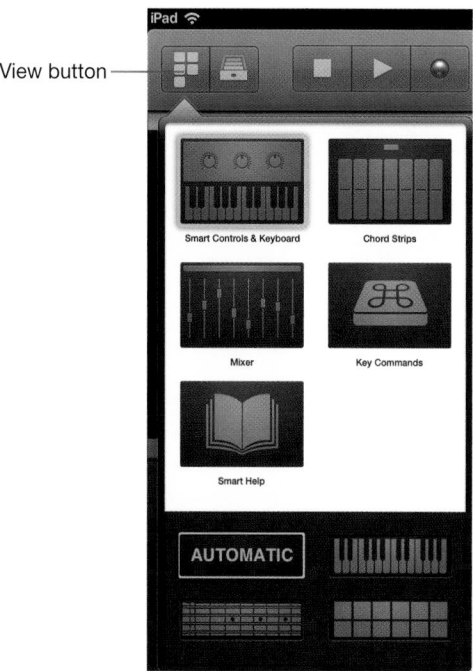

TIP ▶ Tap the keyboard, fretboard, or pads icon at the bottom of the View menu to select those Touch Instruments.

The iPad displays the Smart Controls you customized in the previous exercise, along with a keyboard.

6 Experiment with Logic Remote by touching a screen control and swiping up or down to adjust it; tapping keys to play notes; and swiping a key horizontally to play a glissando.

7 At the top of the keyboard, tap the button marked Glissando.

The button is now marked Scroll.

8 Swipe the keyboard horizontally to move higher or lower on the keyboard.

9 Tap the button marked Scroll.

The button is now marked Pitch.

10 Swipe a key horizontally to pitch the note down or up.

11 At the upper right of the keyboard, tap the Arpeggiator button.

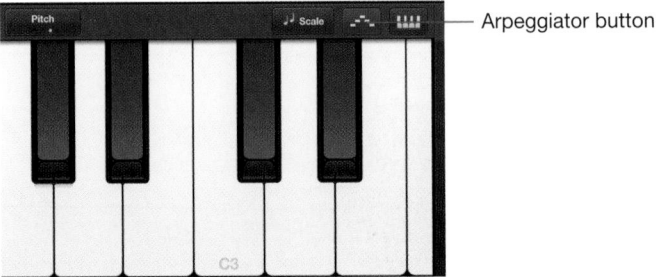
Arpeggiator button

12 Play a chord. The chord's notes are arpeggiated at a sixteenth-note rate. Since you can swipe keys horizontally to bend their pitch, try swiping only some of the notes in the chord to change the arpeggio.

> **NOTE ▸** When a Track Stack is selected, tapping the Arpeggiator button inserts an Arpeggiator MIDI effect plug-in on only the first channel strip within the Track Stack (currently the Nightlife Lead). You will take a closer look at the Arpeggiator MIDI plug-in at the end of this lesson.

13 In the Logic Remote control bar, tap the View button, and choose Mixer to open it.

To the left, you see the Thick Layered Synth channel strip, and three auxiliary channel strips (A1, A2, and A3). To see the two instruments in your layered synth, you need to open the Track Stack.

14 In Logic, click the disclosure triangle in the track header.

The Track Stack opens, and in Logic Remote, you can see the Nightlife Lead and 70s Analog Lead channel strips.

NOTE ▶ The Logic Remote mixer can show up to eight channel strips at a time. In Logic, you can identify which tracks are currently shown on the controller by the thin white bars displayed to the left of the track headers. If you place the mouse pointer over a white bar, a help tag appears with the name of the controller.

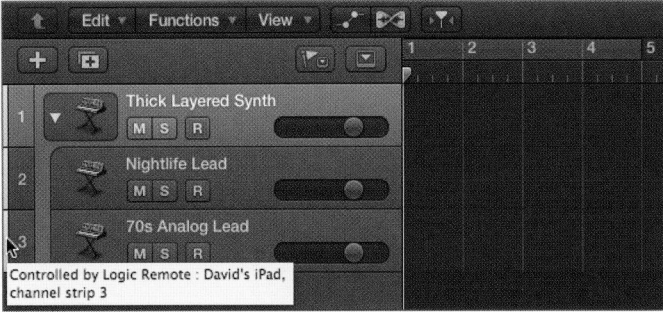

15 Hold down a chord on your MIDI keyboard, and in Logic Remote, swipe the Volume faders and Balance knobs to adjust the mix of the two instruments.

16 In Logic, close the Track Stack.

Let's navigate the project from the iPad.

17 In the Logic Remote control bar, tap the LCD display.

The ruler and playhead are displayed below the control bar.

18 Tap a position in the ruler or swipe the ruler to relocate the playhead.

> **TIP** ▶ Even when the ruler is not showing, you can swipe the LCD display horizontally to show the ruler and relocate the playhead.

19 Tap the LCD display again to hide the ruler.

20 In the control bar, tap the Info button (question mark).

Coaching tips appear for elements of the Logic Remote interface. You can continue using Logic Remote when coaching tips are visible.

21 Tap the Info button again to hide the coaching tips.

22 Tap the View button, and tap Key Commands.

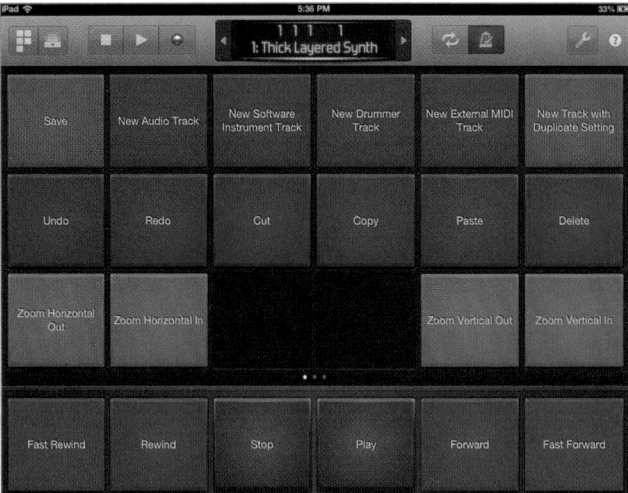

23 Tap the Zoom Vertical In pad a few times. On your Mac, the workspace zooms in vertically.

24 Tap the View button, and tap Smart Help.

Smart Help is a contextual version of the Logic Pro Help. As you move the mouse pointer on your Mac, Smart Help updates to show you the relevant section.

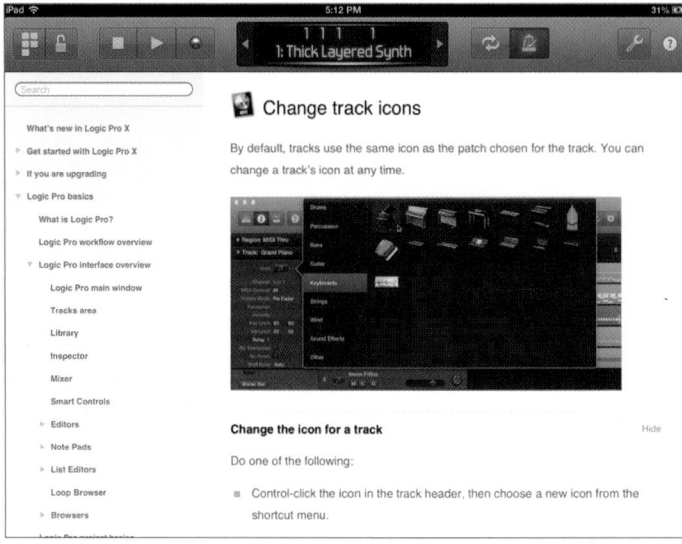

TIP ▶ Next to the View button, tap the Lock button to stop Smart Help from updating when moving your mouse pointer on the Mac.

25 Tap the Settings button, and tap Logic Remote Help to open it.

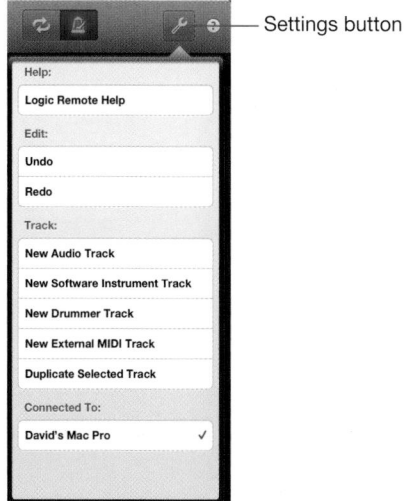

You can use the Logic Remote Help to learn more about the Logic Remote app.

26 At the upper right of Logic Remote Help, tap the Done button to close Remote Help.

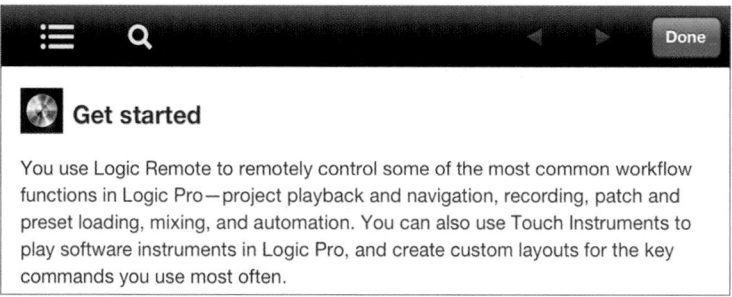

You now know how to remotely control Logic from your iPad. You know how to navigate the song, control the Mixer and the Smart Controls, and play an instrument using the iPad multi-touch screen. If you want to explore further, use the coaching tips or the Logic Remote Help available on your iPad.

Using Step Input Recording

Instead of recording a performance in real-time, you can record notes one at a time. This technique is useful to record musical parts that would be difficult or impossible to perform live. Composers who take the time to choose their notes or chords will also enjoy this technique.

In step input mode, you position the playhead and play a note or chord on your MIDI keyboard. The note(s) are recorded, and the playhead moves one step ahead, ready for you to enter the next note(s). Before you can use step input, you need to identify a MIDI region to receive the notes.

1   On the Thick Layered Synth track, Control-click the workspace in bar 1, and choose Create Empty MIDI Region.

A one-bar MIDI region is created.

2   Make sure the playhead is exactly at 1 1 1 1.

3   Double-click the MIDI region to open the Piano Roll.

4   At the top of the Piano Roll, click the MIDI In button.

The button turns red, indicating that step input recording is enabled.

5   Play a note on your MIDI keyboard.

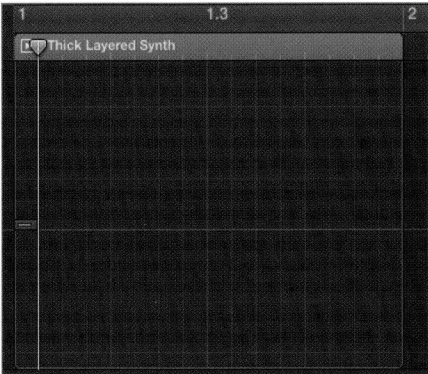

In the Thick Layered Synth region, a sixteenth note is recorded at the playhead position. When you release the key on your MIDI keyboard, the playhead moves forward one sixteenth note. The recorded note has the pitch and velocity of the note you played.

6   Play a chord on your MIDI keyboard.

A sixteenth-note chord is recorded at the playhead position, and the playhead moves forward one sixteenth note.

You can also skip a step by pressing the Spacebar.

7   Press the Spacebar.

The playhead moves forward one sixteenth note.

You can also use the Step Input keyboard to exercise more control over your step input recording.

8 Choose Window > Show Step Input Keyboard (or press Command-Option-K).

Note length buttons

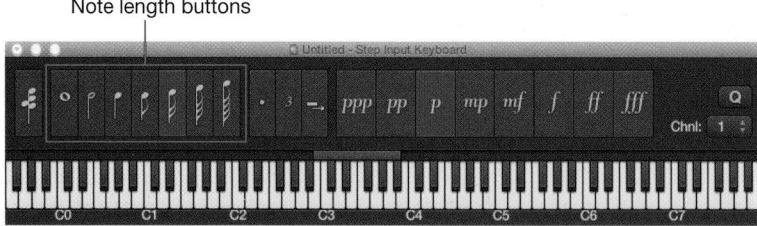

The floating Step Input keyboard opens. When the Step Input keyboard is open, the note length buttons determine the length of the steps.

9 On the Step Input keyboard, click the eighth note button to select it.

10 Play a note on your MIDI keyboard.

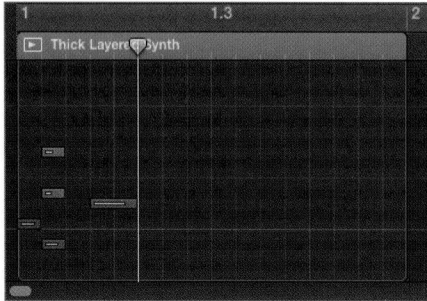

An eighth note is recorded at the playhead position, and the playhead moves forward one eighth note.

If you were recording an eighth-note pattern and wanted to record a single quarter note, you could avoid clicking to change the step value by using the Sustain Inserted Notes feature.

11 Play a note and hold down the key on your MIDI keyboard.

An eighth note is recorded. You need to hold down the MIDI key for the next step, so that the note you are recording remains selected in the Piano Roll.

TIP ▸ You can also release the key on your MIDI keyboard and click the last note recorded to reselect it.

12 On the Step Input keyboard, click the Sustain Inserted Notes button.

You can now release the key on your MIDI keyboard.

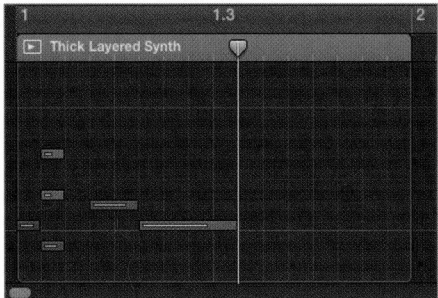

In the Piano Roll, the selected note is lengthened by a step (an eighth note), so it becomes a quarter note. You can click the Sustain Inserted Notes button several times to lengthen any selected note(s) by the current step length.

Try using step input recording techniques to record fast sixteenth-note arpeggios, or even crazy chord patterns. With a little experimentation, you will quickly end up with cool musical phrases that couldn't possibly be performed live.

TIP If you record a wrong note, choose Edit > Undo Create Event (or press Command-Z). The last note recorded is deleted, and the playhead moves one step backward.

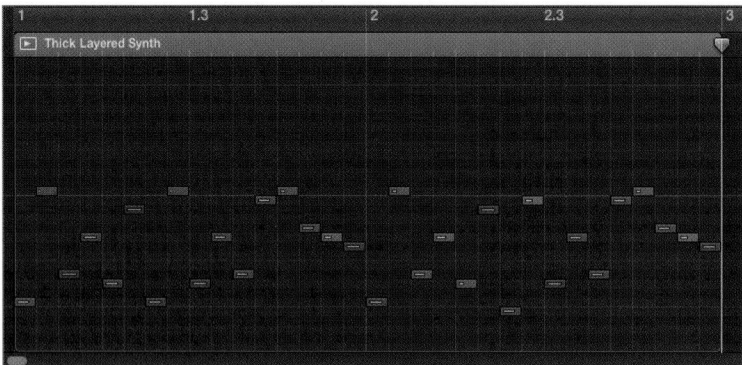

13 At the top of the Piano Roll, click the MIDI In button to turn off step input recording.

14 Listen to the part you recorded.

15 Close this project, and save it only if you want to revisit it later. (You will no longer need it for this book.)

Processing MIDI Notes with MIDI Plug-Ins

MIDI effects are plug-ins that can process the MIDI data coming from the track, whether generated in real time with your MIDI keyboard, or from the MIDI regions on the track during playback, before it reaches the instrument plug-in. A MIDI plug-in may change the pitch and velocity of notes, or even create new MIDI note or controller events.

In this last exercise you will experiment with holding down a chord on your MIDI keyboard, and processing the chord through the Arpeggiator MIDI plug-in, which automatically arpeggiates the chord's notes while staying in sync with the project.

1 Go to Logic Pro X > Lessons and open **05 Dub Beat**. This project has two empty software instrument tracks (Inst 1 and Low Down Dub).

2 In the inspector at the lower left of the channel strip, double-click the Inst 1 name, and rename the channel strip *Synth*.

3   On the Synth channel strip, click the Instrument slot, and choose Retro Synth.

The Retro Synth plug-in opens. This analog modeling instrument can imitate a wide range of classic synths and their specific synthesis techniques. In the Oscillator section at the upper left, four tabs let you access one of the four synthesizer engines: analog modeling (ANALOG), synchronized oscillators (SYNC), wavetable synthesis (TABLE), and frequency modulation (FM).

4   On the Filter display, drag the node slightly toward the upper right while playing some notes on your MIDI keyboard.

The sound acquires more high frequency and sounds brighter and thinner.

TIP ▸ To hear the results of your actions, continue playing your MIDI keyboard as you make adjustments throughout this lesson.

5   In the inspector on the Synth channel strip, click the MIDI FX slot, and choose Arpeggiator.

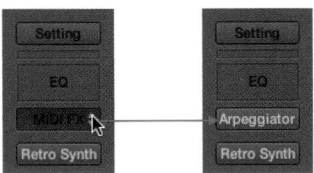

The Arpeggiator opens.

6   Hold down a single note. The Arpeggiator starts repeating it every sixteenth note.

7   Hold down a chord. The Arpeggiator plays one note at a time, from the lowest note to the highest one, every sixteenth note.

8   Press the Spacebar.

You can hear the Low Down Dub beat on track 2. Track 2 uses the Ultrabeat instrument plug-in, which has a built-in sequencer. This is why you can hear the instrument play a beat even though you don't see any MIDI regions on its track.

For the rest of this exercise, feel free to stop and resume playback when you need a break or when you want to focus on the arpeggiated synth.

9   At the top of the Arpeggiator, click Latch.

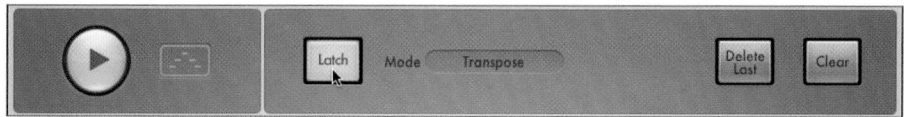

10   Play a chord and release the keys. The arpeggio continues to play.

11   Play another chord to hear the arpeggiated chord.

Next to the Latch button, notice that Mode is set to Transpose. In that mode, you can use your MIDI keyboard to transpose the arpeggio to a different key.

12   Play a single key on your keyboard.

The previous chord is transposed, so it starts on the pitch of the note you played.

NOTE ▶ When Latch is enabled, the Arpeggiator memorized the last chord you played. You can click the Play button at the upper left of the Arpeggiator to stop and start playback.

13   In the Note Order section, click the Down button.

The arpeggio plays from the highest note to the lowest note.

14 Click the Random button.

The notes play in a random order.

15 Click the As Played button.

The notes play in the order they were originally played on the MIDI keyboard.

16 Click the Up button.

17 Drag the Octave Range switch to position 3.

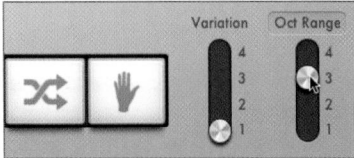

The Arpeggiator repeats over a three-octave range.

18 Set the Variation switch to position 2.

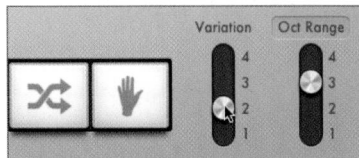

The notes play in a different order.

19 Set the Variation and Octave Range switches back to 1.

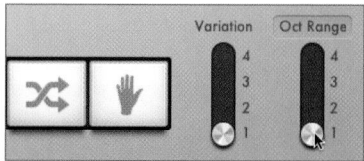

20 Drag the Rate knob down to 1/8.

The Arpeggiator slows down and plays eighth notes. You can also click the Rate field above the knob to directly choose the desired rate.

NOTE ▸ The project tempo is 85 bpm, a slow tempo, and 1/8 is a slow rate, which makes it easy to hear the results of your experiments with the Arpeggiator parameters. Don't hesitate to raise the tempo and the rate after you finish this exercise. With the right pattern and sound, fast arpeggios can be a lot of fun!

At the bottom of the Arpeggiator in the Pattern area, Live mode is highlighted. In Live mode, the notes play at the same velocity you played them on your keyboard. The Grid mode offers more flexibility, but first let's make the Retro Synth more sensitive to velocity, so that lower velocity MIDI notes will trigger lower level notes in the instrument.

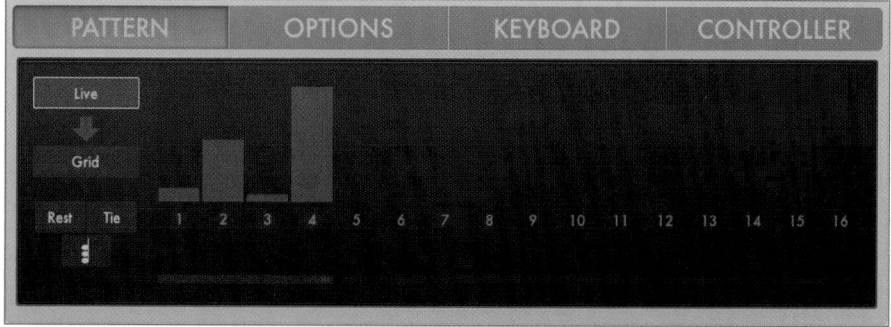

21 In the Retro Synth, at the lower right, drag the Velocity slider (Vel) all the way to the top (1.00).

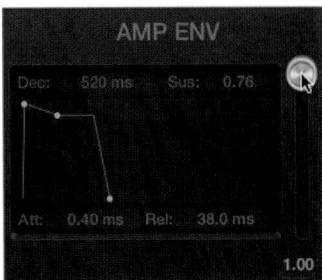

Assuming that you played notes with different velocities, the lower velocity notes now play more quietly. You will now use the Grid mode to customize the arpeggio pattern.

22 In the Pattern area, click the Grid button.

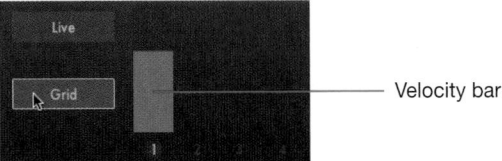

The Arpeggiator is now in Grid mode, and plays all the notes at the same velocity corresponding to the height of the velocity bar on step 1.

23 At the bottom of the Pattern area, from the Pattern pop-up menu, choose Grooving Pulse 01.

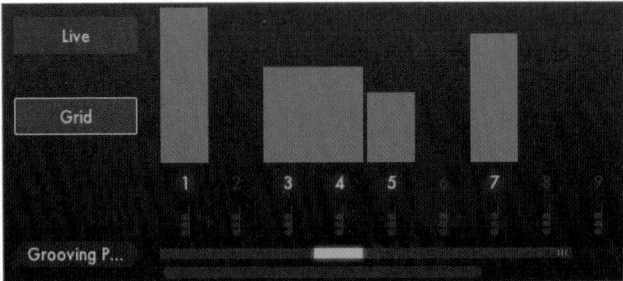

The pattern is loaded to the grid, and you can hear your chord arpeggiated while following the pattern. Note that some of the steps on the grid are turned off, and one note is wider than the others and lasts for two steps.

24 From the Pattern pop-up menu, choose Chordal Jam 01.

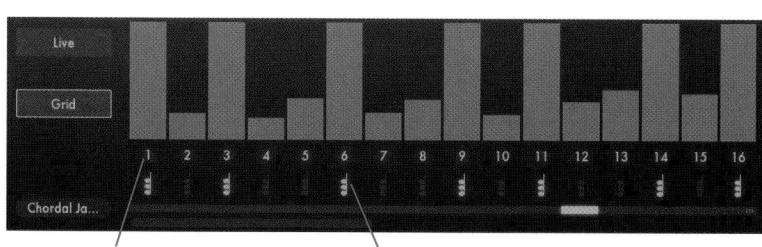

In this pattern, some of the steps have the chord on/off button lit, and they play the whole chord rather than a single note.

25 Feel free to customize the pattern:

▶ Drag a velocity bar up/down to adjust the note velocity.

▶ Drag a velocity bar left/right to adjust the note length.

▶ Click the step number to toggle that step on or off.

▶ Click the chord symbol to make that step play a single note or the whole chord.

26 Now that you have a better grasp on the Arpeggiator, feel free to choose a faster rate with the Rate knob.

While arpeggiators can be a great source of inspiration, they can also become tiresome quickly if they always play the same patterns. One way to keep things fresh is to let the sound of the synth evolve progressively as the arpeggio plays.

In Retro Synth, try playing with the Filter section as you did earlier in this exercise. Also try playing with the amplifier envelope (AMP ENV) by dragging the handles on the display or adjusting the four parameters around the display, Dec(ay), Sus(tain), Att(ack), and Rel(ease). Try making the sound of the synth evolve from long envelopes to very short ones.

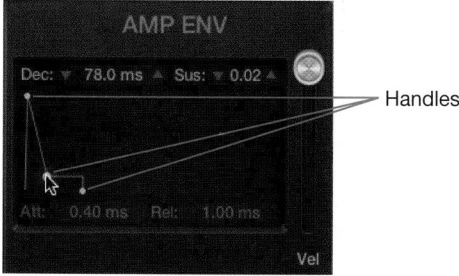

You have used the Arpeggiator MIDI plug-in to process a simple chord played on your keyboard into simple and complex arpeggios. You've learned how to choose different note orders and their variations, and to expand the arpeggio over multiple octaves. You also chose different grid patterns and customized them to make your own.

MIDI plug-ins give you more tools in your arsenal to process MIDI events in real time. Feel free to continue exploring the possibilities, perhaps by choosing different instruments to arpeggiate.

Lesson Review

1. How do you join a new recording in an existing MIDI region?
2. How do you turn on step input recording?
3. How can you time-correct a MIDI region?
4. How do you choose default region parameters for new MIDI recording?
5. What do you need to do before you can punch in on a MIDI track and replace a portion of a MIDI region?
6. How can you change the length of a step when performing step input recording?
7. What type of Track Stack should you create to have MIDI regions on the main track trigger instruments on the subtracks?
8. In the Smart Controls pane, how do you map a screen control to a plug-in parameter?
9. In the Smart Controls pane, how do you assign a screen control to a knob on your MIDI controller?
10. In the Arpeggiator MIDI plug-in, how do you play a chord on specific steps of the pattern?
11. In the Arpeggiator MIDI plug-in, how do you skip a step?

Answers

1. In the project's recording settings, set Overlapping Recordings to "Join with Selected Regions."
2. Click the MIDI In button at the top of the Piano Roll.
3. In the Region inspector, set the Quantize parameter to the desired note length.
4. Deselect all regions in the workspace to access the MIDI Thru settings in the Region inspector.

5. You need to turn on Replace mode.

6. Click the Note Length buttons in the Step Input keyboard.

7. A Summing stack

8. In the Parameter Mapping area, click Learn. Click a screen control to select it, and click a plug-in parameter to map it to the selected screen control.

9. In the External Assignment area, click Learn. Click a screen control to select it, and turn a knob on your MIDI controller until the screen control moves along.

10. Click the chord on/off button below the step number.

11. Click the step on/off button below the velocity bar.

Keyboard Shortcuts

Project

Command-Shift-N	Creates a new empty project
Command-Option-W	Closes the current project

Windows and Panes

Command-K	Opens or closes the Musical Typing window
Command-Option-K	Opens the Step Input keyboard
P	Opens the Piano Roll
B	Opens the Smart Controls
V	Hides or shows all the plug-in windows

Tracks Area

Command-J	Joins the selected regions
Command-Option-S	Creates a new software instrument track
Command-Shift-D	Creates a Track Stack for the selected tracks

6

Lesson Files
Logic Pro X Files > Lessons > 06 Rock Drums

Logic Pro X Files > Media > Additional Media > Lead Synth.mid

Time
This lesson takes approximately 90 minutes to complete.

Goals
Create and edit MIDI notes in the Piano Roll Editor

Quantize MIDI regions

Create and edit MIDI notes in the Score Editor

Time and Scale Quantize individual notes

Import MIDI files

Select and delete continuous controller events in the Event List

Create continuous controller automation in the MIDI Draw area

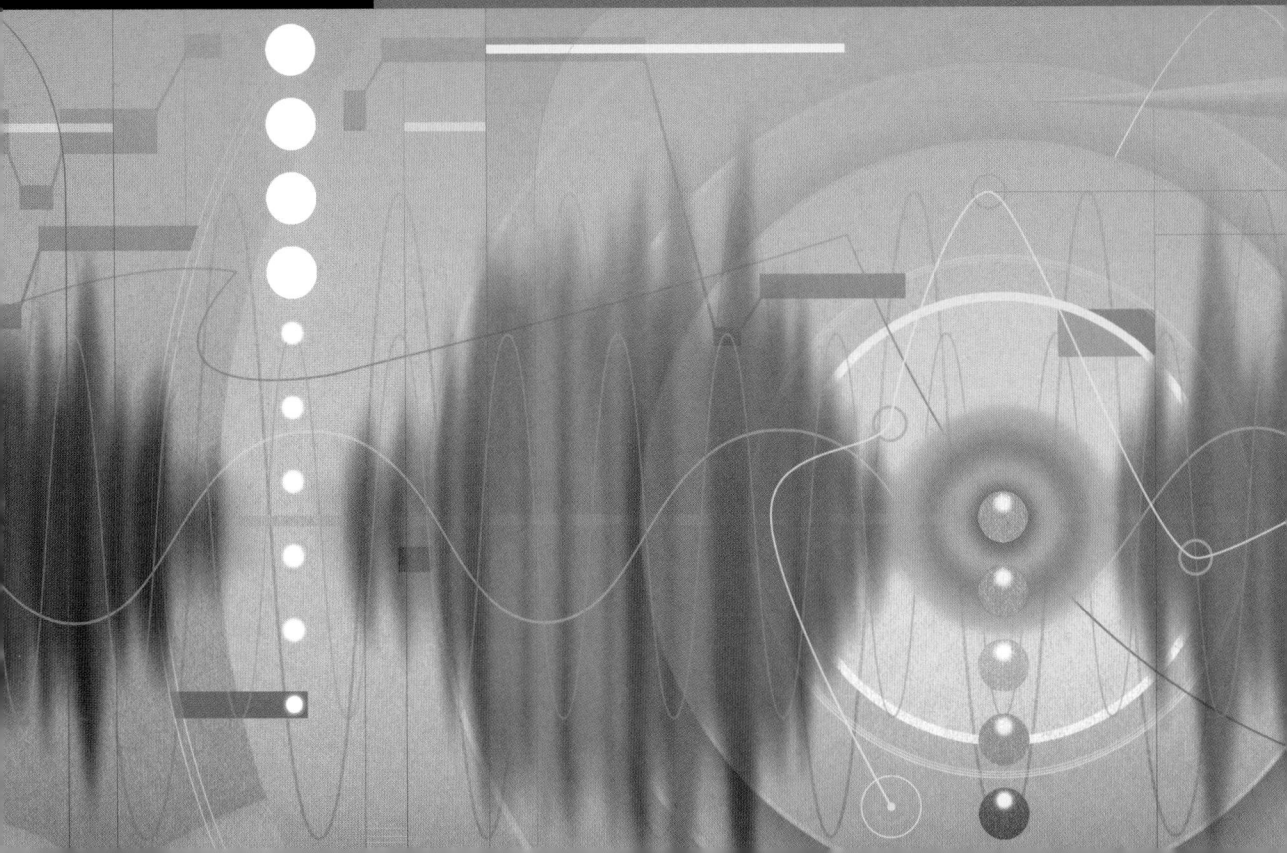

Lesson 6
Creating and Editing MIDI

When you work with MIDI sequences, the flexibility of separating the performance data from a specific instrument gives you total control over the performance data, even after it is recorded. You can open the MIDI region in a MIDI editor to precisely fine-tune each note's position, pitch, velocity, and length. You can edit or add MIDI controller events to automate the instrument's volume, panning, pitch, and many other parameters. You can also write music from scratch, creating notes in MIDI editors using only your mouse, similar to the way you write music on staff paper.

Writing music in MIDI editors is also called *programming MIDI sequences*. Logic includes several MIDI editors for this purpose, and though they all display the same MIDI events, each does so in its own way. For example, the Score Editor shows you musical notes on a staff, and the Piano Roll Editor shows you notes as beams on a grid.

In this lesson, you will program and edit MIDI events using the Logic MIDI editors. You will write a bass line and a syncopated organ groove, import and edit a MIDI file, and program MIDI control automation to breathe life into your MIDI sequences.

Creating MIDI Notes in the Piano Roll Editor

The Piano Roll Editor is the most straightforward MIDI editor in Logic. Its name is inspired by the perforated paper roll used by mechanical player pianos, in which the position and length of those perforations determined the pitches and lengths of notes.

In Logic, the Piano Roll Editor represents MIDI notes as beams on a grid, positioned below a bar ruler, much like the workspace displays regions on a grid below a bar ruler. In fact, most of the techniques for editing regions in the workspace also apply to notes in the Piano Roll Editor.

Creating and Resizing Notes

In the Piano Roll Editor, you create notes by clicking in the grid with the Pencil tool. As you write your musical part using the Pencil tool, you can also use the Pencil tool to resize, move, copy, or delete notes.

You will open a new project that has a basic rock drum track, create a new bass track, and use the Pencil tool to program a simple bass line in the Piano Roll.

1   Open Logic Pro X Files > Lessons > **06 Rock Drums**.

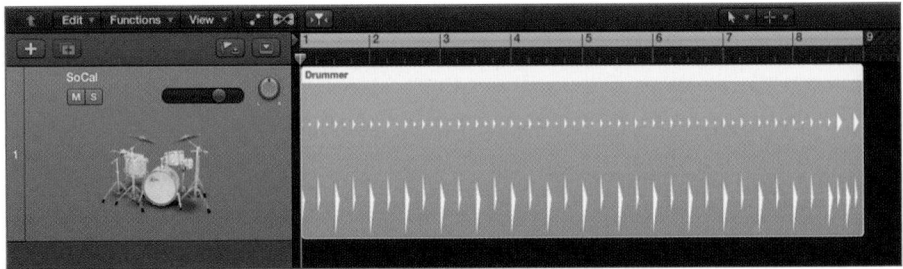

The project contains a single Drummer track looping for eight bars. Listen to the drums. They play a straightforward rock drum pattern with a simple fill at the end of the eight-bar pattern.

2   Choose Track > New Software Instrument Track (or press Command-Option-S).

3   In the control bar, click the Library button (or press Y).

4   In the Library, choose Bass > Stinger Bass.

5   On the Stinger Bass track, Control-click in bar 1, and choose Create Empty MIDI
Region.

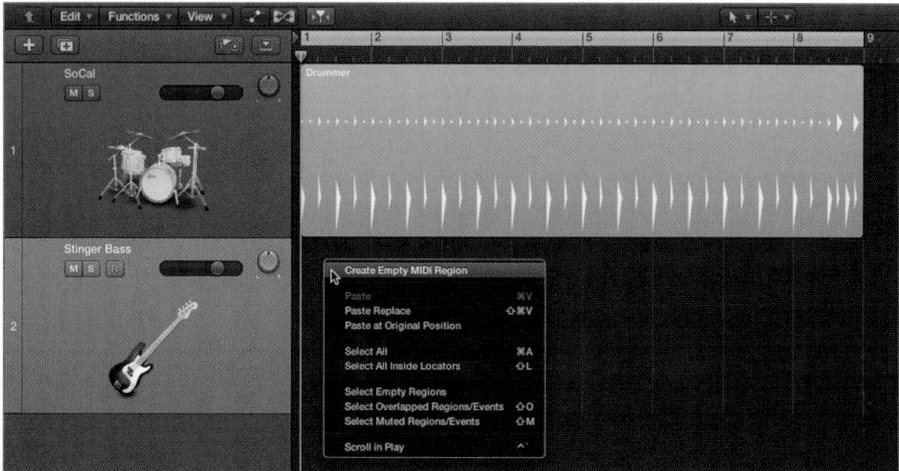

An empty, one-bar MIDI region is created that starts exactly on bar 1.

6   Double-click the new Stinger Bass region.

The Piano Roll opens and displays that region.

7   In the Piano Roll, click the keys on the piano keyboard.

The keys trigger the bass instrument, and you can hear the bass notes.

As you position the mouse pointer over the grid, look at the info display at the top of
the Piano Roll. Scroll down to find A1, two white keys below C2. On the grid, light
gray lanes correspond to the white keys on the piano keyboard, while dark gray lanes
correspond to the black keys.

Info display

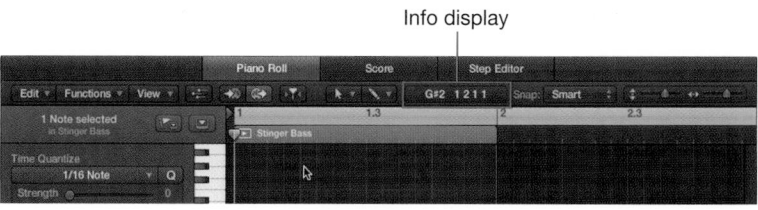

NOTE ▸ If you cannot see the info display, try making the main window wider or close side panes such as inspectors and browsers.

You will now use the Pencil tool, your current Command-click tool, to create notes.

8   Command-click the light gray lane at 1 1 1 1 in front of the A1 note.

Clicking the grid with the Pencil tool inserts a note on the closest grid line to the left, such as clicking at 1 1 1 181 inserts a note at 1 1 1 1.

By default, Logic creates a quarter note. You will resize the note to an eighth note.

9   Position the pointer over the right edge of the note until it changes to a Resize tool.

10 Drag the Resize tool to the left to shorten the note to an eighth note.

The help tag shows the note length as 0 0 2 0, which indicates that the length is 0 bars, 0 beats, 2 divisions, and 0 ticks. By default, the division is set to 1/16, so two divisions make an eighth note.

11 Command-click after the existing eighth note to create a new note at 1 1 3 1.

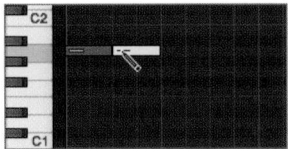

A new note is created with the same length as the previous eighth note.

NOTE ▶ When creating a note, the new note has the same length as the note you most recently created or clicked with the Pencil tool.

You can check the position and pitch of a note by placing the pointer over the note and holding down the mouse button. After a pause, a help tag appears with the information.

This time you will create and resize a note in a single operation.

12 Using the Pencil tool, hold down the mouse button to create a C2 after the last note (at 1 2 1 1) and drag to the right to lengthen the note to a quarter note (0 1 0 0).

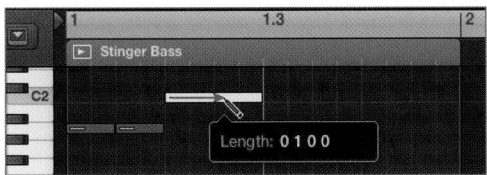

Defining Note Length with Existing Notes

To finish this first bar, you will repeat the same rhythmic motif (two eighth notes followed by a quarter note) on new pitches. You'll select existing notes to create notes of the same length and velocity.

1 Click one of the two eighth notes at the beginning of the bar to select it.

From now on, clicking with the Pencil tool will create eighth notes.

2 Command-click to create a G1 at 1 3 1 1.

3 Command-click to create another G1 at 1 3 3 1.

Now enter the quarter note.

4 Click the quarter note on C2 to select it.

The next note you create will be a quarter note.

5 Create a B1 quarter note at 1 4 1 1.

6 Play your bass line. The melody is nice, but the bass is played too legato.

7 Drag a rectangle around all the notes (or press Command-A) to select them.

8 Drag the right edge of one of the selected notes toward the left to shorten it slightly. After you start dragging, hold down Control to adjust the length with more precision.

9 Listen to the bass line. You can hear the individual notes with more distinction now.

You now have a one bar pattern. You could continue writing the bass line with the Pencil tool, but to go faster you'll repeat the pattern throughout the remaining seven bars of the cycle area.

10 Ensure that all the notes are selected, and choose Edit > Repeat (or press Command-R).

The Repeat Regions/Events dialog opens.

11 Set the Number of Copies to 7, set Adjustment to Bar, and click OK.

In the Piano Roll, the selected notes are repeated on every subsequent seven bars. In the workspace, the region is lengthened to eight bars to accommodate the new notes. Let's zoom out to see how it looks.

12 In the Piano Roll, click the background to deselect all the notes, and press Z.

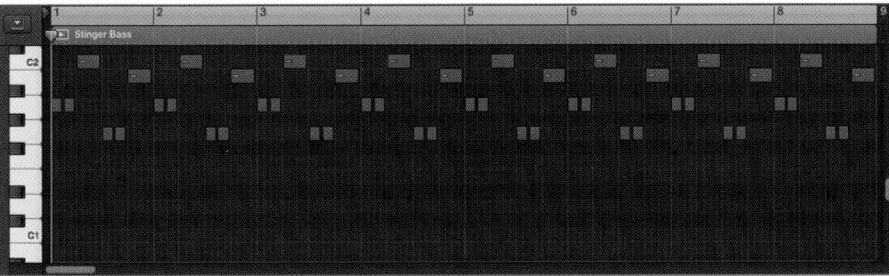

You can see your entire eight-bar bass line.

You used the Pencil tool to create notes, resize them, and define the length and velocity of new notes. Then you used the Repeat Regions/Events dialog to quickly fill up an eight-bar region with your one-bar pattern. Right now the bass line is rather repetitive, but you'll add small variations in the next exercise to make it more exciting.

Editing Note Pitch Using Key Commands

Creating notes with the Pencil tool is fine when you have a clear idea of the pitches you want. But sometimes you may want to experiment with different pitches while listening to the result.

In this next exercise, you will add eighth-note fills to the bass at the end of every two-bar section, and use key commands to select notes and change their pitches.

1   In the Piano Roll, Shift-click the four notes just before bars 3, 5, 7, and 9 to select them.

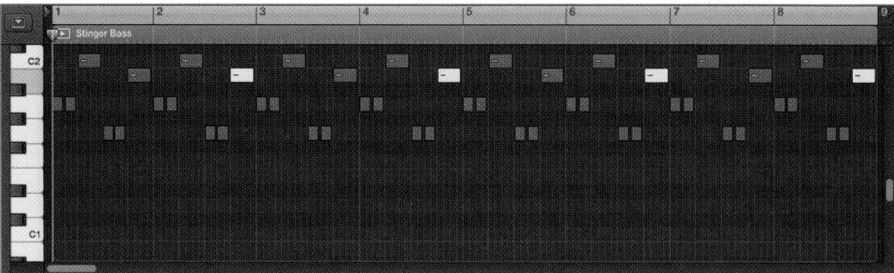

You will now resize the four selected quarter notes to make them slightly shorter than eighth notes and so they don't sound too legato.

2   Drag the right edge of one of the selected notes to the left to shorten all the selected notes to about 0 0 1 160. Remember to start dragging and then press and hold down the Control key to disable snapping.

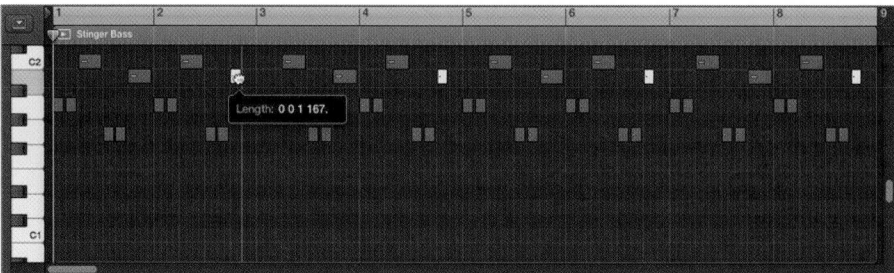

You will now copy the selected notes.

3   Option-drag the first selected note toward the right to 2 4 3 1.

All four selected notes are copied. Now every other bar ends with two eighth notes.

4   Click the background to deselect all notes, and click the last eighth note of bar 2 to select it.

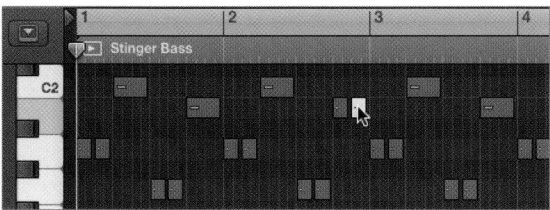

From now on, make sure the Piano Roll always has key focus. You will work with the following key commands to select and transpose notes:

▶   Left/Right Arrow—Selects previous/next note

▶   Option-Up/Down Arrow—Transposes up/down one semitone

▶   Shift-Option-Up/Down Arrow—Transposes up/down one octave

NOTE ▶ If you happen to press Up Arrow by mistake, the Drummer track is selected and the Drummer Editor opens, replacing the Piano Roll. To resume working on the bass, press Down Arrow to reselect the bass track and to reopen the Piano Roll.

5   Press Shift-Option-Down Arrow.

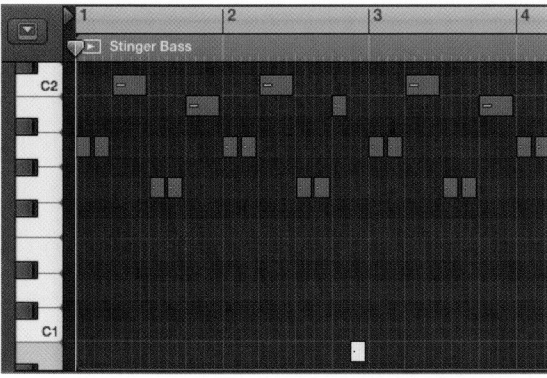

The note is transposed down one octave (from a B1 to a B0).

6   Listen to this new bass fill. It sounds OK, but the B0 note is a bit too low.

7 Press Option-Up Arrow five times to transpose the note up five semitones (from a B0 to an E1).

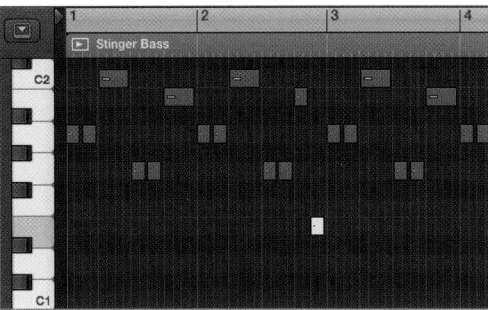

You have several ways to check the pitch of the selected note: Look at the highlighted key on the piano keyboard, position the mouse pointer over the note and look at the info display, or hold down the mouse button over the note and wait for the help tag to appear.

8 Start playback, and keep the song playing for the next few steps; you will continue editing note pitches while listening to the song.

9 Press Right Arrow a few times.

Each time you press Right Arrow, the next note to the right is selected, and its sound is played. This can be distracting when you're trying to focus on the result of your edits.

10 At the top of the Piano Roll, click the MIDI Out button to turn off MIDI Out.

MIDI Out button

11 Press Right Arrow a few more times to select the first of the last two eighth notes in bar 4.

With MIDI Out turned off, no sound is triggered as you select different notes, which makes hearing the song easier.

12 Press Option-Down Arrow three times to transpose the note three semitones lower (from a B1 to a G#1).

13 Press Right Arrow once, and then press Option-Down Arrow three times to transpose the next eighth note to the same pitch (G#1).

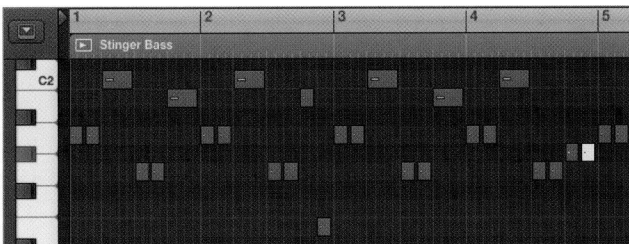

Continue using these key commands to edit the bass fills at the ends of bar 6 and bar 8, choosing pitches that sound good to you.

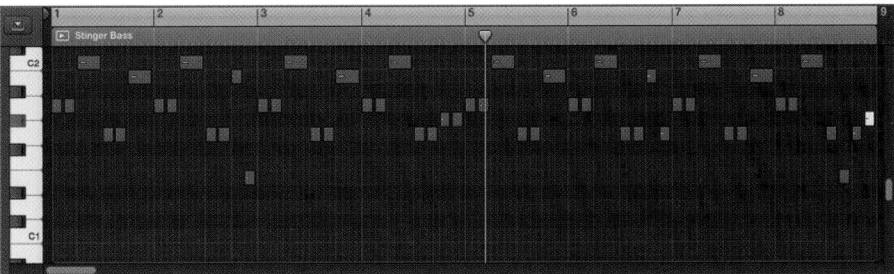

You now have a bass line that repeats the same one-bar pattern for eight bars, with just enough variation in every other bar to keep things sounding fresh.

Editing Note Velocity

When you play a MIDI keyboard, you want to control how loud each note is played. To judge how hard you press the keys, MIDI keyboards measure the speed at which each key is depressed. That speed is called *velocity*. When you press a key, the MIDI keyboard sends a note on MIDI event that contains the key number and velocity value of that note.

Higher velocities usually result in louder notes. Depending on the patch or program you're using, higher velocities may also trigger different sounds or different samples, as they do in the sampler instrument you're using in the Stinger Bass track. Higher-velocity notes trigger samples of a bass string that was actually plucked harder, allowing you to program accents or dynamic variations that sound realistic.

In this exercise, you will use different techniques to change the velocities of notes in the bass line, thereby changing their volumes and timbres, and making your MIDI programming sound closer to a live performance.

1 At the top of the Piano Roll, click the MIDI Out button to enable MIDI Out.

2 Control-Option-drag to zoom in on the first three notes.

3 In the Left-click Tool menu at the top of the Piano Roll, choose the Velocity tool (or press T, and then press 9).

> **TIP** You can also hold down Control-Command to temporarily turn the Pointer tool into a Velocity tool.

4 Using the Velocity tool, drag the first note up or down.

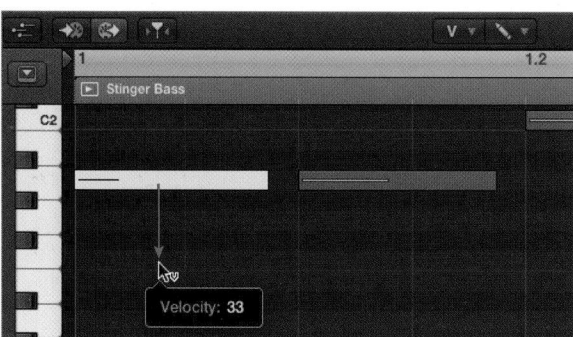

As you drag with the Velocity tool, the MIDI note is triggered repeatedly so that you can hear the sound of the note at different velocities. Notice how higher velocities trigger bass sounds that were plucked harder and have more attack.

The help tag displays the value of the velocity, from 1 to 127.

The velocity value is indicated by the color of the note, ranging from from cold colors (low velocities) to warm colors (high velocities). Velocity is also represented by the length of the line in the middle of the note beam.

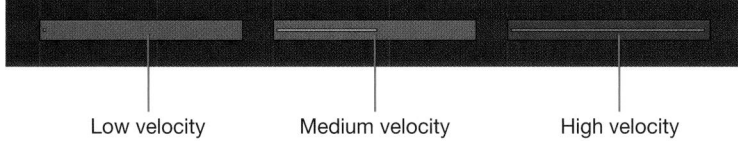

Low velocity   Medium velocity   High velocity

By default, all the notes you previously created have a velocity of 60.

You can add a subtle accent to the first note, but you don't want it to stand out too much, so settle for a velocity of 61. The first bass note now triggers a sound that has slightly more attack than the other notes, but the difference is subtle.

Let's select all B1 and C2 notes and raise their velocities together.

5   Click the background of the Piano Roll, and press Z to zoom out.

6   On the piano keyboard, click the C2 key to select all C2 notes in the region.

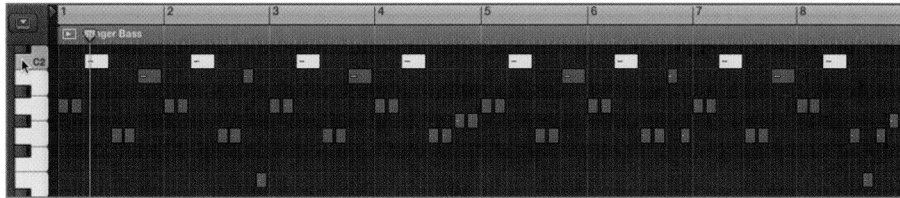

7   Shift-click the B1 key (just below C2) to add all B1 notes to your selection.

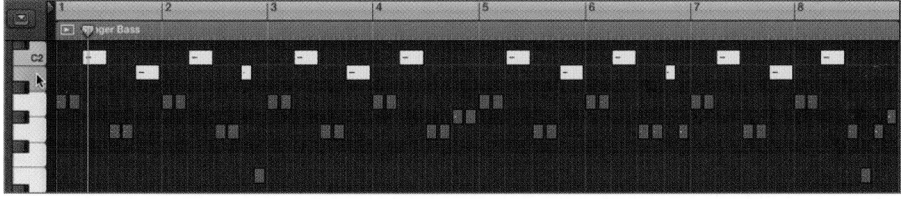

8 Using the Velocity tool, drag one of the selected notes to set the velocity of all the selected notes to 89.

NOTE ▶ When multiple selected notes have different velocities, dragging them with the Velocity tool offsets the velocities of all notes by the same amount, and the differences in velocity between the notes are retained.

9 Press T twice to change the Left-click tool to a Pointer tool.

10 Click the background to deselect the notes.

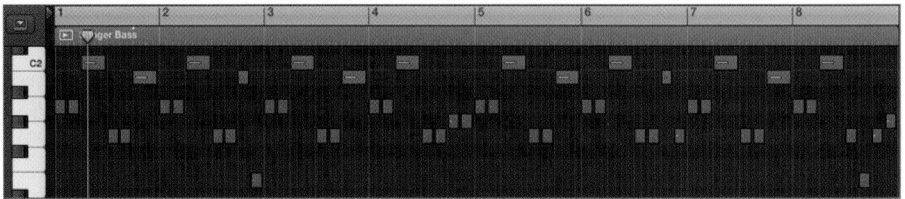

All C2 and B1 notes now have a slightly warmer color because they all have a velocity of 89.

11 Listen to the song. The accents on the quarter notes help make the bass groove better.

Continue adjusting the velocities of individual notes in the bass fills you created in the previous exercise to make them stand out a little, especially at the end of bar 8, during the drum fill on the Drummer track.

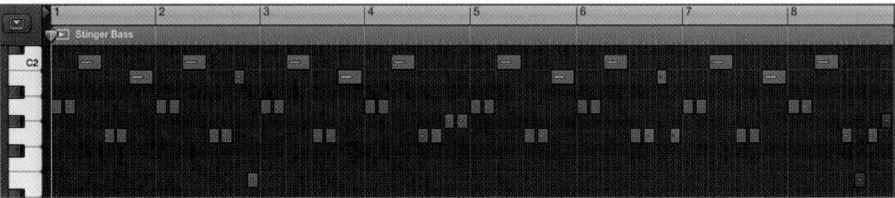

TIP ▶ You can Control-click the Drummer region and choose Convert > Convert to MIDI Region to edit the region in MIDI editors such as the Piano Roll Editor.

Creating MIDI Notes in the Score Editor

The Score Editor displays MIDI notes as standard Western music notation. If you prefer composing with notation, this could become your editor of choice. And even if you don't, you can use it to print sheet music for other musicians.

Creating an Organ Part in the Score Editor

Now that you have a rhythmic foundation with your drums and bass tracks, you will add a new organ track. Using the Score Editor, you will write a part where the left hand alternates with the right hand in a syncopated rhythm.

1   Choose Track > New Software Instrument Track (or press Command-Option-S).

2   In the Library, choose Vintage B3 Organ > Classic Rock Organ, and play your MIDI keyboard to hear the Classic Rock Organ patch.

3   Control-click the organ track in bar 1, and choose Create Empty MIDI Region.

4   At the top of the Piano Roll, click Score (or press N).

5   At the top of the Score Editor, drag the vertical zoom slider (or press Command-Down Arrow a few times) to zoom in.

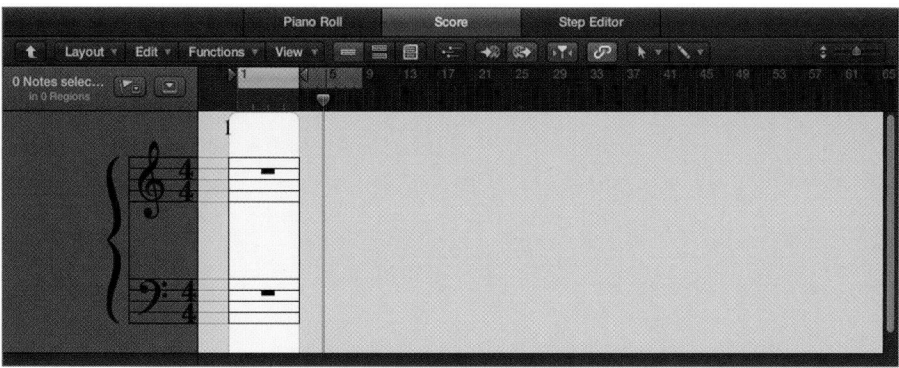

Make sure you can comfortably see both staves (a staff is a set of five lines).

6   In the inspector, from the Part box, drag a quarter note to the top staff in the Score
Editor to create an A3 at 1 1 1 1.

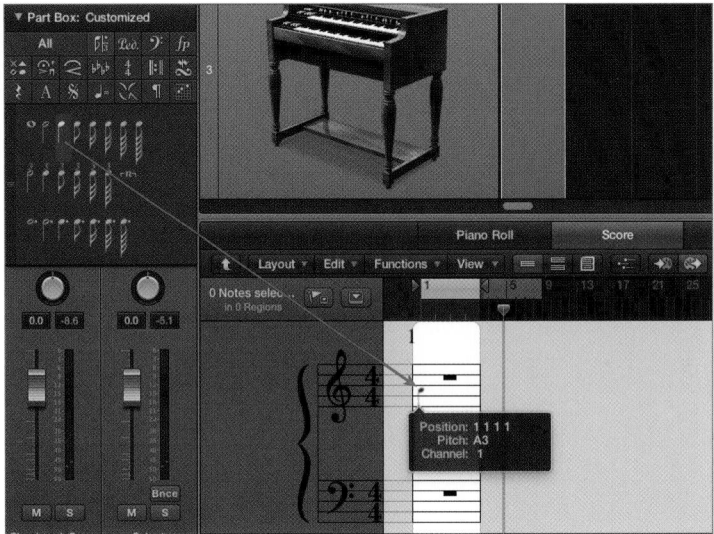

As you drag the note to the staff, you can hear the sound played on the instrument,
and a help tag displays the current position and pitch of the note. Let's copy that A3
to an A2 (one octave below).

TIP ▶ To open the Part box as a floating window, drag it out of the inspector by its
title bar.

7   In the Score Editor, Option-drag the A3 quarter note down one octave to an A2 at the
same position (1 1 1 1).

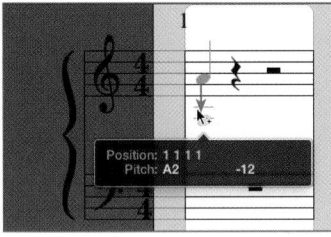

When you release the mouse button, the display updates and the new A2 note is
placed on the lower staff.

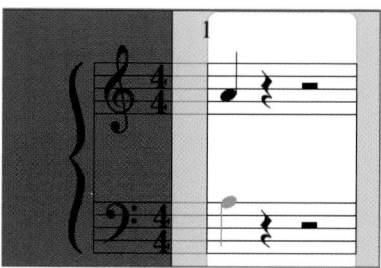

In the Score Editor, deselected notes are black, and selected notes are green.

You will now use the Pencil tool, your current Command-click tool, to create notes.

8   In the Part box, click the eighth note to select it.

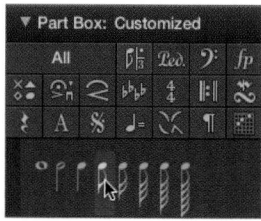

9   On the top staff, Command-drag to create and position a note until its help tag reads Position: 1 2 1 1 and Pitch: E4.

When you release the mouse button, the eighth note is created. It is displayed as a quarter note for now because in the Region inspector, the Interpretation checkbox is selected by default to produce legible music notation. If you want, you can open the Piano Roll to check the exact length of the note you entered.

10 Option-drag the E4 note up to a G4 at the same position (1 2 1 1), and listen to the song.

You have the beginning of a rhythmic organ part. You will now add syncopated notes to make it groove.

11 Drag a rectangle around the A2 and A3 notes at 1 1 1 1 to select them, and Option-drag the notes to 1 2 3 1. Be sure to drag them horizontally to keep the same pitches.

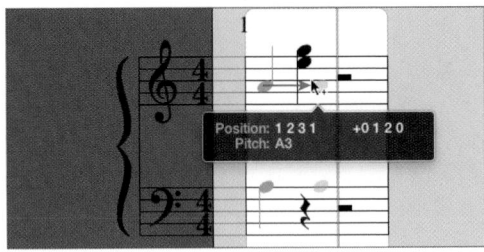

TIP While you're dragging, you can press Shift once to limit the dragging to one direction, either vertical or horizontal. While still dragging, press Shift again to return to the default behavior.

12 Drag a rectangle around the E4 and G4 notes at 1 2 1 1 to select them, and Option-drag them to 1 2 4 1, keeping the same pitches. Then listen to the organ.

The organ plays a grooving pattern. To change the last chord, let's change the pitch of the two last notes.

13 Click the background of the Score Editor to deselect the notes, and drag the last E4 to a D4, and the G4 to an F#4. Listen to the organ.

The new chord at the end gives the pattern more movement. Making some of the notes shorter could improve the groove, as you'll discover in the next exercise.

Adjusting Note Lengths in the Score Editor

As you observed in the previous exercise, the Score Editor doesn't always display the precise note lengths because doing so might make the notation virtually unreadable. However, you can choose to superimpose duration bars on the notes. You can then drag the right edge of the duration bars to adjust the note length in the same way you'd adjust the length of a note in the Piano Roll.

1 In the Score Editor, choose View > Duration Bars > All Notes.

Beams representing the length of the notes appear.

2   Select the A2 and A3 notes at 1 2 3 1.

3   Drag the right edge of the selected notes' duration bars to the left to shorten them to 0 0 0 232 (a few ticks short of a sixteenth note). Listen to the organ.

With the notes shortened, the organ grooves even better now. Let's duplicate the pattern in bar 2.

4   Drag a rectangle around all the notes (or press Command-A) to select them.

All the notes are green.

5   Choose Edit > Repeat Events (or press Command-R).

The Repeat Regions/Events dialog opens.

6   Set the Number of Copies to 1, ensure that Adjustment is still set to Bar, and click OK.

The same pattern is repeated in bar 2. Now you will slightly change the pattern in bar 2 to make the two first notes play on the upbeat.

7   Click the background to deselect all the notes. Select the A2 and A3 notes at the
beginning of bar 2, and drag them to the right to 2 1 3 1.

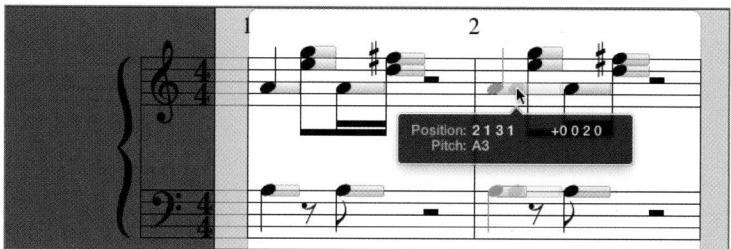

You will now shorten those two notes into eighth notes.

8   Resize the duration bar of one of the two selected notes to 0 0 1 232.

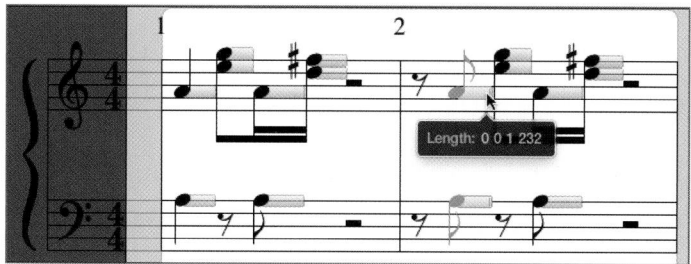

9   Click the background to deselect all the notes.

10   Choose View > Duration Bars > Off.

Using the Score Editor, you entered notes and adjusted their lengths to create an organ
rhythm part. However, some of the notes played by the left hand are displayed on the
upper staff, which makes the score difficult to read. You will fix that in the next exercise.

Adjusting the Score's Display

Let's now adjust the way the Score Editor displays your organ part so that notes played by the left hand are on the lower staff and notes played by the right hand are on the upper staff.

In Logic you have to first select a polyphonic style and then separate the notes into two voices (one for each staff).

1   In the Region inspector, set Style to Piano 1/3.

This choice places all the notes on the upper staff. You can separate them into two voices using the Voice Separation tool.

2   Click the Left-click Tool menu at the top of the Score Editor (or press T), and choose the Voice Separation tool (or press 7).

3   Drag the Voice Separation tool between the A octaves at the bottom and the chords at the top.

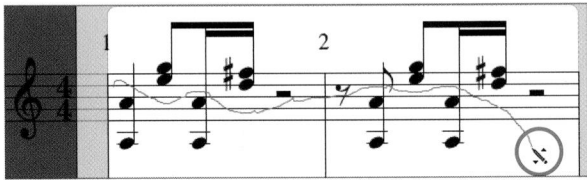

As you drag the Voice Separation tool, it draws a blue line.

> **TIP** ▶ If you make a mistake, don't release the mouse button. Instead, drag to the left to erase your mistake, then resume drawing the blue line.

4 Click the background to deselect all the notes.

The line you drew separates the notes shown on the treble clef from the note on the bass clef. A musician reading the score can clearly distinguish the notes played by the left hand (on the lower staff) from the ones played by the right hand (on the upper staff).

TIP ▶ To print or export a score as a PDF, make sure the Score Editor has key focus, and choose File > Print.

5 Listen to the organ.

You can't hear the notes on the lower staff! That's because when using the Piano 1/3 staff style, separating voices assigns the notes on the upper staff to MIDI channel 1 and the notes on the lower staff to MIDI channel 3. The Classic Rock Organ patch you chose earlier in the Library loads a multi-timbral Vintage B3 instrument plug-in on the channel strip, which uses different MIDI channels to trigger the upper and lower manuals (keyboards meant to be played with the hands) and pedals (keyboard meant to be played by the feet).

Let's open the Vintage B3 plug-in window and look at the MIDI channel assignments.

6 On the Classic Rock Organ channel strip in the Inspector, click the middle of the Vintage B3 plug-in slot to open its plug-in window.

7 At the bottom right of the Vintage B3 plug-in, click Split.

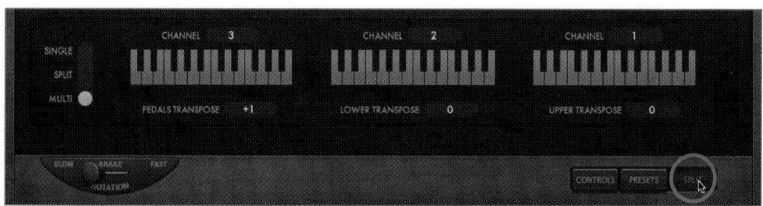

The three keyboards are displayed along with their MIDI channel (CHANNEL) assignments:

▶ Channel 3 triggers the pedals.

▶ Channel 2 triggers the lower manual.

▶ Channel 1 triggers the upper manual.

To have the left hand play the lower manual, you will make channel 3 trigger that lower manual.

8 Above the middle keyboard, set CHANNEL to 3.

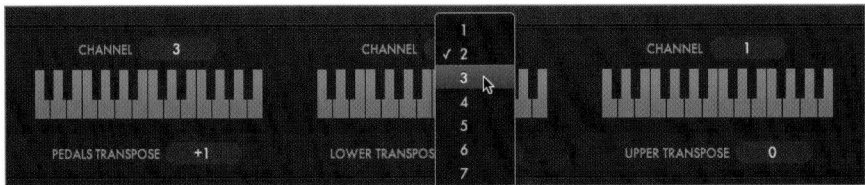

9 Close the Vintage B3 plug-in window, and listen to the organ.

This time you can hear the left hand (the notes on the lower staff, on MIDI channel 3) play the lower manual, while the right hand (the notes on the upper staff, on MIDI channel 1) play the upper manual.

Let's fill up the rest of the cycle area.

10 In the control bar, click the Editors button (or press E) to close the Score Editor.

11 In the workspace, place the mouse pointer in the upper right of the Classic Rock Organ region to get the Loop tool, and then drag to the right to extend the loops to the end of the cycle area.

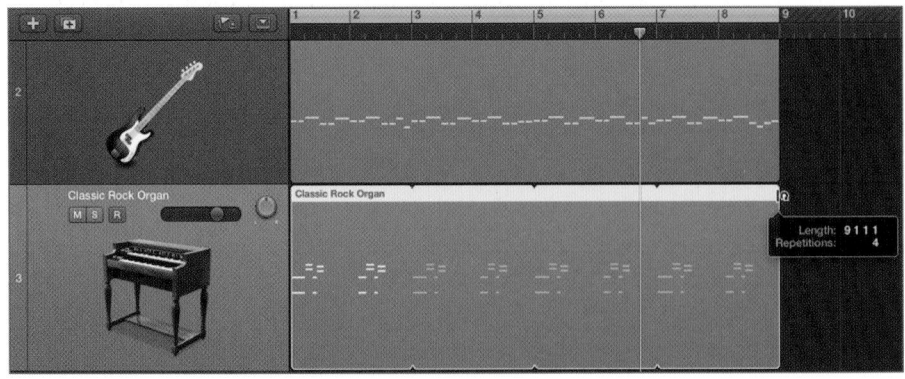

12 Listen to the song. The organ pattern sounds good, and the small rhythmic variation at the beginning of every other bar helps the groove.

In the Score Editor, you've created notes by dragging them from the Part box, copying existing notes, or using the Pencil tool. Finally you adjusted their lengths using duration bars. You have a grooving organ part that complements the drums and bass.

Importing a MIDI File

MIDI events recorded by software and hardware MIDI sequencers (including Logic) can be saved in standard MIDI file (SMF) format. Most sequencers can export and import standard MIDI files, which makes it easy to open them in multiple software sequencers, or share them with others.

In the following exercise, you will import a MIDI file containing an eight-bar synth performance that you'll edit later in the Event List.

1 In the control bar, click the Browsers button (or press F), and at the top of the Browsers area, click All Files.

The All Files Browser displays all the files on your hard drive that can be used by Logic: audio files, MIDI files, movie files, and Logic and GarageBand projects.

2 At the top of the All Files Browser, click the Home button to list the contents of your home folder.

3 Navigate to Desktop > Logic Pro X Files > Media > Additional Media and drag **Lead Synth.mid** to bar 1 at the bottom of the workspace.

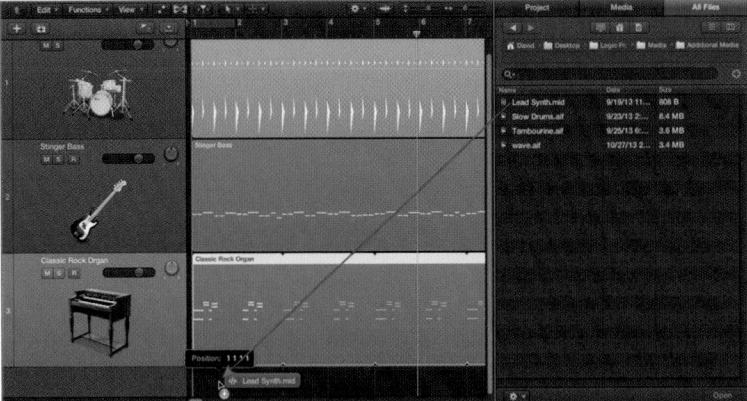

A new software instrument track is created, and a Steinway Grand Piano patch is loaded by default. An eight-bar region named Lead Synth is created on the track. The gray vertical bars in the region represent MIDI control events.

4 Listen to the song. You can hear a piano, but it's panned to the left and a little too low in volume.

5 In the Steinway Grand Piano track header, drag the Volume slider up, and drag the Pan knob to the center position. Start playback.

TIP ▶ In Logic, you can return most parameters to their default values by Option-clicking them. This is particularly useful to bring a Volume fader back to zero or a Pan knob to the center.

As the playhead jumps to bar 1 (the beginning of the cycle area) and playback starts, the Volume slider and the Pan knob revert to their original positions. MIDI files can contain controller volume and pan events, and when Logic plays those events, it uses them to set the volume and pan settings of the track. You'll use the Event List later to delete them.

6   Stop playback, and press Return to go to the beginning of the song.

TIP ▸ To export a MIDI region(s) as a standard MIDI file, select the region(s) in the workspace, and choose File > Export > Selection as MIDI File.

Editing MIDI Data in the Event List

The Event List shows MIDI events as text and numbers. Unlike other MIDI editors—such as the Piano Roll Editor or the Score Editor—which can be more convenient for creative tasks, the Event List displays all the MIDI events in a region, along with the exact numerical values of their attributes (such as MIDI channel, key number, velocity, and so on). While you probably won't use the Event List to compose, it can be a very powerful troubleshooting tool.

You will now open a MIDI file (that you imported in the previous exercise) in the Event List to locate and delete those MIDI events responsible for automatically setting the volume and pan on the channel strip.

1   In the control bar, click the Lists button to open the Event List.

The Event List displays all the MIDI events inside the selected Lead Synth region. You can see Control, Note, and C-Press (channel pressure, or aftertouch) events. A thin white horizontal playhead scrolls the events during playback. At the top of the Event

List, the first two MIDI events are a volume and a pan event. They are responsible for setting a specific volume and pan to the channel strip when playing that region. Let's delete all MIDI events that are not notes.

You can use the event type buttons to filter the events displayed.

2   Click the Notes event type button to disable it.

Note events are hidden. You will now delete all the Control and C-Press events.

3   In the Event List, choose Edit > Select > All (or press Command-A).

4   Choose Edit > Delete (or press Delete) to delete all the Control and C-Press events.

5   Click the Notes event type button to enable it.

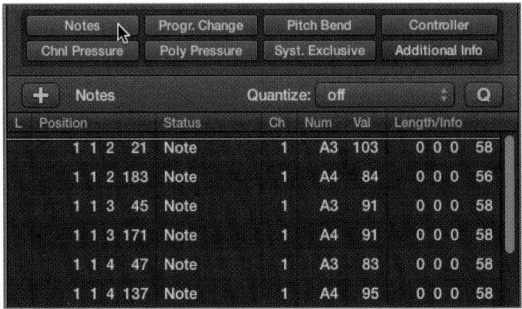

Notice that only Note events remain in the Lead Synth region.

6   Raise the volume and center the pan of the Steinway Grand Piano track and listen to the song.

This time the Volume slider and Pan knob in the track header stay put, and you can hear your piano loud and centered. Let's change the patch to a synth.

7   In the workspace, make sure the Steinway Grand Piano track is selected, and in the Library, choose Synthesizer > Lead > Citrus Fuzz. Listen to the song.

The synth plays a lot of fast notes, and then plays a very simple melody. You will breathe new life onto the synth performance later in this lesson by inserting your own controller events.

Quantizing Pitches, Scales, and Timings of MIDI Notes

In this exercise you will quantize note pitches to certain keys and scales, forcing them to snap to the nearest note in that key. You will also quantize their timings to a grid, and adjust the strength of the quantizations to retain some of the human feel from the original performance.

1   In the workspace, double-click the Lead Synth region to open it in the Piano Roll Editor, and press Z to see all the notes.

2   Select all five notes in bars 4 and 5.

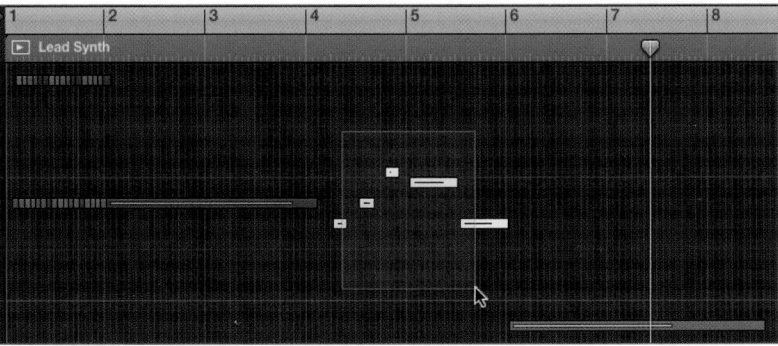

Let's try to play the selected notes in another key.

3   In the Piano Roll inspector, from the left Scale Quantize pop-up menu, choose A. Listen to the song.

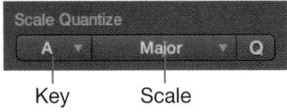

The notes jump to pitches in the key of A Major. You can use the Scale Quantize feature to experiment with playing a melody or chord progression in different keys. In this case, though, the original notes worked best.

4   From the Scale Quantize pop-up menu, choose Off to return the notes to their original pitches. Listen to the song again.

This time pay attention to the timing of the selected notes. It sounds as if the notes are really behind the beat.

5   Press Z to zoom in on the selected notes.

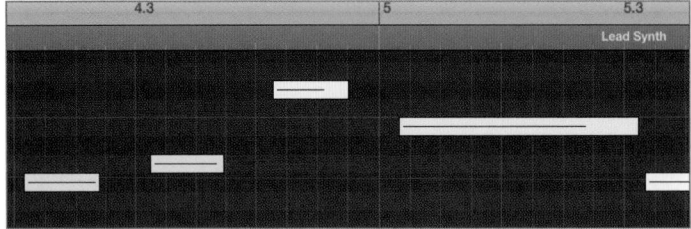

On the grid, you can see that the notes start late.

6   In the Piano Roll inspector, from the Time Quantize pop-up menu, choose 1/4 Note.

The notes snap to the nearest beat.

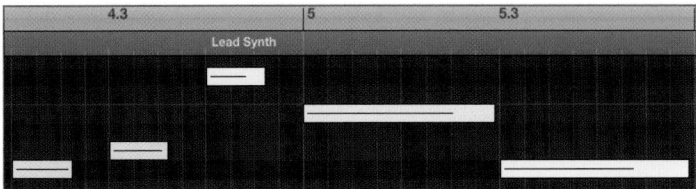

Listen to the song. The notes you've quantized are perfectly in time. But rather than snapping the notes to a rigid grid, you want to retain some of the original feel using the Time Quantize Strength slider.

As the song plays, the Piano Roll constantly updates its display to show the position of the playhead. After you've stopped playback, the notes you wanted to see are still selected, so you can press Z to bring them back into view.

7   Press Z. The selected notes fill the Piano Roll.

8   In the Piano Roll inspector, drag the Strength slider down to 50.

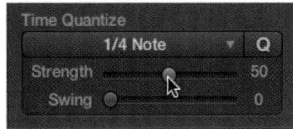

The notes are now positioned halfway between their original positions and the nearest quarter note on the grid.

9   In the Piano Roll, click the background to deselect all notes, and press Z to display all the notes. Listen to the song.

The synth's timing sounds better, but it still retains a bit of its original laid-back feel.

Creating a Crescendo Using Note Velocity

In the following exercise, you will employ a new technique to edit the velocity of the very fast notes at the beginning of the synth region, and make them play a crescendo (scaling note velocities from lower to higher values).

1   At the top of the Piano Roll, click the MIDI Draw button (or press Command-Y).

MIDI Draw button

The MIDI Draw area opens at the bottom of the Piano Roll.

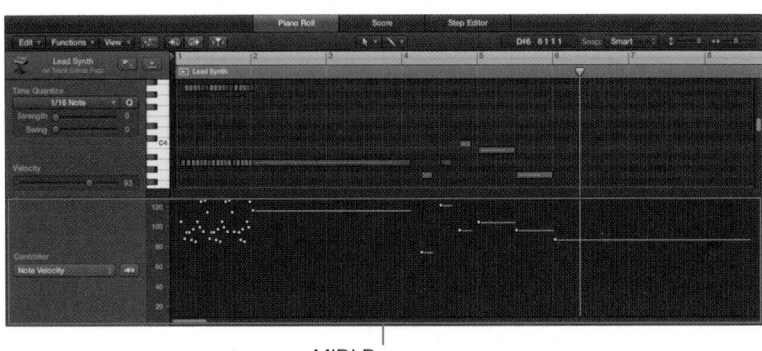

MIDI Draw area

TIP ▶ If you need more display space to work in, choose Window > Open Piano Roll (or press Command-4) to open a full-screen Piano Roll window.

The MIDI Draw area displays the velocity of each MIDI note as a node, along with a line representing the length of the note. The height of each node represents the velocity of the note above it on the grid. You adjust the velocity of a note by vertically dragging the node (not the line).

2   Drag up the node of the first note in bar 4 to raise its velocity.

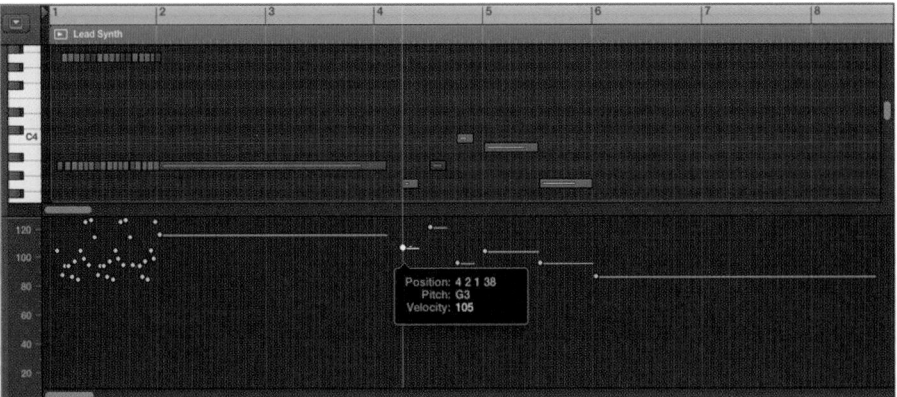

As you drag the node, a help tag shows you the position, pitch, and velocity of the note. When you release the mouse button, the color of the note beam in the Piano Roll updates to reflect the new velocity.

3   Listen to the fast notes at the beginning. They all sound fairly loud. You will now draw a line in the MIDI Draw area to create a crescendo in bar 1.

4   In the MIDI Draw area, drag with the pointer to draw a line up from the lower left to the beginning of the long, sustained note at bar 2.

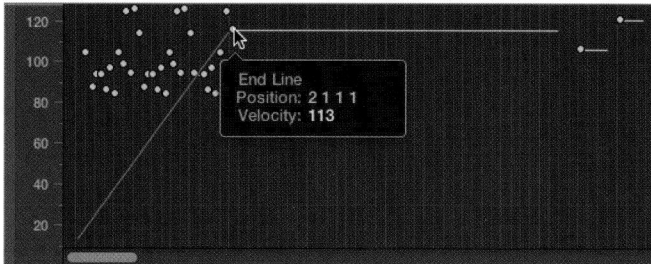

The note velocities are aligned to the green line you drew.

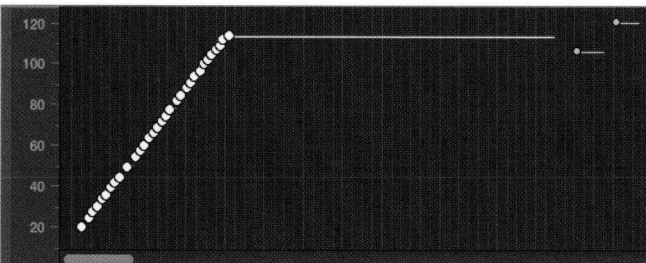

5   Listen to the synth. You can hear the notes crescendo; however, the first few notes are very soft and you can barely hear them.

Let's raise the velocity of all the notes while keeping the crescendo you just drew.

6   In the Piano Roll inspector, drag the Velocity slider all the way up, and listen to the synth.

The velocities of all the selected notes are raised by the same amount, and the crescendo is now louder. In fact, the crescendo could use a gentler slope so that the sustained note in bar 2 doesn't have such a high velocity.

7 With the notes still selected, in the MIDI Draw area, drag down the node of the sustained note at bar 2.

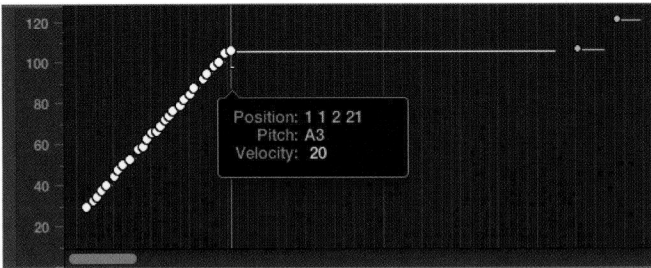

This time the note velocities are adjusted proportionately. For example, if you dragged one selected note velocity to half of its value, then the velocities of all the other selected notes are also halved. This gives your crescendo a gentler slope.

8 Listen to the synth. It is now easier to hear the first few notes, but the last note is no longer too loud.

TIP You can also use MIDI Draw in the Score Editor by clicking the MIDI Draw button at the top; and in the Tracks area by selecting one or more regions and choosing View > MIDI Draw > Autodefine (or pressing Command-Y).

Creating and Editing MIDI Continuous Controllers

When playing a MIDI keyboard, you can add expression to your performance using knobs, sliders, wheels (such as the pitch bend and modulation wheels), or a volume pedal. Manipulating those controllers sends a stream of control events that represent the movement of the controller knob and trigger an action on the instrument.

When programming MIDI, you can draw a stream of control events to alter an instrument's volume, pitch, and other parameters. In the following exercises, you will use the Logic MIDI editors to automate pitch bend and modulation in the synth MIDI region.

MORE INFO ► Control data is often referred to as region-based automation, as opposed to track-based automation, which you'll explore in Lesson 10.

Automating Pitch Bend Data in MIDI Draw

Adding pitch glides at the beginnings or ends of notes can make a MIDI sequence sound musical. Let's enliven your synth performance by bending the pitch in various places, and adding a vibrato at the end of a sustained note.

1   In the MIDI Draw inspector, from the Controller pop-up menu, choose Pitch Bend.

The MIDI Draw inspector shows an empty canvas, ready for you to draw pitch bend automation. First, you will draw a pitch drop from the beginning to the end of the fast notes in bar 1. You can use the Pencil tool, your current Command-click tool, to enter new control points.

2   At the upper left of the MIDI Draw area, Command-click to create a control point.

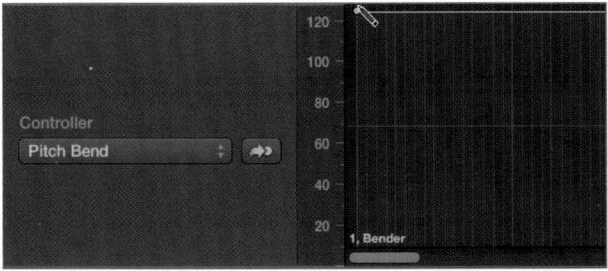

TIP ► You can also double-click with the pointer to create control points.

3   In the lower part of the MIDI Draw area, Command-click at bar 2 to get a value of about –62. Listen to the first bar of the synth.

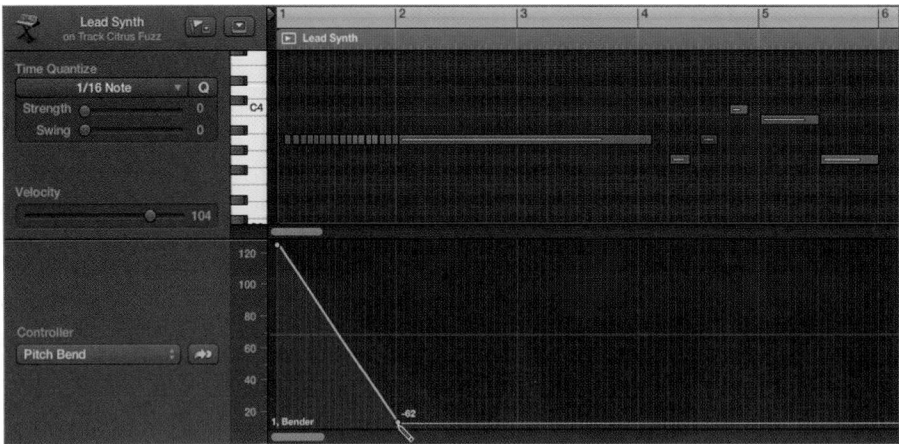

You can hear the fast notes drop down in pitch throughout bar 1. However, the rest of the notes play at the wrong pitch. To play the remaining notes at their correct pitches, you must return the pitch to the horizontal gray middle line, which represents the position of the 0 value (the center position on a MIDI keyboard's Pitch Bend wheel).

4   A little before bar 3, Command-click to create a control point on the horizontal green line that has the same value as the previous control point you created.

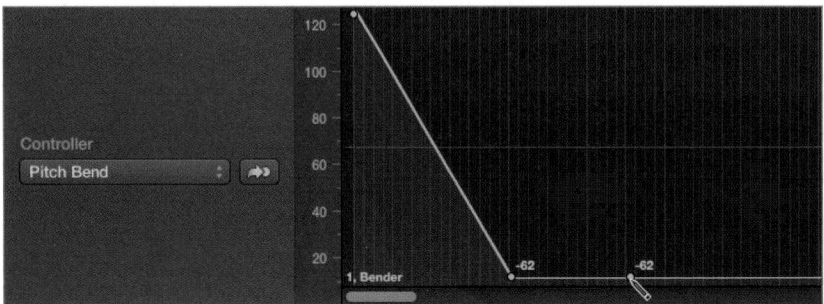

Predicting the exact value of a control point you create can be a bit tricky in the MIDI Draw area. If you didn't get the right value, use the Pointer tool to drag the control point up or down to the same value as the previous control point.

TIP ▶ To delete a control point, double-click it with the Pointer tool. To delete multiple control points, drag around them to select them, and then press Delete on your keyboard.

5 A little after bar 3, create a control point, and drag it to a value of 0. Listen to the synth.

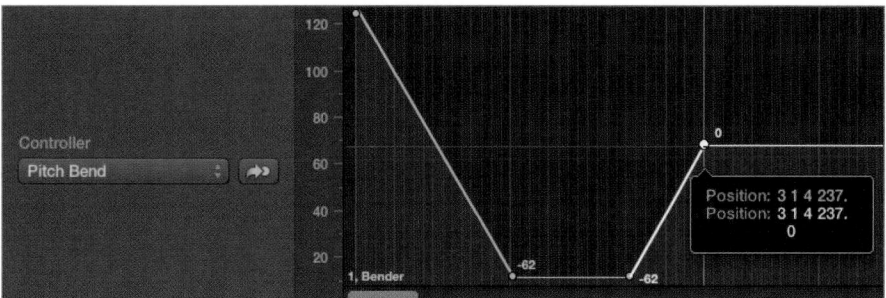

The pitches of the fast notes in bar 2 drop over a range of four semitones, then the sustained note is bent at bar 3, going back up two semitones. You will make the pitch variations more pronounced by increasing the pitch bend range.

The MIDI pitch bend events do not include any pitch bend range information, so it's up to the instrument receiving the events to determine which pitch bend range to use. As with the instrument used here, most instruments default to a range of two semitones above or below the original pitch. And most instruments allow you to adjust the pitch bend range. You will now open the ES2 instrument plug-in on the Citrus Fuzz channel strip in the inspector to adjust its pitch bend range.

6 On the Citrus Fuzz channel strip, click the middle of the instrument slot.

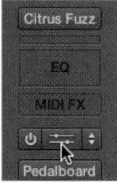

The ES2 plug-in opens.

Pitch bend range

7   In the ES2, set the upward Bend range field to 12 semitones (one octave).

Upward Bend range ——— Downward Bend range

The downward Bend range field is set to *link,* which means that the downward Bend range value is set the same as the upward Bend range value. You can now bend notes up to one octave above or one octave below the original pitch.

8   Listen to the synth. The fast notes at the beginning drop down two octaves, then the sustained note comes back up one octave to the original pitch.

However, unless you got very lucky, the beginning of the sustained note sounds out of tune. You most likely need to adjust the pitch bend value in that section to make sure that it is all the way down (so that part of the note is exactly one octave lower than the original pitch of the note).

9   Close the ES2 plug-in window (or press Command-W).

10 In the MIDI Draw area, drag down the horizontal line between the two control points in bar 2 all the way to a value of –64. Listen to the synth again.

This time the beginning of that sustained note sounds in key, exactly one octave below the original pitch.

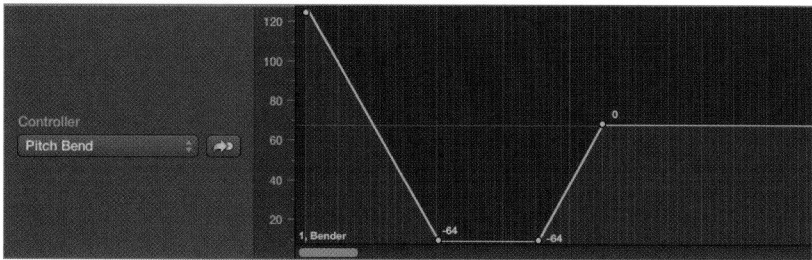

Holding down Control-Shift turns the pointer into an Automation Curve tool you can use to curve the lines joining two control points of different values. (You can't curve a horizontal line.)

11 Control-Shift-drag the line between the –64 and 0 values (around bar 3).

Drag up or down to create a convex or concave curve, respectively. Drag left or right to create a horizontal or vertical S curve, respectively.

> **TIP** To create more complex shapes, drag the Pencil tool to draw the desired automation.

12 Control-Shift-drag that same line to the right to create an S curve.

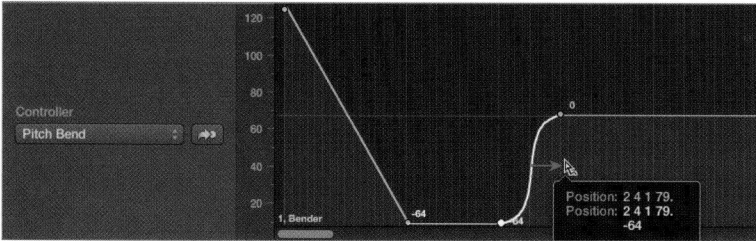

The pitch glide in the middle of the sustained note is now a little faster.

> **TIP** In MIDI Draw, Control-Shift-click a curved line to revert to a straight line.

Copying MIDI Control Data in MIDI Draw

Let's continue automating the pitch bend data in the Lead Synth region. You will raise the next three notes in bar 4 from lower pitches to their correct pitches at the beginning of each note. Then, create the desired pitch bend automation for one note, and copy it to the two other notes.

1 In the Piano Roll, zoom in on the three quarter notes in bar 4.

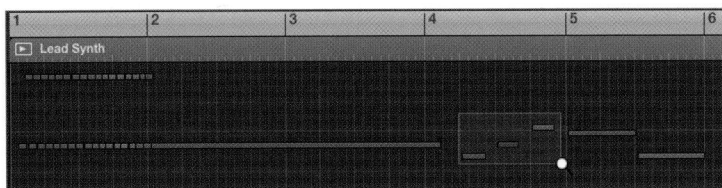

2 Command-click the green line to create a control point to the left of the first note, and make sure it has a value of 0.

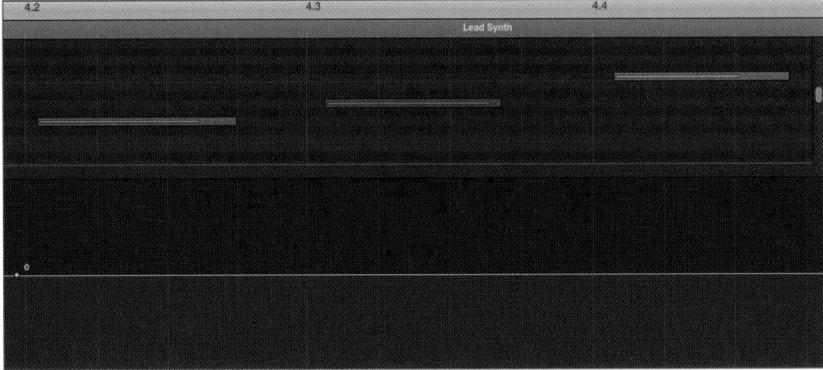

3 Create a control point about halfway down, and drag it horizontally between the previous control point and the beginning of the note.

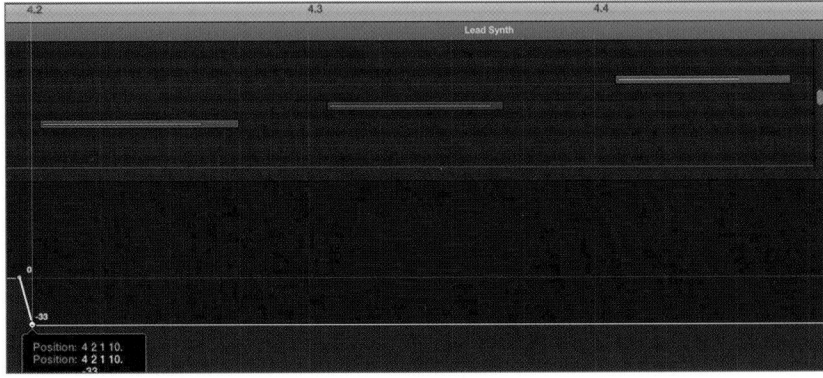

4 Create a control point a little before the middle of the note with a value of 0. Listen to your synth.

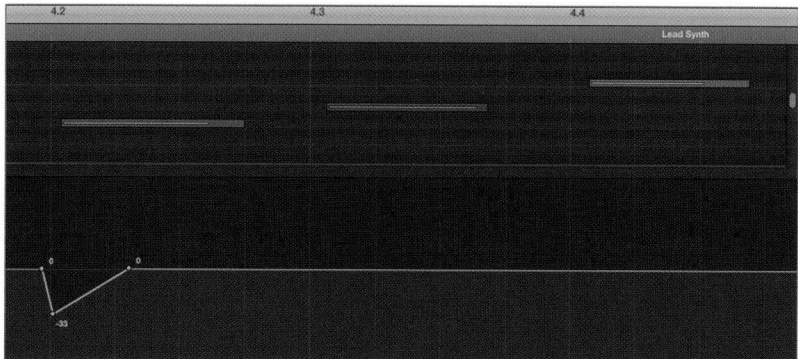

The note now starts on a low pitch and raises up to the correct pitch (similar to the way Frank Sinatra often glided up into the correct pitch).

You will now apply the same pitch bend automation to the two following notes.

5   At the bottom of the Piano Roll, drag the horizontal scroll bar to scroll back to the three notes in bar 4.

6   Drag a selection rectangle around the three control points at the beginning of the first note.

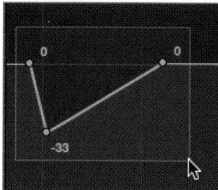

7   Option-drag the selected pitch bend data to the beginning of the second note.

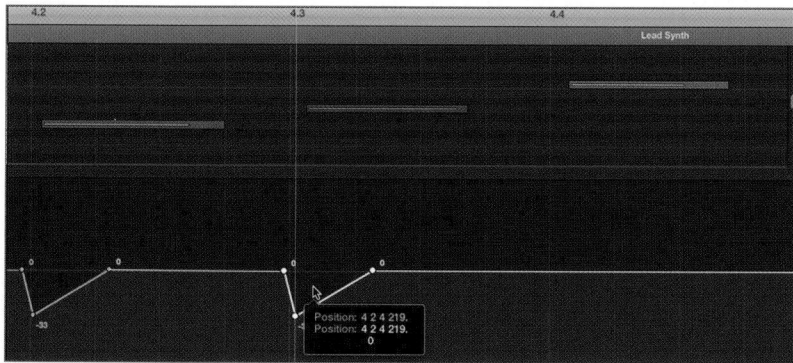

8 Option-drag the selected pitch bend data below the second note to the beginning of the third note. Listen to your synth.

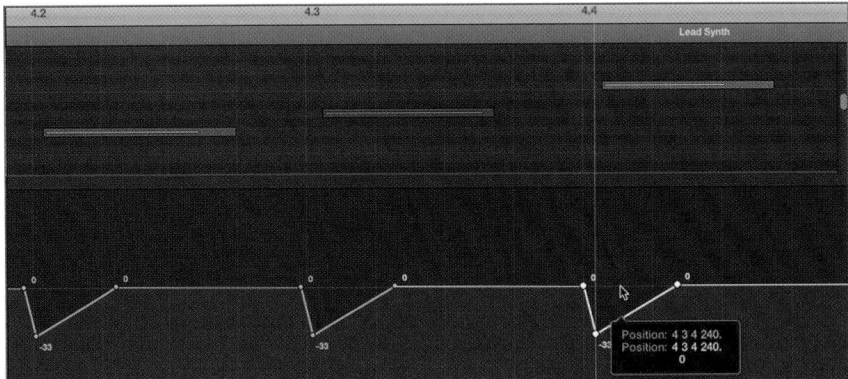

All three notes have their pitches raising to their correct pitches at the beginning of each note, which makes them more expressive.

9 Using the techniques you've learned in this exercise, drop down the pitch of the last sustained note in the region an entire octave before the end of the note (around bar 8).

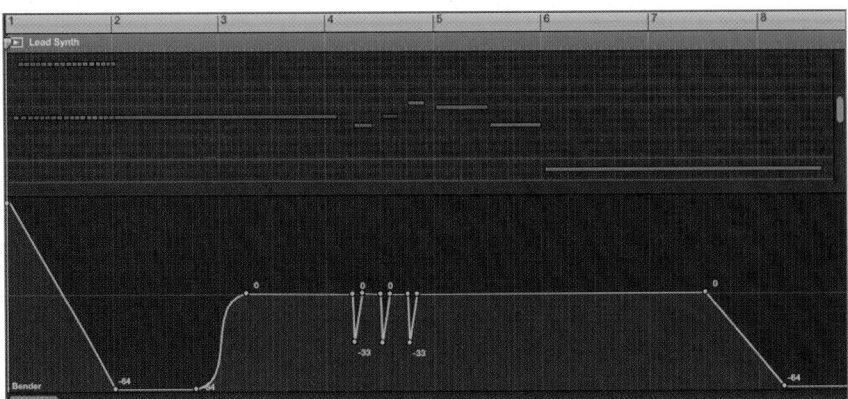

Automating Modulation Data in MIDI Draw

When listening to singers or string players, you may notice that they often use vibrato, and tend to use it more toward the end of sustained notes. On synthesizers, the modulation wheel (often located to the left of the keys) frequently controls the depth of the vibrato. You will now add some modulation automation to the synth to add vibrato to the end of the first sustained note.

1   In the MIDI Draw inspector, from the Controller pop-up menu, choose Modulation.

2   At bar 3, in the very bottom of the MIDI Draw area, Command-click to create a control point with a value of 0.

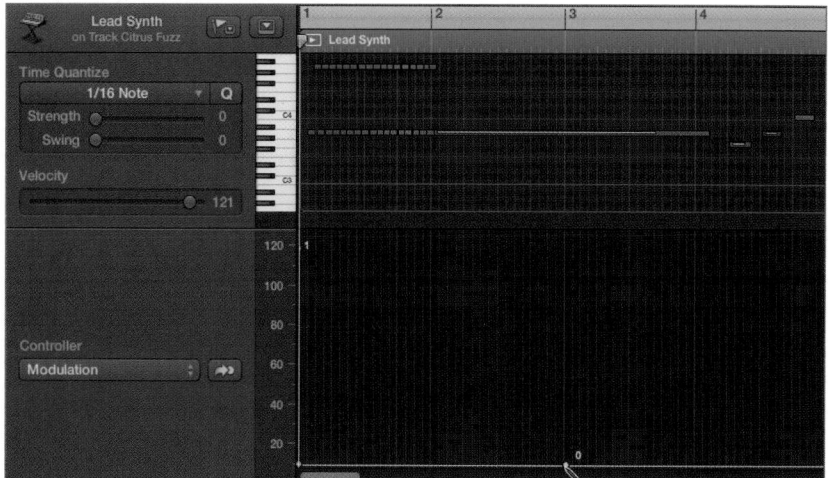

Notice that Logic creates another control point with the same value at the beginning of the region.

NOTE ► If the control point you entered doesn't have the right value, drag down the horizontal line between the two points to adjust both values simultaneously.

3   In the middle of bar 3, at the very top of the MIDI Draw area, Command-click to create a control point with a value of 126. Listen to your synth.

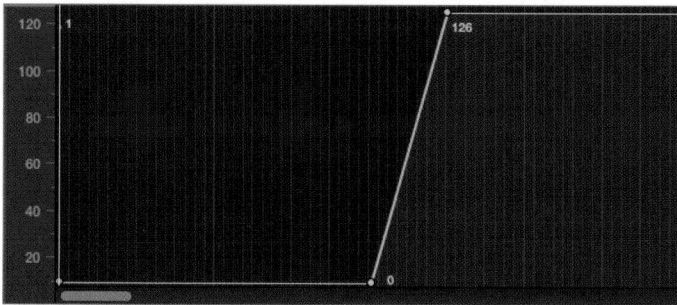

You can hear the vibrato effect come in after the sustained note's pitch goes up an octave at bar 3. However, the vibrato currently stays at its maximum value for the remainder of the region.

4 In the MIDI Draw area, create a control point with a value of 126 right after the end of the sustained note.

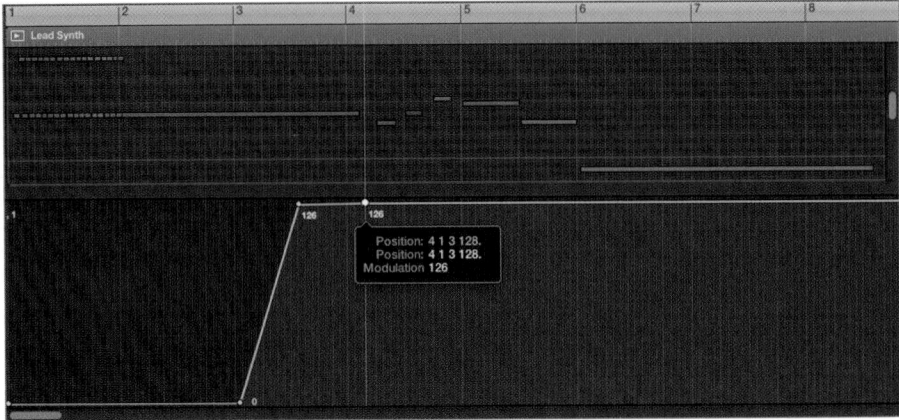

5 Create a control point with a value of 0 after the point you just created, but before the beginning of the next note. Listen to your synth.

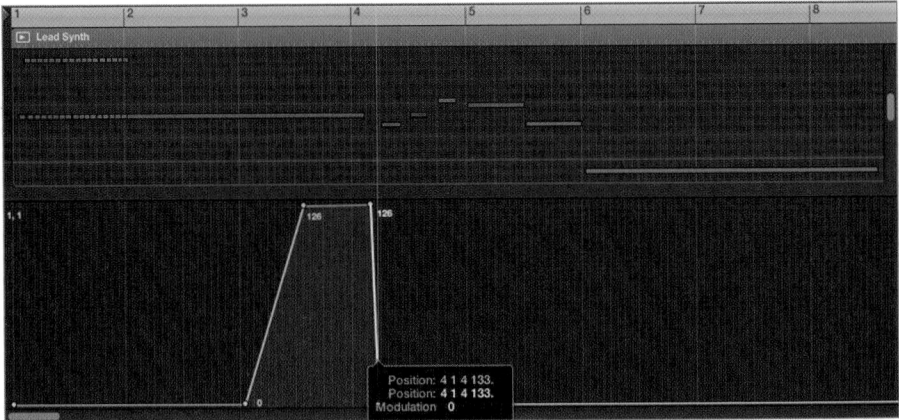

Now the vibrato applies only to the first sustained note, and the next notes don't have any. This synth is now much more expressive than it was when you originally imported its MIDI file into the project. You will now add some audio effects to add even more life to the sound.

6   In the control bar, click the Smart Controls button (or press B).

7   Drag the Delay knob to about three quarters of its range, and drag the Scream knob halfway up.

8   Listen to the song, and adjust other Smart Controls knobs as you listen to their effect on the synth sound.

9   Now that you're done editing the synth, you can turn it down (try about –10 dB), then turn the organ down a bit as well (around –4 dB). It may seem like the mix is weaker, so turn up your monitoring level on your audio interface (or by clicking the speaker icon in the Mac main menu bar) to compensate.

Bringing down the synth and organ should result in more clearly hearing the drums and bass.

In this lesson, you used three different MIDI editors—the Piano Roll Editor, the Score Editor, and the Event List—to create and edit note and control data. But they can do so much more! The MIDI editors in Logic are powerful tools that include numerous options and features.

When trying to perform a specific task, don't hesitate to look through an editor's local menu, or to Control-click an event or an area of the editor to access the shortcut menus. Chances are, you will find the feature you are looking for and discover even more useful features you wouldn't have imagined.

Lesson Review

1. How do you create an empty MIDI region?

2. How do you create notes in the Piano Roll Editor?

3. How do you adjust note lengths in the Piano Roll Editor?

4. How do you adjust the velocity of notes in the Piano Roll Editor?

5. How do you create notes in the Score Editor?

6. How do you adjust note lengths in the Score Editor?

7. How do you create a crescendo using note velocities?

8. How do you create control data?

9. How do you curve lines in MIDI Draw?

10. How do you copy a section of automation in MIDI Draw?

Answers

1. In the workspace, Control-click a software instrument track, and from the shortcut menu, choose Create Empty MIDI Region.

2. Click with the Pencil tool.

3. Drag the right edge of the note beam to resize the note.

4. Drag notes vertically with the Velocity tool.

5. Drag notes from the Part box, or select a note value in the Part box and click the staff with the Pencil tool.

6. Choose View > Duration Bars > All and drag the right edge of the duration bars.

7. In the MIDI Draw inspector, ensure that Velocity is chosen, and draw a line in the MIDI Draw area.

8. Choose a controller in the MIDI Draw inspector, and click the Pencil tool to create control points.

9. Hold down Control-Shift and drag a line between two control points of different values.

10. Drag a rectangle around control points to select them and Option-drag the selection.

Keyboard Shortcuts

Editing

Command-A	Selects all

Piano Roll

Left Arrow	Selects the note to the left of the selected note
Right Arrow	Selects the note to the right of the selected note
Option-Up Arrow	Transposes the selected note up one semitone
Option-Down Arrow	Transposes the selected note down one semitone
Shift-Option-Up Arrow	Transposes the selected note up one octave
Shift-Option-Down Arrow	Transposes the selected note down one octave

Windows and Panes

N	Opens the Score Editor
E	Opens the Editors area
F	Opens the Browsers area
D	Shows or hides the List editors
Command-Y	Shows or hides the MIDI Draw area
Command-4	Opens a Piano Roll window

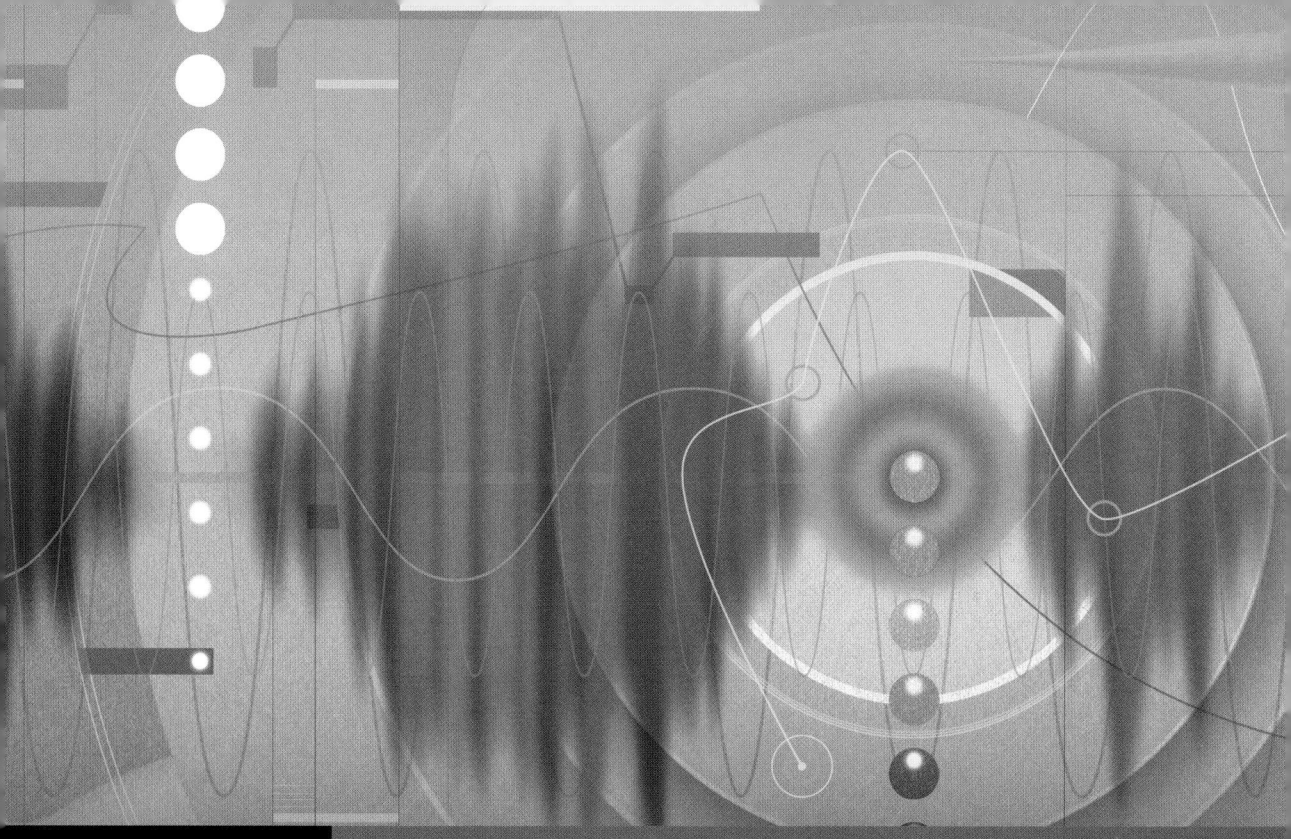

Building a Song

7

Lesson Files

Time

This lesson takes approximately 90 minutes to complete.

Goals

Match a project tempo to an audio file's tempo

Create Apple Loops

Add tempo changes and tempo curves

Apply tape or turntable speed-up and slow-down effects

Make one track follow the groove of another track

Use Varispeed effects

Edit the timing of an audio region

Edit note pitches in an audio region

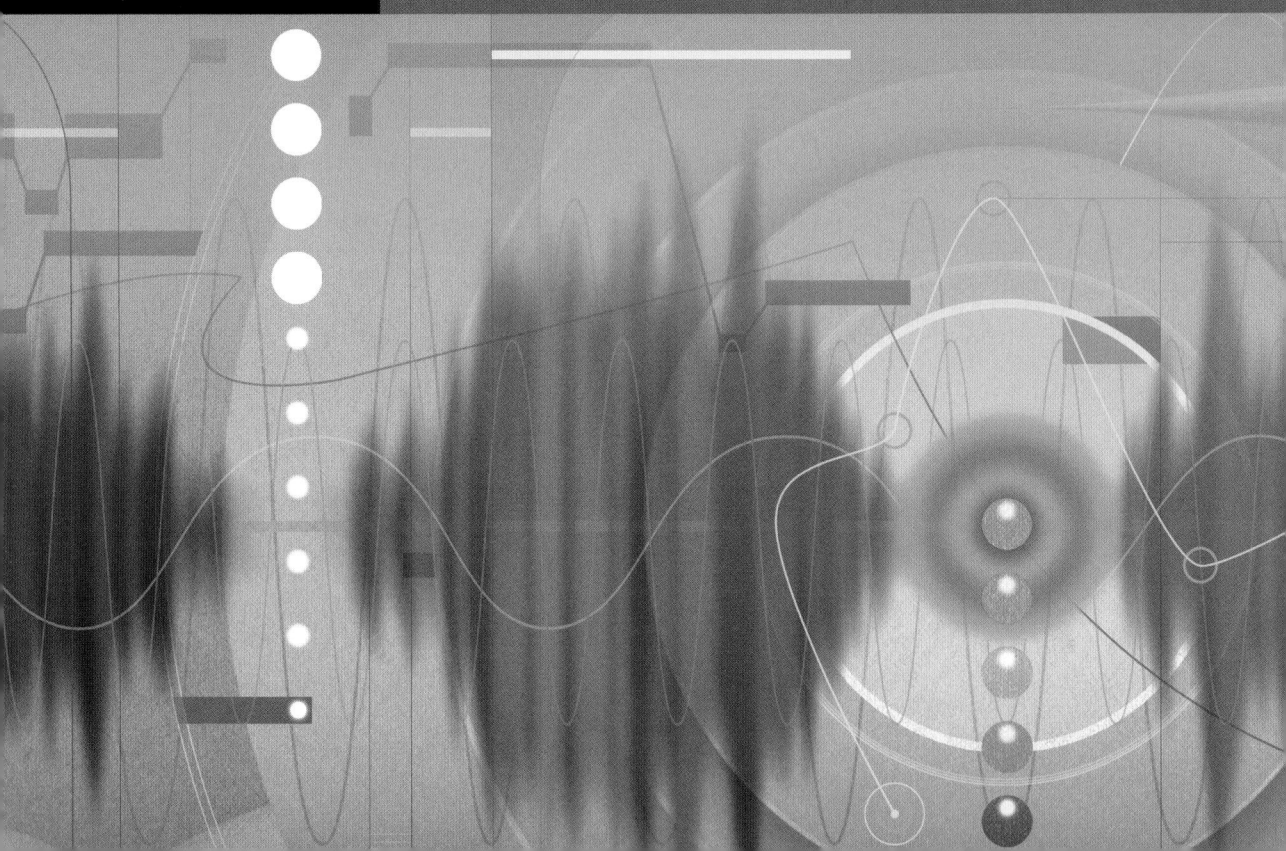

Editing Pitch and Time

The use of loops and samples has become omnipresent in modern music. New technologies encourage experimentation, and it is more and more common to find, say, a sample of a Middle Eastern instrument in a modern rock song, a sample of classical music in a pop song, or a sample of a pop song in a hip hop track.

Mixing prerecorded material into a project can lead to exciting results, but the material must be carefully selected to ensure that it seamlessly blends into the project. The first challenge is to match the prerecorded musical material's tempo with the project's tempo.

Even when you record your own performances, precisely correcting the pitch and timing of an individual note can help you realize the perfection expected by a demanding audience. As with any tool, you can use note correction to fix imprecisions (or mistakes) in the recording, or you can use it creatively. Furthermore, special effects such as Varispeed and tape speed-up or slow-down can provide new inspiration.

In this lesson, you will match the tempo and groove of audio files to make sure they combine into a musical whole. You'll manipulate the project tempo to add tempo changes and tempo curves, apply Varispeed and Speed Fade effects, and use Flex editing to precisely adjust the position and length of individual notes and correct the pitch of a vocal recording.

Setting a Project Tempo by Detecting the Tempo of a Recording

While listening to various recordings, you've found a recording of drums you like because of the way it grooves at its original tempo. To build a project around it, you need to adjust the project's tempo to match the recording. When the two tempos match, you can use the grid to edit and quantize regions, or add Apple Loops and keep everything synchronized.

In this exercise, you will import a drums recording into a new project, let Logic detect the tempo of the drums, and set it as the project tempo.

1   Choose File > New (or press Command-Shift-N).

2   In the New Tracks dialog, choose Audio, and click Create.

3   In the control bar, click the Browsers button (or press F).

4   With the All Files tab selected, navigate to Desktop > Logic Pro X Files > Media > Additional Media, and drag **Slow Drums.aif** to bar 1 on the audio track.

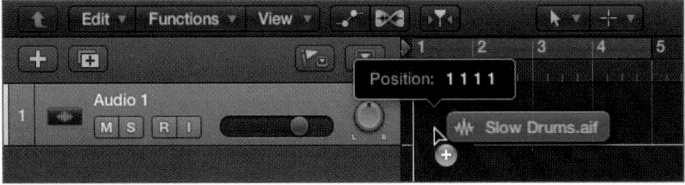

The new Slow Drums region spans about 25 bars at the current project tempo (120 bpm).

5   In the control bar, click the Metronome button (or press K) and listen to the drums.

At first, the metronome plays twice as fast as the drums, which were probably recorded at close to half the current project tempo (close to 60 bpm). After a few bars, the metronome and the drums drift out of sync.

6   In the workspace, with the Slow Drums region selected, choose Edit > Tempo > Adjust Tempo Using Beat Detection (or press Option-Command-T).

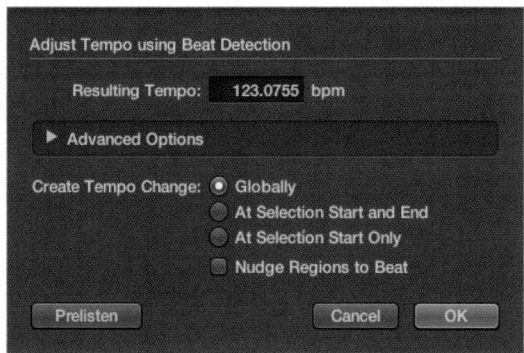

The "Adjust Tempo using Beat Detection" dialog opens, and identifies a resulting tempo of 123.0755 bpm. However, the drums tempo is actually half as fast.

7   In the dialog, click the Advanced Options disclosure triangle.

8   In Advanced Options, set Adjust Value By to 1:2.

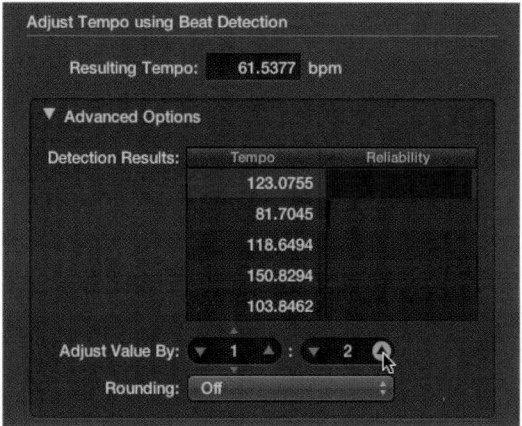

At the top of the dialog, the tempo is adjusted by a ratio of 1/2 with a resulting tempo of 61.5377 bpm. It's rare to work with a tempo that has so many digits after the decimal point, so let's round off that value.

9   From the Rounding pop-up menu, choose 1 Decimal to create a resulting tempo of 61.5 bpm.

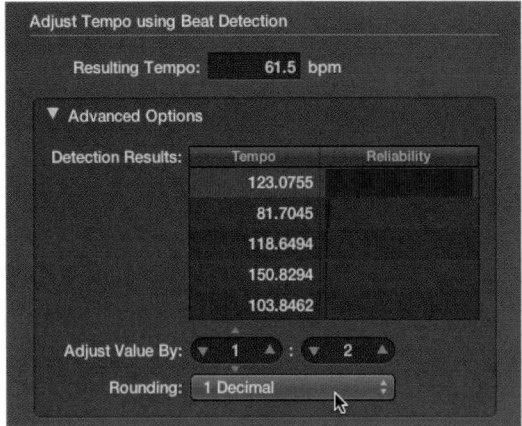

10 Click OK.

In the LCD display, the tempo is rounded to the nearest integer, and is displayed as 62 bpm. Let's switch to the custom LCD display to see the exact tempo.

11 In the LCD display, click the note and metronome icons, and choose Custom.

The custom LCD display shows the exact tempo with four decimals, 61.5000 bpm.

12 Listen to the song. The drums are perfectly in sync with the metronome; in fact the metronome is often inaudible because it is masked by the drums.

13 Click the Metronome button (or press K) to turn it off.

Now that you've set the project tempo to match the drums tempo, you can add Apple Loops and they will automatically match the tempo of your drums. You can also use the grid in the workspace to cut an exact numbers of bars in a region, which you'll need later in this lesson to cut a drum loop.

Using and Creating Apple Loops

Apple Loops are AIFF or CAF format audio files containing additional information that allows them to automatically match the tempo and key when they're imported into a Logic project. They also contain descriptive information (such as instrument, mood, genre, and scale) that helps you search the vast library of loops using the Loop Browser.

Using the Loop Browser

You were introduced to the Loop Browser in Lesson 1 when you previewed and chose loops to create a project. You will now use it to add two Apple Loops to your drums track.

1   In the control bar, click the Apple Loops button (or press O).

2   At the top of the Loop Browser, from the Loop pop-up menu, choose Hip Hop.

Let's try to find a couple of loops that were recorded at a tempo close to the current project tempo (61.5 bpm).

3   At the top of the results list, click the Tempo column header.

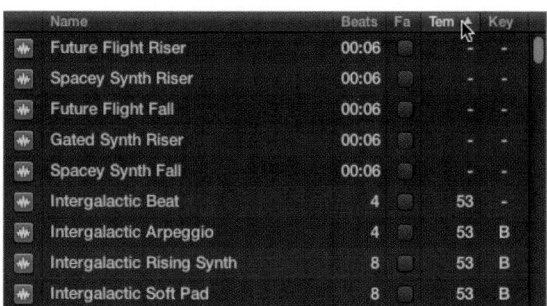

In the results list, the loops are reordered by ascending tempos. Note that the first few loops do not have any tempo information, because they don't contain any rhythmic material.

4   Click Intergalactic Beat to preview it.

That loop sounds as if it would work with the drums recording.

5   Drag Intergalactic Beat to the workspace, below the drums track at bar 1.

6   Place the mouse pointer over the upper-right edge of the Intergalactic Beat region so it turns into the Loop tool, and then drag to loop the region until bar 12.

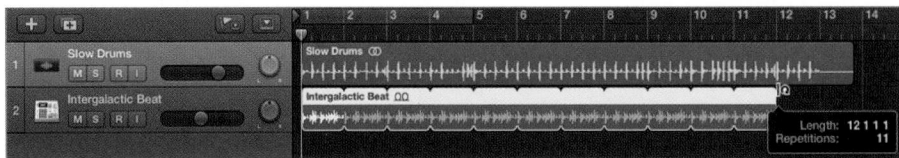

Let's add a synth loop.

7   In the Loop Browser, click Intergalactic Rising Synth to preview it.

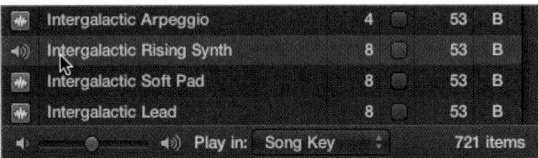

Intergalactic Rising Synth plays in the current project key, which is C, by default. The loop's original key, displayed in the results list, is B. Let's listen to the loop in its original key.

8   At the bottom of the Loop Browser, from the "Play in" pop-up menu, choose Original Key.

The loop now plays in B.

9   Drag Intergalactic Rising Synth to bar 2 below the tracks in the workspace.

NOTE ▶ Apple Loops are automatically transposed to match the root note of the project's key signature. However, they do not match the tonality, so loops sound the same, for example, in C major and in C minor.

10 Loop the region until bar 13.

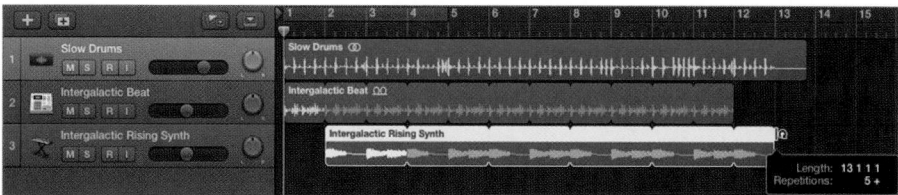

Listen to the song. The synth loop is once again playing in the key of the project, C.

You will now stop the drums on track 1 at the same position as the Intergalactic Beat loop.

11 Command-drag the Slow Drums region from bar 12 to the end of the region.

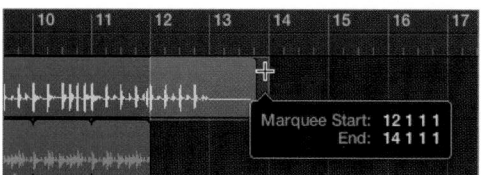

Make sure that your marquee selection starts exactly on 12 1 1 1, but don't worry if the marquee selection goes beyond the end of the region (since there's nothing to delete after the region).

12 Press Delete. This creates a click sound at the end of the Slow Drums region that you'll fix later.

The Slow Drums region now ends at bar 12, as does the Intergalactic Beat loop on track 2.

Setting a Project's Key Signature

Loops generally sound more natural when they're played in their original keys. Their sound is closer to their producer's original intention, and with no transposition to process, the timbre of the loop is closest to the original recording, and you hear fewer artifacts (distortion resulting from the time-stretching or pitch-shifting process).

Let's change the key of the project to B minor, the original key of the synth loop you imported on track 3.

1   In the control bar, click the Lists button.

2   At the top of the Lists area, click the Signature tab.

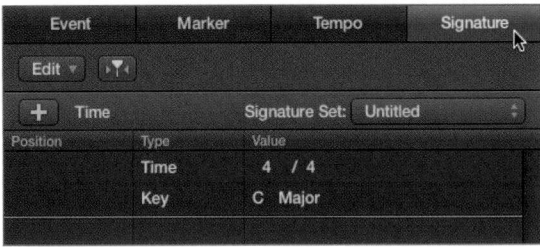

The Signature list shows the Time and Key signatures. The default key signature is C major.

3   In the Value column, click the scale (Major).

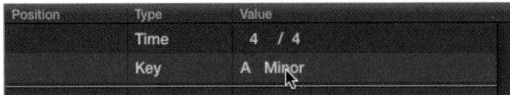

The Key Value changes to A minor, the relative minor of C major. (Relative keys share the same notes, but have different tonal centers.)

4   Click the key (A), and from the pop-up menu, choose B.

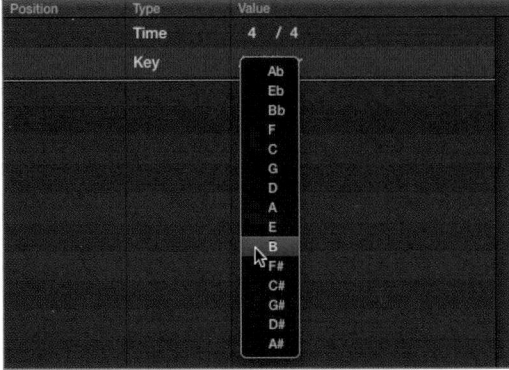

The Key signature is now B minor.

5   Click the Lists button to close the Signature list.

6   Listen to your song. The Intergalactic Synth plays in the new project key, B. Note that rhythmic loops without pitches are not affected by the project's key, so the Intergalactic Beat loop on track 2 isn't transposed.

Creating Apple Loops

When you want to catalog a section of an audio recording so you can reuse it in future projects, you can save it as an Apple Loop. The Apple Loop will be indexed in the Loop Browser so that you can easily find it later, and it will automatically match the tempo (and, when appropriate, the key) of the project into which you import the loop.

In the next exercise, you will first divide the first four bars of drums, and save them as a new Apple Loop.

1   Command-drag to select the first four bars in the Slow Drums.1 region from 1 1 1 1 to 5 1 1 1.

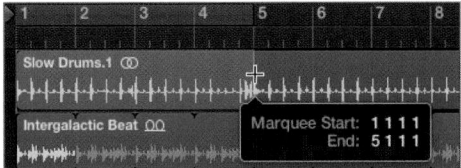

2   In the control bar, click the Apple Loops button (or press O) to open the Loop Browser.

3   Using the Pointer tool, drag the selected section of the drums to the Loop Browser.

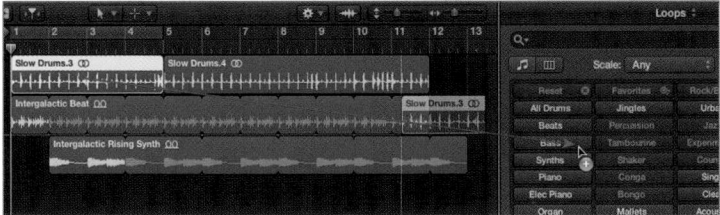

As soon as you click the marquee selection, it is divided as a new region. When you release the mouse button over the Loop Browser, the "Add Region to Apple Loops Library" dialog opens.

4 In the dialog, enter or choose the following:

▶ Name: *Slow Drums*

▶ Type: Loop

▶ Scale: Neither

▶ Genre: Rock/Blues

▶ Descriptors: All Drums > Kits

5 Click the Acoustic, Clean, Dry, Grooving, and Part descriptor buttons. Descriptors deter-mine which keyword buttons you'll later select in the Loop Browser to find that loop.

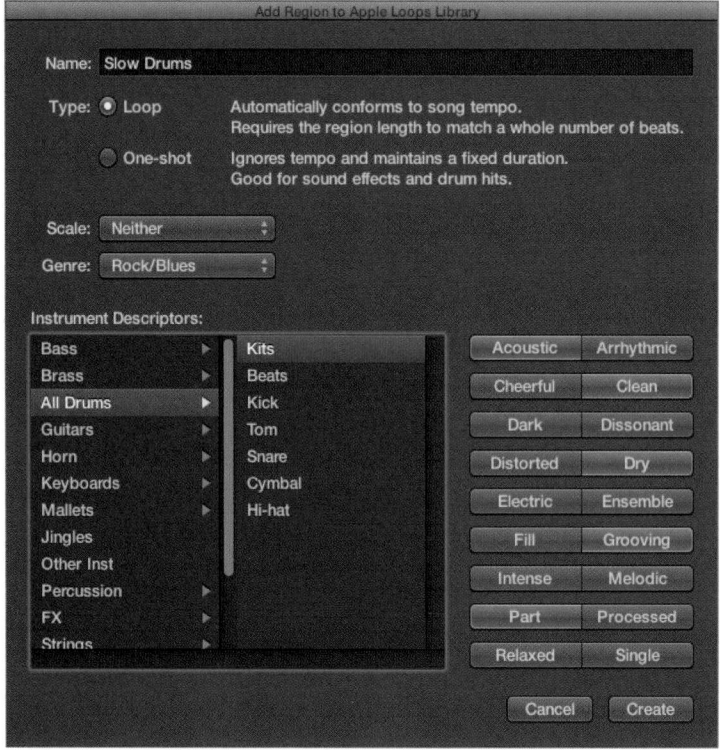

NOTE ▶ When dragging a region to the Loop Browser, you can create loops only when the number of beats in the region is an integer. This function uses the project tempo to tag the transient positions and works best for audio files that match the project tempo. If the selected region's number of beats is not an integer, the Type parameter will be set to One-shot and dimmed, and the resulting Apple Loop will not automatically match a project's tempo and key.

6 Click Create.

Logic bounces the section as a new Apple Loop and indexes it in the Loop Browser. You will come back to the current project shortly, but for now let's find the new loop in a new project.

7 Choose File > New (or press Command-Shift-N) to open a new project, but do not close the current project.

8 Create a track of any type, and open the Loop Browser.

9 In the Loop Browser, in the search field, type *Slow Drums*.

10 In the results list, click Slow Drums to preview it.

The loop plays at the current project tempo, 120 bpm. Notice that in the results list, Slow Drums does not have a key associated with it.

11 As the loop continues playing, experiment by changing the tempo and key of the project in the LCD display. The loop matches the project tempo, but not the project key.

Tempo —┘   └— Key signature

12 Click the loop to stop previewing it.

13 Choose File > Close to close the new project, and do not save it.

You are back in the original project.

14 Close the Loop Browser.

> **TIP** You can also drag a MIDI region on a software instrument track to the Loop Browser to create a green Apple Loop. Green Apple Loops, like the blue Apple Loops you've already used, can be applied as audio regions on audio tracks, or as MIDI regions on software instrument tracks, giving you the additional flexibility of being able to edit the sound of the instrument and the MIDI events.

Creating Tempo Changes and Tempo Curves

When you want to vary the tempo throughout a project, you can use the global Tempo track to insert tempo changes and tempo curves. All MIDI regions and Apple Loops automatically follow the project tempo, even when tempo variations occur in the middle of a region. For non–Apple Loops audio regions (such as the Slow Drums region on track 1), you first have to turn on Flex for the tracks containing the regions to make those regions follow the project tempo.

Creating and Naming Tempo Sets

In this exercise, you will create a new tempo set, and name both the current and new tempo sets. You will create a new tempo curve in the new tempo set, and later switch between the original tempo and the new tempo curve.

1   At the top of the track headers, click the Global Tracks button (or press G).

Below the ruler, the global tracks open. For this exercise, you need to see only the Tempo track.

2   Control-click a global track header, and choose Hide Arrangement from the shortcut menu.

The Arrangement track is hidden.

3   Repeat step 2 to hide the Marker and Signature tracks.

Only the Tempo track remains. Before you start editing the tempo, you will create a new tempo set and name both the current and the new sets.

4   In the Tempo track header, from the Tempo pop-up menu, choose Tempo Sets > Rename Set.

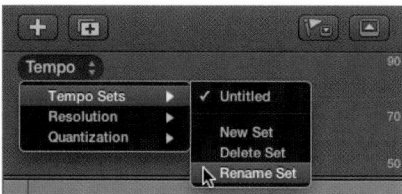

A text field appears on the Tempo track header.

5   Enter *Original*.

6   From the Tempo pop-up menu, choose Tempo Sets > New Set.

A new tempo set is created with a default value of 120 bpm. A text entry field appears, ready for you to enter a name for the new set. In this set, you will make the tempo go gradually faster, so let's name it Accelerando.

7   Rename the new tempo set *Accelerando*, and listen to the song.

Both Apple Loops play at the new tempo (120 bpm), but the drums on track 1 continue playing at their original tempo. To make them follow the project tempo you need to choose a flex mode for their track, but only when the track is playing at its correct tempo.

8   From the Tempo pop-up menu, choose Tempo Sets > Original. The project tempo is 61.5000 bpm, the correct tempo of the drums performance.

9   Select the Slow Drums track header (track 1).

10   Open the Track inspector, and set Flex Mode to Flex Time - Slicing.

This mode slices the audio where it detects a transient, and moves the slices without time-stretching them, which typically works great for drums.

11   In the Tempo track, from the Tempo pop-up menu, choose Tempo Sets > Accelerando. Listen to the song.

This time, all three tracks follow the default 120 bpm tempo of the new tempo set.

Creating Tempo Changes and Tempo Curves

You now have two tempo sets, and will edit the new one to create a tempo that starts at a 62 bpm tempo and progressively ramps up to about 75 bpm, dropping abruptly to 40 bpm for the last sustained note of the synth.

1   In the Tempo track, drag the tempo line down to 62 bpm.

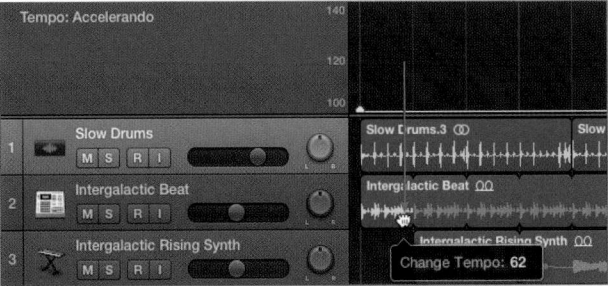

Although the line seems to stop at the bottom edge of the Tempo track, keep dragging down until you see the desired tempo value displayed in the help tag. When you release the mouse button, the scale on the right in the Tempo track header updates and you can see the new tempo.

Let's insert a tempo change at bar 11.

2   In the Tempo track at bar 11, position the mouse pointer above the tempo line so that it no longer looks like a hand, and then double-click to insert a new tempo change, aiming for a value of 75 bpm.

A new tempo control point is inserted at bar 11. You probably didn't get the exact value you had in mind, but that's an easy fix.

3   Place the pointer over the line to the right of the new tempo change so that it changes to a Hand tool. Then drag up or down to a value of 75 bpm. Listen to the tempo change.

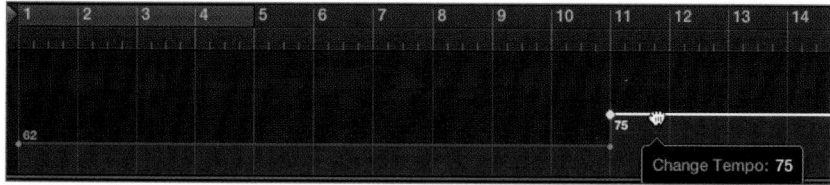

TIP ▶ To reposition a tempo control point, horizontally drag the vertical line below the tempo change.

The tempo changes abruptly at bar 11. To smooth the tempo change, you're going to accelerate the tempo from 62 bpm at bar 1 to 75 bpm at bar 11.

4   At bar 11, position the mouse pointer on the control point below the 75 bpm control point. The pointer turns into the Finger tool.

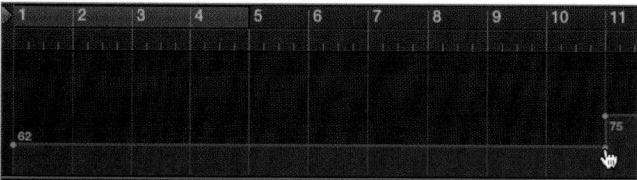

5   Using the Finger tool, drag the control point to the left.

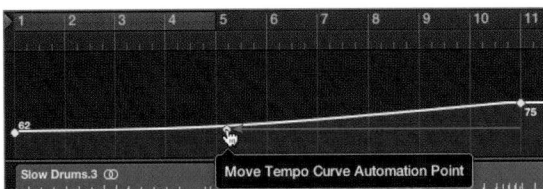

You can precisely adjust the tempo curve by dragging the control point farther to the left, up, or in both directions.

6   Listen to the song. The tempo now ramps up progressively between bar 1 and bar 11.

Let's slow the tempo at bar 12.

7   Double-click below the tempo line at bar 12, and drag the new tempo line to 40 bpm. Listen to the ending.

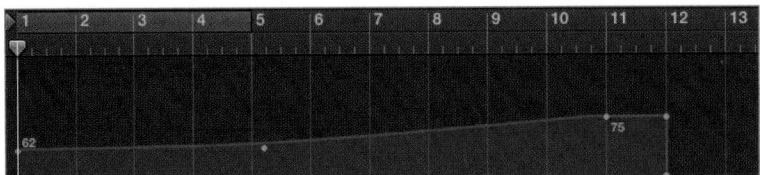

Although the drums seem rather fast in bar 11, the last synth note in bar 12 plays very slowly. You can probably hear a click at bar 12, so let's have a closer look.

8   At the top of the track headers, click the Global tracks button (or press G) to close the global tracks.

9   At bar 12, zoom in closely on the end of the last Slow Drums region on track 1.

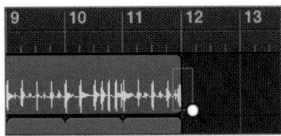

If you zoom in close enough, you can see that the attack of the next drum hit is still inside the region. You need to shorten the region a tiny bit to remove that attack.

10 Position the mouse pointer at the bottom right of the region, and drag to the left to hide the unwanted attack.

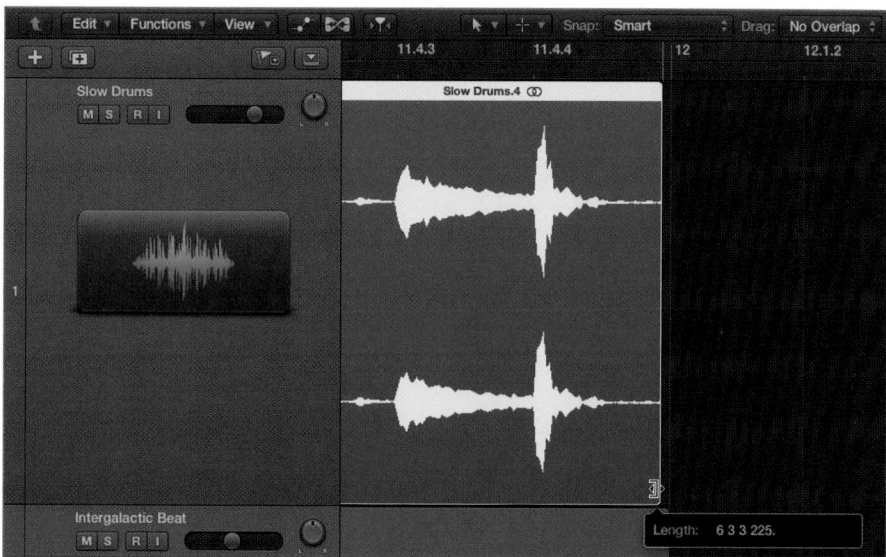

11 Zoom out and listen again. The click at bar 12 is gone.

You can create complex tempo maps to add excitement to your arrangements. Sometimes, a chorus that's a bit faster than the rest of the song is all an arrangement needs to really take off. Or you can use tempo curves to create the classic ritardando at the end of a song. All your Apple Loops and MIDI regions will automatically follow the tempo map, and you can use a flex mode for each audio track you want to follow along.

Adding a Turntable or Tape Slow-Down Effect

When you stop a turntable with the stylus on the record, or stop a tape machine while keeping the playhead in contact with the magnetic tape, the result is a sound that drops in pitch as it slows down. This highly recognizable effect has recently regained popularity along with its opposite—the sound rising in pitch as speed increases when the tape transport or turntable starts.

You will now apply the turntable stop effect to the last sustained synth note at the end of the song. First, you need to turn that last loop into an individual region.

1 Using the Marquee tool, Command-drag over the last loop on the synth track (from 12 1 1 1 to 13 1 1 1) to select it.

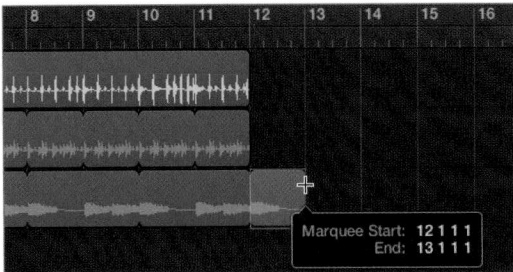

2 Using the Pointer tool, click the Marquee selection.

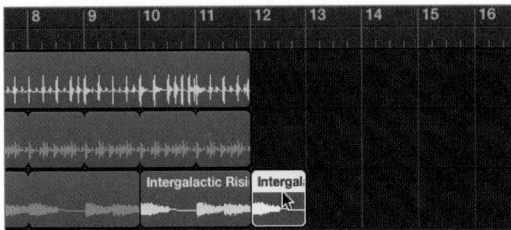

The last two loops are turned into regions.

3 Control-Shift-drag over the region end to create a fade-out.

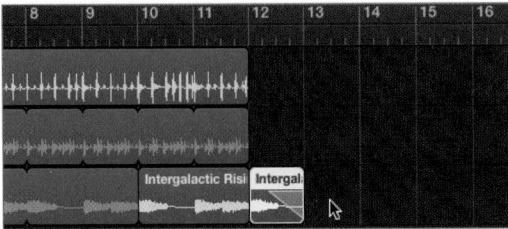

Let's turn that volume fade into a speed fade.

4 Control-click the fade-out, and choose Slow Down from the shortcut menu.

In the workspace, the fade-out turns orange, indicating that it is now a speed fade.

5   Listen to your fade. It sounds just like a tape stopping!

You can adjust the length and curve of the speed fade just as you would a volume fade.

6   As you listen, adjust the fade's curve and length as follows:

▶   Control-Shift-drag the middle of the fade to adjust its curve.

▶   Control-Shift-drag the left edge of the fade to adjust its length.

7   Choose File > Close Project without saving the project.

You just used a speed fade to create a realistic tape slow-down effect, but you can use speed fades for many kinds of effects. Try applying multiple rapid speed fades to short regions to create DJ scratching effects. Or add a speed fade at the end of a kick sample to make it drop in pitch.

Making One Track Follow the Groove of Another Track

Playing all tracks at the same tempo is not always sufficient to achieve a tight rhythm. You also need to make sure they play with the same groove. For example, a musician may play slightly late to create a laid-back feel, or he may add some swing to his performance by delaying only the upbeats. On yet another track, notes may be placed on a rigid grid.

To learn how to get your tracks in the same groove, you will open a new project with a drummer playing a swing groove, and then make a shaker on another track follow the groove of the drummer.

1   Open Logic Pro X Files > Lessons > **07 Swing Groove**, and listen to the song.

Even though both tracks play at the same tempo, they are not synchronized. The drums (track 1) are playing a hip hop shuffle groove while the shaker is playing on a straight sixteenth note grid. Feel free to solo the individual tracks to clearly hear each instrument's feel.

Let's zoom in so you can see the individual drum hits on the waveforms.

2 Press Return to go back to the beginning of the project.

3 Press Command-Right Arrow nine times to zoom in on the first two beats (so you can clearly see 1 and 1.2 in the ruler).

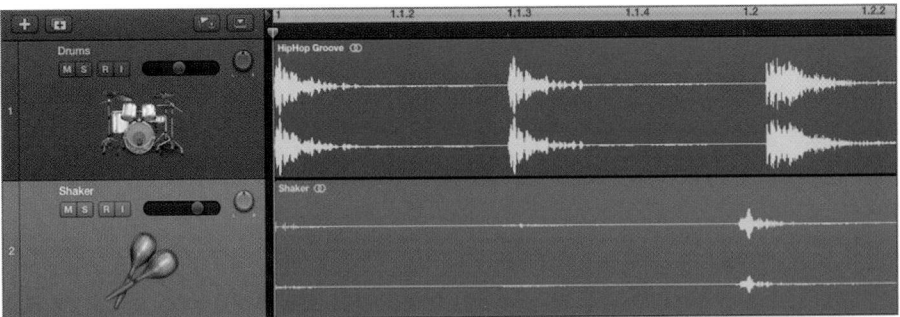

Below the 1.2 grid mark in the ruler, you can clearly see that the waveforms on the two tracks are out of sync.

To make the shaker follow the groove of the drums, you need to set the Drums track as the groove track.

4 Control-click a track header, and from the shortcut menu, choose Track Header Component > Show Groove Track.

At first glance, nothing seems to have changed in the track headers.

5 Position the mouse pointer over the track number (1) of the Drums track.

A gold star appears in place of the track number.

6 Click the gold star.

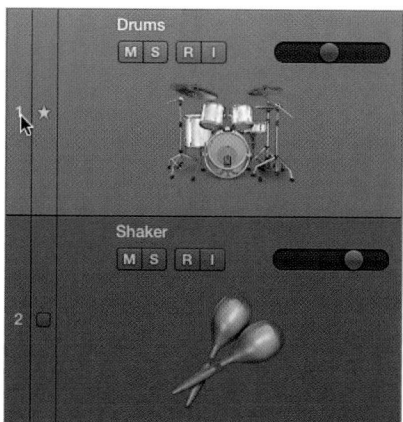

The gold star appears in a new column on the track header, indicating that the Drums track is now the groove track. On the Shaker track header, in the same column, you can select the checkbox to make that track follow the groove track.

7   On the Shaker track, select the Match Groove Track checkbox.

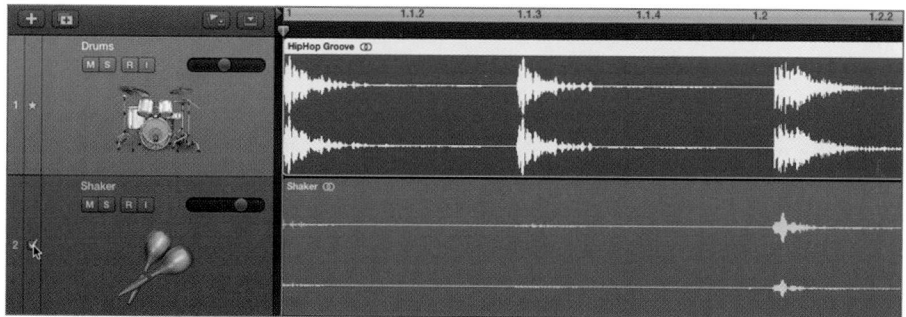

The waveform on the Shaker track updates so that the notes are in sync with the notes on the groove track.

8   Listen to the song. The shaker now follows the groove of the drums, and they play in sync.

9   Solo the Shaker track.

10 While listening to the shaker, deselect and select the Match Groove Track checkbox to compare the original performance with the new groove.

When the checkbox is deselected, the shaker plays straight eighth notes and sixteenth notes. When the checkbox is selected, the shaker plays the same hip hop shuffle feel as the drums.

11 Unsolo the Shaker track.

12 Choose File > Close Project without saving the project.

Groove tracks work with all track types (audio, software instrument, and Drummer tracks). Experiment by applying the groove of a sample to your MIDI programming, or making a Drummer track follow the groove of a live bass recording.

Change the Playback Pitch and Speed with Varispeed

In the days of analog tape recording, engineers performed all sorts of tricks by changing the tape speed. Many major albums were sped up ever so slightly during the mixing process to add excitement to tracks by raising their tempos. This simultaneously raised the pitch, giving the impression of the vocalist reaching higher notes in the most emotional passages of the song. On the other hand, engineers would sometimes slow the tape during recording, so that a musician could play a challenging passage at a more comfortable tempo. When played back at its regular speed during mixdown, the recording created the illusion of the musician playing faster. DJs are probably the biggest users of Varispeed techniques, which gives them control over the tempo and pitch of a track, allowing for seamless transitions from one track to the next.

Logic takes this concept a step further, offering both the classic Varispeed—which, like a tape or record player, changes both the pitch and the speed—and a Speed Only mode, which allows you to change the speed without changing the pitch.

1 Open Logic Pro X Files > Lessons > **07 Little Lady**, and listen to the song. In the LCD display in the control bar, you can see that the song is in the key of A minor and its tempo is 152 bpm.

To use the Varispeed feature, you must add the Varispeed display to the control bar.

2 Control-click the control bar, and from the shortcut menu, choose "Customize Control Bar and Display."

In the LCD column of the "Customize Control Bar and Display" dialog, the Varispeed option is dimmed. To be able to turn it on, you first need to choose the custom LCD display.

3   In the LCD column, from the pop-up menu, choose Custom.

4   Below the pop-up menu, select Varispeed, and click OK.

A new Varispeed display appears in the control bar.

5   In the Varispeed display, drag the 0.00% value up to 6.00%.

The Varispeed display is shaded in orange. The tempo value turns orange, too, indicating that the song is no longer playing at its normal tempo due to the Varispeed feature. To the right of the control bar, the Varispeed button turns orange to indicate that the feature is enabled.

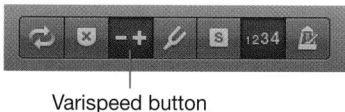

Varispeed button

6   Listen to the song.

The song plays faster, but retains its original pitch. Let's check the song's current tempo.

7 In the Varispeed display, click the % symbol, and from the pop-up menu, choose Resulting Tempo.

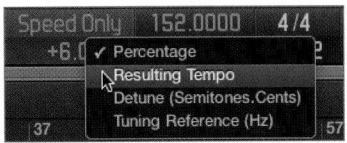

The Varispeed display shows the resulting tempo of 161.120 bpm. You can now use the display to set the desired playback tempo.

8 Double-click the 161.120 tempo value, and enter *140* bpm.

The song plays slower, but still at its original pitch. This would be perfect for practicing a part by playing along with your instrument. You could even record your part at this speed, and then turn off Varispeed to play the whole song (including your newly recorded part) at the normal speed.

Now let's apply the classic Varispeed effect that changes both the playback speed and pitch.

9 In the Varispeed display, click Speed Only, and from the pop-up menu, choose Varispeed (Speed and Pitch).

10 Listen to the song.

Now the song plays both faster and higher in pitch. This is the classic Varispeed effect available on tape machines and turntables.

11 In the Varispeed display, click the bpm symbol, and from the pop-up menu, choose Detune (Semitones, Cents).

12 Double-click the –1.42 detune value, and enter *–2.00*.

13 Listen to the song.

Now the song plays slower and pitched down by two semitones. If your vocal soloist isn't at the top of his game that day and can't reach his usual high notes, you could record at this slower speed, and later turn off Varispeed to play the whole song at the higher pitch.

14 In the control bar, click the Varispeed button to turn it off.

Editing the Timing of an Audio Region

You were introduced to Flex Time editing in Lesson 3 when you used it to tighten the rhythm of a few dead notes on a guitar. You will now go further and explore other Flex Time editing techniques while examining what happens to an audio waveform "under the hood."

Time Stretching the Waveform Between Transient Markers

You will dive deeper into Flex Time editing by using it to correct the timing of a guitar.

1 From the global Marker track, drag the Breakdown marker (at bar 75) into the upper half of the ruler.

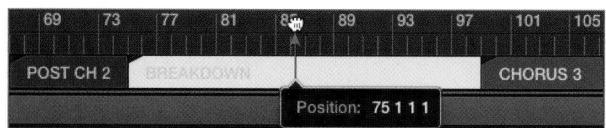

A cycle area is created that corresponds to the Breakdown marker.

2 Solo the two Gtr Bridge tracks (tracks 13 and 14).

3 Listen to the first three bars of the Breakdown section.

The two guitars on the soloed tracks play the same rhythm, but in two places (bar 75, beat 2; and bar 77, beat 2) the guitars are not hitting the notes together.

4 In the Tracks area menu bar, click the Flex button (or press Command-F).

Flex button

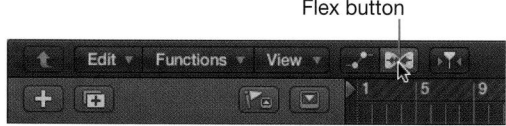

The Tracks area is zoomed in vertically, and each track header shows a Flex button and a Flex pop-up menu.

5 Zoom in and scroll the workspace so you can see the beginning of the Gtr Bridge L region (at bar 75) at the upper left of the workspace, right below the ruler.

6 Click the lower half of the ruler at bar 75 to position the playhead. Click track 13 to select it, and drag the zoom sliders (or press Command-Arrow keys) to continue adjusting your zoom level so that you can see the three first beats of bar 75 in the ruler (the 75, 75.2, and 75.3 grid marks).

Remember that zooming with the zoom sliders or the Command-Arrow keys keeps the playhead at the same horizontal position in the workspace, and the selected track at the same vertical position in the Tracks area. Here, the beginning of the Gtr Bridge L region stays anchored at the upper left of the workspace.

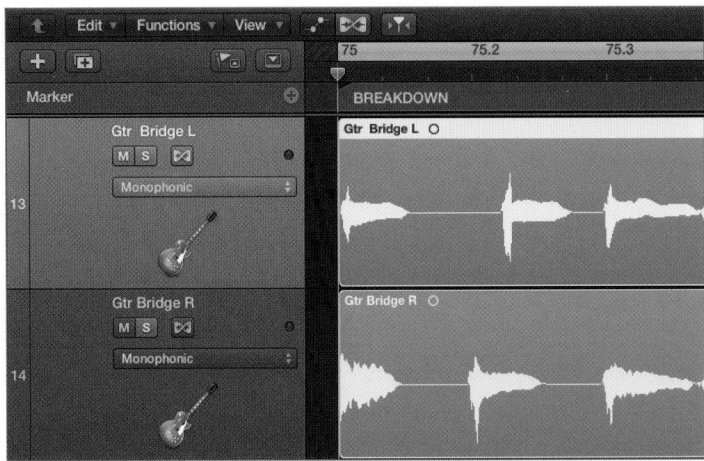

7   In the Gtr Bridge L track header (track 13), click the Flex button.

Flex editing is turned on. The region on the track is darker, and transient markers appear where Logic detected the attack of a new note. Logic automatically detects the most appropriate Flex Time mode for the track, which is set to Monophonic.

NOTE ▶ Monophonic mode is intended for instruments that produce only one pitch at a time (vocals, wind). Polyphonic is used with instruments that play chords (piano, guitar), and Slicing is for moving notes without time-stretching any audio (good for drums).

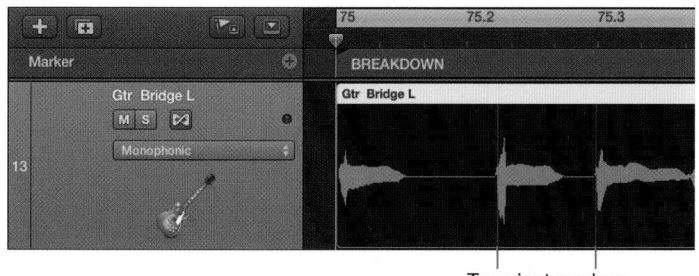

Transient markers

On track 13, the second note in the region is late. It should be in time with the second note of the Gtr Bridge R region on track 14 (under the 75.2 grid mark in the ruler).

8   In the upper half of the waveform, place the mouse pointer over the transient marker of the second note.

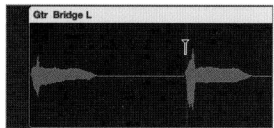

The mouse pointer turns into a Flex tool and looks like a single flex marker. This symbol indicates that clicking or dragging will insert a flex marker on the transient marker.

When you drag the flex marker, the waveform is stretched between the region beginning and the flex marker, and between the flex marker and the region end. Let's try it.

9   Drag the Flex tool to the left to align the flex marker with the second note of the track below.

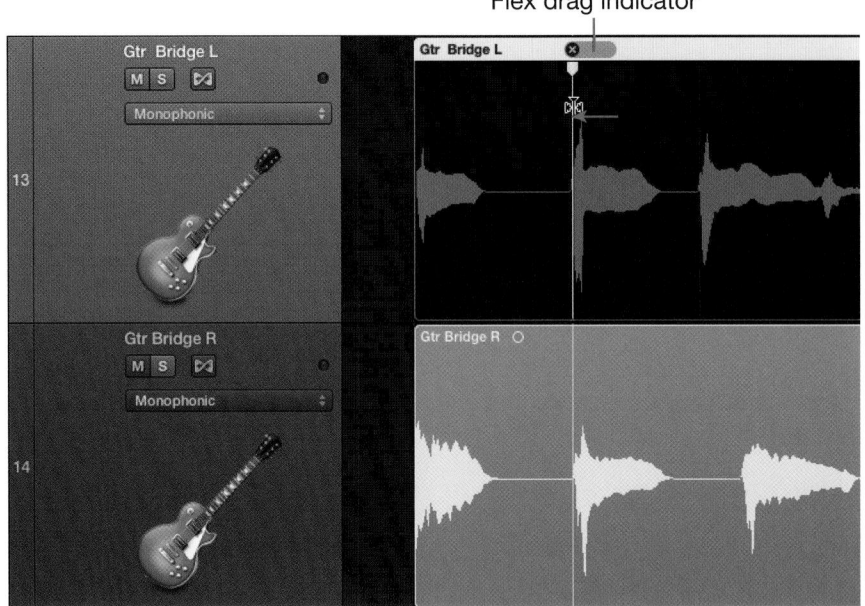

Flex drag indicator

When the mouse pointer is positioned over a flex marker, a flex drag indicator in the region header above the flex marker shows how the flex marker was moved from its original position. You can click the X symbol inside the flex drag indicator to delete that flex marker (and return the waveform to its original state).

After you release the mouse button, the flex marker looks like a white vertical line.

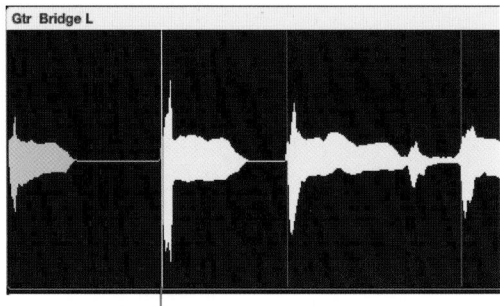

Flex marker

The waveform to the left of the flex marker is blue (time-compressed) and the waveform to the right of the flex marker is white (time-expanded). As a result, all the notes to the right of the flex marker have changed their positions, which is not what's wanted here.

10 Choose Edit > Undo (or press Command-Z).

11 In the lower half of the waveform, place the mouse pointer over the transient marker of the second note.

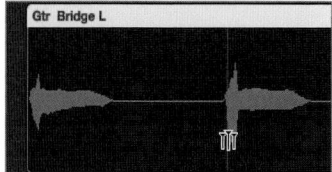

The Flex tool looks like three flex markers. Clicking it creates three flex markers:

▶ On the transient marker you're about to drag

▶ On the transient marker before (which will not move)

▶ On the transient marker after (which will not move)

12 Drag the Flex tool to the left to align the note with the second note of the track below.

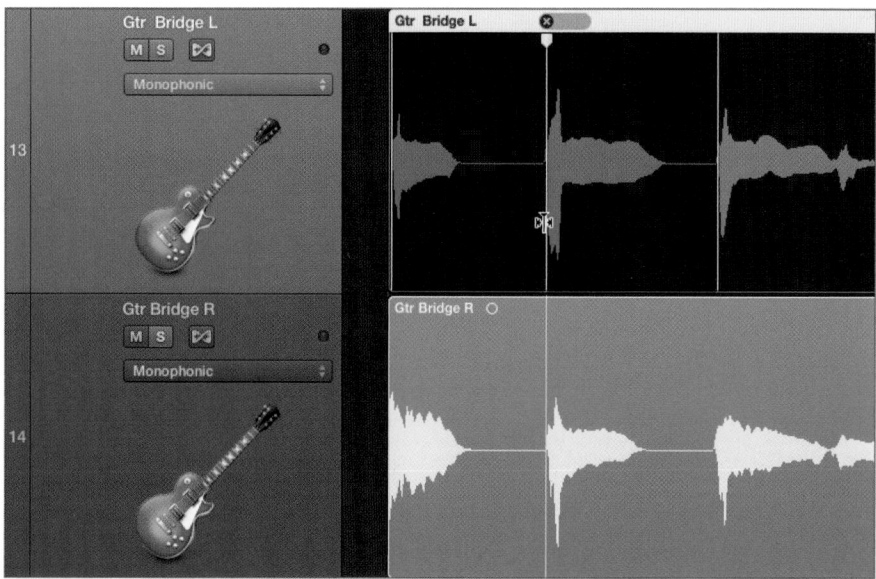

The first note is time compressed, the second note is time expanded, and the rest of the region remains unaffected.

13 Listen to the edit.

The timing sounds much better than in the original. However, the first note is now slightly shorter, and the second note longer. It's a subtle difference, but in the next exercise you will use another technique to get a tighter result.

14 Choose Undo > Dragging (or press Command-Z) to undo the change.

Moving Waveform Sections Without Time-Stretching

In the previous exercise, you applied the Flex tool to time-stretch a waveform using either the previous and next transient markers or the region's beginning and end points as boundaries.

Now you will use the Marquee, your current Command-click tool, to select a section of the waveform, and move it without time-stretching any of the audio region.

1 In the Gtr Bridge L region, Command-drag the second note, starting on the transient marker.

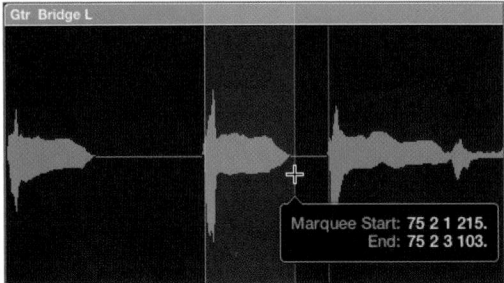

Positioning the mouse pointer in the upper half of a marquee selection turns the pointer into the Hand tool, which lets you move the selected waveform without time-stretching any of the material around it.

2 Drag the upper half of the marquee selection to align the selected note with the second note in the guitar track below.

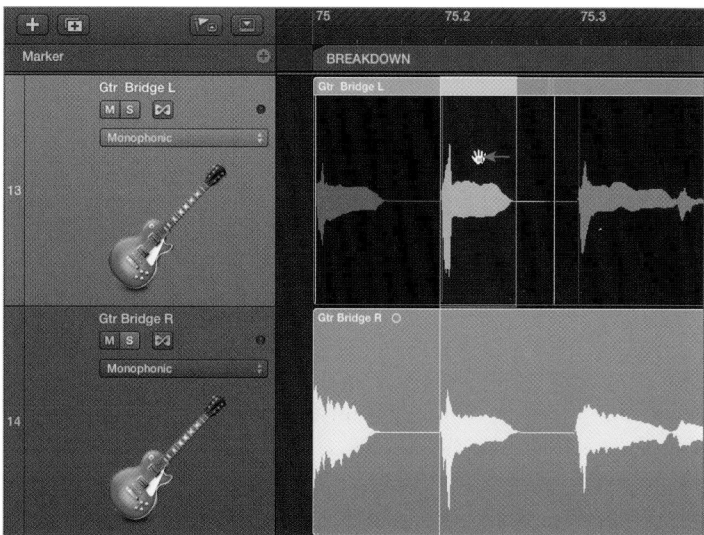

3   Listen to the result. The two guitar tracks sound really tight together until the second note of bar 77 when the Gtr Bridge L plays early.

4   Scroll to the second note of bar 77. Select the note using the Marquee tool, and then drag it to the right to align it with the corresponding note on the track below.

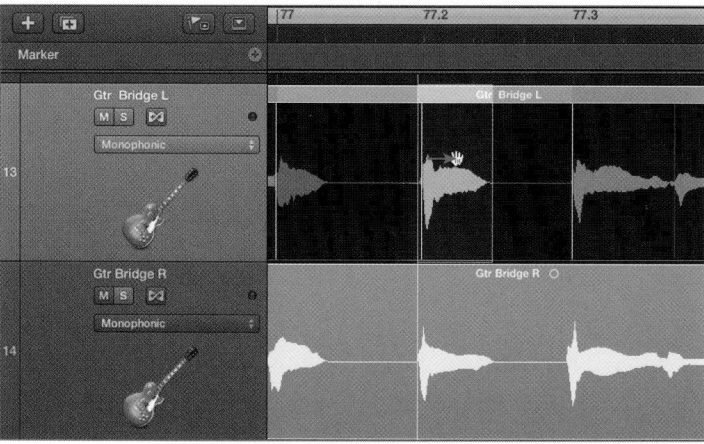

5   Listen to the result. Now both guitars sound tight.

6   Unsolo both guitar tracks.

In the next exercise, you will edit the timing of the bass tracks in the Dropdown section, so keep your current zoom level.

Time Stretching a Single Note

Let's use the Flex tool to lengthen a bass note.

1   In the workspace, scroll up to see the two bass tracks (tracks 9 and 10).

You will stretch the single note at bar 79, first in track 9, and then in track 10.

2   Scroll and zoom as necessary so you can see the single bass note at bar 79.

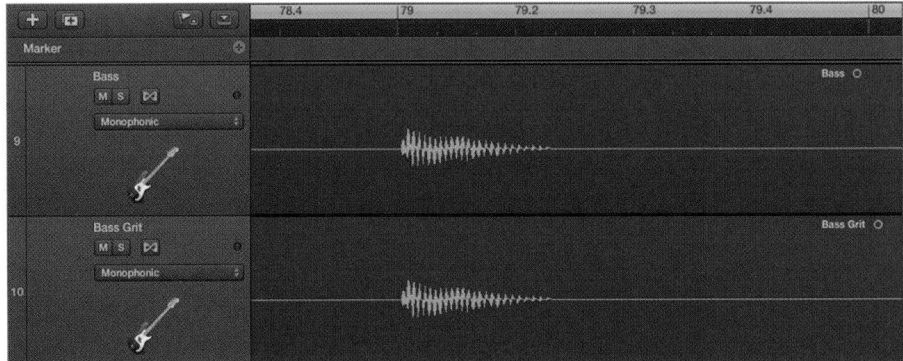

3   In the Bass track header (track 9), click the Flex button.

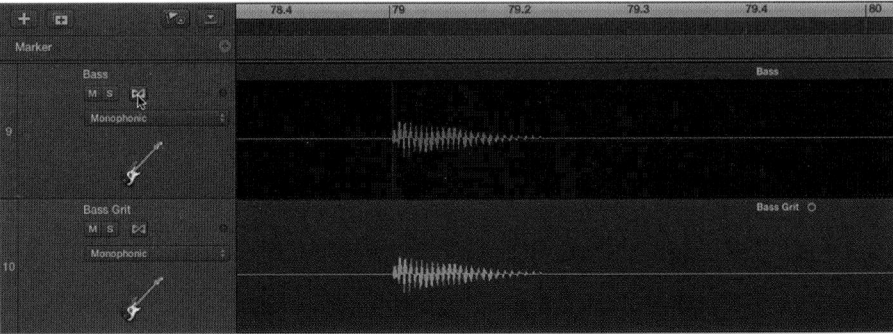

At bar 79, you can see a transient marker at the beginning of the note.

4   Position your mouse pointer in the lower half of the waveform, over the end of the note.

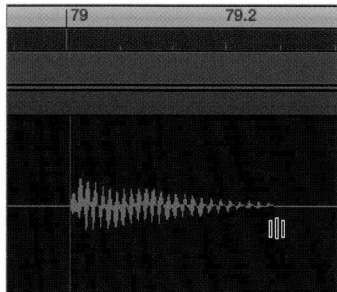

The mouse pointer looks like three vertical lines because it is not located over a transient marker. Clicking creates three flex markers:

▶   At the location you click

▶   On the transient marker before (which will not move)

▶   On the transient marker after (which will not move)

5   Drag the Flex tool to the right to end the note on 79.3.

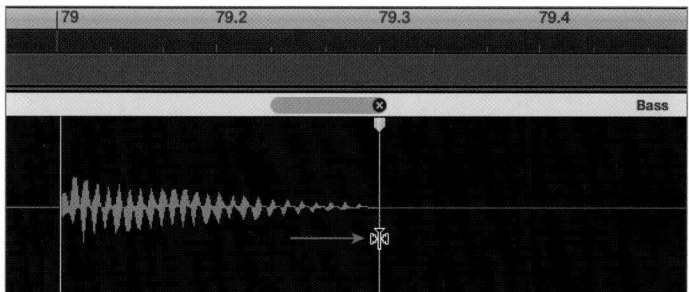

The three flex markers are created, and the note is lengthened. The flex markers on the transient before (at bar 79) and after (end of bar 82) ensure that the rest of the region before and after the lengthened note stays unaffected.

6   Turn on flex for the Bass Grit track (track 10), and lengthen the corresponding note by the same amount.

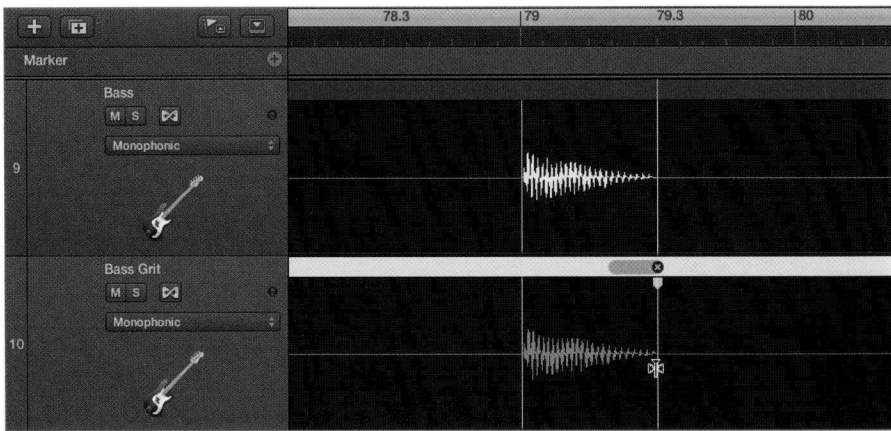

7 Listen to the result.

The bass note at bar 79 is sustained for a longer time. Don't hesitate to solo the two bass guitar tracks, and to turn the Flex buttons on and off in the two bass track headers to compare the before and after results.

8 Click the background, and press Z to see the whole song.

Tuning Vocal Recordings

Hitting pitches perfectly on every single note can be a challenge for singers. Tuning software allows you to correct pitches in a recording. It can be useful for saving an emotional take that contains a few off-pitch notes, or even to refine the pitch of a good performance.

Editing Note Pitches in the Workspace

In Logic, Flex Pitch allows you to automatically correct the pitch of all the notes in a region, or to precisely edit the pitch curve of a single note, along with the amount of vibrato. In this exercise, you will use Flex Pitch to tune the vocals on the Verse track (track 24).

1 Solo the Verse track (track 24), and listen to the second verse (at bar 43).

The singer has a bluesy singing style with some sung parts and some spoken parts. You can hear the pitch glide between notes, and she usually applies vibrato at the end. Some of the pitches are slightly off and will benefit from pitch correction.

2   Zoom in on the second Verse region (at bar 43).

3   Click the Verse track header to select it, and then click its Flex button.

Transient markers appear over the region.

4   In the Verse track header, from the Flex pop-up menu, choose Flex Pitch.

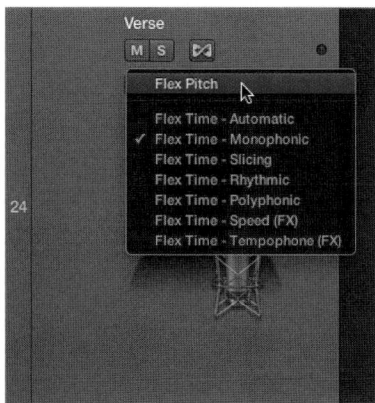

On the region, the transient markers disappear, and you see vertical bars of various heights that represent the pitches detected for each note:

▶   A line in the center of the waveform indicates a perfect pitch.

▶   A bar going up indicates that the note is sharp.

▶   A bar going down indicates that the note is flat.

The height of the bar represents the deviation of the detected pitch from the perfect pitch.

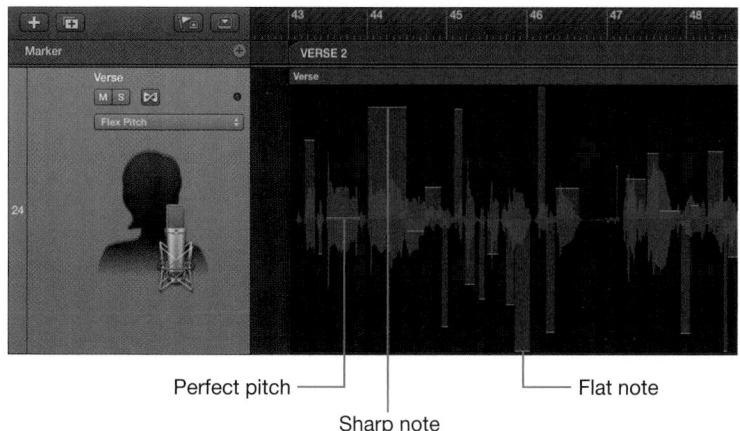

5   Drag the Verse 2 marker into the upper half of the ruler to make the cycle area match the position of the marker.

6   Control-click the Verse region, and from the shortcut menu, choose "Set all to Perfect Pitch."

All the bars in the region snap to the center of the waveform, indicating that all the notes are in tune.

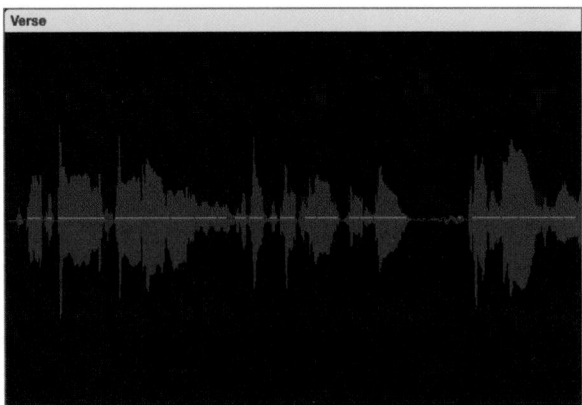

7   Listen to the results.

The notes are corrected to the closest pitches on a chromatic scale while retaining their original pitch drift and vibrato. This fix works well for most notes, but a few issues remain. At the beginning of bar 44, the words "get on" were corrected to the wrong pitch and sound flat.

8   Control-click the Verse region, and from the shortcut menu, choose "Set all to Original Pitch" to return the notes to their original pitches.

You can edit the pitch of individual notes in the region.

9   At the beginning of the region, Control-click the first bar (for the word "pack"), and
from the shortcut menu, choose "Set to Perfect Pitch."

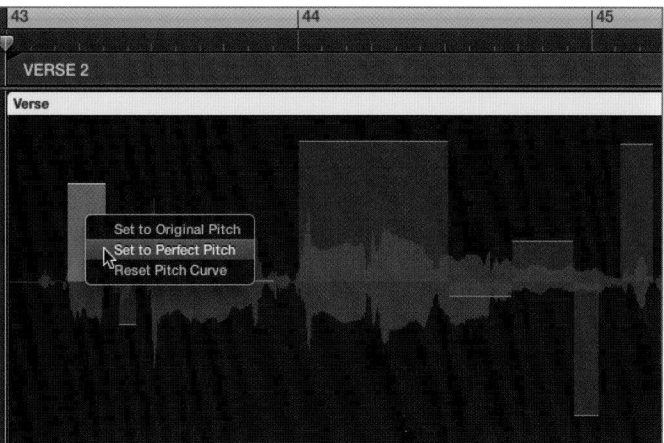

The bar becomes a line in the center of the waveform, indicating that the note is
tuned to a perfect pitch.

You can also drag bars up and down to manually tune a note.

10   At bar 44, drag up the horizontal line corresponding to the words "get on."

The singer is bending her pitch at the beginning of those two words, so it's best to
tune them by ear.

11   Drag horizontally from the beginning to the end of each word ("get" and "on"). You can
hear the pitch ramp up on each word as the singer bends the note. Find the horizontal
position to hear the highest pitch at the end of the first word ("get"), and then try to
drag only vertically to hear the pitch as you adjust it. You may need to zoom in closer.

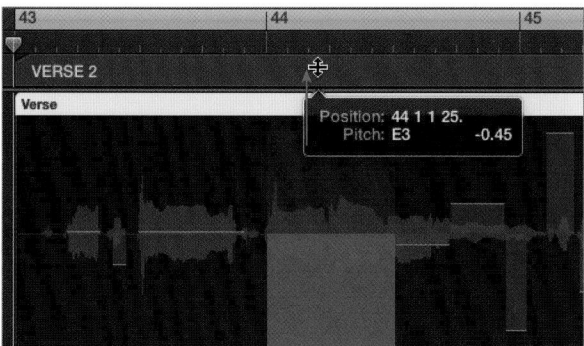

You need to drag farther up than the top of the region to tune this note. As you do so, the help tag no longer shows a D#3, but an E3, and the upward bar turns into a downward bar. Flex Pitch no longer considers the note to be a sharp D#3, but a flat E3.

12 Listen to Verse 2.

The singer alternates sung lines with spoken lines. It's best not to tune the spoken lines. You can continue tuning the desired notes by selecting a few at a time. You may need to zoom out a bit for the next step.

13 Drag the Pointer tool in bars 47 and 48 to select the words, "Tell me why, you still hang around."

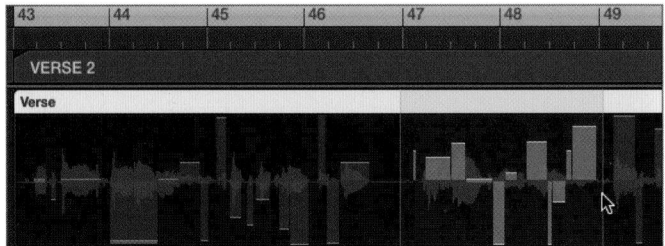

14 Control-click one of the selected bars, and from the shortcut menu, choose "Set to Perfect Pitch."

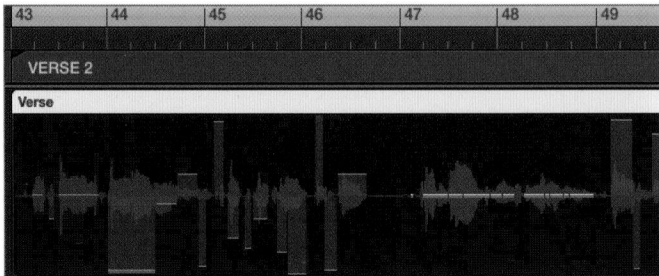

All selected notes are tuned to the perfect pitch.

15 Zoom out to see the whole song.

Editing Note Pitches in the Audio Track Editor

Tuning notes in the Tracks area is quick and easy. However, you sometimes need more flexibility and control over the exact pitch curve of a note. The Audio Track Editor gives you that control over the amount of pitch drift at the start or end of notes, and the amount of vibrato you want to retain.

1   Drag the Verse 1 marker into the upper half of the ruler.

2   On the Verse track (track 24), select the first Verse region (at bar 11).

3   In the control bar, click the Editors button (or press E), and click the Track tab to open the Audio Track Editor.

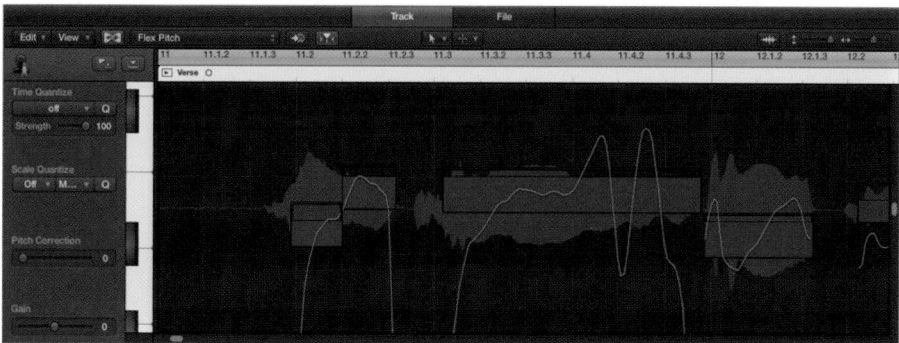

In the Audio Track Editor menu bar, the Flex button is on, and the Flex Pitch mode is selected.

As in the Piano Roll Editor, the note pitches are represented as beams on a grid. (You may need to scroll up or down to see the note beams.) On the grid, light gray lanes correspond to the white keys on the piano keyboard, and dark gray lanes correspond to the black keys. The section of a note beam that intersects with the closest lane is colored, while the height of the hollowed-out section of the beam represents the amount of deviation from the perfect pitch. When a note plays at the perfect pitch, it sits exactly on a lane, and the beam doesn't have any hollowed-out section.

On top of the frame, a light-gray line represents the pitch curve so that you can see pitch drifts and vibrato.

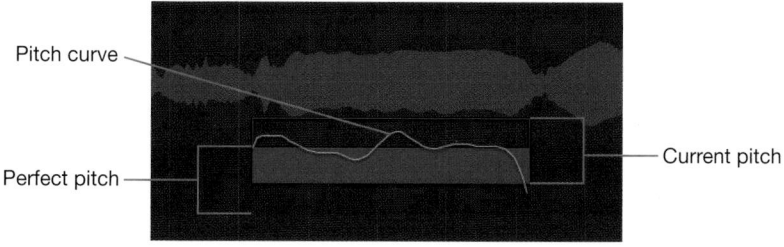

4   Play the first three notes of the verse ("Here you come").

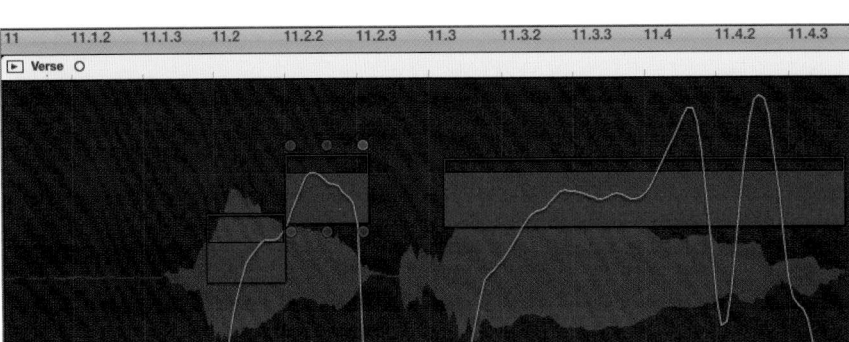

The first two notes (the words "here you") are short and their pitches sound good so you will leave them unchanged.

The third note ("come") goes sharp at the end, and you will fix that.

5   Control-click the beam, and from the shortcut menu, choose "Set to Perfect Pitch."

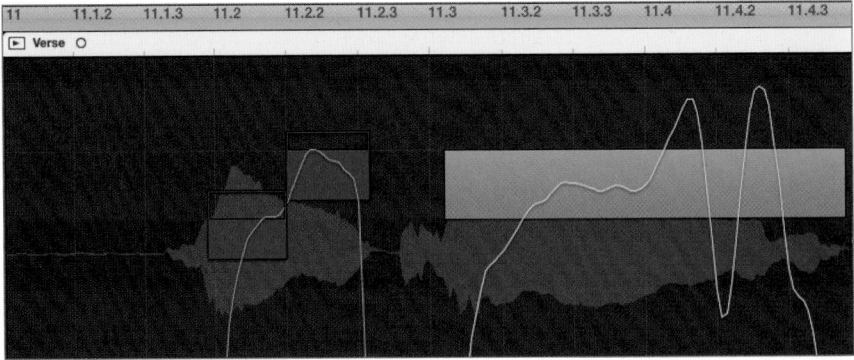

The beam snaps to the closest lane, and the entire beam is colored, indicating that the note plays at the perfect pitch.

Note that at the beginning of the note, the singer raises her pitch to the correct pitch, holds the pitch fairly straight for a short amount of time, adds a wide vibrato, and then drops in pitch at the end.

As you position the mouse pointer in the vicinity of the colored beam, hotspots appear around the beam that allow you to perform various adjustments.

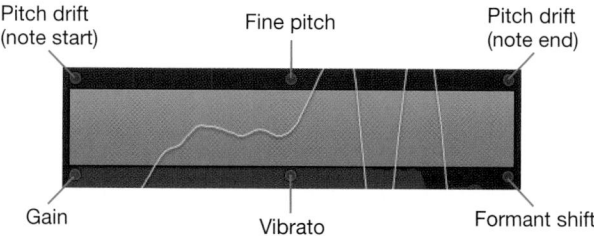

6 Drag the lower-mid hotspot to set Vibrato to 0%.

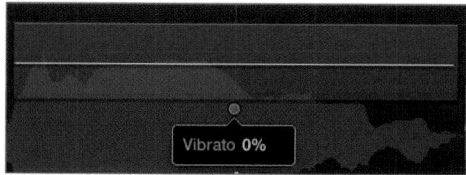

The pitch curve of that note is flat lined.

7 Listen to the result.

The word "come" now has a constant pitch without any drift at the beginning or end, and without any vibrato. The pitch is perfect, but it sounds unnatural.

8 Drag the lower-mid hotspot to set the Vibrato to 50% to halve the pitch deviations around the perfect pitch.

9 Drag the upper-left hotspot to set the Pitch Drift to 0.62 at the note start.

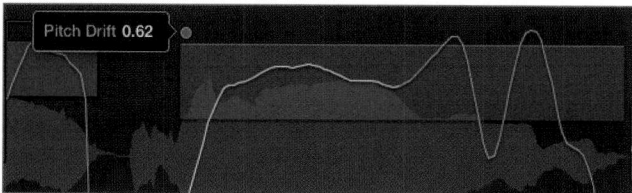

10 Listen to the result.

It sounds as if the singer attacks the note with the correct pitch, which works well if you want a straight pitch. However, for this verse, it sacrifices the bluesy feel imparted by the pitch slurs and wide vibrato.

11   Control-click the note, and choose Reset Pitch Curve from the shortcut menu.

The pitch curve is back to the original, but the note stays on its perfect pitch.

12   In the Tracks area, drag the left edge of the cycle area to bar 17.

13   Unsolo the Verse track (track 24), and listen to a few bars at the beginning of the cycle area.

On the first beat of bar 18, the beginning of the word "sun" is very flat. In fact, the note is so flat that Logic detected its correct pitch as D#3 below, even though the singer meant to reach the E3 above.

14   Drag up the upper-mid hotspot to set the Fine Pitch to 0 on an E3 note.

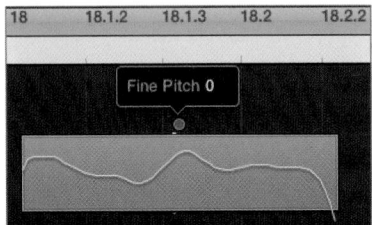

As you drag the Fine Pitch hotspot vertically, you can hear the pitch of the point in the pitch curve at the location of your mouse pointer. In this case, after you click the Fine Pitch hotspot, you can drag to the right about halfway between the middle of the note and the end of the note, where the pitch curve is fairly stable in the middle of the beam. Then drag up while listening to the pitch.

NOTE ▶ Sometimes, pitch correction can alter the timbre of a sound, especially when you play a note several semitones away from its original pitch. At some point, pitching up a vocal makes the singer sound like a chipmunk, whereas pitching it down makes the singer sound like a hulking monster. Dragging the Formant hotspot up or down helps you adjust the timbre to make it sound more realistic.

15   Feel free to correct more note pitches in the two regions on the Verse track, using the different hotspots around the note beams to adjust the fine pitch, the pitch drifts at the start and end of the note, and the amount of vibrato in the pitch curve.

16   In the Tracks area menu bar, click the Flex button (or press Command-F).

The Flex display is hidden, but all your Flex edits remain active.

You now have a large repertoire of techniques you can use to edit the tempo of a project and the timing of its regions, and you can make a track follow the groove of another track. Mastering these techniques will give you the freedom to use almost any prerecorded material in your projects, so keep your ears tuned to interesting material you could sample and loop for your future songs.

Flex Time and Flex Pitch editing can help you correct imperfections in a performance, bringing your material to a new level of precision. Using Varispeed, turntable speed-up and slow-down effects, and Flex Time and Flex Pitch editing techniques, you have a full palette of special effects that can add ear candy to your productions.

Lesson Review

1. How do you detect the tempo of an audio region and apply it to your project?
2. How do you create an Apple Loop that follows the project tempo?
3. How can you add tempo changes and curves?
4. How do you apply a tape or turntable speed-up or slow-down effect?
5. How do you make one track follow the groove of another?
6. How do you turn on Flex editing?
7. How do you time stretch an audio region using the region's start and end points as boundaries?
8. How do you time stretch an audio region using the previous and next transient marker as boundaries?
9. Using Flex Pitch, where can you edit the pitch of notes inside an audio region?
10. When Flex Pitch is turned on for a track, how do you quickly tune an entire audio region?
11. How can you edit the pitch curve?

Answers

1. Select the audio region in the workspace, and choose Edit > Tempo > Adjust Tempo Using Beat Detection.
2. Select a region in the workspace, ensure that its length has an integer number of beats, and drag it to the Loop Browser.

3. Open the global tracks, and on the Tempo track, double-click away from the tempo line to create a tempo change. Drag the control point that appears at the vertical of your tempo change to the left and/or up to adjust the tempo curve.

4. Add a fade-in or a fade-out, control-click it, and from the shortcut menu, choose Speed Up or Slow Down.

5. Ensure that the track headers show groove tracks; then click over the track number to set the groove track, and select the Match Groove Track checkbox in the other track(s).

6. Choose a flex mode for the selected track in the Track inspector, or turn on the Flex button in the Tracks area menu bar and enable the Flex button for the desired track.

7. Assuming there are no pre-existing flex markers in the region, drag the Flex tool on the upper half of the waveform.

8. Drag the Flex tool on the lower half of the waveform.

9. In the workspace, or in the Audio Track Editor

10. Control-click the region, and choose "Set All to Perfect Pitch" from the shortcut menu.

11. Using Flex Pitch editing in the Audio Track Editor, drag the six hotspots around a note beam.

Keyboard Shortcuts

Editing

Option-Command-T	Opens the "Adjust Tempo using Beat Detection" dialog
Command-F	Toggles Flex view on and off

Windows and Panes

G	Opens the global tracks

8

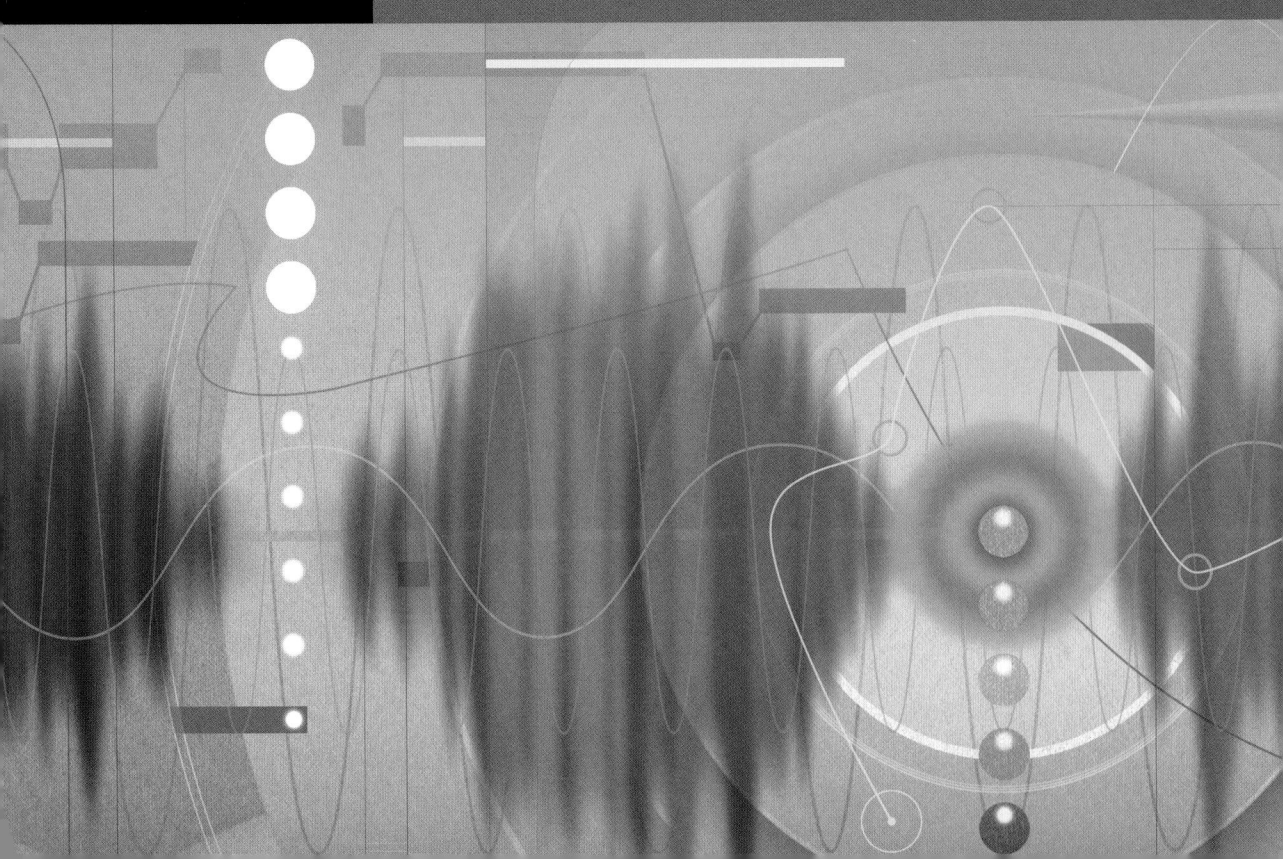

Editing an Arrangement

In previous lessons, you recorded and edited audio and MIDI regions of raw musical material. Your next step is to arrange that material into a song: copying and repeating some elements, removing others, and assembling only those elements that communicate your song's message.

In this lesson, you will start with a song that already has a good basic arrangement and bring it to completion, using existing material to fill in missing elements, and clever editing to repeat layered kick samples on multiple tracks. After adding a break between two sections to create a suspension and capture attention, you will shorten another break that is too long.

Previewing the Song

Before you start editing an arrangement, you must hear the song and get to know its structure and instrumentation.

You can use markers in the Marker track to visually identify sections in a project. In this exercise, you will navigate a song using existing markers that help you familiarize with its structure. Using Solo mode, you'll identify and audition individual tracks.

1   Open Logic Pro X Files > Lessons > **08 Raise It Up.**

2   Click the Marker Track button.

Marker Track button

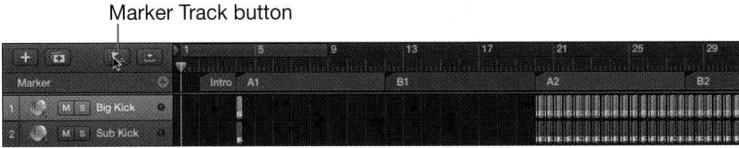

The Marker track opens with markers that identify the sections of the song (Intro, A1, B1, A2, B2, Break, Breakdown, and Outro).

TIP ▶ To create new markers, position the playhead where you want to place the marker, and click the Add Marker (+) button.

3   Listen to the song.

In the A1 and B1 sections, the kick sounds rather weak, except for the first kick at the beginning of A1. You will later repeat the first kick samples on tracks 1 and 2 to fill in both sections.

In the workspace, regions are color-coded to help identify the instruments they represent. From top to bottom, the drums and percussions are blue, the bass is brown, guitars are yellow, keyboards are green, and vocals are purple and pink.

TIP ▶ To show track colors on the track headers, Control-click a track header, and choose Track Header Components > Show Track Color Bars.

To fully understand how the song is arranged, listen to individual instruments. You can click the track header Solo buttons to play each track individually, but soloing and unsoloing one instrument after another to preview them isn't very efficient. Let's use the Solo mode instead.

4   In the control bar, click the Solo button (or press Control-S).

The LCD display and the playhead turn yellow to indicate that Solo mode is on. All the regions in the workspace are dimmed to indicate that they are muted. In Solo mode, only the selected regions play.

5   On the Percussions track (track 8), click the Percussions region to select it.

The region is shaded in yellow to indicate that it is soloed.

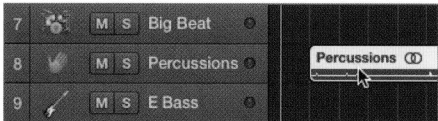

6   Listen to the beginning of the project.

You can hear the selected Percussions region in isolation, and identify which percussion instruments were recorded on that track: handclaps, tambourine, and shaker at the beginning, then more percussions come in at various places throughout the song.

You can click a track header to quickly select all the regions on a track.

7   Click the Banjo 1 track header (track 10) to select all the regions on the track.

8   Listen to the beginning of the project.

The banjo plays with a guitar distortion effect. It sounds thin and nasal in the intro, and then a bit fuller in the A1 section. In the Inspector, look at the EQ display at the top of the Banjo 1 channel strip. You can see the EQ curve change at bar 4. That automated change of the EQ parameters used track automation, which you will learn about in Lesson 10.

9   Start playback at the beginning, and before the end of the Banjo 1 region in A1, click the Piano region on track 15. The Piano region is selected, and after a little delay, you can hear the piano. Stop playback.

To avoid the delayed reaction of Solo mode when changing the selection, you can stop playback, select a new region, and resume playback. If you quickly press the Spacebar to stop playback, click the desired region, and press the Spacebar again, you can become very effective at listening to different regions in the workspace.

Let's listen to the Nana regions at the bottom of the workspace.

10 Drag around all the pink Nana regions at bar 38 to select and solo them.

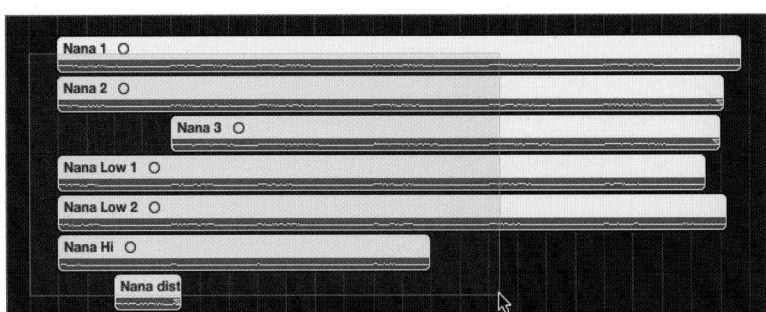

An easy way to start playback at the beginning of the selected regions is to use the "Play from Selection" key command.

TIP ▶ You can customize the control bar to add a "Play from Selection" button.

11 Press Shift-Spacebar (Play from Selection).

The playhead jumps to the beginning of the selected regions and playback starts. You can hear multiple voices singing "Nah nah nah…" at various octaves. Between the sections when they're singing, you can hear their headphone mix bleeding through their microphones. You will later remove that extraneous sound between sung sections.

12 Continue selecting regions and pressing Shift-Spacebar to hear those regions in Solo mode.

13 Stop playback.

14 In the control bar, click the Solo button (or press Control-S) to disable Solo mode.

By now you should be more familiar with the song, and the sections you're about to edit: the kick drums in the A1 and B1 sections, and the "nah nah" backup vocals at the end.

Copying Material to Fill in Parts

When using samples to build a rhythmic part, you often need to repeat the same sample (or group of samples) throughout an entire section. Depending on the length of the sample(s) pattern, you may need to repeat it on every beat, every bar, or every couple of bars. You can use several techniques to repeat sample patterns in the workspace.

Looping Regions with the Loop Tool

In this exercise, you'll use the Loop tool to loop a kick sample at the end of the Breakdown section, and then convert the loops into regions for individual editing.

1   On the Big Beat track (track 7), zoom in on the small region at bar 44.

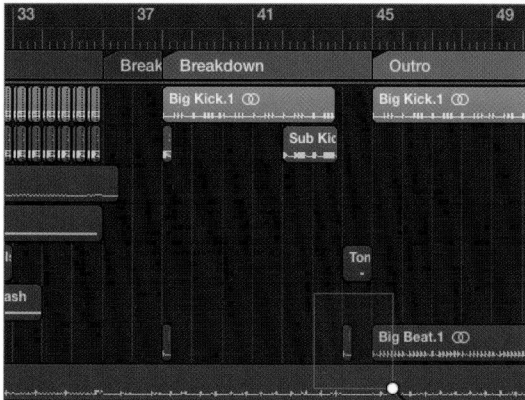

The Kick region is exactly one eighth note long, so looping the region will repeat the kick on every eighth note.

2   Place the mouse pointer at the upper left of the Kick region to choose the Loop tool, and drag to 44 3 3 1, for a total of five repetitions.

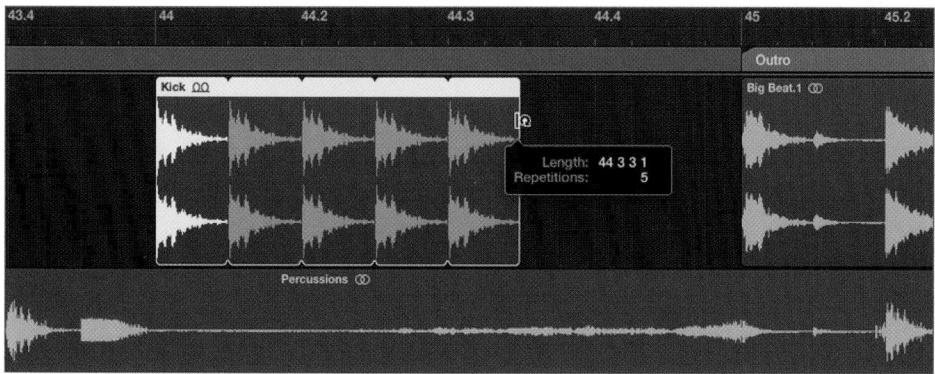

Let's convert those loops to regions.

3   Control-click the Kick loops, and from the shortcut menu, choose Convert > Convert Loops to Regions.

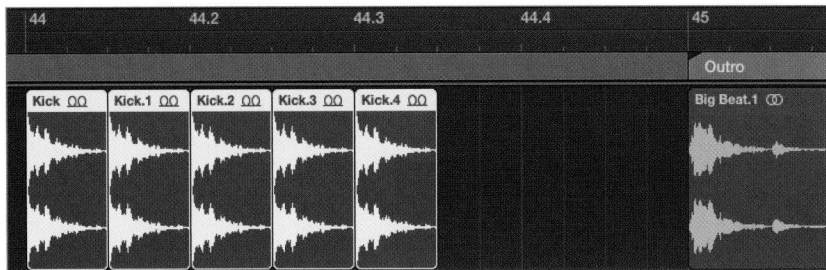

The loops are replaced by individual regions; but because they are all selected, resizing one of them would resize all of them by the same amount.

4   Click the workspace background to deselect all regions.

5   Resize the first Kick region to about half its size.

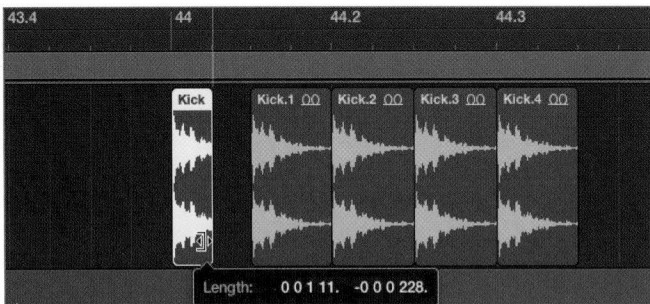

6   Resize the three following kicks in ascending lengths, leaving the last one (Kick.4) unchanged.

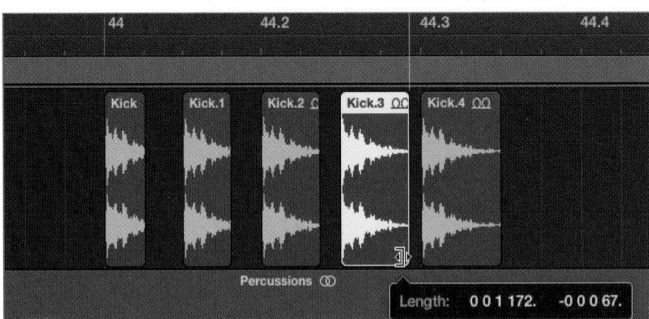

7   Double-click the lower half of the ruler (above the Marker track) to start playback a little before the first kick at bar 44.

The five kicks on the Big Beat track punctuate the Breakdown section with authority, announcing the new Big Beat rhythm in the Outro section.

> **TIP** ▶ To continue playback past the right edge of the workspace without the need to update the workspace to follow the playhead, in the Tracks area menu bar, click the Catch button to turn it off. The Catch button is automatically turned back on when you locate the playhead or start playback, and turned off when you zoom or scroll horizontally.

Catch button

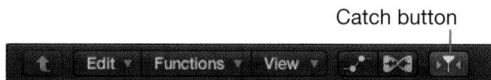

8   Stop playback.

9   Click the background, and press Z to zoom out.

By converting loops to regions, you can start arranging using the simplicity of the Loop tool, and complete your arrangement by leveraging the flexibility of individual regions.

Using Folders to Determine the Length of a Loop

In Logic, folders are regions that can contain other regions. Folders are a powerful arrangement tool, because when you pack regions into a folder, you can edit that folder as a single region, and the regions inside the folder will be edited accordingly.

When you loop a region in the workspace, the length of the region determines the length of the loop. If you wanted to loop a drum sample on every beat, but the sample's audio region was shorter than one beat, you could first pack the region into a folder that can then be resized to any length and looped. Then, the length of the folder determines the length of the loop.

In this exercise, you'll pack the sample on the Big Kick track (track 1) into a folder to loop it on every beat throughout the A1 and B1 sections.

1   Control-Option-drag around the two kick drum samples at the beginning of the A1 section.

The Big Kick region is less than a beat long, and if you looped it now, the loops wouldn't be in sync with the grid.

2   Click the Big Kick region at bar 4 to select it.

3   In the Tracks area menu bar, choose Functions > Folder > Pack Folder.

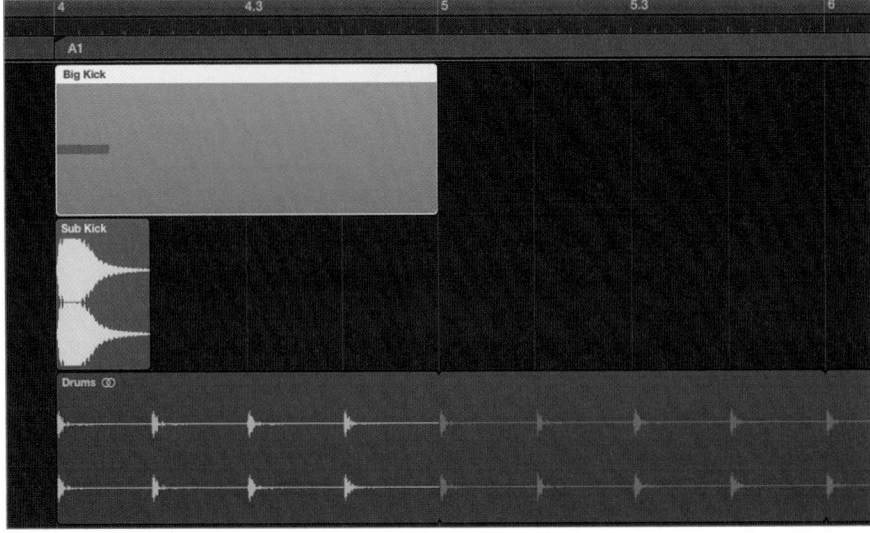

TIP ▶ You can use folders to pack multiple regions on the same track or on multiple tracks.

The region is packed into a folder that is one bar long. Looping it now would repeat the kick on every bar. Let's resize the folder to repeat the kick on every beat.

4   Position the mouse pointer at the lower-right corner of the folder, and shorten the folder length to one beat (0 1 0 0).

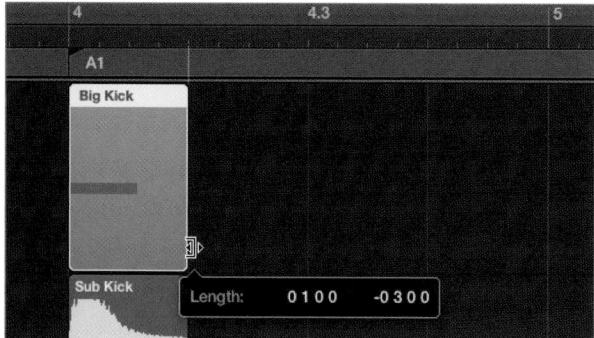

When you want to edit the region(s) inside a folder, you can double-click the folder to display its contents.

5   Double-click the Big Kick folder.

The folder opens, and the Tracks area displays its contents: a single Big Kick audio region. In the ruler, two markers show the folder's beginning (bar 4 beat 1) and end (bar 4 beat 2).

6   In the Tracks area menu bar, click the Display Level button.

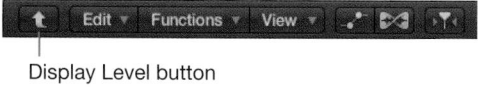

Display Level button

The folder closes, and the top-level Tracks area is visible again.

TIP ▸ You can also close a folder by double-clicking the background of the workspace.

7   Control-Option-click the workspace to zoom out.

8   In the Region inspector, select the Loop checkbox (or press L) to loop the selected region.

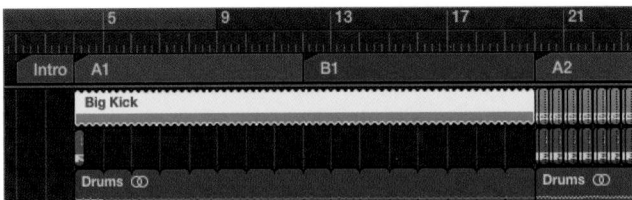

The region loops, and the loops stop where the next region on the track begins (at the beginning of the A2 section).

9   Listen to the A1 and B1 sections.

The Big Kick sample now plays every beat in those sections, making the kick drum sound fuller overall. You will repeat the kick drum sample on track 2 to complete the layered kick drum sound.

Cloning Audio Regions

Clones are regions that refer to the original region from which they were created. Resizing the original region or any of its clones resizes them all equally. Clones are very helpful when you are arranging regions you may have to later resize simultaneously.

You will now place clones of the kick drum sample on track 2 on every beat to fill the A1 and B1 sections, and later shorten the original and all of its clones in a single operation to adjust the kick drum's sustain.

1   On track 2, select the kick drum sample at the beginning of the A1 section.

You were introduced to the Repeat Regions/Events dialog in Lesson 6 when repeating MIDI notes in the Piano Roll. You will now use the same dialog to create multiple clones from the selected audio region.

2   Choose Edit > Repeat (or press Command-R).

3   In the Repeat Regions/Events dialog, use the following settings:

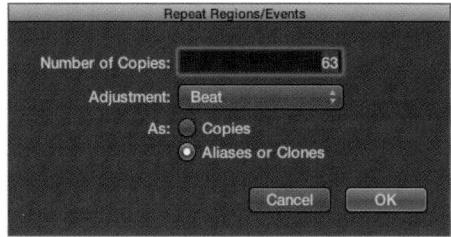

▶   Number of Copies = *63*

▶   Adjustment = Beat

▶   As = Aliases or Clones

NOTE ▶ When you select "Aliases or Clones," the type of region selected in the workspace determines the result: MIDI regions create aliases, and audio regions create clones. An alias doesn't contain any MIDI data of its own and always plays the MIDI data contained in the source region.

TIP ▶ To create a single alias or clone, Shift-Option-drag a MIDI or audio region.

4   Click OK.

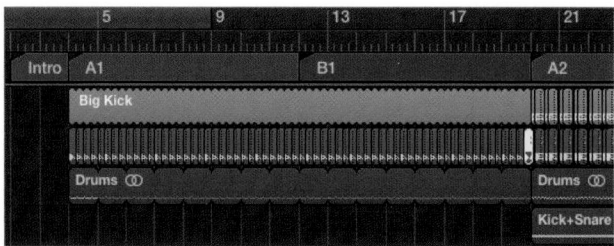

Logic creates 63 clones of the original region placed on every beat in sections A1 and B1.

5   Listen to the A1 section.

You may now be able to hear a faint low-frequency sound throughout the section.

6   Solo the Sub Kick track (track 2), and listen to the A1 section again.

Each kick drum is sustained until the next one hits, which creates a low-frequency drone. Let's shorten the samples so you can clearly distinguish between each kick drum sound.

7 Zoom in on the first few regions in the A1 section of the Sub Kick track (track 2).

The regions are connected, and you see the sustain tail of each kick end where the next kick starts.

8 Resize the first region to shorten it slightly.

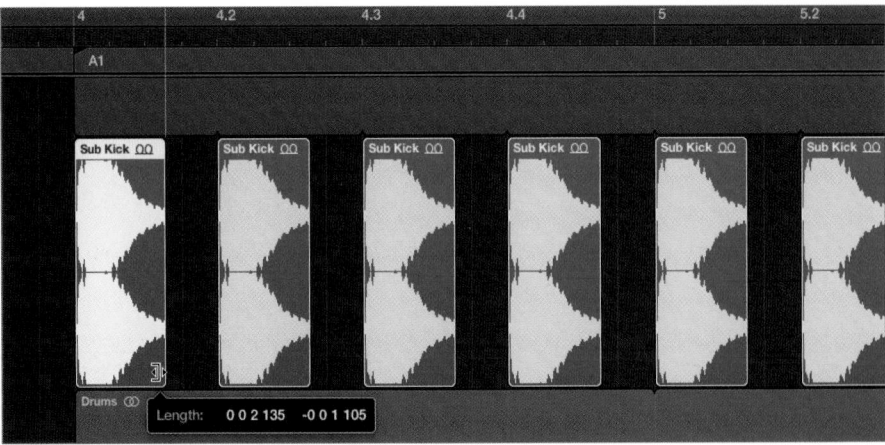

The original region and all its clones are resized by the same amount, which places silence between all the kick drum samples.

9 Listen to the Sub Kick track in the A1 section.

You can now hear silence between the kick drums on that track, and you no longer hear the low-frequency sound. However, the ends of the Sub Kick regions now click, a problem you will resolve using fade-outs.

Adding Batch Fades

Editing multiple regions can result in click sounds at each edit point. To remove the click sounds, you can easily apply the same fade to multiple selected regions using the Region inspector.

The first step is to select all the regions you want to fade. Selecting many small regions can be challenging: Zoom in and you won't see them all, zoom out and you may have difficulty distinguishing what is and isn't selected. Fortunately, you can use the locators to precisely determine which regions are selected.

1 Control-Option-click the workspace to zoom out.

   You could drag to select all the Sub Kick regions in the A1 and B1 sections. However, the regions are so small you might not be sure that you selected the last B1 region without selecting the first region in the next section.

   In Logic, clicking a track header selects all the regions on that track. However, when Cycle mode is turned on, only those regions within the locators are selected.

2 Drag a cycle area corresponding to the A1 and B1 sections (from 4 1 1 1 to 20 1 1 1).

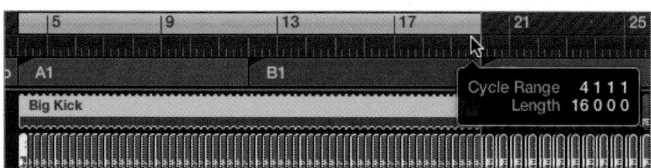

3 Click the Sub Kick track header (track 2) to select all the Sub Kick regions within the locators.

You can now use the Region inspector to batch apply fade-outs.

4   In the Region inspector, double-click to the right of the Fade Out parameter to activate the data field.

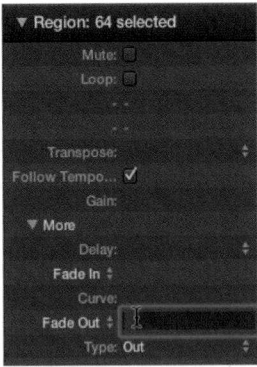

5   Enter *100* (ms).

A 100 ms fade-out is added to the end of each selected region.

6   Zoom in on a few regions on the Sub Kick track to see the fade-outs placed on those regions.

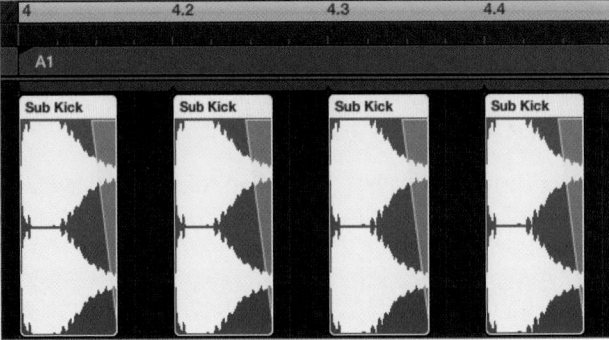

7   Listen to the result.

You can now hear the boomy sub kick sample on every beat, but with a shortened sustain tail, and without click sounds at the end of each sample.

8   Unsolo the Sub Kick track.

9   Control-Option-click the workspace to zoom out.

10 In the control bar, click the Cycle button (or press C) to turn off Cycle mode.

11 Listen to the beginning of the song. In the A1 and B1 sections, the kick now sounds deep and strong.

You now know several ways to copy, clone, repeat, and loop regions. You can pack regions of odd lengths into a folder and easily adjust its length for looping, and use batch fades to remove click sounds at the end of the regions.

Rendering Multiple Regions

In previous exercises, you created many loops and clones, and added fades to those cloned regions. When working with many small regions in the workspace, you may accidentally edit a region's length, position, or fade and not notice the accidental change unless you zoom in closer. To avoid this error, you can render several regions and their fades into a single new audio file.

1 Make sure the Sub Kick regions in sections A1 and B1 on track 2 are still selected.

2 Choose Edit > Join > Regions (or press Command-J).

A dialog opens asking you to confirm the creation of a new audio file.

3 Click Create. On the track, all the selected Sub Kick regions are replaced by a long Sub Kick audio region that spans the A1 and B1 sections.

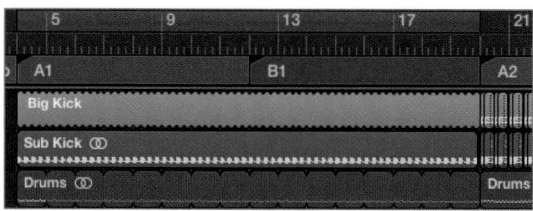

On the Big Kick track, a folder region loops throughout the two sections. You will bounce that section in place to create a new audio file on a new track, and then drag it back to the existing track.

4 Click the Big Kick region or one of its loops in the A1 or B1 sections to select the region and all of its loops.

5   Control-click the looped region, and choose Bounce and Join > Bounce in Place (or press Control-B) to open the Bounce Regions In Place dialog.

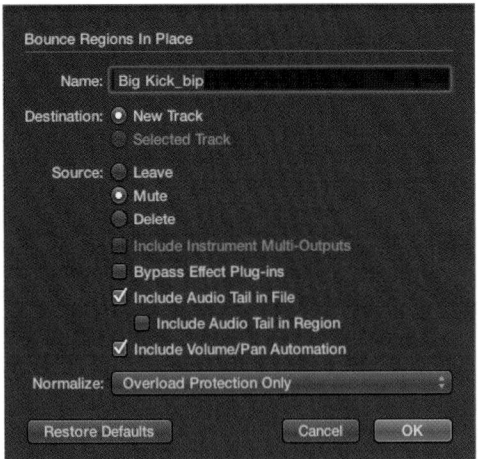

This dialog includes multiple options to determine whether to bounce with or without the effect plug-ins, and how to manage the source material.

6   In the Name field, enter *Big Kick*.

7   Set Source to Delete.

The current selection will automatically be deleted after the new audio file is created. You will be dragging the new audio file back to the Big Kick track, so you need to ensure that the new file remains unprocessed by the plug-ins, the Volume fader, and the Pan knob.

8   Select Bypass Effect Plug-ins.

Now the selected regions will not be processed by the plug-ins on the Big Kick channel strip to create the new audio file.

9   Deselect Include Volume/Pan Automation.

Doing so ensures that the bounced audio will not be processed by the Volume fader and Pan knob on the channel strip.

Normalize automatically adjusts the level of an audio file so that it peaks at or below 0 dBFS. However, in this case you want to retain the original level of the sample.

10 Set Normalize to Off.

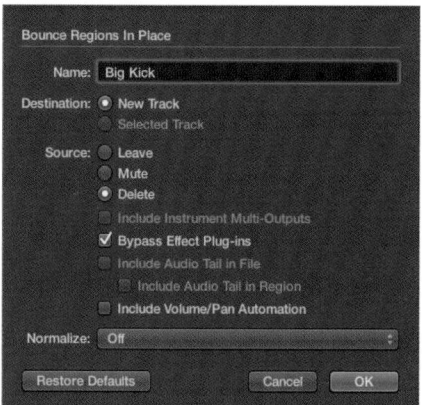

11 Click OK.

A new sixteen-bar Big Kick audio region appears on a new Big Kick track (track 2). Let's move that region back to the original Big Kick track (track 1).

12 Drag the Big Kick region on track 2 to track 1.

Because track 2 is now empty, you can delete it.

13 Select track 1.

14 Choose Track > Delete Unused Tracks.

The second Big Kick track created earlier is deleted.

Adding and Deleting Sections

Artists often become so involved in the creative process that they may not see the big picture when developing an ideal structure for their song. Producers and A&R representatives may suggest adding an introduction, making the chorus come in earlier, or shortening the song so its length is more suitable for radio play. Sometimes a shorter radio mix will be produced along with a longer mix for the album.

In the following exercises, you will save an alternative arrangement, insert one new section, and cut another to make the song more exciting.

Saving an Alternative Arrangement

Saving alternative versions can allow you to freely explore creative tangents while remaining able to return to previous versions of the project. In Logic, a project's alternatives are saved within the project file, itself. When the project is open, you can switch between different alternatives in the File menu.

Let's create a new alternative for your song, and rename the two alternatives. Later you'll continue editing the new alternative, and at the end of this lesson you'll go back to the current alternative.

1   Choose File > Save (or press Command-S).

All the edits you've performed to this point are now saved in the current project file, Raise It Up.

2   Choose File > Alternatives > New Alternative.

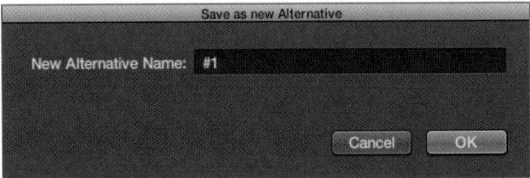

The "Save as new Alternative" dialog opens. Because you later will create a second break section, let's call this new alternative "Two Breaks."

3   In the New Alternative Name field, enter *Two Breaks*, and click OK.

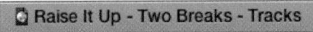

In the title bar, the new alternative's name (Two Breaks) appears next to the project name (Raise It Up).

Let's name the previous version you saved at the beginning of this exercise.

4   Choose File > Alternatives > Edit Alternatives.

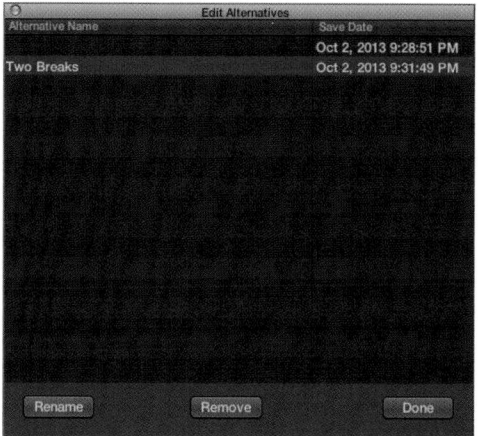

The Edit Alternatives window opens, listing all the alternatives created for the current project, and the dates when they were saved. Buttons allow you to rename or remove selected alternatives.

5   Double-click the first line below the Alternative Name header, rename the first alternative *Original*, and click Done.

You now have two alternatives of the same project. You saved Original at the beginning of this exercise, and you are currently working on the new alternative, Two Breaks.

Adding a Section

A good arrangement carefully balances new elements to keep listeners excited with repeating sections that return listeners to familiar territory and inspire them to hum along or dance. Adding a short pause before going back to a familiar section creates a suspension in time that surprises listeners and reclaims attention.

In this exercise, you will insert one bar of silence between the B1 and A2 sections, and use existing material in the song to populate that new break. In Logic, the position and length of the cycle area determine where the new section will be inserted and how long it will be.

1   Listen to the transition from the B1 section to the A2 section.

You can hear the vocals from the end of the B1 section ("yeah") overlap the vocals at the beginning of the A2 section ("I was"). When vocals from two consecutive sections overlap, adding a break or a pause between the two sections gives them space, as if you allowed the singer to breathe between two phrases.

Alignment guides are currently turned on in this project. If you tried to drag a cycle area in the A2 section, Logic would snap to the beginning and end of all the small regions in tracks 1 and 2, which would make it challenging to drag the cycle area that you want. Let's turn off the alignment guides.

2 In the Tracks area menu bar, choose View > Alignment Guides to turn them off.

3 In the upper half of the ruler, drag a one-bar cycle at bar 20.

4 Choose Edit > Cut/Insert Time > Insert Silence at Locators (or press Control-Command-Z).

All the regions are divided at bar 20. The regions to the right of bar 20 are selected and moved one bar to the right, leaving an empty bar below the cycle area.

You will copy the first region in the Banjo 1 track to this new break section. That region doesn't start on a downbeat, so let's enable snapping to make sure that the copy has the same position relative to the bar as the original.

5 In the Tracks area menu bar, click the Snap pop-up menu, and make sure "Snap Regions to Relative Values" is selected.

6 From the Snap pop-up menu, choose Bar.

7 In the Banjo 1 track (track 10), hold down the mouse button over the first region, Intro Banjo.

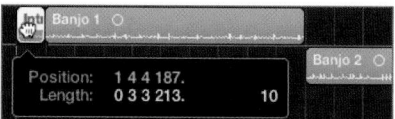

The help tag displays the position of the region (1 4 4 187).

8 Option-drag the Intro Banjo region to 19 4 4 187.

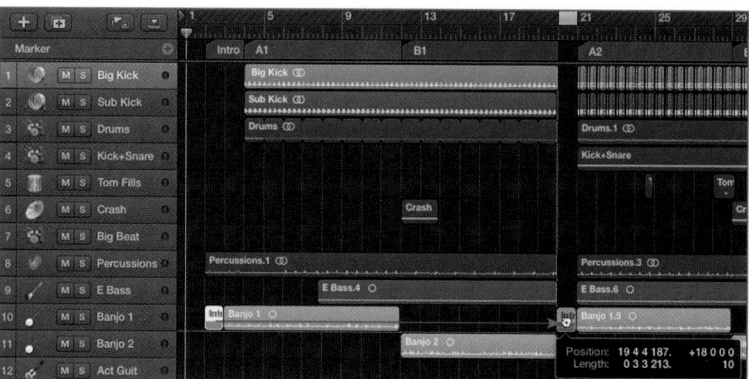

As you drag the region, it snaps to the same relative position in every bar (1 4 4 187, then 2 4 4 187, and so on), making for easy positioning without losing the timing of the performance in reference to the grid.

9 When you release the mouse button, an alert asks if you want to copy the track automation along with the region.

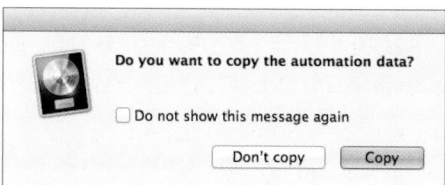

Remember when you listened to the banjo in Solo mode at the beginning of this lesson? You noticed that the EQ was automated, which gave the banjo a thinner sound during the intro. That same thinner sound would work great for this break, so let's copy the automation along with the region.

10   Click Copy.

Now let's add a tom fill to this new break section.

11   On the Tom Fills track (track 5), hold down the mouse button in the region just before bar 25.

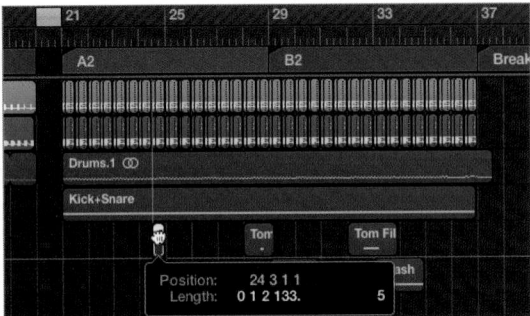

The help tag displays a position of 24 3 1 1, indicating that the region starts in the middle of bar 24. Snapping will ensure that you can drag the region only to the middle of a bar.

12   Option-drag the Tom Fills region to 20 3 1 1.

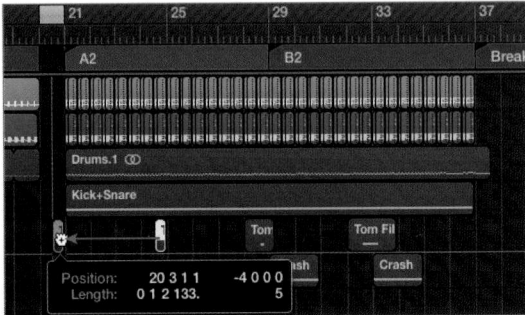

An alert asks you if you also want to copy the automation.

13   Click Copy to copy the automation with the region.

14   In the ruler, click the cycle area to turn off Cycle mode.

15 Listen to the new break.

It sounds good, but there's an issue with the vocal at the beginning of the A2 section. The vocals actually started a bit before the beginning of the A2 section, so they were divided when you inserted a bar of silence. Now the beginning of the sentence ("I was") is sung before the break, and the rest of the sentence is sung after the break ("under the ground").

16 Zoom in on the Lead Vox track (track 19) so you can comfortably see the small region at the end of the B1 section and the beginning of the Lead Vox region in the A2 section.

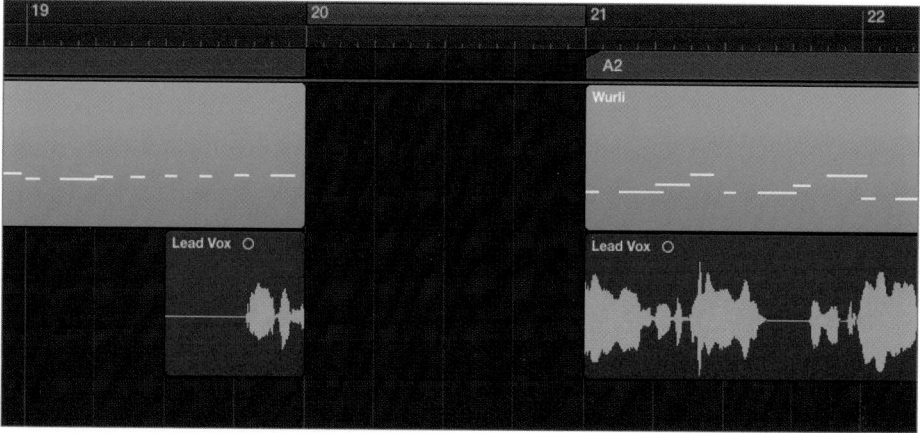

17 At the end of the B1 section (the end of bar 19), select the small Lead Vox region, and press Delete to remove it.

An alert asks you if you want to erase the automation at the region location.

18 In the alert, click Erase.

The Lead Vox region at the beginning of the A2 section is now missing the beginning of the sentence ("I was"). However, the region still references the original audio file, so resizing the region from the left will recover the part that was cut.

Because you will need to drag with more precision, you will set the Snap mode back to Smart.

19 In the Tracks area menu bar, from the Snap pop-up menu, choose Smart.

20 Position the mouse pointer on the lower-right corner of the Lead Vox region at the beginning of the A2 section, and drag to the left to 20 4 1 1.

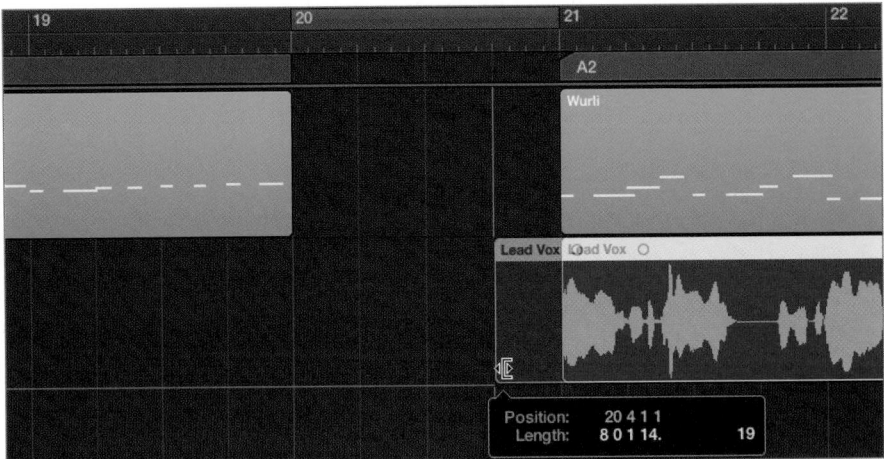

21 Zoom out and listen to your new break section by starting playback at the beginning of the song. At bar 20, you may hear clicks at the end of some audio regions. Feel free to zoom in and add fade-outs to remove the clicks.

The song has a two-bar intro, then plays two different eight-bar sections (A1 and B1). At the end of the B1 section, you can clearly hear the "yeah" on the vocals because no other vocals overlap them. Instead of the expected return to an A section, you get a one-bar break where most instruments pause. The thin banjo sound and the tom fill are just enough material to capture attention, and the beginning of the new sentence ("I was") at the end of the break pulls the listener into the next A2 section.

Cutting a Section

If adding a section can increase excitement, cutting part or all of a section can be equally effective to sustain the song's flow and energy. While arranging the song, you may not realize that a section is too long. Later in the process, as the song approaches completion, you can experiment by skipping parts of the song, and cutting a part when you decide the song works better without it.

You will now skip areas of your song using the locators, and remove part of a section. First, let's skip over the Breakdown section.

1 Play the song from around bar 35 to around bar 49.

The song comes out of the B2 section into a two-bar Break section, then a seven-bar Breakdown section introduces new backup vocals that continue during the Outro. Let's listen to the song without that Breakdown section.

2   In the Marker track, drag the Breakdown marker to the ruler.

Cycle mode is on, and the cycle area matches the marker. To turn the cycle area into a skip cycle area, you have to swap the left and right locators.

3   In the ruler, Control-click the cycle area, and choose "Swap Left and Right Locator."

The cycle area is replaced by a skip cycle area.

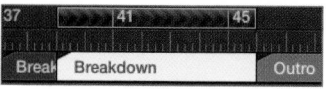

Let's play the song without the Breakdown section.

4   Listen to the song by starting playback a couple of bars before the Break.

When the playhead reaches the end of the Break, it jumps to the Outro, thereby skipping the Breakdown section.

Now that it's omitted, the breath of fresh air that the Breakdown section created is also missing. Instead, let's try skipping the Break section.

5   Move the skip cycle area to bar 37, and resize it to two bars to match the Break marker.

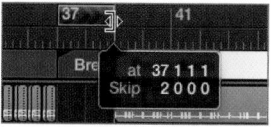

6   Start playback a few bars before the Break marker.

The transition between the B2 section and the Breakdown section is too abrupt. Let's skip only half of the Break section.

7   Stop playback, and resize the skip cycle area to one bar long so that it skips bar 37.

8   Start playback a few bars before the Break marker.

The timing is better. The break sounds empty now, but you can later add a section of bass. Let's cut the section below the skip cycle area.

9   Stop playback, and choose Edit > Cut/Insert Time > Cut Section Between Locators (or press Control-Command-X).

The section below the skip cycle area is cut, and all the regions that were previously to the right of the skip cycle area move one bar to the left to fill the void. Let's bring back the bass section from the cut first half of the Break section.

10 Zoom in on the bass below the skip cycle.

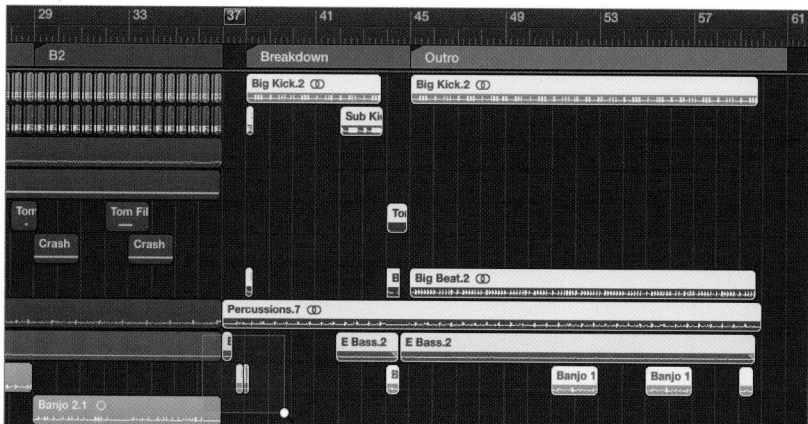

In the Tracks area menu bar, the Drag mode is set to No Overlap. In that mode, regions are automatically resized to ensure that they never overlap as the result of an edit. You will now lengthen the already-long E Bass.5 region.

11 Drag the lower-right corner of the E Bass.5 region to the right, over the short E Bass.8 region, ending it a little past the end of the skip cycle.

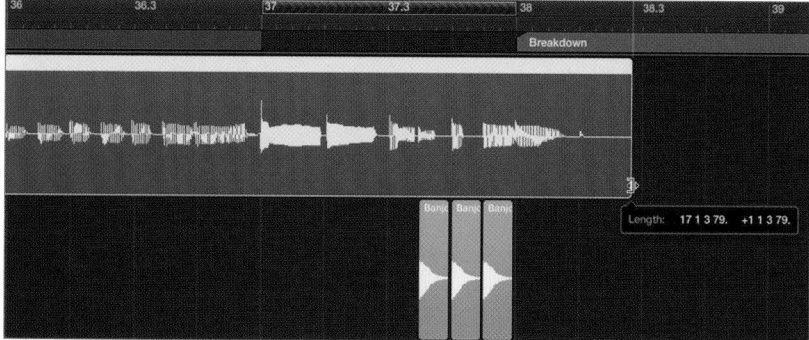

The short E Bass.8 region is removed.

Note that Cycle mode is still on. You'll have to turn it off if you don't want the play-head skipping the new one-bar break.

12 Click the skip cycle area to turn it off.

13 Zoom out, and listen to the new break.

The break now sounds perfect. The bass plays a fill, and the banjo, percussions, and keyboard (Wurli) play the last three eighth notes before the Breakdown section.

Cutting Regions to Remove Silence or Noise

When you are recording musicians who sing or play in only parts of your song, you may end up with long audio regions that have silence or noise between their performances. Cutting those silent or noisy sections cleans up your project, and produces individual audio regions for each part of their performance, so you can arrange and rearrange those parts more easily.

Muting or Deleting Marquee Selections

You can use the Marquee tool to select those sections between the performances, and then apply key commands to delete or mute them.

1   In the Nana 1 track header (track 24), click the Solo button.

In the workspace, all the regions on other tracks are dimmed, so you can easily see which track is soloed.

2   Click the Nana 1.1 region to select it, press C to enable Cycle mode, and press Command-U (Set Locators by Regions/Events/Marquee).

The cycle area matches the position and length of the Nana 1.1 region.

3   Zoom in on the beginning of the Nana 1.1 region.

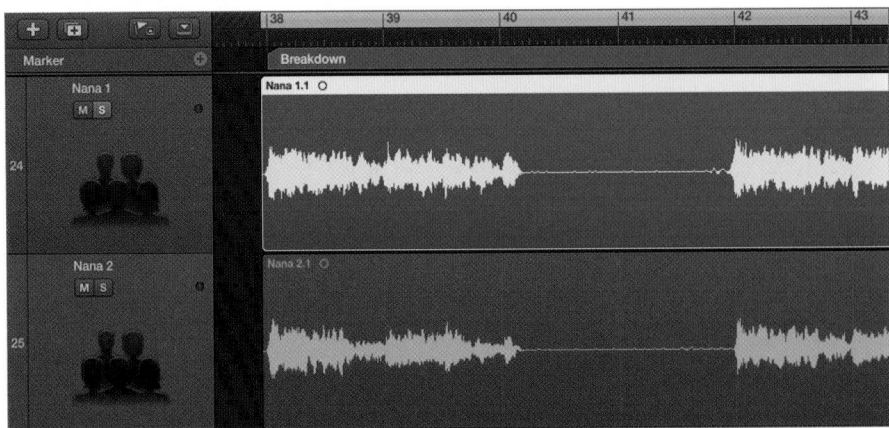

On the waveform, you clearly see where the vocalists are singing. When they're silent, the waveform is flat. But if you look close enough it's not completely flat, which indicates that you may have unwanted noise in the recording.

4   Listen to the soloed track until bar 42.

When the vocalists are not singing in bars 40 and 41, their headphone mix bleeds through their microphone. Let's remove that unwanted section using the Marquee tool, which is your Command-click tool.

5   Command-drag over the flat section of the waveform in bars 40 and 41.

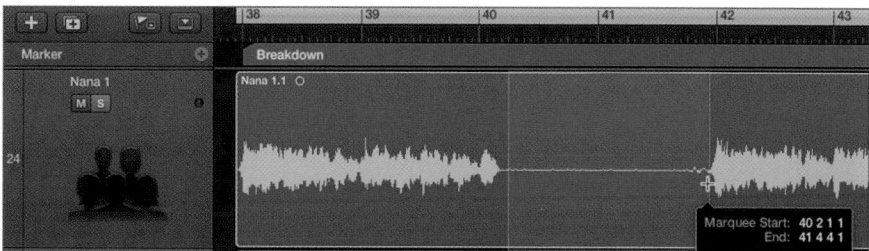

6   Press Delete.

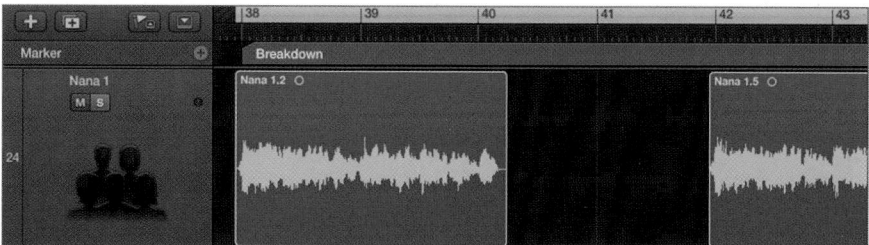

The marquee selection is cut, leaving you two regions on the track.

7   Listen to the result and note that you no longer hear extraneous sound in bars 40 and 41.

8   Using the same technique on the Nana 1 track, continue removing the noises between the singing until you reach bar 57.

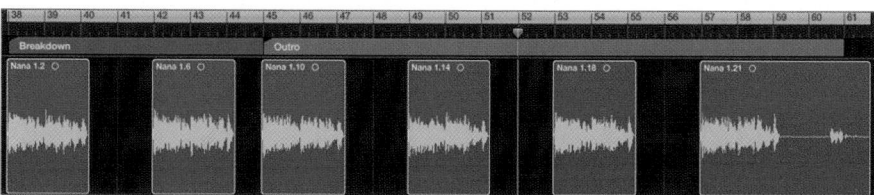

9 Listen to the last region by double-clicking the lower half of the ruler at bar 57 to start playback.

At the end of bar 60, the singers sing "Nah nah nah," and then you can hear a faint laugh. They most likely sang that last part as a joke because it wasn't part of the arrangement. When you're not sure whether or not to remove a part, you can mute it. Later, if you change your mind, you can easily unmute the regions you want to restore.

10 In the last region on the Nana 1 track, Command-drag starting with the flat waveform in bar 59 and including the little waveform near the end.

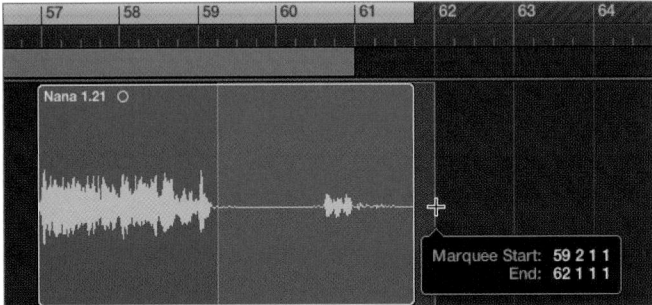

11 Press Control-M (Mute Notes/Regions/Folders on/off).

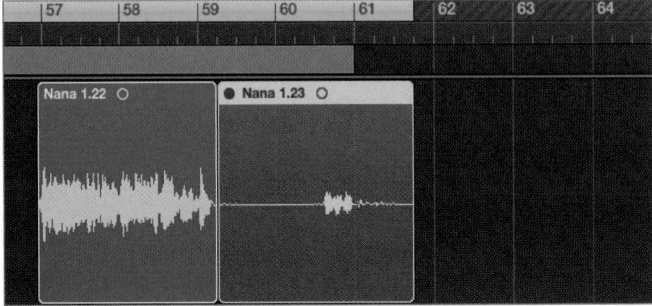

The portion of the region you selected is divided into a new, muted region. If you later decide that you want to play it, you can select the region, and press Control-M to unmute it.

Dividing Regions by Removing Silence

In the previous exercise, you used the Marquee tool to select unwanted portions of an audio region, and deleted or muted the selected sections using key commands. Although the Marquee is a powerful audio editing tool, continuing to manually edit all the Nana regions would be time-consuming.

To finish editing the remaining Nana regions, you will use Strip Silence, a feature that automatically cuts portions of an audio region that fall below a specific volume threshold.

1   Zoom out vertically so you can see all the Nana tracks (from track 24 to track 30).

To quickly solo or mute multiple tracks in the Tracks area, you can drag an interface button in a track header down or up to emulate the way sound engineers mute or solo multiple channel strips by sliding a finger across the buttons on a mixing board.

2   In the Nana 2 track header (track 25), drag the Solo button down to the last track (track 30).

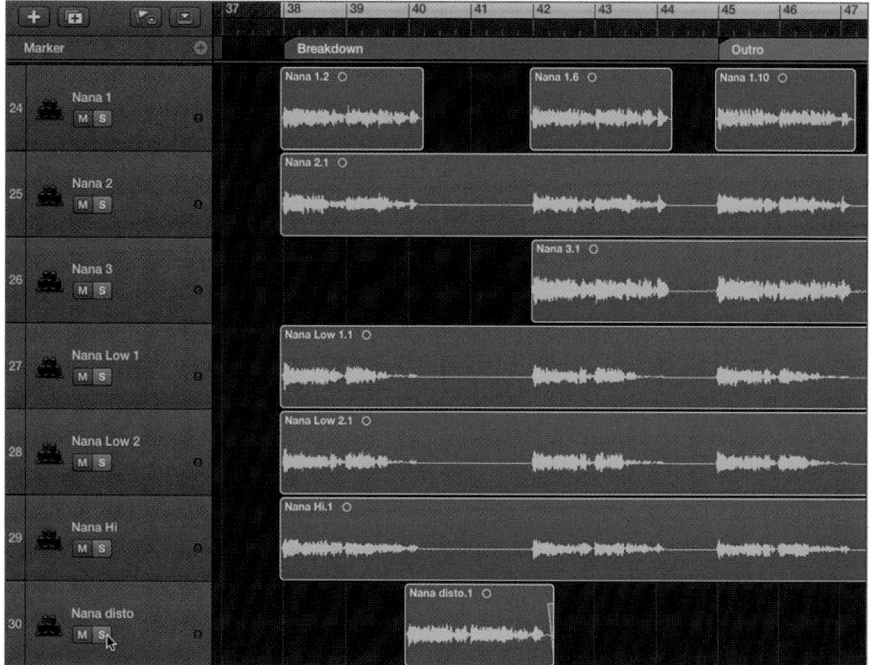

Track 24 was already soloed, so now tracks 24 through 30 (all the Nana tracks) are soloed.

3   Listen to the soloed tracks. You can hear noise (mostly headphones bleeding) between the sung sections.

Let's apply Strip Silence to the Nana 2.1 region (on track 25).

4   Select the Nana 2.1 region.

5   Choose Functions > "Remove Silence from Audio Region" (or press Control-X).

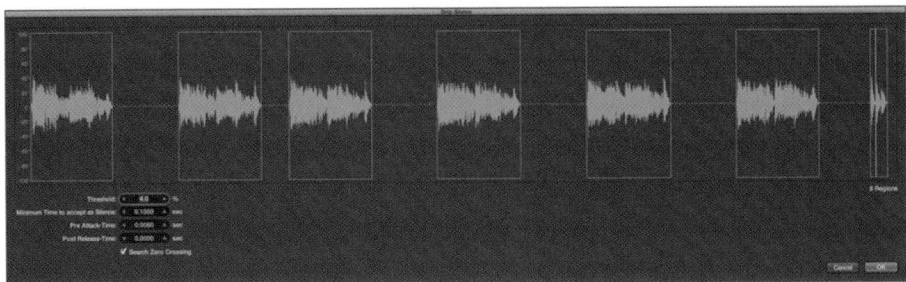

The Strip Silence window opens, showing how the region will be edited. To the left of the waveform, a scale allows you to measure the amplitude of the waveform from 0% to 100%. Below the waveform, the Threshold parameter is set to 4.0%, so Strip Silence will remove any audio that drops below 4%.

To the right in the Strip Silence window, two small regions will be created where you'd prefer to create only one. This occurs because in that short section, the audio went below the 4% threshold for a short period. You will now increase the "Minimum Time to accept as Silence" value a little to ensure that Strip Silence cuts a region only when the audio stays under the 4% threshold for 0.5 seconds or longer.

6   In the Strip Silence window, set the "Minimum Time to accept as Silence" to 0.5000 sec.

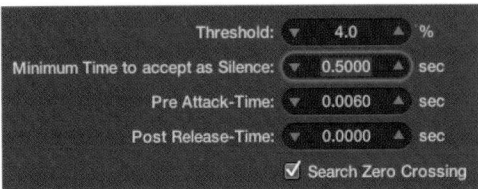

In the Strip Silence window, the values adjust by whole increments of the digit you drag. So you drag the first digit to the right of the decimal point to change the value from 0.1000 to 0.5000 sec.

In the Strip Silence window, the two short regions at the end are replaced by a single region.

7   Click OK.

On the Nana 2 track, the regions are divided so that the silence between the performances is removed.

8   Select the Nana 3.1 region (on track 26).

9   Choose Functions > "Remove Silence from Audio Region" (or press Control-X).

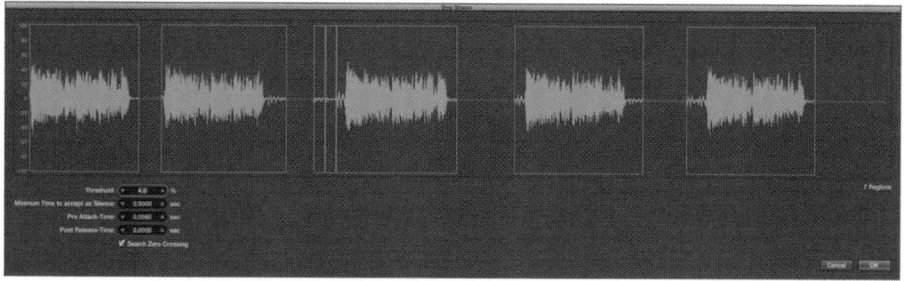

This region has more noise than the previous one. Some of the noise is over the 4% threshold, and Strip Silence is about to create several regions with only noise in them (just before the third sung section). To avoid it, you need to raise the Threshold above the noise level.

10   Drag the Threshold value up to 6.0%.

In the Strip Silence window, the two small regions containing noise disappear.

11   Click OK.

12   Click the Nana Low 1.1 region on track 27, and press Control-X to open the Strip Silence window.

One of the sung sections appears in two regions.

13 Set the "Minimum Time to Accept as Silence" to 0.6000 sec, and click OK.

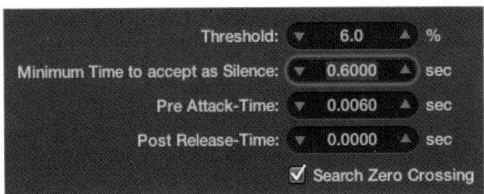

On the Nana Low 1 track (track 27), regions are created for each sung section. You will apply the same Strip Silence settings to the two remaining sections.

14 Select the Nana Low 2.1 region (track 28), press Control-X to open the Strip Silence window, and click OK.

15 Select the Nana Hi.1 region (track 29), press Control-X, and click OK.

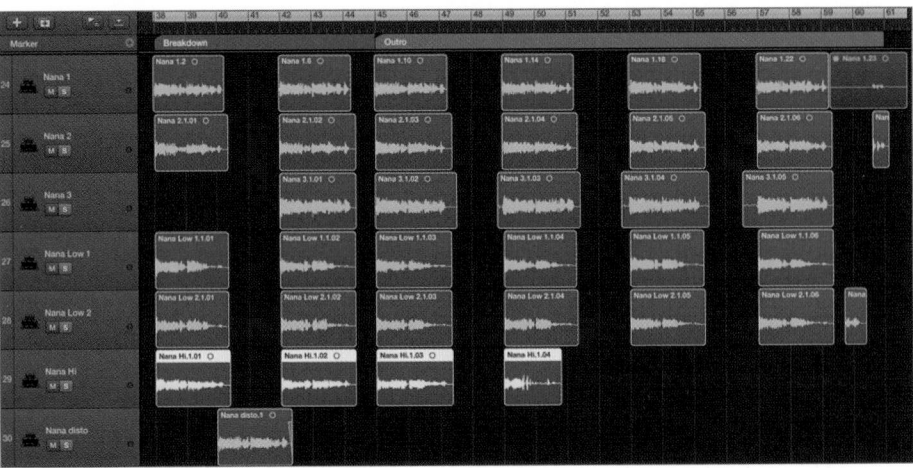

All the regions on the Nana tracks were divided to remove the unwanted sounds between the sung parts. Working with each sung section as an individual region will make the editing and arranging process easier.

16 Listen to the soloed tracks.

The sounds between the sung sections were removed, although you may hear some clicks at the edit points.

You will continue working on this vocal section in the next exercise, so keep the Nana tracks soloed.

Arranging the Resulting Regions

Now that you have each sung section in an individual region, you can easily edit and arrange those sections by muting or deleting unwanted regions, copying existing regions where performances are missing, and replacing a bad performance with a good one.

1   Start playback at bar 59, and listen to the end of the Outro section.

    On the Nana 2 track (track 25), the last region contains the same "Nah nah nah" performance you muted on the Nana 1 track. Let's mute that region.

2   Select the last region on track 25, and press Control-M to mute it.

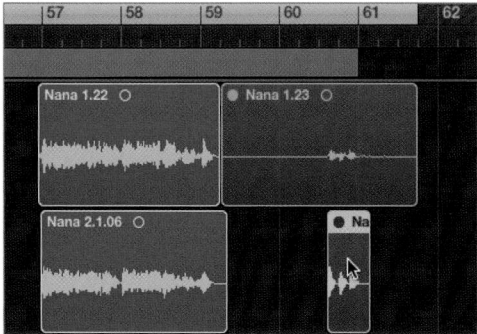

You will now listen to a bad performance and delete it.

3   On the Nana Hi track (track 29), select the last Nana region (at bar 49), and in the control bar, click the Solo button (or press Control-S).

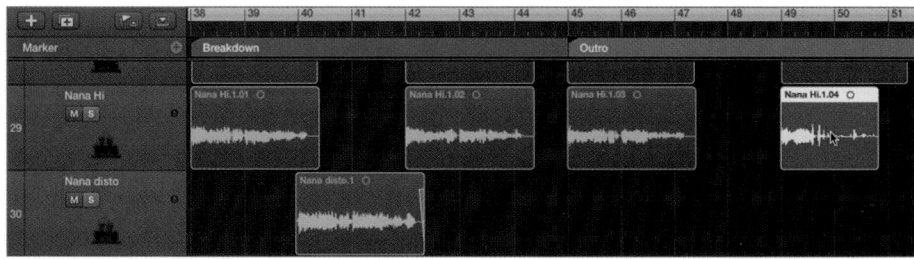

In the workspace, all other regions are dimmed and the selected region is shaded in yellow to indicate that it is soloed.

Cycle mode is still enabled, so pressing the Spacebar would start playback at the beginning of the Breakdown marker, several bars before the region you want to hear. Instead, you'll use the "Play from Selection" key command (Shift-Spacebar).

4   Press Shift-Spacebar to start playback at the beginning of the soloed region.

The singer goes flat on the first note, strains to hit the high pitch, laughs, and gives up. Let's delete this region.

5   Press Delete.

To replace the deleted passage, you'll copy the first region on the Nana Hi track to bar 49 using snapping to ensure an accurately placed copy.

6   In the Tracks area menu bar, from the Snap pop-up menu, make sure that "Snap Regions to Relative Value" is selected, and choose Bar.

7   Option-drag the first region on the Nana Hi track (track 29) to copy it to around bar 49.

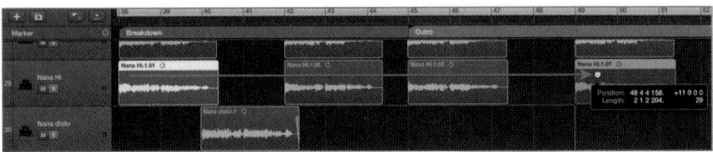

The copied region snaps to 48 4 4 158, retaining the same relative position as the original region.

NOTE ▶ To ensure that the region you drag doesn't snap to the beginning and ends of regions on other tracks, make sure that Alignment Guides are not selected in the Tracks area View menu.

8   Copy the region twice more to 52 4 4 158 and 56 4 4 158.

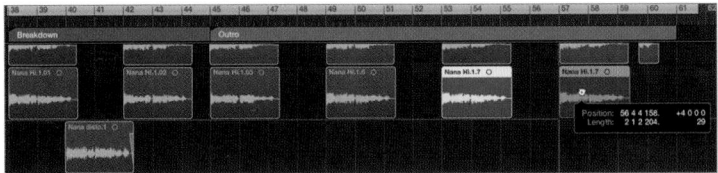

9   In the control bar, click the Solo button (or press Control-S) to turn off Solo mode.

You are done editing this project, so let's listen to the whole song.

10   Click the Cycle button (or press C) to turn off Cycle mode.

You will now use the "Solo off for all" key command to unsolo all the soloed tracks in your project.

11 Press Control-Option-Command-S to unsolo all tracks.

12 Click the background, and press Z to display the whole song.

13 Listen to the entire song.

Pay close attention to the sections you edited in this lesson. The kick drums you looped and repeated earlier in the A1 and B1 sections are now blending into a commanding, layered kick drum sound that drives the beginning of the song. At bar 20, the short one-bar break creates an exciting suspension that transitions into the A2 section. The one-bar bass fill leading into the Breakdown section is just the right length, carrying the listener into the powerful Nana backup vocals throughout the Breakdown and Outro sections.

You saved different project alternatives before you started editing the arrangement, so you can now go back to your original alternative.

14 Choose File > Save (or press Command-S).

15 Choose File > Alternatives > Original.

The current alternative closes, and the older version of the song opens. Note the absence of the break at bar 20, the two-bar break at bar 36, and the unedited Nana regions at the bottom right of the workspace.

Remember that a successful arrangement balances repeated elements and new elements. Repeating melodies and grooves gives the listener a chance to become familiar with the song, sometimes to the point of singing along or dancing. Adding small breaks to the arrangement suspends time in the flow of the song, and helps renew interest.

As you produce more music, you will become increasingly adept at determining what makes a good arrangement. Try to analyze the arrangements of the songs you love, and incorporate some of those ideas into your own compositions.

Lesson Review

1. How do you use the Solo mode?

2. How do you create a marker?

3. How do you pack regions into a folder?

4. How do you open and close a folder?

5. How can you insert a new section into a project?

6. How do you skip a section when playing a project?

7. How can you remove background noise between performances on a track?

8. How can you quickly select many small regions on the same track in a section of a song?

9. How do you drag a region while ensuring that it retains its position relative to the bar lines?

10. How do you quickly solo or mute multiple tracks in the Tracks area?

Answers

1. Select the regions you want to solo, and in the control bar, click the Solo button (or press Control-S).

2. Position the playhead where you want to place the marker, and in the Marker track header, click the Add Marker button.

3. Select the regions to pack, and choose Functions > Folder > Pack Folder.

4. Double-click a folder to open it. Double-click the background of the workspace, or click the Display Level button, to close a folder.

5. Adjust the cycle area to identify the length and position of the section to insert, and choose Edit > Cut/Insert Time > Insert Silence at Locators.

6. Create a skip cycle area by Control-clicking the cycle area, and from the shortcut menu, choosing "Swap Left and Right Locator."

7. Use Strip Silence to remove all the portions of a region that fall below a specific level threshold.

8. When Cycle mode is enabled, click a track header to select all the regions between the locators on that track.

9. In the Snap pop-up menu, make sure "Snap Regions to Relative Values" is selected, and choose Bar.

10. Hold down the Solo or Mute button on a track header and drag up or down.

Keyboard Shortcuts

Editing

Command-R	Repeats selected regions or events
Command-J	Renders selected regions into a new region
Control-B	Opens the "Bounce in Place" dialog
Control-Command-Z	Inserts an empty section between the locators
Control-Command-X	Cuts the section between the locators
Control-X	Opens the Strip Silence window
Control-M	Mutes or unmutes the selected regions or marquee selection

Tracks

Control-Option-Command-S	Unsolos all soloed tracks

Navigation

Command-U	Sets the locators to match the selected regions or events, or the marquee selection
Control-S	Toggles the Solo mode
Shift-Spacebar	Starts playback at the beginning of the selected region(s)

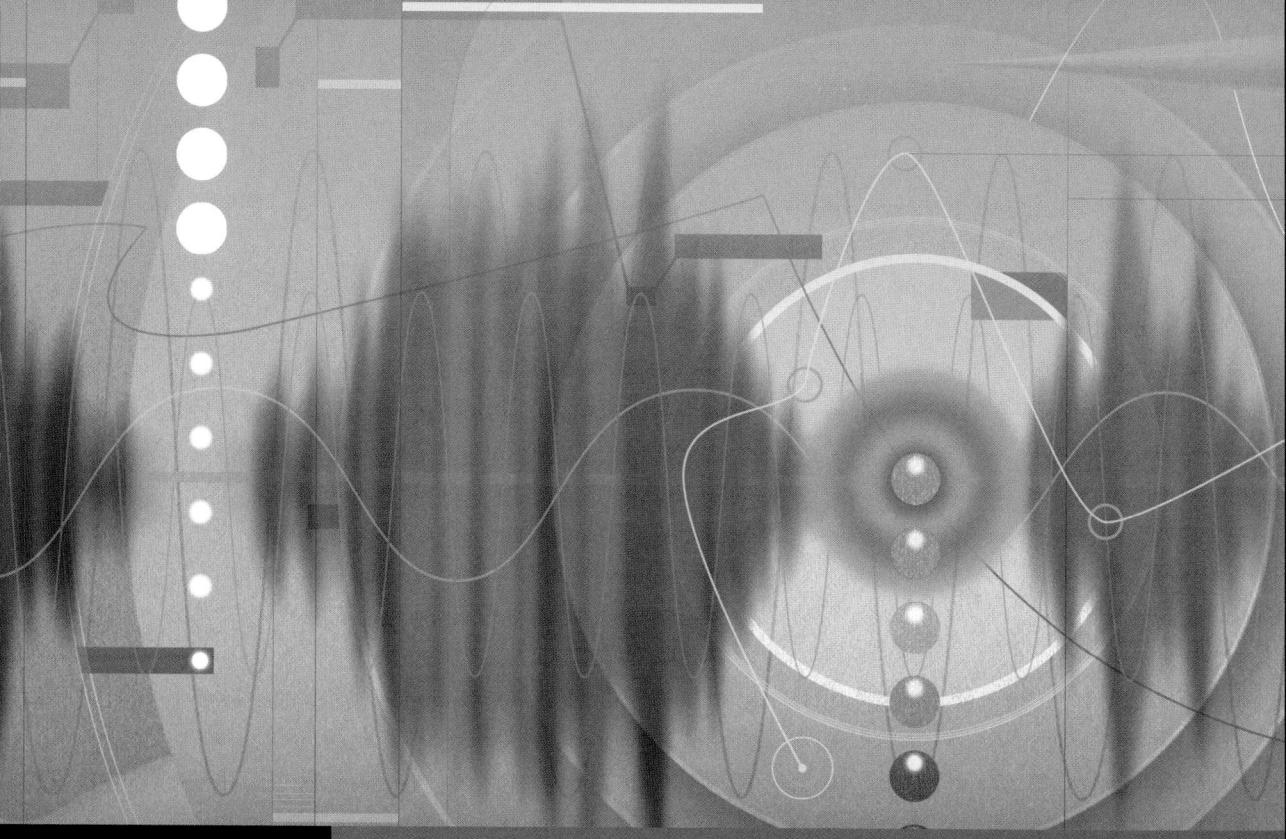

Mixing and
Automating a Song

9

Lesson Files   Logic Pro X Files > Lessons > 09 BIG

Time   This lesson takes approximately 90 minutes to complete.

Goals   Use folder and summing stacks

Use screensets

Use effects plug-ins

Adjust volume levels and pan positions

Filter frequencies with an equalizer plug-in

Process with bus sends and auxiliary channel strips

Add depth with delay and reverberation plug-ins

Use compressor and limiter plug-ins

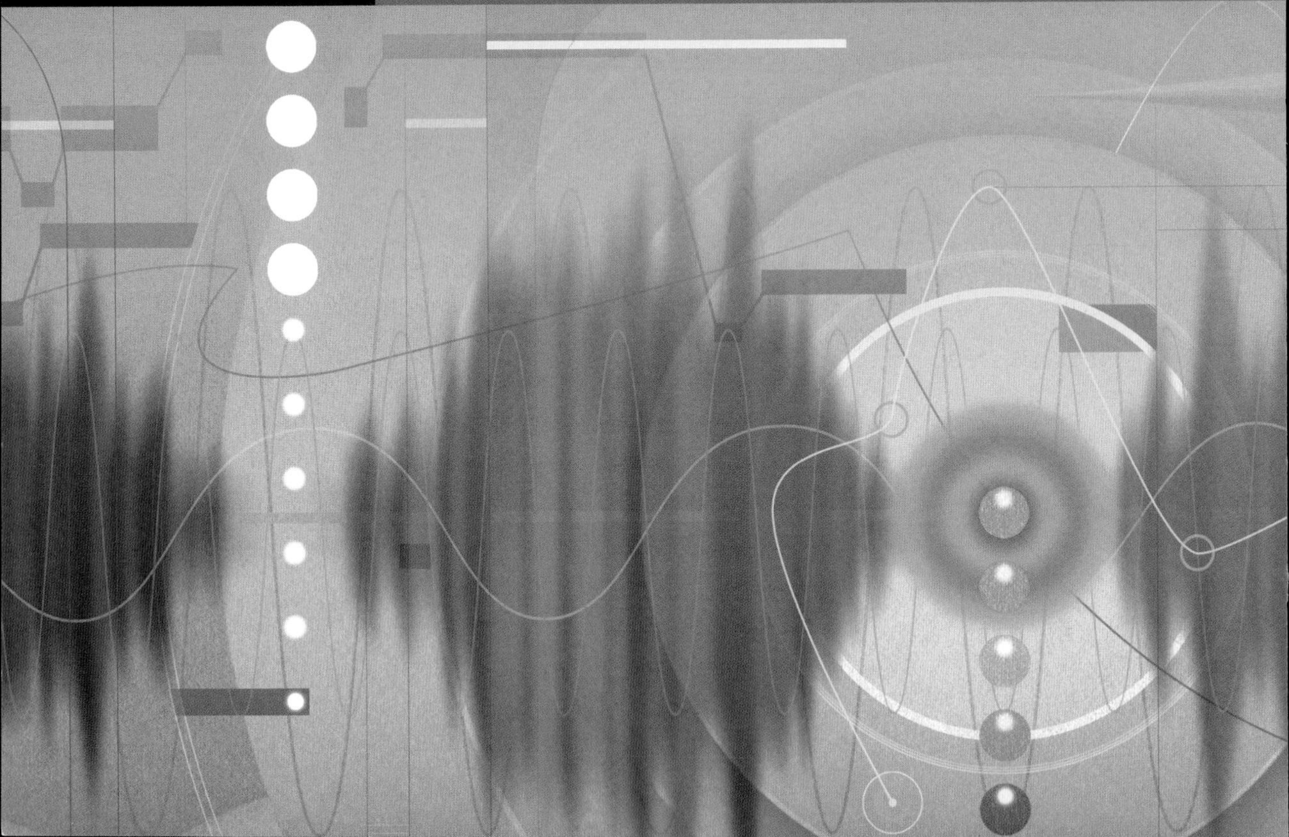

Mixing

Mixing is the art of blending all the instruments and sounds into a sound field. A good mix can make the difference between an amateur demo track and a professional production. Mixing should carefully balance two goals: blending all the elements into a cohesive whole, and at the same time, keeping them sufficiently defined so that listeners can distinguish among them. In other words, make the musicians sound as if they are playing in the same room, while ensuring that they don't mask each other and muddy the mix. A good mix is like a completed puzzle, in which all the pieces (all the instruments) fill their proper places in the sound field without overlapping.

With those goals in mind, you can adjust four parameters of an instrument to define its space in the sound field. You can adjust the instrument's volume, its lateral position in the sound field, its distance, and its frequency spectrum. Those parameters are interrelated, and changing one often means that you will need to readjust the others.

When mixing, it's also fundamental to be faithful to the genre of the song. In Lesson 7, you worked with a song (Little Lady) that had a rather dry mix because the indie rock song genre didn't call for many effects, and you wanted to stay close to the raw live performance sound of a rock band.

You will work with an indie folk song in the context of a modern pop production that will benefit from a variety of processing effects. A more complex arrangement with more layered instruments also means that you must pay more attention to each instrument's place in the mix. While Logic allows you to mix in various surround formats such as Quadrophonic, 5.1, or even 7.1, you'll focus on stereophonic mixing in this lesson.

Organizing Windows and Tracks

A little organization can go a long way toward making your mixing session more productive. It can save time by minimizing the need to constantly open and close panes, or zoom and scroll the workspace to locate tracks or navigate the song. The more you streamline your workflow, the easier it will be for you to focus on finding a place in the mix for each specific sound or instrument.

Using Track Stacks to Streamline the Workspace

As you build an arrangement, you may find yourself layering multiple instruments to get a fuller sound. Modern pop productions also often use short sound effects in strategic positions in the song that add ear candy and help renew excitement throughout the arrangement. As the track count increases, the Tracks area becomes bloated, making it increasingly more difficult to find the tracks you want to adjust.

In Logic, Track Stacks allow you to display a group of tracks as a single track in the Tracks area. The stack can be opened when you need to access individual tracks. In the next exercise, you will create a folder stack for all the drums and percussion tracks in the song, freeing the Tracks area of the tracks that don't need further work.

1   Open Logic Pro X Files > Lessons > **09 BIG**.

2   Listen to the song.

The mix sounds good, but a few instruments need work. Feel free to solo some of the tracks to listen to them in isolation. The electric guitar on the E Guit Hi track (track 25) sounds dry. Adding a guitar amplifier modeling plug-in will give it character. Using a tremolo plug-in to process the acoustic guitars on tracks 16 and 17 will add a bouncy groove to the Interlude section at bar 29.

Later, you'll mix the vocals (tracks 27 through 31) by adjusting their pans, levels, and EQ settings; and adding delay and reverberation.

The drums and percussion tracks on tracks 1 through 9 are fully mixed and don't need further attention, so you will now create a track stack for them.

3   Make sure the Kick track (track 1) is selected.

4   Shift-click the Percussions track (track 9) to select tracks 1 through 9.

5   Choose Track > Create Track Stack (or press Command-Shift-D).

In the Track Stack dialog, you can choose between a folder stack and a summing stack. Let's learn the difference.

6   Make sure Summing Stack is selected, and click the disclosure triangle next to Details.

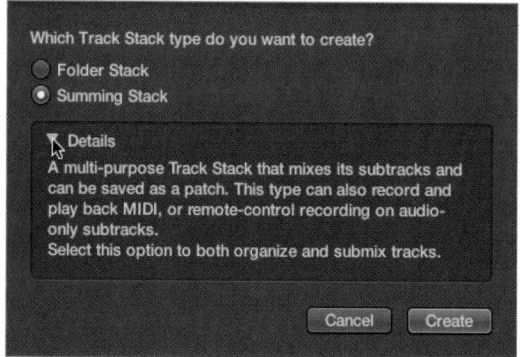

You used a summing stack in Lesson 5 to create a layered synth patch. In a summing stack, all the subtracks are routed to the main track's auxiliary channel strip where their submix can be further processed by plug-ins and then routed as desired. In this case, however, there's no need to further process the drums and percussions, and a folder stack is the tool for the job.

7   In the Track Stack dialog, select Folder Stack.

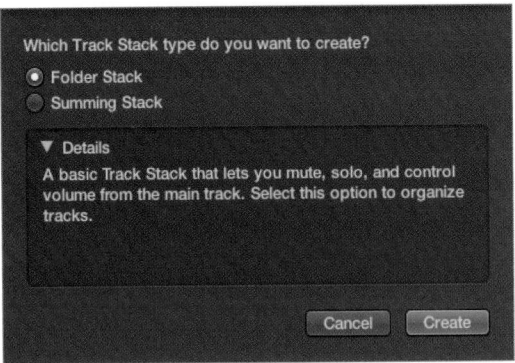

Folder stacks do not affect the routing of the subtracks, which makes them the right choice for organizing tracks that don't need to be submixed.

8   Click Create.

All the selected tracks are placed into a Track Stack on track 1. The Tracks area is streamlined, which will make it easier to find your way around the remaining tracks. In the Inspector, note that the Track Stack's main track channel strip (to the left) shows a Volume fader and Mute and Solo buttons, but has no Audio FX slot. The subtracks inside the folder stack are still routed directly to the Output channel strip, and no audio signal goes through the main track's channel strip.

Let's rename this track stack.

9   On the folder stack track header (track 1), double-click the track stack name, and enter *Drums+Percu.*

When working with very high track counts, consider creating track stacks for groups of instruments (such as drums, guitars, keyboards, and vocals) to streamline your workspace.

Using Screensets to Switch Between the Tracks Area and the Mixer

When first exploring the mixing process in Lesson 1, you may have noticed how much of a challenge navigating the workspace can be when the Mixer pane is open at the bottom of the workspace. In this lesson, you will use two screensets to save different window layouts. One screenset will display your main window, and the other will include your Mixer. As you work on the mix, you can recall each of these screensets using key commands.

Let's create the two screensets and study their behaviors.

1   At the top of your screen, look at the main menu bar.

The Screenset menu displays the number of the current screenset (1).

2   Click the Screenset menu to open it.

The menu lists only one screenset, with a default name in parentheses, Screenset 1 (Tracks). Let's create a new one.

3   Press 2.

NOTE ▶ If you use an extended keyboard with a numeric keypad, make sure that you press the 2 key on the alphanumeric keypad. You can use the numerical keypad to go to the markers in the Marker track.

A new screenset is created with a main window of a different size and zoom level from screenset 1.

4   Choose Window > Open Mixer (or press Command-2).

A Mixer window opens on top of the main window. You won't need the main window in screenset 2, so you can close it.

5   Click the main window beneath the Mixer window to bring it to the top, and press Command-W to close it.

Let's make the Mixer window bigger.

6   At the left of the Mixer window title bar, click the window zoom button.

Window zoom button

The Mixer window occupies the full width of the screen.

7 Click the Screenset menu.

The menu lists the two screensets with an appropriate default name for each.

8 From the Screenset menu, choose Screenset 1 (Tracks), or press 1.

Screenset 1 is recalled, and you can see the main window.

By default, screensets are unlocked. You can open multiple windows, adjust their sizes and positions, open the desired panes, choose different tools, and so on, and the screenset will memorize your layout.

9 Make sure that no regions are selected, and press Z to zoom in on the regions so that they occupy the entire workspace. If necessary, scroll to adjust the display as desired.

10 Press 2 to recall screenset 2, and press 1 to recall screenset 1.

Screenset 1 is recalled with the zoom and scroll adjustments you made in step 9.

When you're happy with the arrangement of a screenset, you can lock it to make sure that it always returns in that state.

11 From the Screenset menu, choose Lock.

Locked screenset

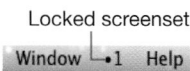

A dot appears next to the Screenset menu to indicate that the current screenset is locked. Let's observe the behavior of a locked screenset.

12 Zoom in on a region, change the tools in your tool menus, open some panes such as a Browser and an editor, and open some windows from the Window menu.

13 Press 1 to recall screenset 1.

The screenset is recalled in the state it was when you locked it, and all the changes you made in step 12 are lost.

14 Press 2 to recall screenset 2.

15 From the Screenset menu, choose Lock to lock screenset 2.

You have adjusted the layout of two screensets to easily switch between the main window and the Mixer window using the number keys. You've also locked those screensets, which gives you a quick way to recall them in their current states.

Customizing a Locked Screenset

In the previous exercise, you observed that locked screensets are always recalled in the state in which you locked them. When you want to customize a screenset that was previously locked, you can unlock it, apply the desired changes, and lock it again.

You will now customize the Mixer window in screenset 2 to display only the tools you need in this lesson.

1 Make sure you are in screenset 2 (the Mixer window), and from the Screenset menu, choose Unlock.

After making a decision during a mixing session, locating the components you need on the correct channel strip in the Mixer can be frustrating. By default, the channel strips in the Mixer window show you nearly all the available channel strip components. Because you won't need to access channel strip settings, you can hide the Setting buttons at the top of the channel strips.

2 In the Mixer window, choose View > Channel Strip Components > Setting Menu to deselect it.

At the top of the channel strips, the Setting buttons disappear.

3 Using the same method, hide the MIDI effects, Group, and Automation areas.

You can display track numbers on channel strips to make identifying them easier.

4   In the Mixer window, choose View > Channel Strip Components > Track Number to
select it.

Track numbers appear below the track names.

Some of the track, plug-in, and output names are abbreviated to fit the narrow channel strips. For example, the track name on the first channel strip on the left is displayed as "Dru…Percu," and the Output slot of most channel strips is displayed as "St
Out." You can choose to view wide channel strips, which are easier on the eyes and
avoid name abbreviations.

5   In the Mixer, click the Wide Channel Strips button.

Narrow Channel Strips button ———  ——— Wide Channel Strips button

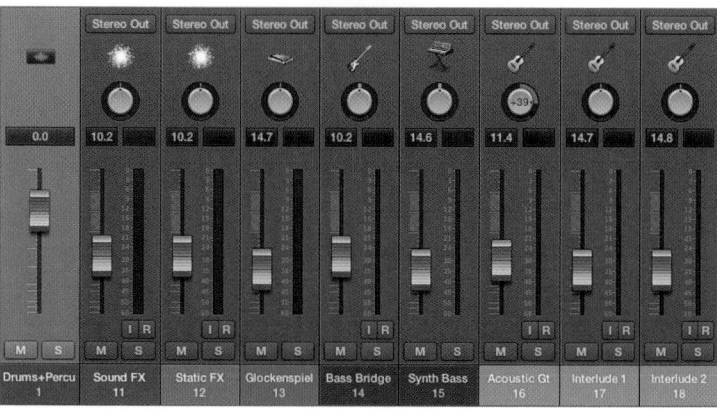

The channel strips grow wider. The first channel strip now displays the full track name, "Drums+Percu," and the outputs of most channel strips now display "Stereo Out."

To avoid any further changes to this screenset, let's lock it again.

6   From the Screenset menu, choose Lock to lock screenset 2.

7   Press 1 to recall screenset 1.

You took the time to get rid of the clutter in the Mixer, which will reward you later when you have to quickly identify channel strips, see where they are routed, and adjust their settings.

Using the Amp Designer

You can use audio effect plug-ins to sculpt sound and give it character, and help the various parts find their places in the mix. These plug-ins will also give those parts a different timbre, and later, influence how you adjust their levels or EQ (equalization).

The Amp Designer is a plug-in that emulates the sound of a guitar amp, its speaker cabinet, and the microphone used to record it. The plug-in simulates several amp models from famous vintage to modern guitar amps, and produces sounds ranging from clean to devastating high-gain distortion, with every nuance in-between.

Inserting a Plug-in at a Specific Point in the Signal Flow

When processing an instrument with multiple plug-ins, the order of the plug-ins influences the resulting sound. A guitar that is EQ'ed then distorted will not sound the same as a guitar that is distorted then EQ'ed.

In this song, the electric guitar on track 26 was recorded direct without using a guitar amp. To start your mix, you'll apply the Amp Designer plug-in to give the guitar a vintage low-gain distortion tone. A couple of plug-ins were already placed on the guitar channel strip, and you will insert the Amp Designer before those two plug-ins so that the guitar is distorted first by the amp and then processed by the other plug-ins.

1   In the Marker track, drag the CH2 marker to the ruler.

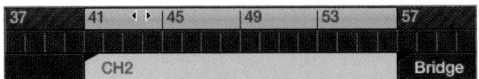

Cycle mode is turned on, and the cycle area corresponds to the CH2 marker where the E Guit Hi (track 26) plays for the first time in the song.

2   Press the Spacebar to start playback.

The guitar plays a staccato rhythm with short, clean-sounding chords on every beat.

3   Select the E Guit Hi track (track 26), and click its Solo button (or press S) to hear it independently.

The guitar has the really clean and dry sound typical of direct guitar recordings.

In the Inspector, look at the E Guit Hi channel strip. Two plug-ins (a Compressor and a Channel EQ) are in the audio FX section. At the top of the channel strip, the EQ display shows the rather drastic EQ curve of the Channel EQ plug-in. That EQ will later help give the guitar its place in the mix, but let's turn it off for now, so that you can clearly hear the effect of the Amp Designer.

4   Place the mouse pointer over the Channel EQ plug-in slot, and click the power button that appears to the left.

The frequency range of the guitar is extended. It sounds fuller, but still clean and dry. On the channel strip, the EQ display is dimmed to indicate that the Channel EQ plug-in is turned off.

Let's insert an Amp Designer plug-in before the Compressor.

5   Place the Pointer tool at the top of the Compressor plug-in so that you see a white line above the plug-in.

The white line indicates where the plug-in will be inserted in the signal flow of the channel strip.

6   Click the white line, and choose Amps & Pedals > Amp Designer.

The Amp Designer plug-in opens. On the channel strip, the Amp Designer plug-in (Amp) is inserted at the top of the Audio FX section, which means that the dry guitar sound on the track will be processed by the Amp Designer, then by the Compressor, and finally by the Channel EQ (after you turn it back on).

In the Amp Designer graphic interface, you can see the amp and its parameters (Gain, EQ, Reverb, and so on), and to the right, the cabinet and the microphone. At the bottom, pop-up menus allow you to choose a model, and to customize the model by selecting the desired amp, cabinet, and microphone.

TIP ▶ Press V to hide or show all open plug-in windows.

The guitar tone now has the character of a guitar plugged into an amp, and you can hear the amp's reverb.

7   Press the Spacebar to stop playback.

Inserting an Amp Designer plug-in on your dry guitar track produces a sound that is very close to the sound of a mic'ed guitar amp cabinet. The modeled amp gives you the sound you want (and great flexibility) without the hassle of dealing with high acoustic sound levels.

Customizing an Amp Model

A great way to personalize the sound of a guitar amp is to pair it with a specific guitar cabinet and microphone. To further customize the amp, you can change the amp's EQ and Reverb types, and adjust the position of the microphone in front of the cabinet.

Throughout this exercise, take time to experiment with various models, and tweak the amp knobs to get a feel for the many sounds that the Amp Designer can produce. As you customize and fine-tune your guitar amp, don't forget to unsolo the guitar occasionally to hear how your changes affect the perception of the guitar within the entire mix.

1   Press the Spacebar to start playback.

The amp gives the guitar a clean sound. Let's raise the gain to get a crunchier distortion sound.

2   On the amp, turn the Gain knob all the way up.

The guitar has a nice crunchy distortion. Let's try another color of reverb.

3   From the Reverb pop-up menu, choose Boutique Spring.

Reverb pop-up menu

The reverb has the biting high-frequency sound typical of the spring reverb units found on some vintage guitar amps. The guitar sound has a lot of reverberation, which makes it seem far away. Let's bring the guitar forward a little more.

4   Turn down the Level knob to a position between 8 and 9 o'clock.

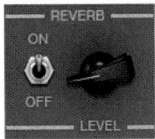

The volume of the reverb lowers, and it now sounds as if the guitar moves a little closer.

If you are listening on speakers that have an extended frequency range, or on head-phones, you may hear a low rumble coming from the guitar amp. At the bottom of the speaker cabinet, look at the Mic pop-up menu. The current microphone, a ribbon mic, has an extended range of frequencies that captures all the low-frequency content coming from the cabinet. A ribbon mic is a good choice when you're looking for a fuller sound. However, in this busy mix, a full guitar sound would have to fight for attention with the other instruments in the arrangement. A more focused sound will help the guitar find its place in the frequency spectrum of the mix without masking the other instruments.

5   From the Mic pop-up menu, choose Dynamic 57.

The low rumble is tamed, and the guitar has a sharper sound that more easily cuts through the mix.

At the bottom of the Amp Designer, look at the Model, Amp, and Cabinet pop-up menus. The British Combo model is a combination of a British amp and a British 2x12 cabinet. To create your own hybrid guitar amp model, you'll choose another cabinet.

6   From the Cabinet pop-up menu, choose Vintage British 4x12.

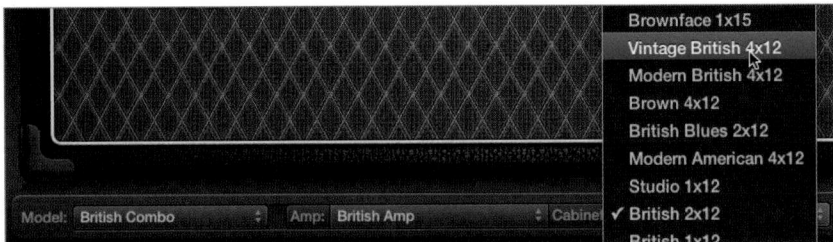

The guitar sound becomes a little less aggressive.

You can now further sculpt the sound of the guitar by carefully positioning the microphone in front of the speaker.

7   Place the mouse pointer over the speaker cabinet.

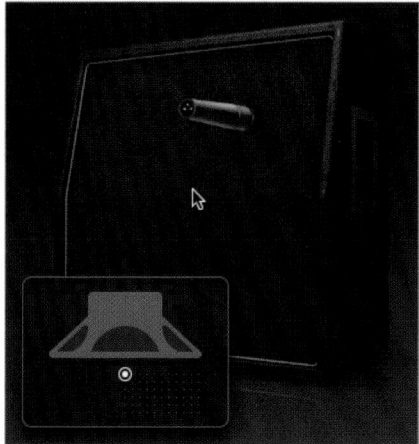

A graphic appears that displays the position of the microphone in front of the speaker (represented as a white dot).

8   Drag the white dot over the graphic while listening to its effect on the guitar sound.

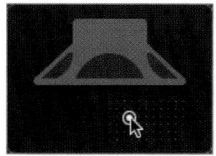

The mic position strongly influences which cabinet-generated frequencies are picked up by the mic. When the mic is aligned with the center axis of the speaker, you hear the maximum level of high frequencies, and the guitar sounds brighter and more present. Moving the mic off-axis tends to *scoop* the frequency spectrum, lowering the mids and emphasizing the lows.

Try to place your mic slightly off the speaker's axis and not too close to the speaker, as seen in the previous figure.

TIP When you have chosen a speaker cabinet and a mic, and positioned the microphone, you can click the disclosure triangle in front of the Mic menu to work with a smaller Amp Designer window.

You will now adjust the EQ to give the guitar a more focused sound with less low and high frequencies and more mid-range frequencies.

9   In the EQ section, turn down the Bass and Treble knobs, and turn up the Mids knob to the positions shown in the following figure.

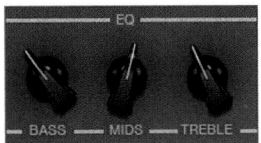

The guitar sound is slightly more rounded and focused, though still quite aggressive. You can tame its brightness with the Presence knob.

10   Option-click the Presence knob.

The Presence knob jumps to its middle position (12 o'clock), and the sound loses some of its aggressive bite.

There are two stages of distortion in the Amp Designer. Previously, you used the Gain knob to adjust the level of distortion introduced by the preamp stage. You will now adjust the Master knob to reduce the saturation introduced by the power amp.

11   Drag the Master knob to 1 o'clock.

While the guitar still has the nice crunch created by the gain in the preamp stage, it has less of the power amp stage saturation and sounds clearer. Turning down the Master knob also turns down the volume of the amp. To compensate, you can drag the Output slider, which adjusts the output volume of the plug-in without affecting the tone.

12 At the bottom right of the Amp Designer, drag the Output slider up to –3.0 dB.

13 Close the Amp Designer plug-in window.

14 Stop playback.

The guitar now has a focused, crunchy, distorted sound that faithfully emulates the famous tone of vintage low-gain British amps. It has just enough distortion to thicken the tone, while adding character to the guitar and not muddying the harmony of the chords.

When customizing and adjusting amp settings, remember that all settings interact, and the quest for the ultimate guitar tone is rarely a sequential process. Trying a different mic probably means you'll have to correct its position, and choosing a new speaker cabinet may require you to readjust the Gain and EQ.

> **TIP** ▶ Don't restrict the Amp Designer to dry guitar tracks! It can work wonders to add sizzle to a drum track, warm up a digital synth, or give an edge to a vocal track.

Adjusting Levels and Pan

Adjusting the level of each instrument may seem like the most obvious part of the mixing process, and you will usually start setting levels as you build the song. However, the perception of an instrument's loudness changes during the mixing process, and you will often have to readjust the level of an instrument after you add an effect to it or change its EQ settings, or when you mix other instruments that influence listener perception of that first instrument.

Positioning instruments to the left or the right of the stereo mix is a good way to separate them and make it easier for the listener to distinguish between them.

Now that you've adjusted the guitar amp to your desired guitar tone, you will unsolo the guitar track to hear how it interacts with the other instruments in the mix. You'll turn on the EQ plug-in you turned off earlier, and adjust the guitar's volume and pan to help it find its place in the mix.

1 On track 26, click the Solo button (or press S) to unsolo the guitar, and start playback.
The guitar sounds good but it's quite loud and full.

2   In the Inspector, place the mouse pointer over the Channel EQ plug-in, and click the power button to turn it on.

The drastic EQ curve completely removed a good part of the low frequencies, which really helps focus the guitar sound, which is now thinner, and almost nasal. That result wouldn't sound good for a solo guitar recording; but in a busy mix, it allows the guitar to play at a low volume and still cut through the mix.

3   On the E Guit Hi channel strip, drag the Volume fader down to –16.6 dB.

You probably feel that the level of the guitar is now so low that it almost disappears. When you spend a lot of time adjusting the sound of an instrument, it can be difficult to detach yourself from it and shift your focus to the song as a whole.

To find the right level for the guitar, turning it all the way down and listening to the whole mix (without the electric guitar) for a while may help. Then slowly raise the level of the electric guitar. (Closing your eyes ensures that you use your ears, and are not influenced by any preconceived notion of what value the fader should be.) When you feel that the electric guitar adds texture to the song without taking away from the other instruments (especially the vocals), you've found the right level.

4   On the E Guit Hi channel strip, drag the Volume fader all the way down to –∞.

Listen to at least one entire chorus without the guitar to become accustomed to the sound of the instrumentation in that section. Notice that the acoustic guitar (track 16) is panned to the right, leaving room for an equivalent instrument to the left of the stereo field.

5   Slowly drag the Volume fader up to –16.6 dB.

This time you can hear the guitar find its place in the mix. Listen to how it interacts with the vocals. However, every time the singers sing "Big," they mask the guitar chord. To avoid this issue without raising the volume of the guitar, you can move the electric guitar away from the center position. To complement the acoustic guitar and balance the mix in the stereo field, you'll pan the electric guitar to the left.

6   Drag the Pan knob down to –55.

The guitar is located on the left of the stereo field, where the vocals no longer mask it. The ostinato rhythmic chord pattern adds energy to the chorus, but stays out of the way and lets the vocals shine.

Submixing Tracks and Processing the Submix

When working with an ensemble of related tracks—such as the elements of a drum kit, an ensemble of backup vocalists, or two guitars doubling the same part—you can submix the signal of the group of tracks, and process the submix. Instead of using one plug-in for each individual track, a single plug-in can process the submix. Using one plug-in rather than multiple plug-ins saves CPU resources and lets you adjust the effect more quickly.

Submixing with a Summing Stack

In this exercise, you'll use a summing stack to submix two guitars doubling the same part in the Interlude section, and observe how the Track Stack affects the routing of its sub-tracks in the Mixer.

1 In the Marker Track, drag the Interlude marker (at bar 29) up to the ruler.

The cycle area corresponds to the Interlude marker.

2 Listen to the Interlude section.

Two acoustic guitars (on tracks 17 and 18) play the same sustained chords. To make this section more exciting, you will later process the guitars through a tremolo plug-in. For now, let's look at the signal flow of the two guitar channel strips in the Mixer.

3 Press 2 to recall screenset 2.

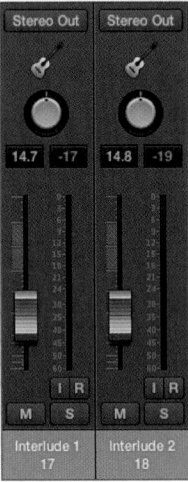

In the Mixer, look at the Interlude 1 and Interlude 2 channel strips (17 and 18). Both of them are routed to the Stereo Output (the Output channel strip located to the right in the Mixer).

TIP ▶ Double-click an output or send destination on a channel strip to select the corresponding destination channel strip.

Let's create a summing stack for the two Interlude tracks.

4 Press 1 to recall screenset 1.

5 Select the Interlude 1 track header (track 17).

6 Shift-click the Interlude 2 track header (track 18) to select both Interlude tracks.

7 Choose Track > Create Track Stack (or press Command-Shift-D).

8 In the Track Stack dialog, select Summing Stack.

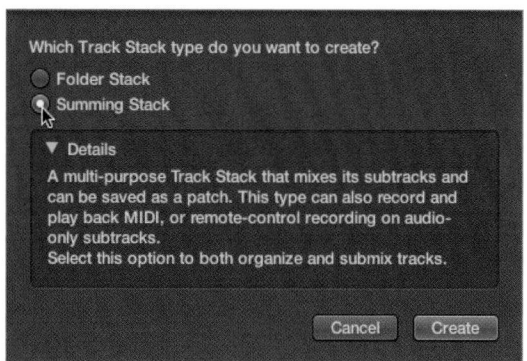

9 In the Track Stack dialog, click Create to create the track stack.

10 Press 2 to recall screenset 2.

The outputs of the subtracks are set to Bus 2, and their signal is routed to the input of the main track (Sum 2), also set to Bus 2. On the Sum 2 channel strip, two plug-ins (Compressor and Channel EQ) are loaded by default, but they are turned off.

Processing the Guitars with a Tremolo Plug-in

You will now insert a Tremolo plug-in on the summing stack to process the submix of the two guitars. When multiple channel strips are selected in the Mixer, their settings are linked. To insert a plug-in on only one of the selected channel strips, you must first ensure that multiple channel strips aren't selected.

1 Press the Spacebar to start playback.

Playback starts at the beginning of the Interlude section. (You can't see it currently, but in the previous exercise, you created a cycle area corresponding to the Interlude marker.)

Currently, the three channel strips that form the new summing stack are selected in your Mixer. If you tried inserting a plug-in on one of the selected channel strips, all the selected channel strips would have that same plug-in inserted in the corresponding slot. You need to deselect the three channel strips so that you can insert a plug-in to only one of them.

2   Click the name of any channel strip in the Mixer to select that channel strip.

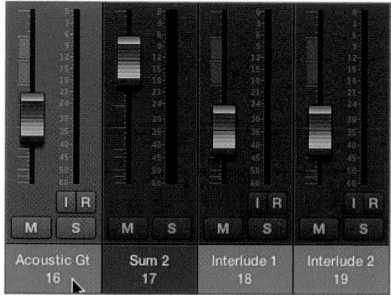

You can now insert a plug-in on only the Sum 2 channel strip.

3   On the Sum 2 channel strip (17), click below the Channel EQ plug-in in the Audio FX area, and choose Modulation > Tremolo.

On the Channel strip, the Tremolo plug-in is inserted after the Channel EQ plug-in, and the Tremolo plug-in opens.

The guitar keeps moving in the stereo field. This can be useful when you want an auto-pan effect, but in this case, you want a simple tremolo effect in which the volume of both sides of the guitar's stereo signal goes up and down simultaneously.

4   At the lower right of the Tremolo plug-in, drag the Phase knob down to 0°.

Both sides of the guitar's stereo signal now simultaneously go up and down in volume, creating a bouncy feel. Let's speed up the effect.

5   In the Tremolo plug-in, set the Rate to 1/8.

The Tremolo makes the guitar bounce up and down in volume every eighth note, which adds a rhythmic effect to the interlude, and novelty to the section. The side effect is that the guitars are now perceived to be softer in the mix. To compensate, you can use the Volume fader of the Sum 2 channel strip.

6   On the Sum 2 channel strip, drag the Volume fader up to +4.0 dB.

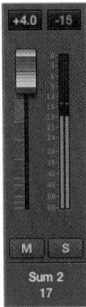

The tremolo effect sounds great, but the two guitars feel confined in the center of the stereo field, along with the Glockenspiel (channel strip 13). Not many instruments are playing during the interlude, so you can spread the guitars apart to add width to their mix.

7   Pan the Interlude 1 channel strip all the way to the left, and pan the Interlude 2 channel strip all the way to the right.

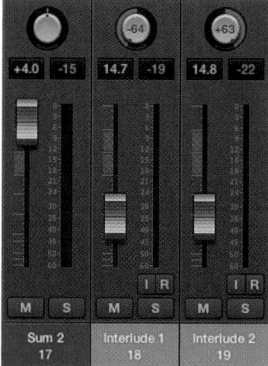

The guitars are spread out to each side of the stereo field, leaving more room in the center for the glockenspiel. The mix is wider, giving an impression of space, and each instrument has its own place in the stereo field.

Although you are done working with the Tremolo plug-in, there's no need to close its window, as you will now recall screenset 1. And since screenset 2 was locked before you opened the Tremolo plug-in, that plug-in will not be reopened the next time you recall screenset 2.

8   Stop playback.

9   Press 1 to recall screenset 1.

10 On track 17, click the disclosure triangle next to the track icon to close the summing stack.

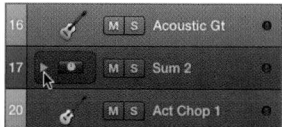

You used a track stack to sum two guitars onto a single channel strip, allowing you to process them as an ensemble. The Tremolo plug-in you added to the Sum 2 channel strip makes the guitars bounce in volume, and spreading the guitars in the stereo field produces a wider stereo mix, while giving breathing room to the individual instruments.

Using an EQ Plug-in

The sound of an instrument comprises several frequencies mixed together in varying amounts. By applying an EQ plug-in to attenuate or boost certain ranges of frequency, you can alter the timbre of the sound, much as you would change the sound of your music player by tweaking the bass or treble EQ settings.

EQ plug-ins can shape the sound of your instruments, focusing them in a specific frequency range and helping each instrument cut through the mix without boosting the overall level of its channel strip. Equalizing (EQing) an instrument can also decrease unwanted frequencies in its recording and keep it from masking another instrument in the same frequency range.

To shape the frequency spectrum of a vocal track, you will use the Channel EQ plug-in to attenuate some of its low rumbling while boosting some of the high frequencies to give it some air.

1   In the Marker track, drag the V2 marker up to the ruler, and start playback.

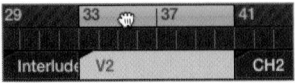

Feel free to keep repeating the V2 section throughout the whole exercise, or to stop and restart playback as you choose.

Several layered vocal tracks are located at the bottom of the workspace. You will solo one vocal track that hasn't yet been processed and EQ it.

2   Select the Ami Vox track (track 29) so that you can see its channel strip in the Inspector, and then solo it.

3   At the top of the Ami Vox channel strip, double-click the EQ display.

In the Audio FX area, a Channel EQ plug-in is inserted in the first available slot, and the Channel EQ window opens.

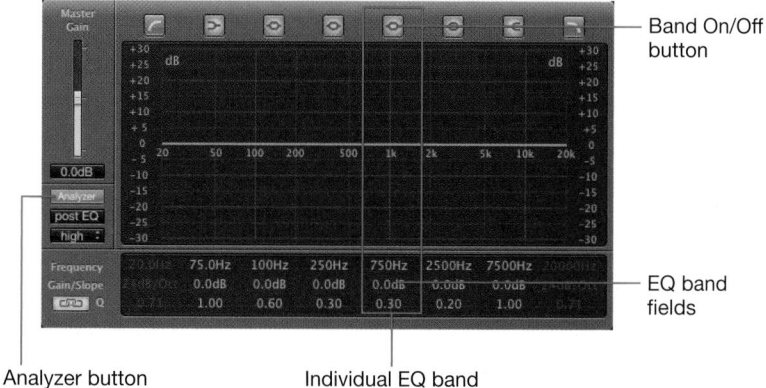

Band On/Off button

EQ band fields

Analyzer button   Individual EQ band

The Channel EQ plug-in allows you to adjust eight bands of EQ. You can toggle a band on and off by clicking the button at the top of that band. By default, the first and last bands are turned off, and all the other bands are turned on. Each band's settings are shown below the graphic display in the EQ band fields. All the bands that are turned on by default have their Gain parameters set to 0.0 dB; and in the graphic display, the EQ curve is flat, which means that the Channel EQ is not currently affecting the audio signal on the channel strip.

Clicking the Analyzer button turns on the frequency analyzer, which displays the frequency spectrum curve of the sound on the graphic display when the track is playing.

TIP ▶ By default, the frequency analyzer displays the frequency spectrum of the sound at the output of the Channel EQ plug-in. You can click the Pre/Post EQ button below the Analyzer button to switch the frequency analyzer to pre EQ. It will then display the frequency spectrum of the sound at the input of the Channel EQ, before being processed by the Channel EQ plug-in.

4   Click the Analyzer button.

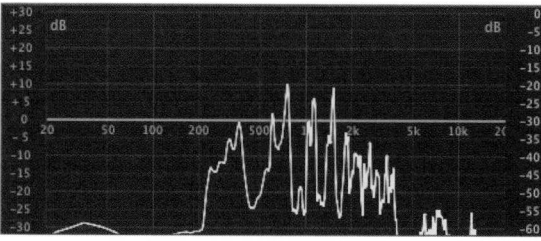

A curve appears in the graphic display, showing the sound's frequency spectrum in real time. Listen closely to the vocals as you watch the occasional movement in the very low range of frequencies (to the left). Feel free to raise your monitoring volume on your audio interface, or use the Volume fader on the Ami Vox channel strip. You can hear some low-frequency noises in the recording, especially at the beginning of bar 35. In vocal recordings, those low-frequency noises are often generated by the singer accidentally touching the mic stand, or by the mic cable rubbing against the mic stand.

You will filter out those very low frequencies to attenuate the unwanted noises.

5 To the left, click the first Band On/Off button to turn on that EQ band.

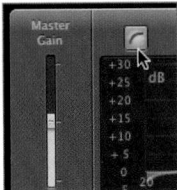

The first EQ band's shape appears on the graphic display. You can see that the low frequencies are slightly attenuated around 20 Hz.

6 In the parameter section below the graphic display, drag the Frequency parameter of the first band up to 400 Hz.

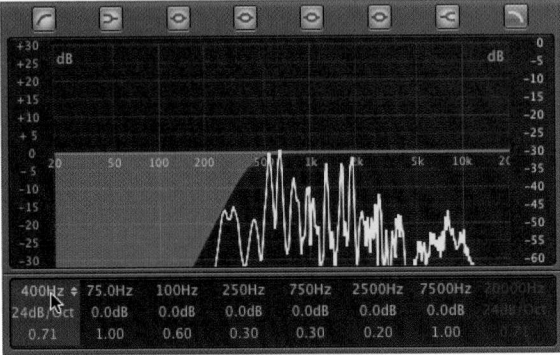

The EQ band shape updates in the graphic display. In the frequency curve displayed by the Analyzer, you can watch the low-frequency content disappear from the vocal signal. You can hear the low-frequency noises completely disappear. However you've changed the timbre of the vocals, and they now sound a bit thinner, almost as if coming from a cheap sound system.

You have to adjust the Frequency parameter of that first band so that the low-frequency noises are attenuated as much as possible without affecting the vocals.

7   Drag the Frequency of the first band down to 220 Hz.

You can hear the full vocal sound, and not the low-frequency noises. Mission accomplished!

Now you will attenuate the low/mid frequencies to remove the "mud" from the vocals. Instead of adjusting the numerical settings in the parameter section, you'll drag the pointer in the graphic display to adjust the shape of individual bands.

8   Position the mouse pointer over the upper half of the graphic display, and move it from left to right.

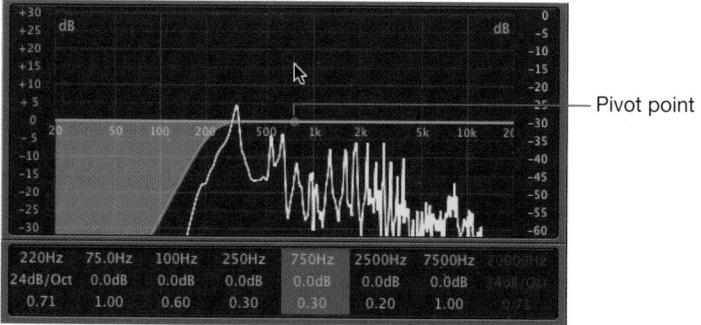

As you move the pointer horizontally, the EQ band fields are shaded in different colors at the bottom of the Channel EQ to show you which EQ band is selected. You can shape the curve of the selected band by dragging in the graphic display:

▶   To adjust the gain, drag vertically.

▶   To adjust the frequency, drag horizontally.

▶   To adjust the Q (or width, or resonance), vertically drag the pivot point (which appears at that band's frequency).

You first need to adjust the band's gain to see its shape on the graphic display.

9   Position the pointer to select the fourth band, which is currently set to a frequency of 250 Hz.

10 Drag down so that the Gain parameter below reads –7.0 dB.

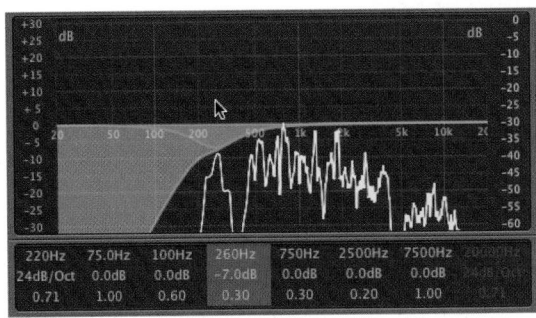

The shape of the selected EQ band appears on the graphic display, and the settings below are adjusted accordingly.

Now, while listening to the vocal, you will adjust both the Q and the frequency of the EQ band you are attenuating.

11 Drag the band to the right to set its frequency to 470 Hz.

12 Drag the pivot point down to widen the band of EQ until the Q field below reads 0.23.

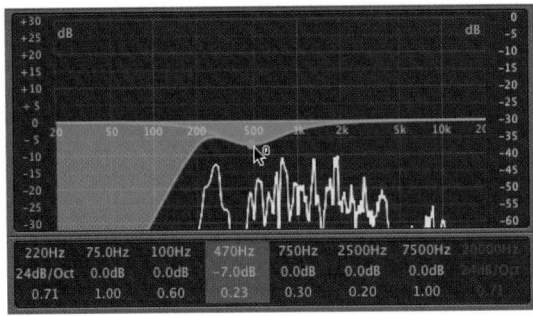

The vocal sounds less muddy already. Remember to click that EQ band's On/Off button to compare the vocal sound with and without that EQ band applied.

Now you can add some air to the vocal by boosting its high frequencies.

13 Drag the values in the EQ band fields, and set the next-to-last EQ band to the following parameters:

▶ Set the frequency to 6800 Hz.

▶ Set the gain to +3.0 dB.

▶ Leave the Q at 1.00.

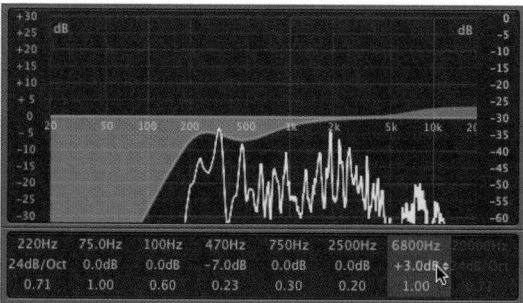

The vocal now sounds a bit less dull, and more present. Let's compare the sound of the vocal with and without the Channel EQ.

14 In the plug-in header, click the On/Off button.

The button is dimmed to indicate that the Channel EQ is off. On the Channel EQ graphic display, the curve disappears because the audio signal is no longer routed through the plug-in.

You can now hear the unprocessed vocal recording. The low-frequency noises are back, and the vocal is boomy and slightly dull.

15 Turn the Channel EQ on. The noises disappear, and the vocals sound clear and distinct.

16 Press Control-Option-Command-S to unsolo the Ami Vox track.

Let's now adjust the level of the Ami Vox track.

17 On the Ami Vox channel strip in the Inspector, drag the Volume fader all the way down.

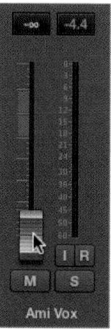

Listen to the verse a few times to become familiar with the sound of the mix without the Ami Vox track.

18 Slowly raise the Ami Vox Volume fader to around –9 dB.

As you try to find the right level for the vocal you just EQ'ed, you may notice that some words are louder than others. You will later use a compressor to give the vocal a more consistent level.

19 Stop playback.

Instead of closing the Channel EQ window, you can recall the current screenset to return it to its locked state.

20 Press 1 to recall screenset 1.

The screenset is recalled, and the Channel EQ window is no longer open.

By applying an EQ plug-in to the vocal, you shaped its frequency spectrum to eliminate unwanted low-frequency noises, and clarify the vocal, establishing its appropriate place in the frequency spectrum of the mix.

Using Delay and Reverberation

In a natural environment, an instrument's sound is reflected by the floor, walls, and ceiling of the room. The sounds of those reflections, combined with the direct sound of the instrument, allow listeners to determine the distance from the instrument to their ears and understand the nature of the acoustic space.

When recording instruments, you can choose to record in an absorbent studio to primarily record the direct sound of each instrument. Then you apply delay and reverberation plug-ins to create artificial reflections, giving you total control over the apparent placement and depth of the instruments.

Adding Delay to the Vocals

Delay can be applied so you can clearly hear the distinct repeats of the sound echoing, or it can be applied with shorter delay times to create an ambience, similar to a reverb.

You will now add a Tape Delay plug-in to a vocal track to create a classic slap-back delay, a vintage effect popularized by the Beatles, who often used it liberally on John Lennon's voice.

1   In the Tracks area, select the Duvid Vox track (track 30) to show its channel strip in the Inspector, and solo it.

2   Start playback.

3   On the Duvid Vox channel strip, in the Audio FX area, click below the Compressor, and choose Delay > Tape Delay.

The Tape Delay plug-in is inserted, and its window opens.

You hear the reflections applied to the vocals as an echo. By default, the Tape Delay is automatically synchronized to the project tempo so that reflections are produced every quarter note. To get a slap-back effect, you needn't synchronize the delay to the grid, and you want the repeats to occur faster.

4   Click the Sync button to disable it.

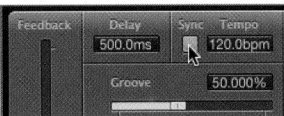

To the left of the Sync button, the Delay time changes from 375.0 ms to 500.0 ms, and you can hear that the repeats are no longer in sync with the song's tempo.

5   Drag the Delay value down to around 100 ms, then Shift-drag the Delay value to fine-tune it to around 88.1 ms.

The delay is now very short, and you can no longer hear distinct repeats. Instead the delay creates an ambiance similar to recording the vocal in a very small reflective room.

You can drag the two Output sliders to the right to adjust the level balance between Dry (the sound not affected by the plug-in) and Wet (the reflections generated by the plug-in). You will bring the Dry signal all the way up to its maximum level, so that you maintain the same level of direct sound as you had before inserting the plug-in.

6   Drag the Dry slider up to 100%.

You can now adjust the level of the delay effect with the Wet slider. Let's make the effect a little more subtle.

7   Drag the Wet slider down to 14%.

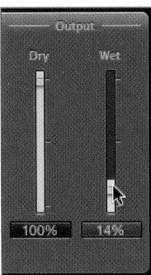

Here again, because you were focused on the sound of the delay, you may feel as if you just turned the effect down so much that you don't hear it any more. To fully hear the effect of the Tape Delay, let's toggle that plug-in on and off.

8   In the plug-in header, click the On/Off button to turn off the plug-in. The vocal sounds much drier.

9   Turn the plug-in back on. The Tape Delay adds a little bit of slap-back echo, creating an ambience while keeping the vocal sound fairly natural.

10   Keep the Duvid Vox track soloed, and stop playback.

Adding Reverb Using Aux Sends

You could insert a reverb plug-in directly into the channel strip of the instrument you want to process, just as you inserted a delay plug-in in the previous exercise. However, when you use reverb to simulate the sound of instruments in a room, applying an individual reverb plug-in for each instrument would require a lot of processing power. You would also have to readjust the parameters of each reverb plug-in every time you wanted to change the acoustics of your artificial room.

Instead, you can use aux sends to route some of the signal from a channel strip to a new auxiliary channel strip. When you have set up an aux channel strip with the desired reverb plug-in, you can add reverberation to any instrument by sending some of its signal to that aux for processing.

In this exercise, you will use a bus send to route a vocal track to an aux, and insert the reverberation plug-in on the aux channel strip. Later you'll send another vocal track to the same aux to give it the same reverb sound.

A track is still soloed from the previous exercise. To unsolo it and solo a new track, you can Option-click the new track's Solo button.

1   Select the Gang Vox 1 track (track 31) and Option-click its Solo button. The Duvid Vox track is unsoloed, and the Gang Vox 1 track is soloed.

2   On the Gang Vox 1 channel strip, click the first Send slot, and choose Bus > Bus 7.

When you click a Send slot and choose an available bus, a new aux channel strip is automatically added to the Mixer. In the Inspector, the channel strip to the right automatically shows the new Aux 6 channel strip, and you can see the signal path from the lead vocal channel strip to the aux channel strip. At the top of the Aux 6 channel strip, the input is set to Bus 7.

TIP ▶ On the left channel strip, click the desired Send or Output slot to display the corresponding output or auxiliary channel strip to the right of the Inspector. When you click a send, make sure that you click the right area of the Send slot to avoid toggling its On/Off button.

Let's insert the reverb plug-in on the aux.

3   On the Aux 6 channel strip, click the top of the Audio FX section, and choose Reverb > Space Designer to insert that plug-in.

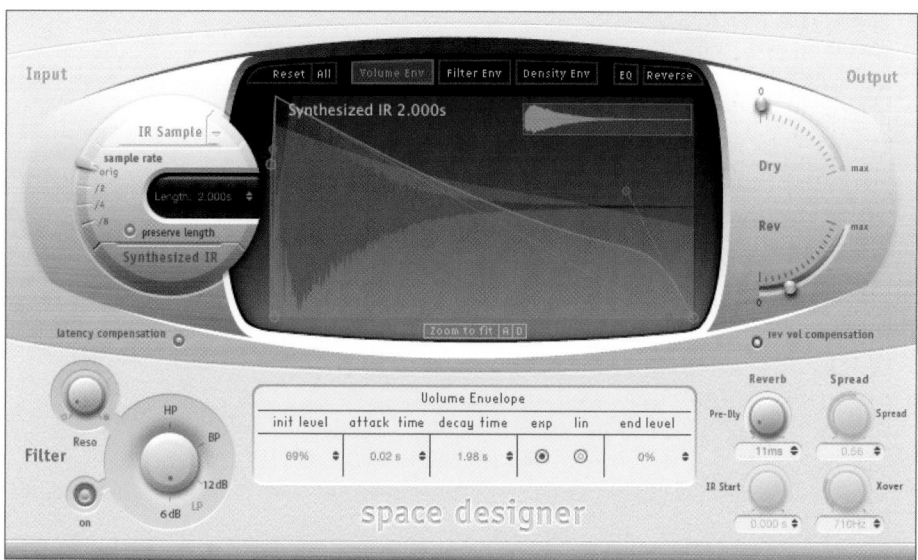

4   In the Marker track, drag the CH2 marker up into the ruler, and start playback.

The vocals sound dry, and no movement appears on the Aux 6 channel strip's meter. On the Gang Vox 1 channel strip, you need to raise the Send level knob to determine how much of the vocal signal you're sending to Aux 6 for processing by the reverb.

5   On the Gang Vox 1 channel strip, Option-click the Send Level knob next to Bus 7.

The Bus 7 send briefly displays the send level (0.0 (dB)), and you can hear the reverb. Let's choose a bigger reverb sound.

6   In the Space Designer plug-in header, from the Settings pop-up menu, choose Large Spaces > Rooms > 02.3s Clean Room.

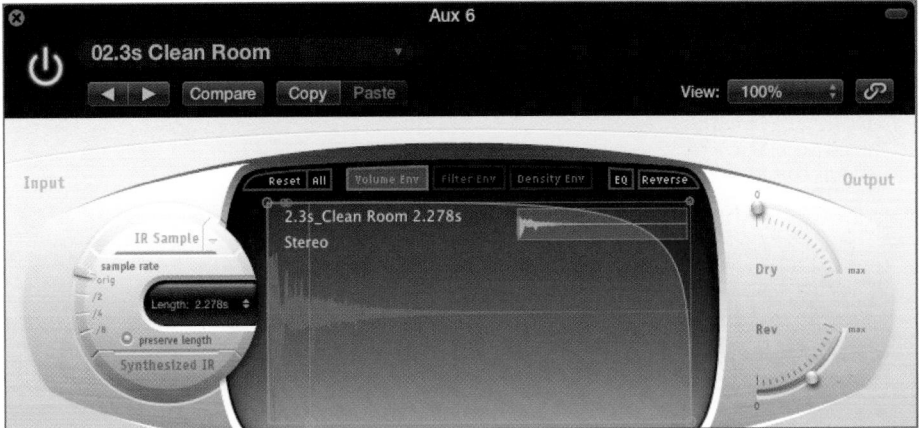

The reverb sound is bigger. In fact, you now have too much reverb. You'll need to adjust the send level on the Gang Vox 1 channel strip to determine how much of the dry vocal sound is routed to the reverb plug-in.

7   On the Gang Vox 1 channel strip, drag the Bus 7 Send Level knob down to around –12.0 (dB).

You can now send the audio signal from any channel strip to Bus 7 to route it to Aux 6 and add the same reverb effect to its sound. The Gang Vox 1 track was doubled on the Gang Vox 2 track, so let's open the Mixer and send the Gang Vox 2 track to the same reverb.

8   Press 2 to recall screenset 2.

Because you previously selected the Gang Vox 1 track in the Tracks area, the Gang Vox 1 channel strip (31) is selected in the Mixer, making it easy to locate.

9   Option-click the Gang Vox 2 channel strip's Solo button. Gang Vox 1 is unsoloed and Gang Vox 2 is soloed. You can hear the dry recording.

10   On the Gang Vox 2 channel strip (32), click the top Send slot, and choose Bus > Bus 7.

11   Drag the Send Level knob up to around –12.0 (dB).

Let's hear both tracks together.

12 Click the Solo button at the bottom of the Gang Vox 1 channel strip.

Both tracks sound as if they are located at the same distance. Let's spread them in the stereo field to widen the ensemble.

13 Pan the Gang Vox 1 to the left and the Gang Vox 2 to the right, choosing Pan values around –40 and +40.

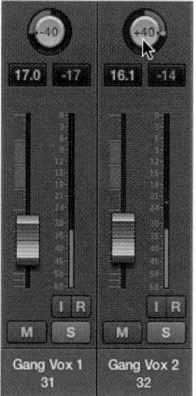

The vocals are spread out in the stereo field and sound closer to you. However, the reverb stayed in the center. Let's look at the Aux 6 channel strip to see what happened.

14 Place the mouse pointer over a Bus 7 send on one of the Gang Vox channel strips, and double-click the 7.

The Aux 6 channel strip is selected (and if necessary, the Mixer scrolls to show it). At the top of the channel strip, the Format button next to the input (Bus 7) shows a single circle, indicating a mono input. Let's fix this.

15 Click the Format button.

Format button

The reverb of each track is positioned according to the track's panning in the stereo field, and the reverb now sounds wider.

16 Press Control-Option-Command-S to unsolo all channel strips.

17 Press 1 to recall screenset 1.

Using Dynamic Processing Plug-ins

The dynamic range of a recording is the difference between the quietest and loudest parts of the recording. Sometimes too much dynamic range in a recording can be a problem because the loudest parts become too loud, and the quietest parts drop to barely audible levels. You can use dynamic processing plug-ins such as a compressor or a limiter to adjust the dynamic range of an audio signal, usually to make the audio signal level more consistent over time.

Dynamic processing can be applied to a single channel strip, a submix of a group of instruments, or to an entire mix.

Using the Compressor

When recording an instrument, the musician rarely plays all the notes at the same volume. Singers need more energy to reach higher pitches, and they relax to sing low pitches, resulting in uneven loudness throughout a melody line. This variation can become a challenge when mixing, as some of the notes stick out and others are buried in the mix.

A compressor attenuates a signal when its level reaches a specific threshold. You can use it to lower the volume of loud notes and then raise the overall level of the instrument to increase the volume of softer notes.

In this exercise, you will apply a compressor plug-in to even out the dynamic range of a vocal track, making sure that you can hear all the words at the same level.

1   In the Tracks area, drag the V2 marker up to the ruler.

2   Select and solo the Ami Vox track (track 29).

3   Start playback.

The level of the vocal recording fluctuates as the singer hits different pitches. On the level meter in the Ami Vox channel strip, you can see higher notes reach higher levels than lower notes.

4   On the Ami Vox channel strip, click below the Channel EQ plug-in, and choose Dynamic > Compressor.

The Gain Reduction meter shows by how many decibels the compressor is attenuating the audio signal. The little bit of activity on the meter indicates that the compressor is barely attenuating the vocals.

NOTE ▸ On channel strips, you can also use the Gain Reduction meter (below the Setting button) to see how much gain reduction is applied by the Compressor plug-in, or any other dynamic plug-in inserted in the Audio FX section.

 — Gain Reduction meter

TIP ▸ Double-click the Gain Reduction meter on a channel strip to open the first compressor or limiter plug-in in the Audio FX section of that channel strip. When no dynamic plug-in is present, double-clicking the Gain Reduction meter inserts a Compressor plug-in in the first available Audio FX slot.

The Gain and Auto Gain parameters help compensate for the gain reduction by applying a constant gain at the output of the compressor (also known as make-up gain). To hear only the gain reduction, let's eliminate the make-up gain.

5   Option-click the Gain slider to set it to 0.0 dB. From the Auto Gain pop-up menu, choose Off.

Without make-up gain, the compressor can apply only gain reduction, so it can only turn down the volume when the vocals reach levels higher than the Threshold parameter. Remember to turn the Compressor on and off as you adjust it to compare the sound of the vocal with and without the compression effect.

From the Circuit Type pop-up menu, you can choose from different models based on vintage hardware compressors. Except for Platinum, which is a transparent compressor, each circuit type adds its own color to the signal.

6   From the Circuit Type pop-up menu, choose Vintage Opto.

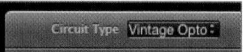

The Gain Reduction meter is inactive. Right now, the compressor isn't having any effect on the vocals. You will now adjust the threshold so that all notes trigger the compressor.

7   Drag the Compressor Threshold down to −34.5 dB.

On the Gain Reduction meter, you can see the compressor being triggered by all the notes, working harder on higher-pitched notes, while barely attenuating the lower-pitched notes.

You can adjust the amount of compression with the Ratio slider, which changes the ratio by which the signal is reduced when it exceeds the threshold.

8   Drag the Ratio slider to 2.0:1.

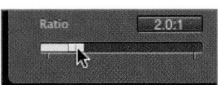

The vocal level sounds more consistent. You can clearly hear the singer even when he sings lower pitches, and higher-pitched notes no longer jump out.

Don't hesitate to experiment using higher ratio values to increase the amounts of compression. Be aware, however, that high ratio values may attenuate the high-pitched notes too much and produce an unnatural-sounding result.

Now that the compressor is reducing the gain, the vocal sounds lower in volume, so you can apply some make-up gain.

9   Drag the Gain slider up to 2.5 dB.

The vocals have roughly the same overall loudness as when you first started compressing them, making it easy to hear the effect of the compressor by toggling it on and off.

10 Stop playback.

11 Unsolo the Ami Vox track, turn off Cycle mode, and close the Compressor plug-in window.

Compressing and Limiting the Mix

On a professional project, you would usually send your final mix to a mastering engineer, who would put a final polish on the audio file using subtle amounts of EQ, compression, reverb, or other processing.

When you don't have the budget to hire a mastering engineer, you can master your own mix by inserting plug-ins on the Stereo Out channel strip, as in this exercise. You will start by using a compressor to make the mix level more consistent throughout the song, and then apply a limiter to raise the perceived loudness without clipping the Stereo Out channel strip audio.

1 Start playback at the beginning of the song.

2 On the Output channel strip, click the Audio FX area, and choose Dynamic > Compressor.

This time you will use a setting designed to emulate the soft compression of analog tape recorders.

3 In the Compressor, from the Setting menu, choose Compressor by Type > Platinum Analog Tape.

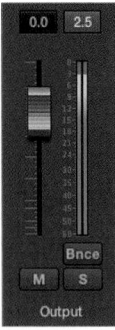

NOTE ► If you've adjusted the volume of the song using the Volume slider that appears in the control bar or the Volume fader on the Master channel strip in the Mixer, make sure you Option-click it now to return it to 0 dB.

The Output channel strip is clipping, as indicated by the red peak level display. In the compressor window, the gain reduction shows a few decibels of gain reduction, but the Auto Gain parameter applies enough make-up gain to make the mix clip.

4   In the Compressor, from the Auto Gain pop-up menu, choose Off.

The peak level display continues to display the most recent maximum peak value. You need to reset it to determine if the new compressor setting still clips the mix.

5   On the Output channel strip, click the peak level display to reset it. The mix is no longer clipping.

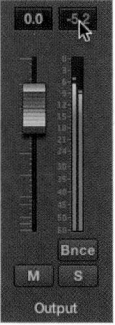

You will now insert a limiter after the compressor to raise the gain without clipping the output. A limiter works similarly to a compressor, but attenuates the signal so that the output signal never exceeds a specific volume level.

6   On the Output channel strip, click below the Compressor, and choose Dynamics > Adaptive Limiter.

The meters to the left display the signal level at the input of the plug-in; the meters to the right display the signal level at the output of the plug-in. At the bottom of the Adaptive Limiter plug-in window, the Out Ceiling is set to 0.0 dB, ensuring that the audio signal will never go over 0 dBFS on the Stereo Out channel strip.

When adjusting the Adaptive Limiter, you should adjust the Input Scale knob to avoid producing red *over* warnings on the input meters. Sometimes a few red overs can be OK, but when in doubt, trust your ears!

7   Drag the Input Scale up to +2.8 dB.

Keep playing the song, and make sure that the overs at the top of the left meter don't turn red all the time.

TIP ▶ At the top of the input meters, you can click the red *over* warnings to reset them.

You can now adjust the Gain knob in the middle of the plug-in window to raise the perceived level of the mix. You now need to pay close attention to what you are hearing. Although it is tempting to raise the gain to produce a louder mix, higher gain settings can introduce distortion.

8 Drag the Gain knob all the way up to 12.0 dB.

You hear the distortion introduced by the Adaptive Limiter, even though the signal is not clipping on the Output channel strip meters.

> **TIP** ▶ When you are not sure how a specific plug-in parameter affects the sound, don't hesitate to turn it all the way up and all the way down to find out. The results probably won't be good, but hearing those extremes will demonstrate how that parameter affects the sound, and you will know what to listen for as you adjust the parameter to a more reasonable setting.

9 Drag the Gain down to around 6 dB.

Even though the Adaptive Limiter's output meters still display *over* warnings, the audible distortion disappears.

10 In the Adaptive Limiter plug-in header, click the On/Off button to toggle it on and off.

The compressor makes your mix sound more consistent. The Adaptive Limiter gives you a nice gain boost on the whole mix and ensures that no clipping occurs at the output.

You have finished your mix using effect plug-ins and adjusting the four main parameters of the instrument sounds (volume levels, pan position, frequency, and distance) to give each sound its own place in the stereo sound field.

Using a Few Tips and Tricks

As with any other art, mixing requires a combination of skill, experience, and talent. It takes practice to learn how to apply mixing techniques efficiently, and even more practice to learn to listen. Here are a few tips and tricks that will help you perfect your craft and become better at mixing your projects.

Take a Break

After you mix for a while, listening to the same song for the hundredth time, you can lose your objectivity and experience ear fatigue. Take frequent short breaks while mixing, and return to the mix with rested ears. You will be able to better judge your results.

Listen to Your Mix Outside the Studio

When you feel that your mix is pretty advanced and you are happy with the way it sounds in your studio, copy it to a portable music player and listen to it in another room, or even better, in your car while driving. You will probably hear things you didn't notice in your studio, and miss things you could hear clearly in your studio. You can take notes and return to your studio to rework the mix. Obviously, the mix will never sound the same in the studio and in the car, but it's the mixing engineer's job to make sure that all the instruments can be heard in most situations.

Compare Your Mix with Commercial Mixes

Compare your mix with commercial mixes you like. Build a small library of good-sounding mixes in the same genre of music as the songs you are mixing. You can open a new Logic project, and place your mix on one track and a professional mix on another track so that you can solo and compare them.

Lesson Review

1. Identify the four main instrumental sound components you can adjust to give each instrument its place in a mix.
2. For what purpose do you use an aux send?
3. How can you make a group of tracks appear as one track in the Tracks area without changing its audio routing?
4. How can you submix a group of tracks, for example, to process the submix with audio effect plug-ins?
5. What does a compressor do?
6. What does a limiter do?
7. In the Inspector, how can you choose which channel strip is displayed in the right channel strip?
8. How do you change the mono or stereo format of the input of a channel strip?

Answers

1. Volume level, pan position, frequency spectrum, and distance.
2. You use an aux send to route some of the signal from a channel strip to an aux channel strip, usually to be processed by plug-ins.

3. Select the tracks, choose Track > Create Track Stack, and choose a Folder Stack.

4. Select the tracks, choose Track > Create Track Stack, and choose a Summing Stack.

5. It attenuates the level of a signal after that signal goes over a certain threshold, giving the signal a more consistent level.

6. It works in a similar fashion to a compressor, but it makes sure that the signal is attenuated so it never goes over a specific output ceiling.

7. On the left channel strip, click any Send slot or the Output slot to display the corresponding channel strip on the right.

8. Click the Format button in the Input slot.

Keyboard Shortcuts

Tracks

Command-Shift-D	Creates a track stack
Control-Option-Command-S	Unsolos all soloed tracks
S	Solos the selected track

Windows

Command-2	Opens a Mixer window
Number keys **(on alphanumerical keypad)**	Recalls the corresponding screenset
V	Hides or shows all plug-in windows

10

Lesson Files   Logic Pro X Files > Lessons > 10 Alliance

Time   This lesson takes approximately 45 minutes to complete.

Goals   Create track automation graphically

Record live track automation

Use the Touch and Latch automation modes

Assign a MIDI controller knob or fader
to remote control the desired parameter

Automate track mute and plug-in bypass

Export the mix as a PCM file

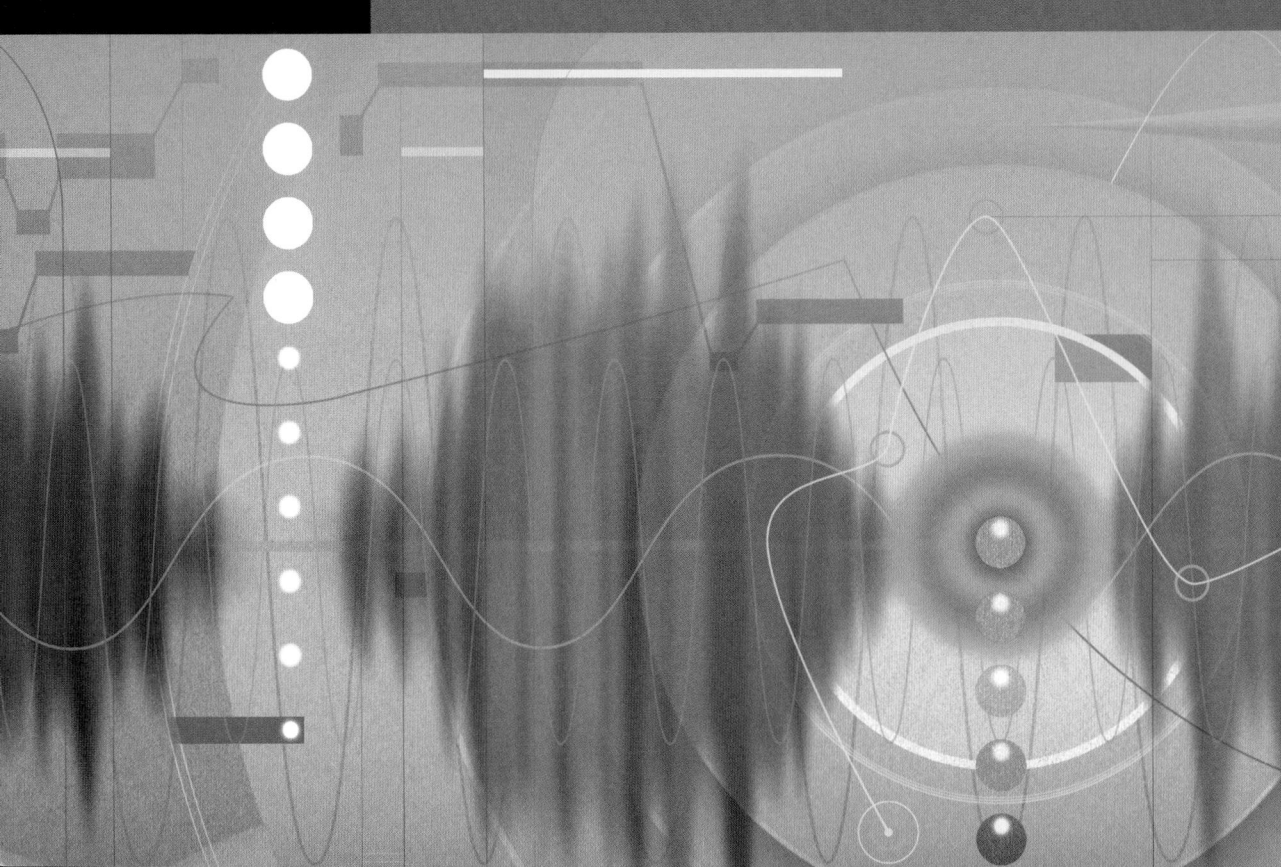

Automating the Mix

When multitrack recorders first appeared in recording studios, they forever changed the way artists produced music. Having separate recordings of individual instruments opened the door for experimentation, and soon artists and producers alike placed their hands on the mixing board during the final mixdown—panning an instrument from left to right or riding a volume fader to change the level of a track throughout a song. Soon enough, two or three pairs of hands weren't enough to perform all the changes needed throughout a mix, and a solution was needed.

Eventually, mixing consoles were designed on which moving a fader also generated a data stream. By recording those data streams onto a separate track of the multitrack tape, the console could automatically recreate those fader movements during playback. This started the era of automated consoles. Today, professional computerized mixing boards and digital audio workstations are fully automated.

In Logic, you can automate almost all the controls on a channel strip, including volume, pan, and plug-in parameters. In this lesson, you will draw and edit offline automation to bring down the volume of a vocoder (a synthesized vocal recording) during the breaks, pan a sound effect from left to right, and turn off a plug-in at the end of a section. You will then record live automation to swipe a low-pass filter over the vocoder, pan the vocoder across the stereo field, and turn off an EQ at the beginning of a section.

Creating and Editing Offline Automation

In Logic, the techniques used to create and edit track-based automation closely resemble MIDI Draw, which you used to graphically edit MIDI continuous controller events in Lesson 6. While MIDI Draw allows you to automate MIDI CC parameters in a region, track automation lets you automate almost any channel strip controls independent of the regions on the track.

Drawing automation graphically is also known as *offline automation*, because it is applied without regard for the playhead position and can be performed while Logic is not playing.

Creating Automation Curves to Adjust Section Volume

When you need to accurately control the volume of an instrument in specific sections of a song, drawing offline automation over the waveform enables surgical precision without the pressure of performing fader movements in real time.

In this exercise, you will add offline volume automation to a vocal track so that the track plays more softly during the breakdowns.

1   Open Logic Pro X Files > Lessons > **10 Alliance**.

2   Play the song, and listen to the Vocoder Chorus track (track 28) in both breakdown sections (at bar 29 and at bar 89).

    NOTE ▶ Remember to use Solo mode along with Shift-Spacebar (Play from Selection) to listen to a specific region or group of regions.

    You will bring the vocals down slightly in those two sections.

3   Select the Vocoder Chorus track (track 28).

4   In the Tracks area menu bar, click the Automation button (or press A).

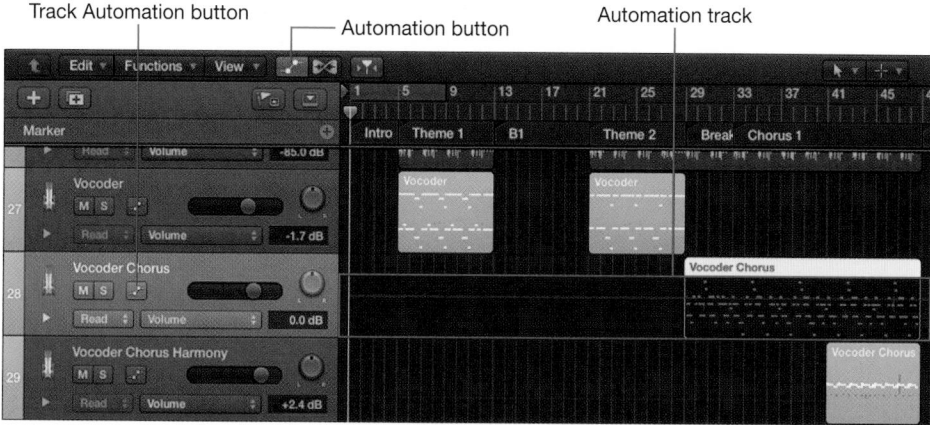

In the Tracks area, tracks must be tall enough to display their automation curves, so the Tracks area is automatically zoomed in vertically. On the selected track, the Track Automation button is automatically turned on, and an automation track shows the currently empty volume automation curve.

TIP When an automation track is shown, you can edit regions (move, copy, resize, and so on) in the thin lane containing the region names.

You will now create a volume automation curve to reduce the volume of the vocoded vocals in the Breakdown at bar 29.

5   On the Vocoder Chorus track, click anywhere in the automation track.

A control point is created at the beginning of the project (bar 1) at the current Volume fader value, 0.0 dB; and the automation curve is shaded yellow to indicate that some automation data is now present.

6   Zoom in on the beginning of the Vocoder Chorus region at bar 29, below the Breakdown marker.

You can create control points by clicking the automation curve.

7   Click the volume automation curve just before and just after the beginning of bar 33 to create two 0 dB control points.

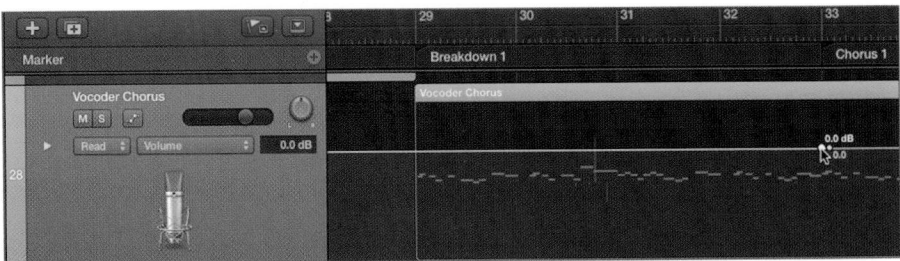

8   Create two more control points before the Vocoder Chorus region beginning at bar 29.

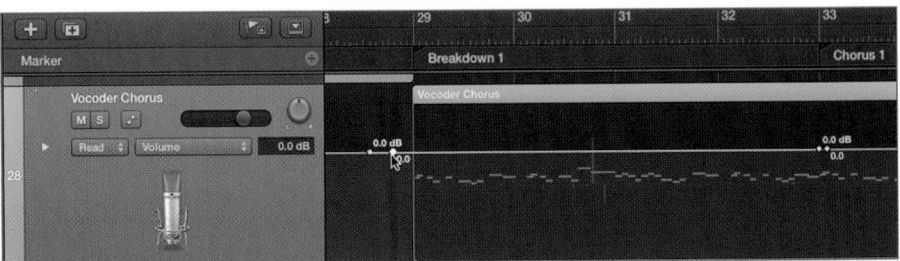

9   In the Breakdown 1 section, drag the automation curve down to –2.6 dB.

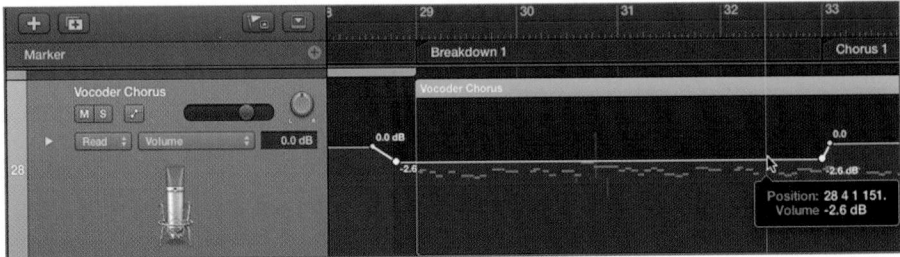

TIP ▶ You can also draw automation curves using the Pencil tool.

10   Start playback before the four control points (at bar 28).

Look at the Volume slider in the track header, or the Volume fader in the Inspector. They both move to reflect the volume automation curve on the track, dropping down from 0 dB to –2.6 dB just before the breakdown, and coming back up to 0 dB at the beginning of the chorus.

If you're not happy with the timing of your automation, feel free to zoom in on any of the control points, and drag them to other locations.

You will now create similar automation in the second breakdown.

11 Scroll to the right until you can see the Breakdown 2 marker (bar 89).

This time, you will use the Marquee tool to select a section of the automation curve, and then drag down the selected section of the curve. To quickly select the entire region, you can Option-click the region with the Marquee tool, your current Command-click tool. Since the automation track is displayed, you'll have to click in the region name area.

12 Command-Option-click the name area of the Vocoder Chorus region to select it with the Marquee tool. The region is highlighted.

13 In the Breakdown 2 section, drag the automation curve down to around –2.7 dB.

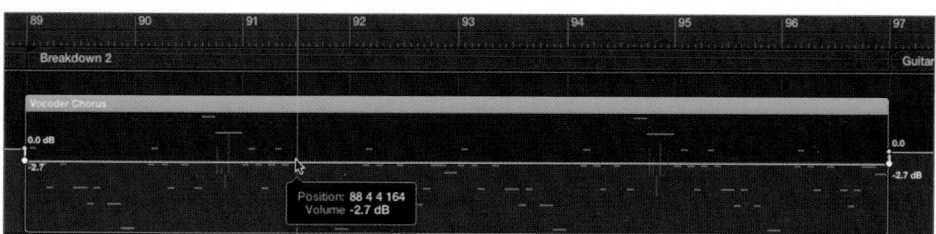

As you drag the line down, you can see two nodes created on each end of the Marquee selection, so dragging the automation curve will adjust the volume only for the selected section.

14 Click the background of the workspace to clear the selection, and press Z to see all the regions.

15 Listen to the Breakdown 2 section by starting playback around bar 88.

At the beginning of the breakdown, the Volume fader in the Inspector drops down from 0 dB to –2.7 dB. At the end of the section, the Volume fader returns to 0 dB.

When you're happy with the automation curve, you can adjust the overall volume level of the track by trimming the automation on the track.

16 In the control bar, click the "Go to Beginning" button (or press Return).

17 Zoom in on the Vocoder Chorus track. In the track header, place the mouse pointer over the numerical display (the parameter value changes to Trim) and drag up to +1.0 dB.

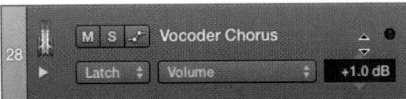

The automation curve for the entire track is raised by 1.0 dB.

18 Click the background, and press Z to zoom out.

Creating Pan Automation

Applying pan automation can be a fun way to create movement in your mix, moving a sound from one side of the stereo field to the other. It is a powerful effect that calls attention to the automated sound, but when used in moderation, can add life to a sound effect.

Let's draw offline pan automation on the first sound effect at the end of the intro to move it from the left speaker to the right speaker.

1 Select the FX rise 1 track (track 7).

2 Control-Option-drag the workspace to zoom in on the first region of the track.

The Track Automation button is dimmed, and the automation curve is not visible.

3 From the Automation Parameter pop-up menu, choose Main > Pan.

Automation Parameter pop-up menu

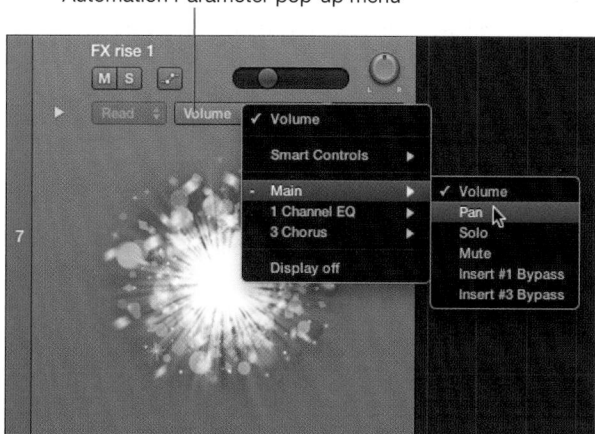

The Track Automation button is automatically turned on, and the pan automation curve appears on the track.

4   Click anywhere on the automation track.

At the beginning of the automation track, a control point is created for the current pan value (0).

To create control points away from the automation curve, you can double-click using the Pointer tool.

5   Double-click the top of the automation track just before the FX rise 1 region.

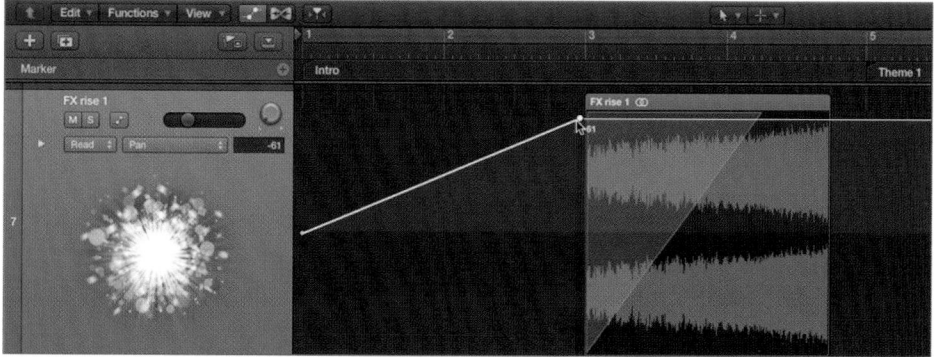

Let's readjust the position of the control point you just created to start the panning effect all the way to the left at the beginning of the sound effect.

6 Drag the control point you just created up as far as you can, and as close as possible to the beginning of the region.

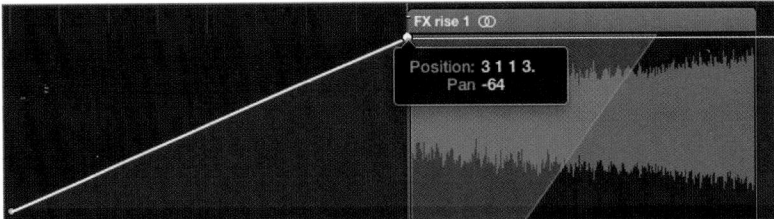

7 Double-click the automation track at the end of the FX rise 1 region.

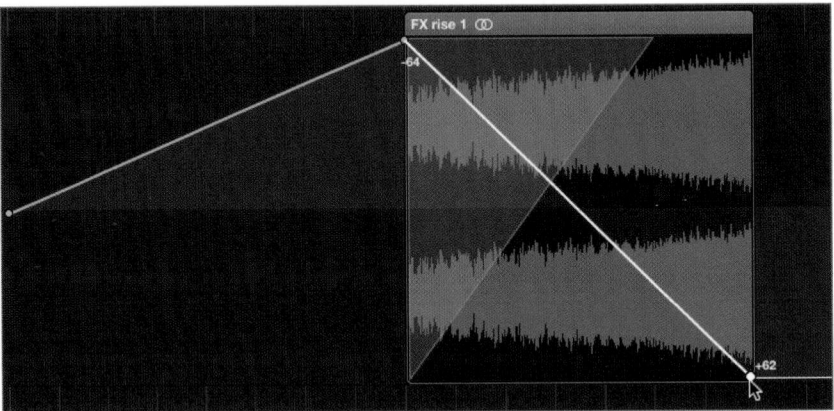

The automation curve goes from the upper left to the lower right of the region, representing the pan position of the track going from the left speaker to the right speaker.

8 Listen to the intro.

The Pan knob in the track header and the Pan knob on the FX rise 1 channel strip in the Inspector reflect the automation curve, moving from center to the left at the beginning of the intro, then from left to right during the FX rise 1 region. You can hear the sound effect move from the left to the right of the stereo field.

Let's look at the pan automation curve for the whole track.

9 Control-option-click the workspace to zoom out.

To quickly zoom in vertically on the selected track, you can use Auto Track Zoom.

10 In the Tracks area main menu bar, choose View > Auto Track Zoom (or press
Control-Z).

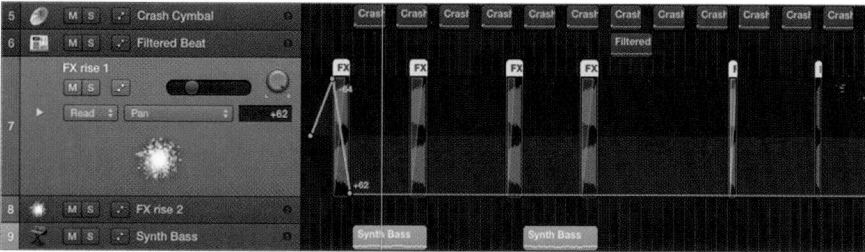

The selected track expands vertically, and you can see its automation curve. Following
the automation curve you created over the first region, the automation curve remains
at a low position throughout the rest of the track. As a result, all the sound effects
after the intro will play on the right side of the stereo field. Let's bring them back to
the center.

11 Between the first two regions on the track, Double-click the automation track to create a control point; and if necessary, drag it to a value of 0.

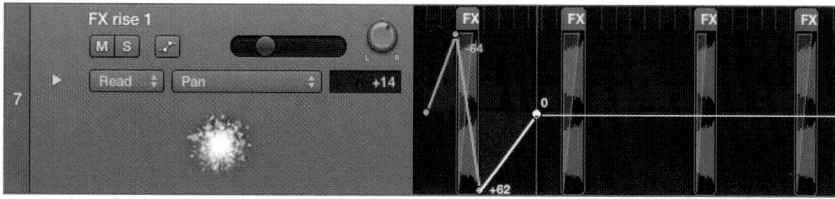

The pan automation curve shows a flat horizontal line after the new control point,
and the rest of the track will play the sound effect in the center of the stereo field.

12 Listen from the beginning of the song to the end of the Theme 1 section.

After the panning effect on the first region, the Pan knob returns to and stays at its
center position.

Creating and Snapping Mute Automation

Mute automation can be very useful when you need an instrument or sound to drop out
instantaneously. While you can edit a region to make it stop playing at a specific point, some
effect plug-ins such as delay or reverberation may continue to produce sound after the playhead moves past the end of the region. Muting the channel strip ensures that the audio signal processed by the plug-ins on the channel strip is no longer routed to the stereo output.

In this exercise, you will mute a reverberant snare drum to stop its ringing at a specific location in the arrangement.

1   Select the Snare track (track 4).

The Snare track expands vertically, while the FX rise 1 track returns to its original vertical zoom level.

You can Option-click a marker to position the playhead at the beginning of that marker.

2   In the Marker track, Option-click the Build-up marker (bar 57).

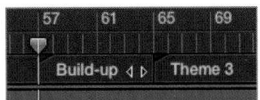

The playhead jumps to the beginning of the marker.

3   Listen to the Build-up section.

At the end of the section, a drum fill ends with a reverberant snare leading into the next section, Theme 3. While the build-up ends with a rising sound effect and a busy drum fill, the Theme 3 section begins with a very intimate mix. To accentuate the difference in ambiance between the sections, you can mute the reverberated snare so that its reverb tail stops abruptly at the end of the build-up.

4   In the Snare track header, from the Automation Parameter pop-up menu, choose Main > Mute.

5   Click anywhere in the automation track to create a control point at the beginning of the track with the current parameter value (mute off).

6   Zoom in on the Snare region at the end of the build-up.

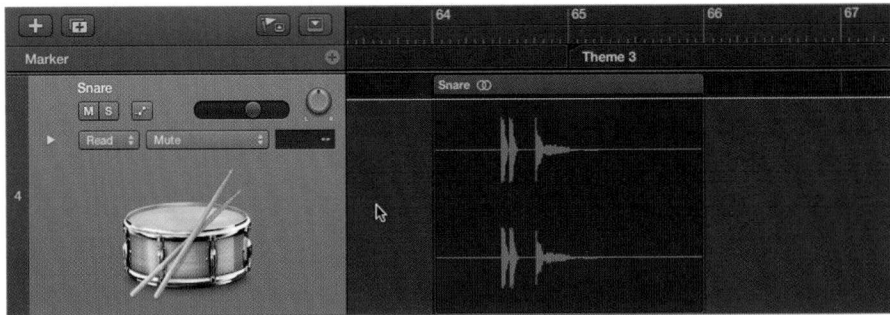

To abruptly cut out the snare exactly before the Theme 3 section, you need to create a control point at exactly 65 1 1 1. You will now use the snap modes to create control points that are aligned with the grid.

7   In the Tracks area menu bar, from the Snap pop-up menu, choose "Snap Automation to Absolute Values."

By default, Logic snaps control points five ticks before the closest grid line. This default behavior can be useful when automating, for example, a compressor that needs to be turned on before a downbeat so it can be triggered by the attack of a note on the downbeat. But, you don't need that default offset here.

8   From the Snap pop-up menu, choose Automation Snap Offset to open the Automation preferences window.

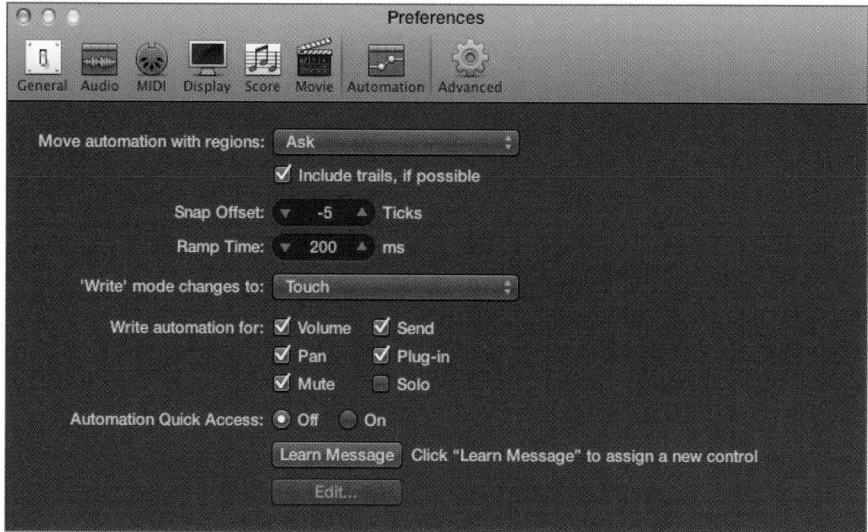

9   In the preferences window, set the Snap Offset to 0 Ticks, and then close the window.

10 At bar 65, double-click in the lower half of the automation track.

A control point with the value Muted is created. Note that the mute parameter has only two possible values (Unmuted and Muted).

Let's check the position of the control point you just created.

11 Over the control point, click and hold down the mouse button.

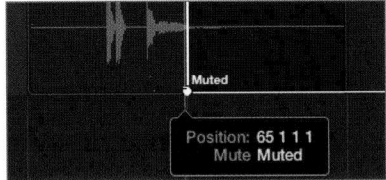

The help tag displays the position of the control point as 65 1 1 1.

12 From the Snap pop-up menu, choose "Snap Automation to Absolute Values" to turn it off.

13 Listen to the build-up.

While you can see that the track is muted at bar 65, you may have difficulty hearing exactly where the snare stops when the whole song is playing. Let's solo the snare.

14 Solo the Snare track, and listen again.

You can hear the snare sound and its reverb effect stop abruptly at bar 65. Let's listen to the Snare track without any mute automation. First you'll position the playhead in a section where the Snare track is not muted.

15 Place the playhead before bar 65, but do not start playback yet.

The Snare track is unmuted.

16 On the Snare track header, click the Track Automation button to turn off the automation on that track.

17 Listen to the build-up.

The Snare track remains unmuted and you can hear the reverb tail sustain past 65 1 1 1.

18 On the Snare track header, click the Track Automation button to turn automation back on.

Let's now unmute the snare for the remainder of the track.

19 At the top of the automation track after the end of the region, double click in bar 66 to unmute the snare.

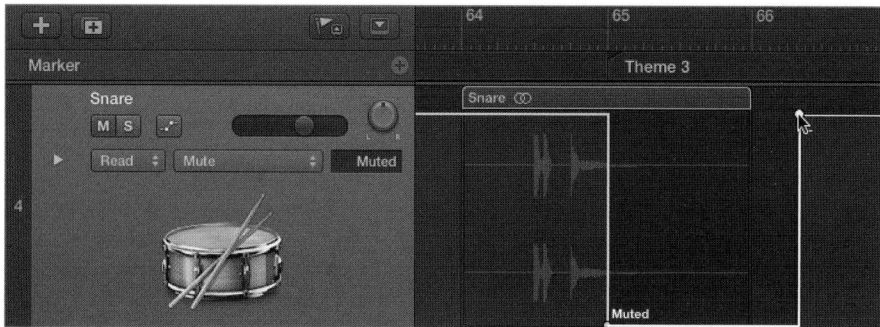

20 Unsolo the snare track.

21 In the Tracks area main menu bar, choose View > Auto Track Zoom (or press Control-Z) to turn off Auto Track Zoom.

Recording Live Automation

While offline automation is a good option when you know in advance what automation movements you want to achieve, you sometimes want to hear the song playing as you adjust channel strip or plug-in controls in real time.

To record live automation, you need to choose a live automation mode for the track(s) you want to automate, start playback, and then tweak the desired plug-in or channel strip controls.

Recording Automation in Touch Mode

When you start playback in Touch mode, any existing automation on the track is read (as if Logic were in Read mode). As soon as you hold down the mouse button on a knob or slider, Logic starts recording the new values. When you release the mouse button, Touch mode behaves like Read mode again, and the automation parameter returns to its original value or reproduces any existing automation on the track.

In this exercise, you will use the Touch mode to automate closing a low-pass filter on the Vocoder track during the build-up.

1   At the beginning of the Build-up section, zoom in on the Vocoder region.

2   In the Marker track, drag the Build-up marker (at bar 57) up to the ruler, and listen to the section.

You will automate one of the bands of the Channel EQ plug-in inserted on the Vocoder channel strip to progressively filter more high frequencies, evolving the vocal sound throughout the first half of the build-up.

3   Select the Vocoder track (track 27), and solo it.

4   In the Vocoder track header, click the Track Automation button to turn it on, and from the Automation Mode pop-up menu, choose Touch.

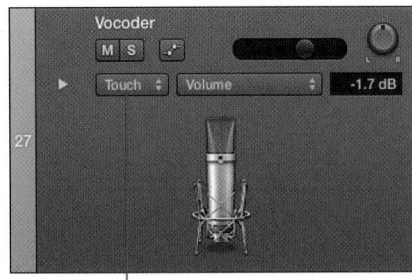

Automation Mode pop-up menu

5   In the Inspector, click the middle of the Channel EQ plug-in to open its window.

> **TIP** ▶ You can also double-click the EQ display at the top of the channel strip to open the Channel EQ plug-in.

In the Channel EQ, you will automate the frequency of the low-pass filter, the last band of EQ all the way to the right.

6   Position the mouse pointer over the low-pass EQ band's frequency.

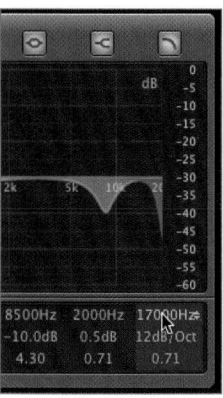

> **NOTE** ▶ Remember that you needn't choose a parameter from the track header's Automation Parameter pop-up menu to record live automation.

You are ready to record live automation. You don't need to put Logic in record mode to record live automation. You need only to put the track in one of the live automation modes (Touch, Latch, or Write) and start playback.

When you record automation in Touch mode, hold down the mouse button until you want the parameter to return to its original level (in this case, after the end of the Vocoder region in the Build-up section).

7   Press the Spacebar to start playback, and in the Channel EQ, slowly drag the frequency value down while listening to the effect on the vocoded voice.

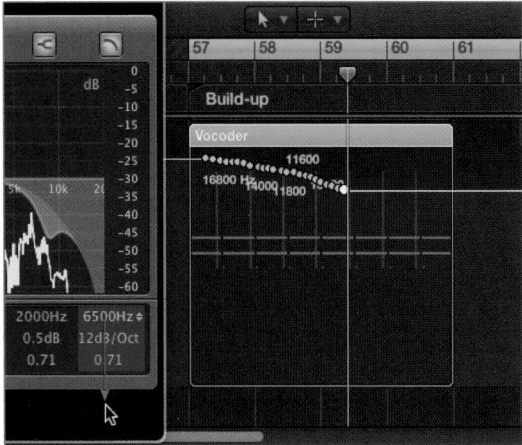

When you first click the frequency parameter in the plug-in window, on the Vocoder track header, the Automation Parameter pop-up menu displays that frequency parameter (2 Channel EQ: High Cut Frequency).

NOTE ▶ High cut is another name for a low pass filter.

As you drag down the frequency during playback, control points are added to the automation curve to record the new frequency values.

8   After the playhead moves past the end of the region, release the mouse button.

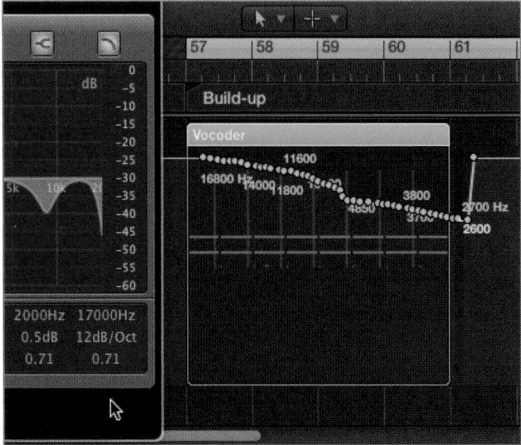

The frequency automation returns to its original value on the track (17,000 Hz).

9   Press the Spacebar to stop playback, and press the Spacebar again to resume playback
at the beginning of the build-up.

In the Channel EQ window, you see the frequency value at the bottom right reflect
the automation curve value at the playhead position. On the graphic display, the EQ
curve changes to reflect the closing of the low pass filter.

10 Stop playback.

If you are not happy with the automation curve you recorded, you can stay in Touch
mode and correct your automation. Let's do so now to drop the frequency a little faster
at the beginning of the section, and slower toward the end of the Vocoder region.

11 Start playback.

As long as you don't touch it, the frequency parameter reproduces the frequency
automation on the track.

12 When you're ready to start correcting your automation curve, drag the frequency
value down in the Channel EQ window.

As soon as you start dragging the frequency parameter, the new values overwrite the
existing frequency automation.

13 Before the end of the region, release the mouse button.

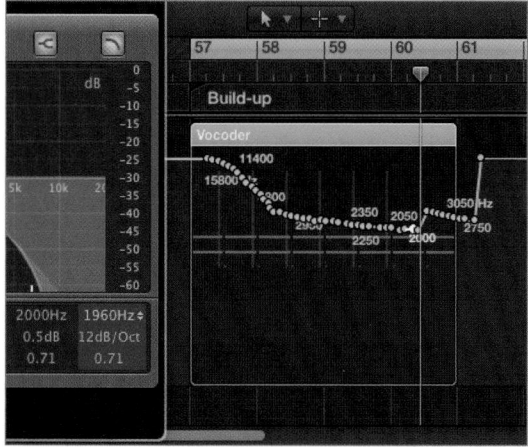

The frequency parameter responds to the existing frequency automation on the track.

> **TIP** ▸ When you release the mouse button in Touch mode, the time it takes for the automation curve to go from the last recorded value to the first existing value is called *ramp time.* The default ramp time is 200 ms, and you can adjust it in Logic Pro X > Preferences > Automation.

14 Stop playback.

Repeat steps 11 through 13 until you are happy with your automation curve.

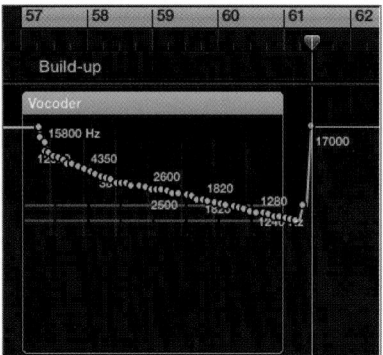

Be careful! A common mistake is to move on to another task and leave the automation mode set to Touch. However, when you do so, any further changes you make to that track's channel strip or any of its plug-in parameters during playback are recorded on the automation track (even if the track is not selected and the Automation button in the Tracks area menu bar is dimmed). To avoid accidentally recording more automation, let's return the automation mode to Read.

15 In the Vocoder track header, from the Automation Mode pop-up menu, choose Read.

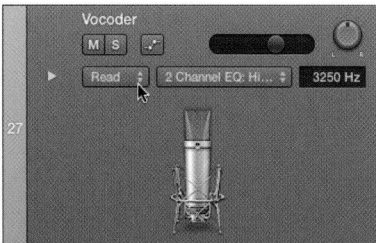

16 Unsolo the Vocoder track, close the Channel EQ plug-in window, and listen to your automation.

In the first half of the build-up, the vocoded vocals start bright and get progressively duller, similar to the effect you hear when walking out of a room where someone is singing. The timbral evolution of the vocal keeps things moving and adds interest to the section.

Recording Automation in Latch Mode

Latch mode works similar to Touch mode, except that when you release the mouse button, the automation continues to record and the parameter stays at the current value. If automation is already present for that parameter on that track, the automation is overwritten until you stop playback.

You will now enable Latch mode to record pan automation on the same Vocoder region you worked with in the previous exercise.

1   Listen to the Build-up section.

     The vocoded vocal stays in the center of the stereo field for the length of the Vocoder region.

2   In the Vocoder track header, set the automation mode to Latch.

     If you started playback now and dragged the Vocoder track's Pan knob, the Automation Parameter pop-up menu would automatically switch to Pan to show you the automation curve you're recording. If you prefer, you can view multiple automation curves for a single track.

3   In the Vocoder track header, click the disclosure triangle next to the Automation Mode pop-up menu.

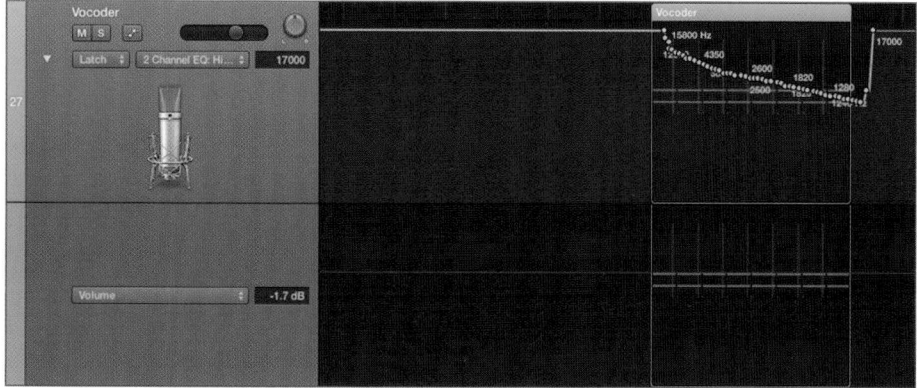

A separate automation subtrack opens below the track. By default, it shows the (currently empty) volume automation curve.

TIP ▶ To open more than one automation subtrack, place the mouse pointer over the subtrack header and click the + (plus sign) button that appears at the bottom. To close an automation subtrack, place the mouse pointer over the subtrack header and click the x button that appears at the top. You can also drag subtracks vertically to reorder them.

You will use pan automation to place the first two bars (bars 57 and 58) of vocoded vocals on the left side of the mix, and the two last bars (bars 59 and 60) on the right side of the mix.

4   Click the cycle area to turn off Cycle mode.

5   Start playback a couple of bars before the Build-up marker.

6   Before the playhead reaches the Vocoder region, drag the Pan knob on the track header to around –40, and release the mouse button.

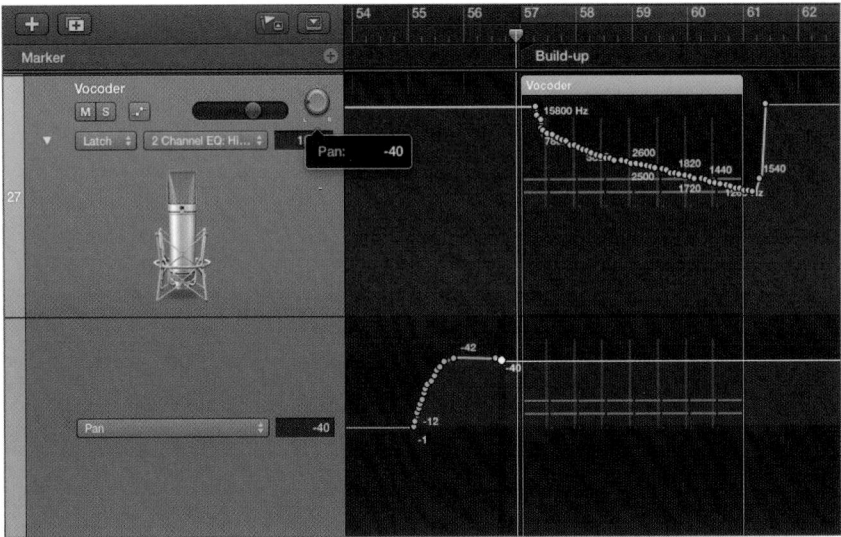

The pan automation is recorded on the subtrack, and the Pan knob remains in the position it was in when you released the mouse button.

7   When the playhead reaches bar 59, quickly drag up the Pan knob to around +40, and then release the mouse button.

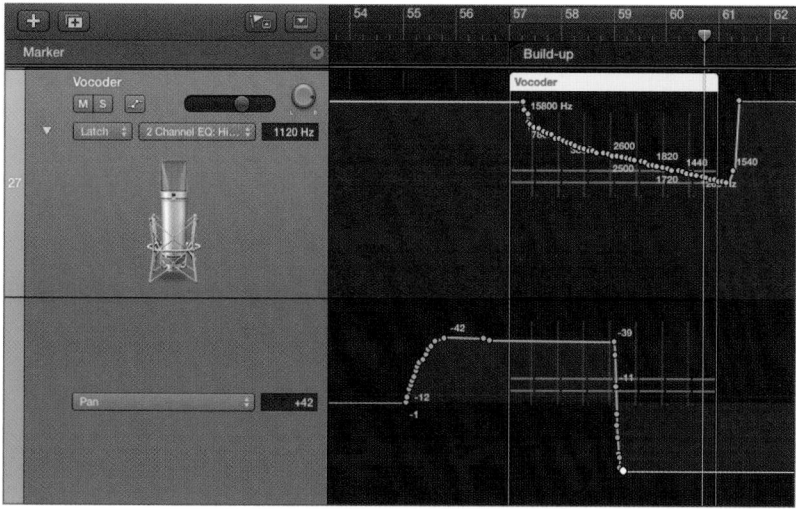

TIP To create sudden breaks in an automation curve, double-click the parameter you're automating (the Pan knob in this case) and type a new value. Then press Return when you want to record the new value on the automation track.

8   After the playhead has moved past the end of the Vocoder region, Option-click the Pan knob.

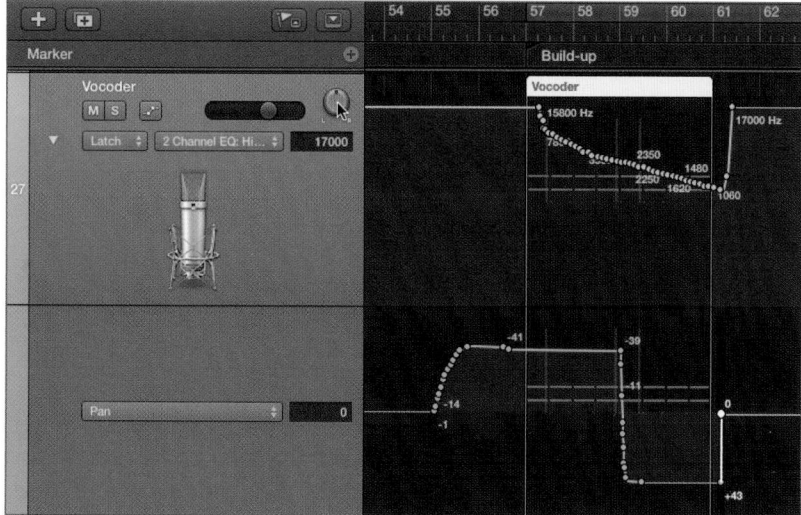

The Pan knob returns to its center position, and the automation curve jumps to the 0 value.

9   Stop playback.

10 On the Vocoder track header, set the automation mode to Read, and click the disclosure triangle to close the subtrack.

11 Listen to the result.

In the build-up, the first two bars of vocals are to the left of the stereo field, and the last two bars are to the right. The vocals moving from left to right in the stereo field renew interest at bar 59, and add excitement to the section.

NOTE ▶ The Write automation mode is rarely used. It erases all automation data as the playhead passes it and records any new movements you make on the channel strip. It can be quite dangerous, as it even erases automation not currently displayed in the automation track.

Recording Plug-in Bypass Automation

Like a guitar player engaging a distortion pedal to play a solo, you'll sometimes want to apply an effect plug-in to only specific sections of a song. Automating the plug-in bypass allows you to turn the effect on and off at specific positions.

You will now add an EQ plug-in to a vocal track, choose a telephone EQ setting, and then automate the bypass of the EQ plug-in so it's turned on only during the first breakdown.

1   Select the Vocoder Chorus track (track 28).

2   Zoom in on the first Vocoder Chorus on the track (at bar 29) to view the entire Breakdown 1 marker.

You can see the volume automation curve you created earlier in this lesson.

3 In the Inspector, on the Vocoder Chorus channel strip, click below the last plug-in in the Audio FX area, and choose EQ > Channel EQ.

4 In the Channel EQ plug-in window, from the Settings menu, choose EQ Tools > Phone Filter Wide Band.

Look at the EQ curve. This setting emphasizes mid frequencies while drastically cutting high and low frequencies to simulate the sound of a voice through a telephone. You will apply this telephone effect to the Breakdown 1 section. Because the track has no previous regions, the EQ can be turned on from the beginning of the song until the end of the breakdown when you will bypass it.

5 In the Vocoder Chorus track header, set the automation mode to Latch.

6 Start playback before the Breakdown 1 marker.

7   At the very end of the breakdown (at bar 33), click the Channel EQ power button to turn it off.

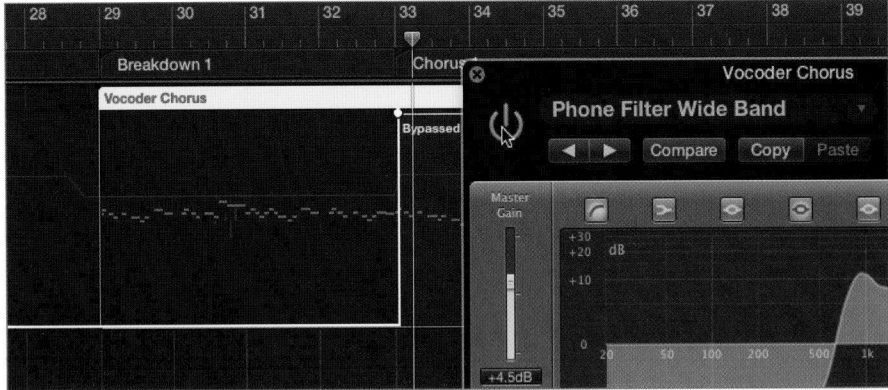

On the track header, the Automation Parameter pop-up menu displays the Insert #7 Bypass parameter, and on the track, the plug-in is bypassed (turned off) at the end of the breakdown.

If you are not happy with the timing of the Bypassed control point, you can zoom in and drag it to adjust its position.

8   Stop playback.

9   On the Vocoder Chorus track header, set the automation mode to Read.

10   Listen to the result.

The vocoded vocal has a narrow band of frequencies during the breakdown, then the Channel EQ is turned off at bar 33 and the vocoded vocal has a full frequency range sound throughout the rest of the song.

11   Close the Channel EQ plug-in, and zoom out.

Using MIDI Controllers

Recording live automation by dragging onscreen sliders and knobs with the mouse can be a powerful means of expression, but nothing beats the feel of a real fader or knob under your fingers. Adding a control surface to your Logic setup allows you to map different knobs to the desired channel strip or plug-in parameters to remotely control those parameters to record live automation.

Many supported control surfaces (such as the Logic Remote) are automatically detected by Logic, which also will automatically assign their faders and knobs.

> **MORE INFO ▸** To learn more about supported control surfaces, choose Help > Logic Pro Control Surfaces Support.

When the controls are not automatically mapped—for example, when control knobs are used on a MIDI keyboard that isn't a supported device—you can manually assign the physical knobs to the parameters you want to automate.

> **NOTE ▸** If your control surface is a MIDI keyboard that does not have a controller knob of any kind, you can use the modulation wheel to perform the following exercise. Any device sending MIDI CC events can be assigned to any channel strip or plug-in parameter.

Using Automation Quick Access

Automation Quick Access allows you to assign a single controller knob to the automation parameter that is currently displayed on the selected track. You need to assign the controller knob only once, and you can then use it to control any parameter on any track. Just select a track and choose the desired parameter from the Automation Parameter pop-up menu.

In this exercise, you will slowly fade out the entire song at the end. To record automation curves for the Output channel strip, you must first create a track for that channel strip.

1   In the Inspector, Control-click the Output channel strip, and from the shortcut menu, choose Create Track.

An Output track appears below the selected track in the Tracks area.

2   In the Tracks area, drag the Output track header to the bottom of the Tracks area.

3   In the Output track header, from the Automation Parameter pop-up menu, choose Volume.

The Track Automation button is automatically turned on.

4   Choose Logic Pro X > Preferences > Automation (or press Option-A).

5   At the bottom of the Automation window, turn on Automation Quick Access.

TIP ▶ To turn on Automation Quick Access, you can also choose Mix > Enable Automation Quick Access.

An alert message asks you to assign a controller to Automation Quick Access.

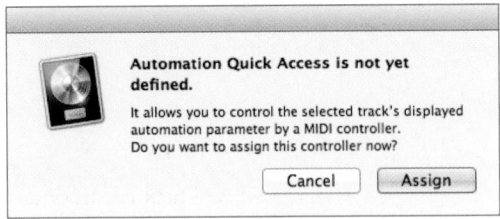

6   Click Assign.

7   On your MIDI controller, turn a knob all the way up then all the way down.

In the Inspector, the Output Volume fader moves accordingly.

8   Turn the controller knob back up so that the Output is set to 0 dB.

9   Close the Automation preferences window.

10   In the Output track header, set the automation mode to Latch.

11   Start playback at the beginning of Chorus 3 (at bar 105).

12   Slowly turn down the knob on your controller to record a slow fade-out throughout the Chorus 3 section.

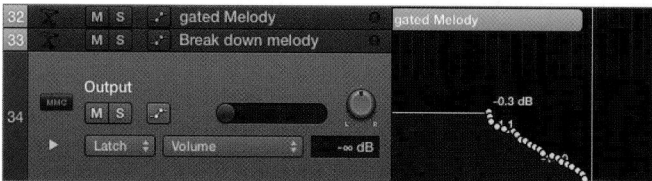

The controller knob allows you to remotely control the Output channel strip Volume fader and record its automation. From now on, you can select any track, and the controller knob you assigned to Automation Quick Access can control the parameter selected in that track's Automation Parameter pop-up menu.

13   Set the Output track's automation mode to Read.

14   Select the Guitar Solo track (track 17).

15   In the Guitar Solo track header, from the Automation Parameter pop-up menu, choose Main > Pan.

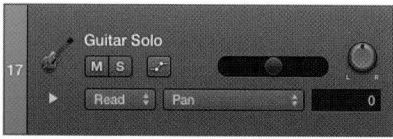

16   On your MIDI controller, turn the controller knob assigned to Automation Quick Access up and down.

The knob now controls the Pan knob on the Guitar Solo track. Feel free to set the track to the Touch or Latch mode, start playback at the beginning of the Guitar Solo section (at bar 97), and then turn the knob to automate the position of the guitar solo in the stereo field. Make sure that you set the Automation Mode pop-up menu back to Read when you're finished.

You are now done automating this project so you can hide all the automation curves.

17 In the Tracks area menu bar, click the Automation button to disable it.

In the workspace, all the automation tracks are hidden, and on the track headers, the Automation button and menus disappear.

Using knobs on a control surface to tweak plug-in parameters in real time can be a lot of fun as you discover new ways to "play" the plug-ins as musical instruments. Make sure that you keep this technique in mind when you feel an instrument or a section of a song is a little static or repetitive and could benefit from automation.

Bouncing the Mix

In Lesson 1, you exported a finished mix to an MP3 file. To come full circle, in this final lesson, you will bounce your automated mix at the highest quality available: an uncompressed PCM file.

First, you will zoom out so that you can see the entire song in the workspace.

1 Click the background of the workspace, and press Z to view the entire song.

Note where the last regions end at bar 114. When you are not sure of the exact end of a song, zoom in on the end of the last regions, and play the final few bars. Sometimes effect plug-ins such as reverberation and delay still produce sound long after the end of the song!

2 Choose File > Bounce (or press Command-B) to open the Bounce dialog.

3 In the Destination column, ensure that PCM is selected, and set the End field to 114.

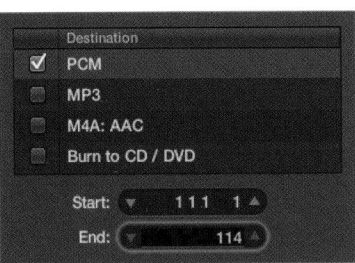

Leave the Mode set to Offline.

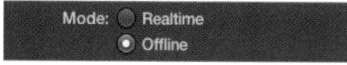

While Realtime mode lets you hear your song while it's bouncing in real time, Offline mode takes advantage of your CPU to complete the operation as fast as your Mac can process it, which can save a lot of time.

The Normalize function automatically adjusts the level of the file so that it peaks at or below 0 dBFS. If you have used mastering plug-ins to ensure that the Output peak meter peaks at 0 dBFS, you do not need Normalize.

4   Set Normalize to Off.

Leave all the PCM parameters (to the right) set to their default values.

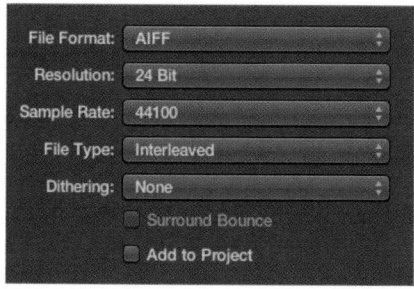

▶   The File Format choices—AIFF, Wave, and CAF—all produce the same sound quality. (Each has its own features, as discussed in Lesson 2, "Choosing the Recording File Type.") The File Format you choose depends mostly on which format is needed for further processing, such as mastering.

▶   The (bit depth) Resolution is set to 24 Bit, which is the best sound quality.

▶   The Sample Rate is set by default to the project sample rate. You should change this only if you want to convert the bounced file to a new sample rate.

▶   The File Type is Interleaved, which is the most common file type used.

▶ Dithering can make a subtle difference in very quiet sections of a song, or when a song is fading in or out. It is recommended to dither only once and at the very end of the production of a song, so leave it off if you intend to have the song mastered.

▶ When you select "Add to Project," the bounce file is added to the Project Audio Browser.

5 Click Bounce.

A Bounce Output 1-2 dialog opens, and you can choose a filename and a location for the bounced file.

6 Name the file *Alliance* (the name of the song), press Command-D to save it to the desktop, and click Bounce.

A progress window appears, and in the Tracks area, you can see the playhead move faster than real time as the bounced file is created.

When the progress window disappears, your bounced file is ready.

7 Press Command-Tab to go to the Finder.

8 In the Finder, choose Finder > Hide Others (or press Command-Option-H).

9 On your desktop, click **Alliance.aif**, and press the Spacebar to play the final version of the song.

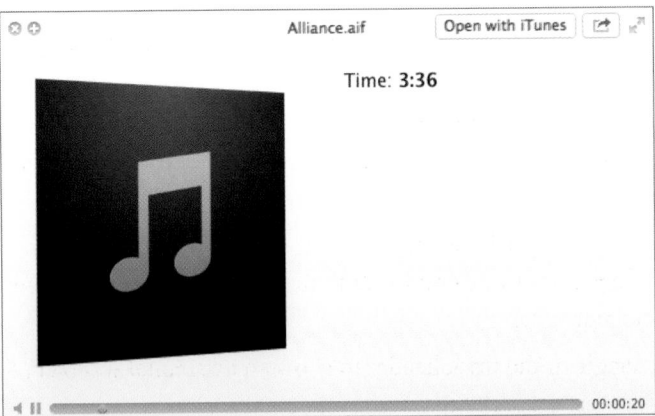

Using automation, you have taken your song to a new level, adjusting the volume and adding EQ automation to vocoded vocals to change their sounds in different sections. You have drawn offline automation on the track, and recorded live automation using both the mouse and a control surface. Let your imagination run wild, and try to think of other applications to automate your own projects.

Lesson Review

1. How can you create a control point on the automation curve?
2. How can you create a control point away from the automation curve?
3. How can you quickly adjust the value of a parameter for a given section of a track?
4. How can you trim an automation curve?
5. How can you create control points that snap to the grid?
6. What differentiates Touch mode from Latch mode?
7. How can you view multiple automation curves on the same track?
8. How do you assign a controller knob to Automation Quick Access?
9. How do you determine which parameter the knob assigned to Automation Quick Access controls?

Answers

1. Click the automation curve.
2. Double-click the automation track using the Pointer tool.
3. Use the Marquee tool to select the desired section, and drag the selected automation curve up or down.
4. Place the mouse pointer on the numerical display in the track header and drag vertically.
5. In Automation preferences, adjust the Snap Offset. Choose "Snap Automation to Absolute Values," and double-click the automation track to insert control points on the grid.
6. After you drag a parameter in Touch mode, when you release the mouse button, the parameter returns to the previous value on the automation curve; in Latch mode, the value remains at the current value.
7. Click the disclosure triangle in the track header to show an additional subtrack, then click the + (plus sign) in the subtrack to create another subtrack.

8. In the Automation preferences, turn on Automation Quick Access. An alert asks you to assign a controller knob. Click Assign, and turn the knob of your choice up and down to assign it.

9. Automation Quick Access always controls the parameter displayed in the Automation Parameter pop-up menu on the selected track header.

Keyboard Shortcuts

Tracks

A	Shows or hides automation tracks in the Tracks area
Control-Z	Automatically zooms vertically on the selected track

Windows

Option-A	Opens the Automation preferences window

Various

Command-B	Opens the Bounce dialog
Command-Tab	Goes to the next application
Command-Option-H	Hides all other applications

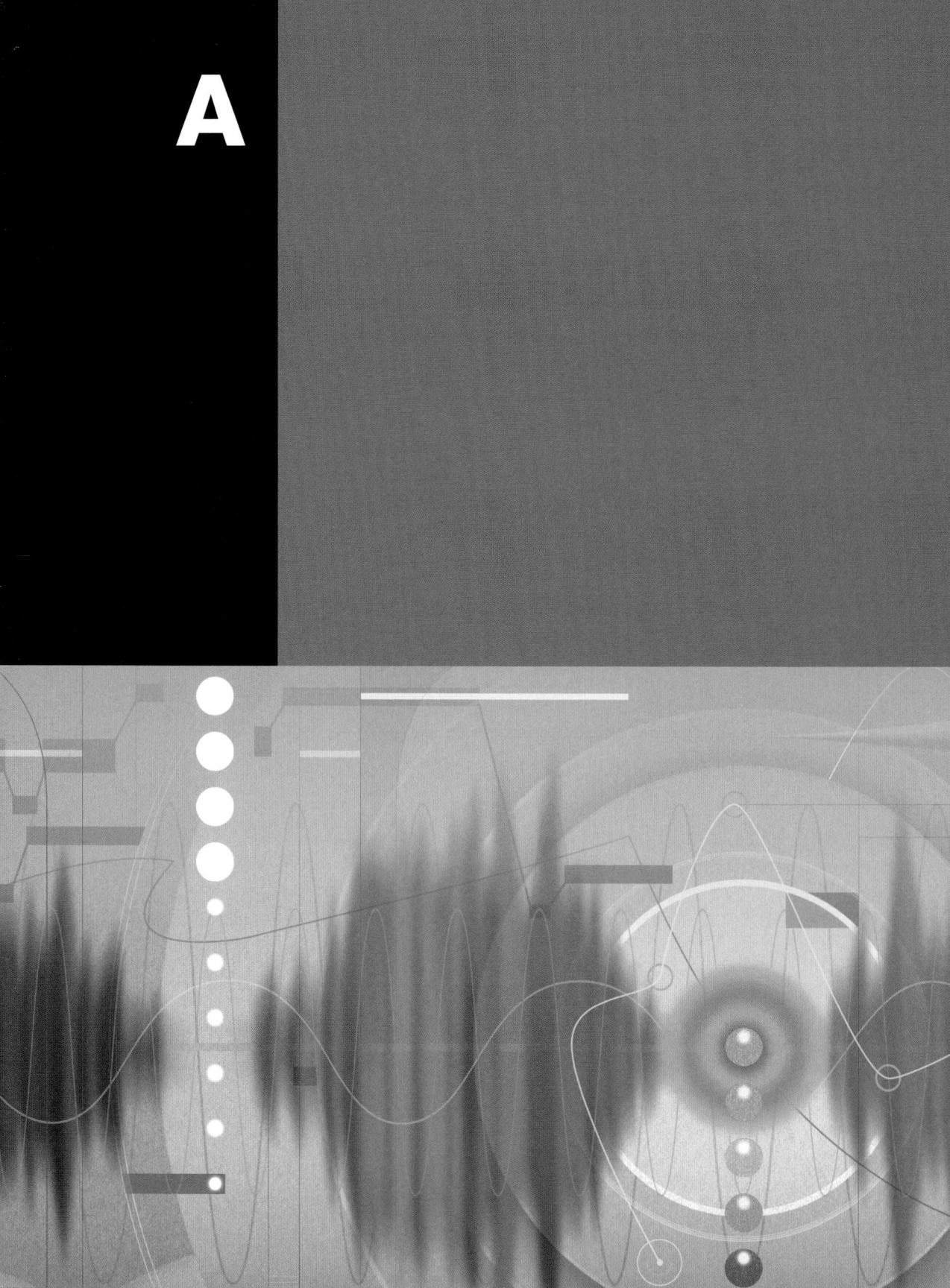

A

Appendix **A**
Using External MIDI Devices

Although Logic includes a wide array of software instruments and supports third-party Audio Units software instruments, you may sometimes want to use Logic to trigger a hardware synthesizer or sampler, or even a software instrument in another software application.

In the following exercises, you will set up hardware instruments to access them from Logic, first using the External Instrument plug-in on a software instrument track, then using external MIDI tracks to route MIDI events to a MIDI instrument outside of Logic. You can then record on external MIDI tracks using the same recording techniques you use with software instrument tracks. An external MIDI track can be routed to a hardware MIDI device or to any MIDI-compatible application available on your computer or network.

Using the External Instrument Plug-in

When you want to quickly access an external MIDI instrument, you can use the External Instrument plug-in, which allows you to treat the external device as a software instrument plug-in.

The External Instrument plug-in is inserted in the Instrument slot of a software instrument channel strip. It routes the MIDI data coming from the track to an external MIDI destination you choose in the plug-in, and routes the incoming audio data from the device back to the software instrument channel strip's Instrument slot. The audio data can be processed by audio effect plug-ins in the Audio FX section and routed to a destination in the Logic mixer.

In the following exercise, you'll use the External Instrument plug-in to route MIDI notes to an external synthesizer, and route the audio from the synthesizer back to the Logic Mixer.

1 Choose File > New. In the New Tracks dialog, choose Software Instrument, and click Create.

2 On the Inst 1 channel strip in the Inspector, click the Instrument slot, and choose External Instrument.

A stereo External Instrument plug-in window opens. The MIDI Destination determines where Logic routes the MIDI events from the track; they can be routed to a synthesizer or sampler connected to your Mac with a USB cable, or the MIDI Out port number of a USB MIDI interface. In the latter case, make sure that the MIDI Out port is connected to the MIDI In port on the synthesizer.

3 In the External Instrument plug-in, select the MIDI Destination.

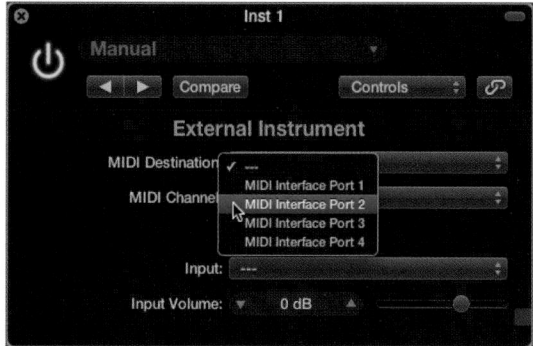

NOTE ▶ By default, the External Instrument plug-in routes the MIDI events to all MIDI channels. If you need to send a specific channel, you can choose one from the MIDI Channel pop-up menu.

To route the audio from the external synthesizer, you need to connect a cable from its audio outputs (two audio outputs for a stereo synthesizer) to instrument audio inputs on your audio interface. You can then select those audio inputs in the External Instrument plug-in.

4   From the Input pop-up menu, choose the audio interface inputs to which you've connected your synth.

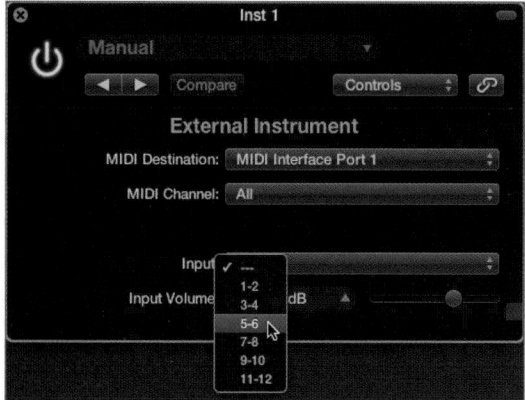

In Logic Pro X, any incoming MIDI data is routed to the record-enabled track in the Tracks area. That data (or, upon playback, MIDI data contained in MIDI regions on the track) is passed on to the External Instrument plug-in, which routes it to the selected MIDI Destination. As the MIDI events reach your synth, they trigger the synth's sound to produce an audio signal. That audio signal is routed back to the External Instrument plug-in and can be processed and routed by the channel strip as with any software instrument.

NOTE ▶ Some synthesizers have a built-in audio interface. To use the synth's audio interface, select the synth as an Input Device in Logic Pro X > Preferences > Audio, under the Devices tab. The synth audio outputs are then available in the External Instrument's Input pop-up menu.

Configuring MIDI Hardware

Logic can identify by name any device that has been configured in Audio MIDI Setup, a Mac OS X configuration tool. Audio MIDI Setup automatically detects USB- or FireWire-connected MIDI devices on your Mac, provided that the necessary drivers are properly installed.

However, MIDI synthesizers connected to a MIDI interface are not automatically detected. You can set up those synths in Audio MIDI Setup. Once that is done, you can access them by name in Logic, so you needn't remember which device is connected to which port on the MIDI interface.

For the purposes of this exercise, we will set up two external synthesizers in Audio MIDI Setup, connected to the Mac via a USB MIDI interface.

1   Open a Finder window.

The Finder is the active application, and its name is displayed to the right of the Apple menu in the main menu bar.

2   Choose Go > Utilities (or press Command-Shift-U) to open the Utilities folder.

3   Double-click Audio MIDI Setup.

Audio MIDI Setup opens, and by default, the Audio window opens.

4   Choose Window > Show MIDI Window.

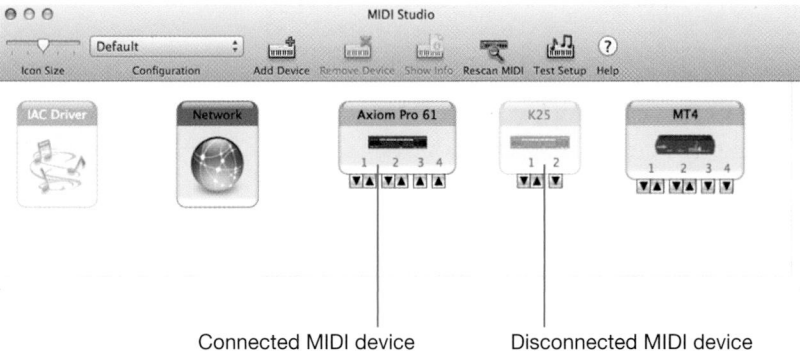

Connected MIDI device   Disconnected MIDI device

You should see an IAC Driver icon, a Network button, and icons for any MIDI devices connected directly to your computer. Devices that were previously, but not currently, connected to your Mac are represented by dimmed icon.

NOTE ▸ If a device connected to your Mac does not appear in Audio MIDI Setup, make sure that you have properly installed the most recent driver for that device.

You can double-click the Network icon to create network MIDI ports, virtual MIDI cables that allow you to connect applications over a wired or wireless network. Existing network MIDI ports are displayed in the Logic Library when an external MIDI track is selected.

You can double-click the IAC Driver icon to create Inter-Application Communication buses, virtual MIDI cables that allow you to connect applications on your computer. Existing IAC buses are displayed in the Logic Library when an external MIDI track is selected.

Let's create an icon to represent the two synths connected to the MIDI interface.

5   Click the Add Device button.

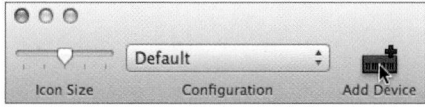

A new external device is created.

6 Click the Add Device button again.

A second new external device is created.

7 Double-click the first new device.

A Properties window appears.

8 In the Device Name field, enter *Synthesizer 1* (or an appropriate name to designate your first synth).

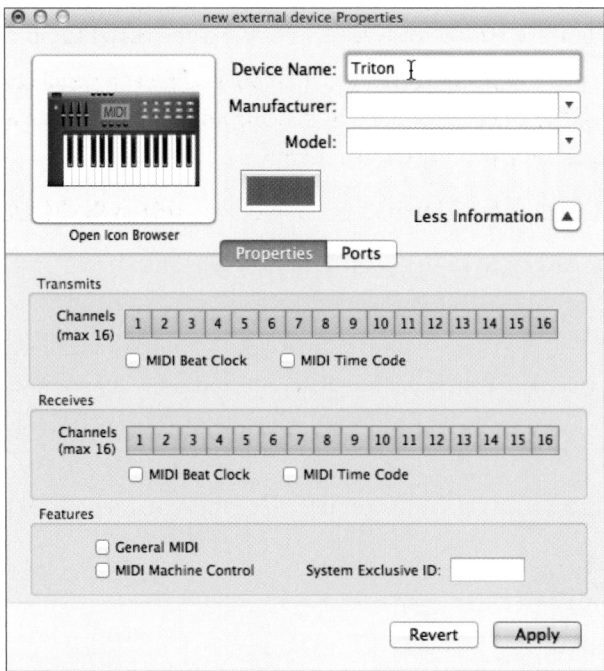

9 Click Apply to rename the device.

10 Close the Synthesizer 1 Properties window.

11 In the Audio MIDI Setup window, double-click the second device to open its Properties window.

12 In the Device Name field, enter *Synthesizer 2*.

13 Click Apply, and close the Properties window.

Now you need to identify the physical connections between the MIDI interface and the synthesizers in Audio MIDI Setup. Because Logic routes all incoming MIDI events to the record-enabled track, you need only to route outgoing MIDI events. For this exercise, let's assume you have a MIDI interface with the following physical MIDI connections:

► MIDI interface MIDI Out port 1 connects to the Synthesizer 1 MIDI In port.

► MIDI interface MIDI Out port 2 connects to the Synthesizer 2 MIDI In port.

You will now enter these connections in Audio MIDI Setup. Feel free to scroll or resize the MIDI window, and to drag the icons representing your MIDI devices to new locations to make it easier for you to connect them.

14 Click the MIDI Out port 1 of the MIDI interface, and drag the cable to the MIDI In port of Synthesizer 1.

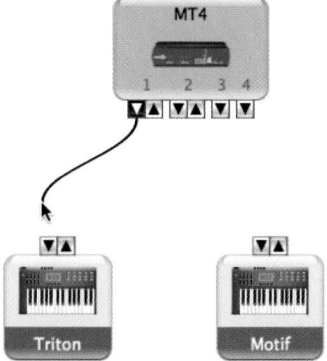

15 Click the MIDI Out port 2 of the MIDI interface, and connect it to the MIDI In port of Synthesizer 2.

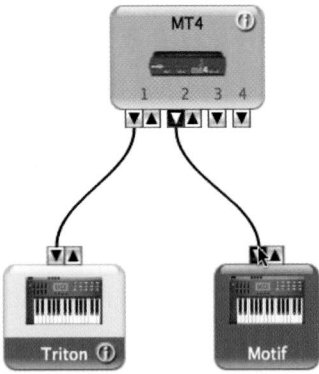

You have now connected the devices in Audio MIDI Setup.

16 Choose Audio MIDI Setup > Quit Audio MIDI Setup (or press Command-Q).

Audio MIDI Setup now knows which MIDI Out port is connected to which device, and the Logic Library will display the Synthesizer 1 and Synthesizer 2 device names you previously entered, replacing MIDI interface Port 1 and MIDI interface Port 2.

> **NOTE** ▶ If you want to record or monitor the audio outputs from the hardware synthesizers in Logic, you must also connect the synthesizers' audio outputs to audio inputs on your audio interface. In Logic, record-enable an audio track to record or monitor those audio inputs. Make sure that you have chosen the desired input number in the input slot of the I/O section on the audio track's channel strip.

Routing External MIDI Tracks

When using external MIDI tracks, you route the MIDI events on the track via the Library. All the devices set up in Audio MIDI Setup appear in the Library (including IAC buses and network MIDI ports), along with all the ReWire applications installed on your computer.

In the next exercise, you will use the Library to choose a destination for an external MIDI track.

1   Open a new Empty Project template, and in the New Tracks dialog, choose External MIDI as the Type. In the Details area, leave "Use External Instrument plug-in" dese-lected, set Output to Off, and then click Create.

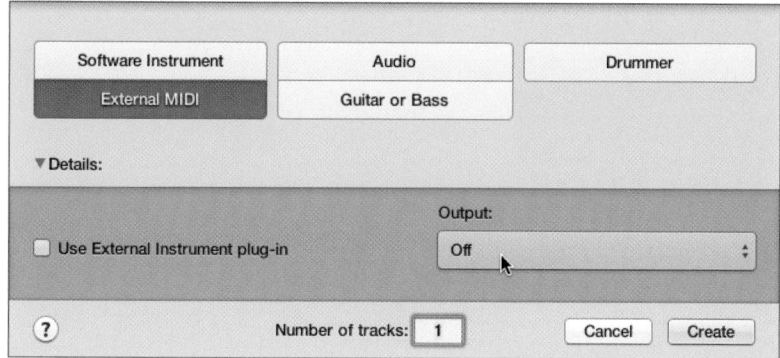

A new external MIDI track is created.

2   In the control bar, click the Library button (or press Y).

The Library displays all the available MIDI destinations for the external MIDI track. (The available destinations depend on your studio setup.)

▶   The GM (General MIDI) device is a multi-timbral instrument that always sends to all existing MIDI Out ports. A *multi-timbral* instrument is one that can respond to more than one MIDI channel at a time to play several sounds (more commonly called *patches* or *programs*) simultaneously. A single MIDI port can transmit 16 MIDI channels simultaneously, and each MIDI channel can play one program. The 16 MIDI channels of the GM device are displayed in the right column.

▶   The Synthesizer 1 and 2 you configured in Audio MIDI Setup are displayed in the list of available MIDI destinations.

▶   The MIDI output ports of any connected USB MIDI interface that aren't cabled into a device in Audio MIDI Setup.

▶   The virtual MIDI input ports of any MIDI synth or sampler connected to your Mac with a USB cable.

You will now assign the selected track to MIDI channel 1 of Synthesizer 1.

NOTE ▶ If you do not have an external MIDI synthesizer or sampler, in the next step choose GM Device instead of Synthesizer 1, then follow along with the steps, but keep in mind you won't hear any sound because no external instrument is connected.

3   In the Library, select Synthesizer 1, and in the right column, select Channel 1.

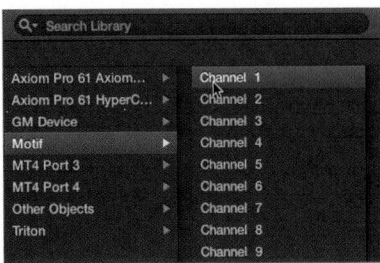

While the track is record-enabled, any incoming MIDI events will be routed to the track. The track header displays the name of the MIDI destination (Synthesizer 1), and the MIDI Channel (1).

In the Inspector, the Arrange channel strip appears, but does not look like the audio and software instrument channel strips. Because the external MIDI channel strip generates MIDI events, it does not have processing plug-in inserts or audio routing settings.

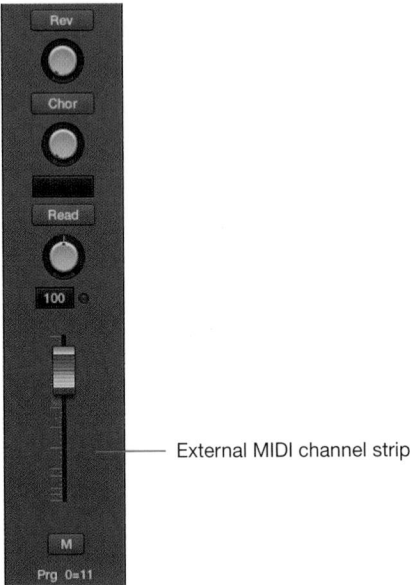

The Volume fader and the knobs on the external MIDI channel strip send MIDI continuous controller events to the external MIDI instrument. Those events allow you to remotely control the external instrument's volume, pan position, and other parameters of the program on that MIDI channel, provided that these parameters are implemented on the external MIDI instrument.

Choosing a Program Remotely

Logic allows you to remotely choose a program or patch on your external MIDI device, which avoids interrupting your Logic workflow, and also allows you to save the programs used on each track in your Logic project file.

1   On the track header, double-click the instrument icon.

The Synthesizer 1's Multi-Instrument window appears.

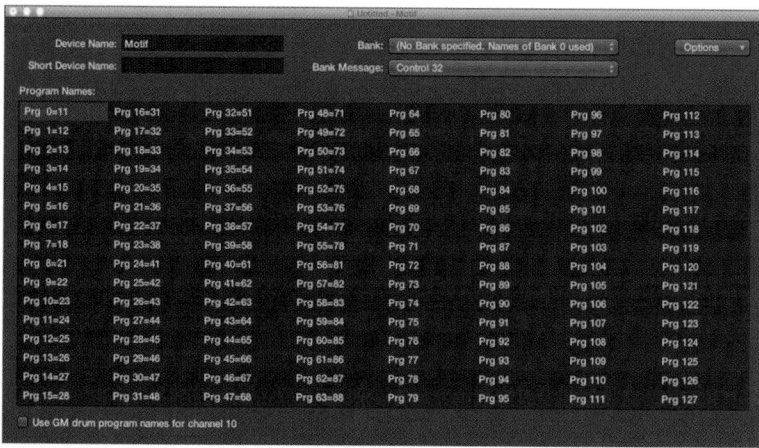

NOTE ▶ The GM Device Multi-Instrument window contains the General MIDI program names.

To transmit program change events from Logic to your synth, you need to select the Program parameter for the track.

2   Open the Track inspector, and select the Program checkbox.

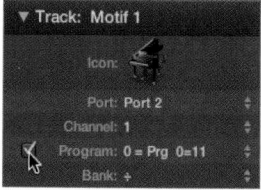

In the Tracks area, the track header displays the program number, and the corresponding program change event (program 0) is sent to your synth.

3   In the Synthesizer 1 Multi-Instrument window, click a program name.

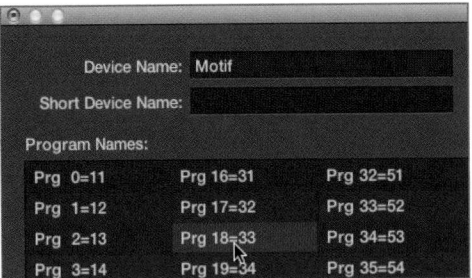

The corresponding program-change MIDI event is sent to the external MIDI instrument. (In the control bar, if you choose the custom LCD display, you can see the program-change event on the MIDI Out activity display.) When you play your MIDI keyboard, you will hear the new sound.

Most instruments have more than 128 programs. To access additional programs, you need to switch to another bank of programs.

4   Click the Bank menu, and choose 1.

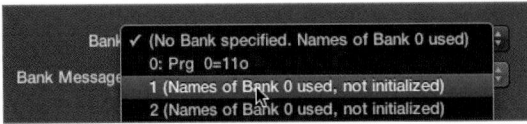

An alert message appears, asking if you want to initialize the bank.

5   Click Initialize.

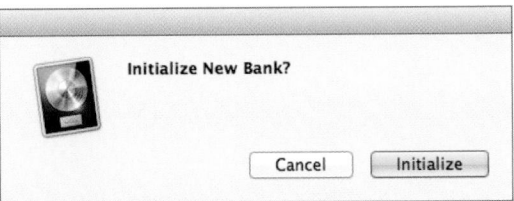

Choosing a bank from the Bank menu sends a bank select MIDI event to the external MIDI instrument that instructs it to switch to the new bank. If your instrument does not react to the bank select event, try choosing another type of bank select event for that instrument in the Bank Message menu (below the Bank menu).

You can name all the programs for your instruments and save the project as a template so that you can choose programs by name, rather than by number.

6 Double-click the first program number, type a name for the first program, and press Return.

TIP ▶ You could repeat this process until you've named all the programs in all the banks, but that could take some time! Instead, search a website devoted to Logic users for a Logic project file in which the desired hardware instruments have already been configured.

If you can't find a Logic template, look online for an electronic voice list, usually in PDF format (and sometimes part of the electronic manual, so start your search with the instrument manufacturer's website). Copy and paste the list of program names for your MIDI device into a text editor (such as Apple TextEdit) and edit it to create a list of 128 names, one per line. Copy all 128 names, and in Logic, at the upper right of the Multi-Instrument window, from the Options menu, choose Paste All Names. Repeat the process for each program bank.

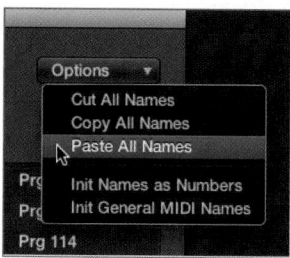

When you are done entering program names for all your instruments, you should save your work. Program names are saved in the project file, not as a general preference; so, unless you save the project, all your program names will be lost. To avoid that, let's save this project as a template.

7   Choose File > Save As Template.

A Save As dialog appears, and the location is already set to the Project Templates folder. All you need to do is name your template.

8   Name and save your template.

Your new template will be available in the Templates dialog that appears when you choose File > New from Template (or press Command-N), in the My Templates collection folder.

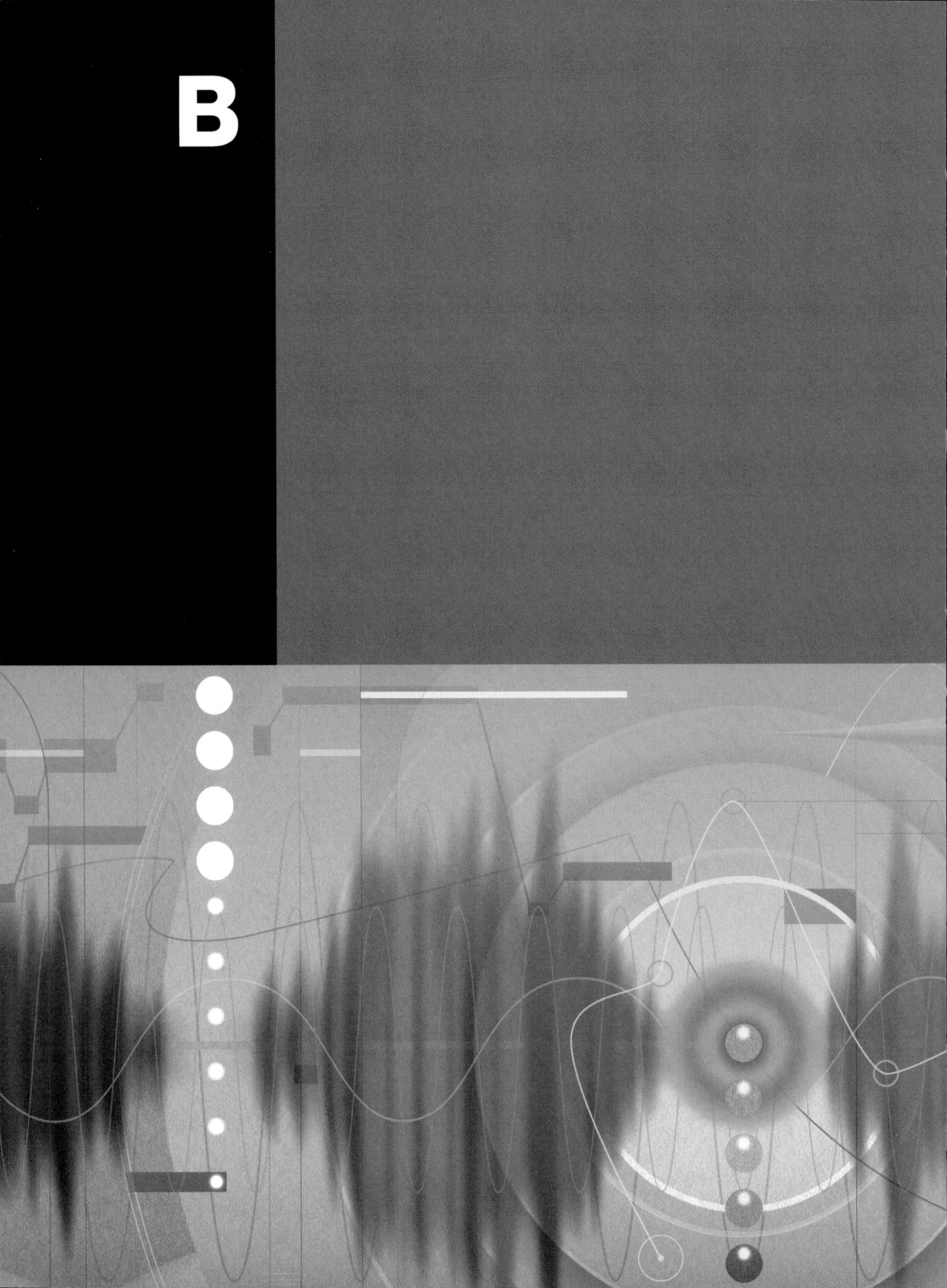

Appendix B

Keyboard Shortcuts (Default for U.S. Keyboard)

Panes and Windows

P	Shows or hides the Piano Roll
N	Shows or hides the Score Editor
I	Shows or hides the inspector
Y	Shows or hides the Library
X	Shows or hides the Mixer
O	Shows or hides the Loop Browser
E	Shows or hides the Editors area
F	Shows or hides the Browsers area
B	Shows or hides the Smart Controls
G	Shows or hides the global tracks
V	Shows or hides all the plug-in windows
T	Shows Tool menu at the mouse pointer position, or hides Tool menu and assigns the Pointer tool to the Left-click tool
Tab	Cycles key focus forward through open panes
Shift-Tab	Cycles key focus backward through open panes
Option-K	Opens Key Commands window

Command-Shift-N	Opens a new file without opening the Templates dialog
Command-Option-W	Closes the current project
Command-Y	Shows or hides the MIDI Draw area
Command-2	Opens a Mixer window
Command-4	Opens a Piano Roll window
Command-K	Opens or closes the Musical Typing window
Command-Option-K	Opens the Step Input keyboard
Number keys (on alphanumerical keypad)	Recalls the corresponding screenset
Option-A	Opens Automation preferences

Navigation and Playback

Spacebar	Plays or stops project
Shift-Spacebar	Starts playback at the beginning of the selected region(s)
Control-Spacebar	Plays or stops selection (in browsers and editors)
, (comma)	Rewinds one bar
. (period)	Forwards one bar
Return	Returns to beginning of project
U	Sets rounded locators to match the selected regions or events, or the marquee selection
Command-U	Sets the locators to match the selected regions or events, or the marquee selection
C	Toggles Cycle mode on and off
R	Starts recording
Command-Control-Option-P	Toggles Autopunch mode

Command-click lower half of ruler	Toggles Autopunch mode
Control-S	Toggles the Solo mode

Zooming

Control-Option-drag	Zooms in on the dragged area
Option-drag by clicking the background of an area	Zooms in on the dragged area
Z	Expands the selection to fill workspace, or goes back to previous zoom level, and shows all regions when no regions are selected
Control-Z	Automatically zooms vertically on the selected track
Command-Left Arrow	Zooms out horizontally
Command-Right Arrow	Zooms in horizontally
Command-Up Arrow	Zooms out vertically
Command-Down Arrow	Zooms in vertically

Channel Strip, Track, and Region Operations

S	Solos or unsolos the selected track
Control-Option-Command-S	Unsolos all soloed tracks
M	Mutes or unmutes the selected track
Control-M	Mutes or unmutes the selected regions or marquee selection
A	Shows or hides automation tracks in the Tracks area
Command-F	Shows or hides Flex editing tools
Command-Option-N	Opens New Tracks dialog
Command-Option-S	Creates a new software instrument track

Command-Shift-D	Creates a Track Stack for the selected tracks
L	Toggles Loop parameter on and off for the selected region(s)
Command-A	Selects all
Command-B	Bounces the project
Command-S	Saves the project
Control-Shift-drag over an audio region border with the Pointer tool	Adds a fade
Option-click with the Fade tool	Removes a fade
Drag, and while dragging press and hold down Control	Disables snapping
Drag, and while dragging press and hold down Control-Shift	Disables snapping with increased placement precision
Command-R	Repeats selected regions or events
Command-J	Renders the selected regions and their fades into a single new audio region
Option-Command-T	Opens the "Adjust Tempo using Beat Detection" dialog
Control-B	Bounces selected regions onto a new track
Control-Command-Z	Inserts an empty section between the locators
Control-Command-X	Cuts the section between the locators
Control-X	Opens the Strip Silence window
Command-Z	Undoes the last action
Shift-Command-Z	Redoes the last action

Project Audio Browser

Shift-U   Selects unused audio files

Piano Roll Editor

Left Arrow   Selects the note to the left of the selected note

Right Arrow   Selects the note to the right of the selected note

Option-Up Arrow   Transposes the selected note up one semitone

Option-Down Arrow   Transposes the selected note down one semitone

Shift-Option-Up Arrow   Transposes the selected note up one octave

Shift-Option-Down Arrow   Transposes the selected note down one octave

Finder

Command-D   Selects Desktop from Where pop-up menu in
                                    Save dialog

Command-H   Hides current application

Option-Command-H   Hides all other applications

Command-Tab   Cycles forward through open applications

Shift-Command-Tab   Cycles backward through open applications

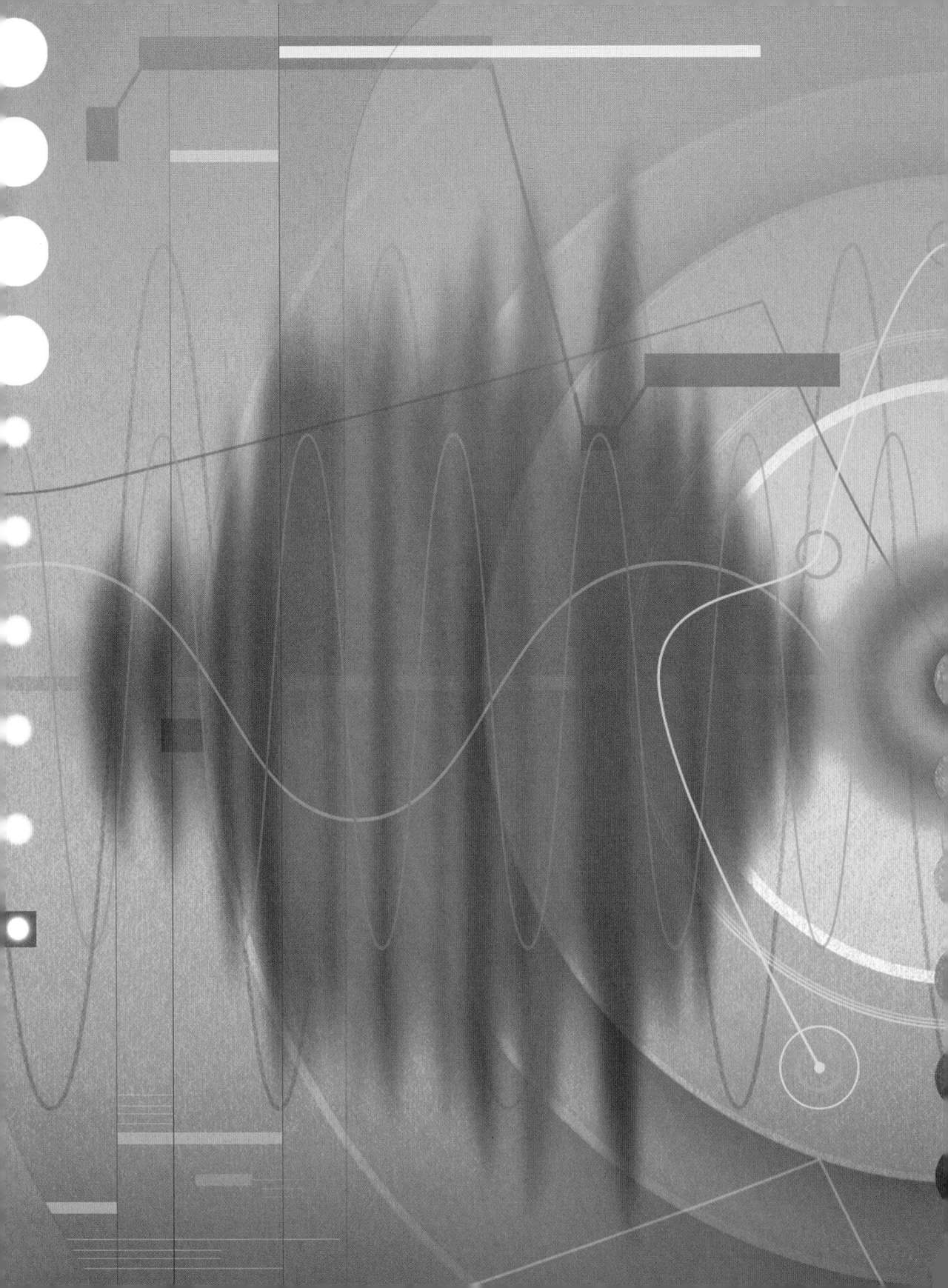

Glossary

AAC A digital coding standard used to compress audio files and distribute them over the Internet

aftertouch MIDI data type generated by additional pressure on keys after they have been struck. Aftertouch is also known as *pressure*.

AIFF (Audio Interchange File Format) A cross-platform file format supported by a large number of digital video and audio editing applications. AIFF audio can use a variety of bit depths, but the two most common are 16- and 24-bit.

alias A region in the workspace that mirrors a MIDI region somewhere else. You cannot edit an alias, only a real region, but any change to a region will be reflected in its aliases. To create an alias, Shift-Option-drag the original MIDI region to a new location.

anchor A temporal reference point, or the point that Logic Pro uses to snap a region to the workspace's time grid. In the Project Audio Browser and Audio File Editor, the anchor is represented by a small triangle under the starting point of a region.

Apple Loops An audio file format containing recurring rhythmic musical elements or elements suitable for repetition. Apple Loops have embedded metadata that allow Logic to make them automatically match the project's key and tempo. They also have tags that allow you to locate files in the Loop Browser by instrument, genre, or mood.

arming Enabling a track to be recorded

Arrangement track A global track in which arrangement markers can be used to move or copy sections of the region arrangement in the workspace

audio file Any digital audio recording stored on your hard disk. The default storage format for audio files in Logic Pro is AIFF, but you can also record audio files in the CAF and WAVE (BWF) formats.

Audio File Editor An editor in Logic Pro in which stereo or mono audio files are destructively cut, reversed, shortened, changed in gain, and processed in a number of other ways. The Audio File Editor allows sample-accurate editing of an audio file.

audio interface A device that provides audio inputs and outputs to your computer

audio region An area of an audio file registered in the Project Audio Browser for use in the project. It can be placed on audio tracks in the workspace, just as a MIDI region can be placed on software instrument or external MIDI tracks. Audio regions are pointers to portions of audio files.

audio track A track in the Tracks area used for the playback, recording, and editing of audio regions

automation The ability to record, edit, and replay the movements of knobs, sliders, and switches, including volume faders and pan, EQ, and aux send controls

Automation Quick Access A Logic Pro feature that assigns a slider or knob on your hardware MIDI controller keyboard to input track automation data

aux An auxiliary channel strip, either mono or stereo, in the Mixer

B

bar A measure of music, containing a specified number of beats, that establishes the rhythmic structure of the composition

bit depth The resolution (the number of 0s and 1s) of a digital audio sample that influences the dynamic range of a digital audio recording

bounce To combine several tracks of audio into one file

bus A virtual audio cable to route audio between channel strips, for processing or submixing tasks

bypass To temporarily turn off a plug-in

C

Catch A mode that continuously updates the contents of a window to show the position of the playhead. The Catch button shows a playhead.

CD Audio Abbreviation for Compact Disc–Audio; the standard for stereo music CDs uses a 44.1 kHz sampling rate and 16-bit resolution.

channel A discrete path used to transport a signal

channel strip A virtual representation of a channel strip on a mixing console. Each channel strip can contain a number of controls, such as Solo and Mute buttons, a Volume fader, a Pan/Balance knob, Input or Instrument slot, Output slot, Send slots, and MIDI FX and Audio FX slots.

channel strip setting A combination of the plug-ins inserted on a channel strip and their settings that define a sound

clip To feed too much signal through a channel, producing audible distortion. Channel strips have a clip detector.

continuous control number (cc#) The number assigned by the MIDI specification to the MIDI events that are used to control parameters such as volume or pan.

control bar An area at the top of the main window that includes buttons to control Logic playback and recording functions. Several buttons (Record, Pause, Play, Stop, Rewind, Forward) work much like the control buttons on a music player.

control point A position in MIDI Draw and automation tracks (identified by a dot) where data manipulation begins or ends

Core Audio The standardized audio driver for a computer running OS X 10.2 or higher. It allows the connection of all audio interfaces that are Core Audio compatible.

Core MIDI The standardized MIDI driver for a computer running OS X 10.2 or higher. It allows the connection of all MIDI devices that are Core MIDI compatible.

cross-fade To raise the volume of one audio file while simultaneously lowering the volume of another file in a smooth transition

Cycle mode A mode in which you can endlessly repeat a section of a project. To turn Cycle mode on and off, click the Cycle button in the control bar, or click the cycle area in the upper half of the ruler. The left and right locators define the beginning and end positions of the cycle area.

D

dB Abbreviation for *decibels*, a measurement that relates the relative change in the volume of an audio signal

dBFS Short for *decibels Full Scale*, a measurement that measures the volume of a digital audio signal

digital audio workstation (DAW) An electronic system that records, mixes, and produces audio files, such as a Mac running Logic Pro X

driver A software program that allows your computer to communicate with other hardware

E

editor A software interface that helps you manipulate the audio or MIDI data contained in regions on the workspace. The primary MIDI editors are the Piano Roll, the Step and Score Editors, and the Event List. You can edit audio regions in the workspace, Project Audio Browser, and Audio Track and Audio File Editors.

event A MIDI message. The main events are note, control-change, pitch bend, and aftertouch events. MIDI events can be edited in a number of ways.

Event List A list of events and regions that provide access to all recorded event data. Thus, you can directly manipulate events and regions and make precise alterations.

F

fader Generally, a volume control on channel strips.

Fade tool One of the tools in the Tracks area Tool menu that creates a cross-fade when you drag across a section where two audio regions meet. You can also drag the tool over the beginning or end of a region to create a fade-in or fade-out, respectively.

Flex editing A Logic Pro X editing technique that allows you to automatically detect individual notes in an audio region, and precisely adjust each note's pitch, position, and length

folder A container in the Logic Pro workspace for MIDI regions, audio regions, or other folders

General MIDI (GM) A specification designed to increase compatibility between MIDI devices. A musical sequence generated by a GM instrument should trigger similar sounds on any other GM synthesizer or sound module.

G

grid Vertical lines used to map the positions of bars, beats, and divisions (such as sixteenth notes) in various editors

groove track A chosen track in the Tracks area in which timing can be used to influence the timing of other tracks

Hand tool A tool that appears when you click and hold an event or region with the Pointer tool. It is used to move regions or events in the editors.

H

headroom The available dynamic range before clipping or distortion occurs

help tag A small text window that appears when you click-hold an element such as a region or MIDI note and displays that element's position, length, or other information

Insert slot A slot on channel strips in which you can insert a plug-in

I

Inspector The pane at the left edge of the Tracks area containing the Region and Track inspectors, the channel strip of the selected track, and one of the channel strips in its signal flow (usually the output or an aux channel strip)

I/O buffer size The amount of data that the computer buffers at one time when working with audio. Larger buffers ease the burden on your CPU, providing more processing power for plug-ins, but also increase latency when monitoring record-enabled tracks. The buffer size is set in the Devices tab of the Audio preferences.

key command An instruction to Logic Pro that triggers an action, communicated by pressing a key or a combination of keys. Most of the Logic Pro main functions can be activated by key commands.

K

L

latency The delay between, for example, playing your keyboard and hearing the sound. One factor contributing to latency is the I/O buffer size.

Library A pane of the main window that can be opened to the left of the Inspector in which you can open or save your own patches and settings

locators The two positions defining the edges of the cycle area. The locators are displayed in the control bar's custom LCD display, directly to the right of the playhead position.

Logic Remote A free iPad app that functions as a control surface for Logic Pro

loop A region parameter allowing a region to repeat

M

main window The primary working area of Logic. It includes the Tracks area and can incorporate other panes.

marker Used for indicating sections of your project

Marquee tool A crosshair-shaped tool in the Tracks area with which you can select and edit regions or portions of regions

menu bar The bar extending along the top of the computer screen or the top of a window or pane that shows menus and mode buttons

metronome In Logic, a component that produces a sound concurrent with the beat. It can be set with a button in the control bar.

MIDI (Musical Instrument Digital Interface) An industry-standard protocol that enables devices such as synthesizers and computers to communicate. It defines a musical note's key number, and velocity, among other characteristics.

MIDI channel A discrete path for MIDI data. MIDI data flows through MIDI ports in channels, and up to 16 MIDI channels can pass through each port simultaneously.

MIDI Draw A function that lets you create and edit MIDI CC automation in a region by graphically inserting a set of control points, which are automatically connected

MIDI Plug-Ins Plug-ins that can manipulate MIDI data coming from MIDI regions or your MIDI keyboard before the MIDI events reach a software instrument plug-in

MIDI region Data container for MIDI events, shown in the workspace on software instrument or external MIDI tracks. MIDI regions do not contain sounds, but rather contain MIDI events that tell a synthesizer how to produce sounds.

Mixer A virtual mixing console used to display all channel strips used in a project that mirrors the number and order of tracks in the Tracks area. In the Mixer, you can also change a channel strip's volume or panorama (pan) position, insert DSP effects, or mute and solo channel strips.

mixing The process of shaping the overall sound of a project by adjusting the volume levels and pan positions, adding EQ and other effects, and using automation to dynamically alter aspects of the project.

MP3 A digital coding standard used to compress audio files to reduce file size.

multi-timbral Describes an instrument that can use several MIDI channels simultaneously to trigger the timbres of multiple instruments/programs

Musical Typing An interface that allows you to use your computer keyboard as a MIDI controller keyboard

mute To silence a region or the output of a channel strip

Mute tool A tool that stops a region or event from playing when you click with it

nondestructive Said of an audio editor that does not change the source audio files in the course of editing

N

output channel strip Channel strip type in the Mixer that controls the output level and balance for the physical stereo output of your audio interface

O

P

patch one or several channel strip settings that can be recalled and saved in the Library

PCM (Pulse-code modulated audio) Uncompressed digital audio data that may be included in AIFF, WAV, and CAF format files

Pencil tool A tool used to draw various types of information in an editor

Piano Roll Editor It displays note events as horizontal beams. Events can be cut, copied, moved, and resized in a similar fashion to regions in the workspace.

playhead A vertical line with a triangle at the top, located in the Tracks area and in other horizontal time-based editors, that indicates where you are in a project. In play mode, a project usually begins playback from the playhead position. You can position the playhead with the mouse by clicking the lower half of the ruler.

plug-in A small software application that adds functions to a main program. Logic Pro plug-ins include audio effects, MIDI effects, and software instruments.

Pointer tool The default selection tool, shaped like an arrow. It is in the tool-box of every pane and window.

preferences Parameters that affect the behavior of Logic and are applied independently of the currently open project

programs Synthesizer sounds

Project Audio Files Browser A tab in the browsers area, used to manage the audio files used in your project

punch in, punch out A technique that allows you to interrupt playback and record audio as the project is playing. It can be automated in Logic Pro.

Q

quantize To correct the positions of notes so that they conform to a specific time grid

R

region A rectangular beam that represents a container for audio or MIDI data and is found on tracks in the workspace. There are different types: audio regions, MIDI regions, folders, and take folders.

Region inspector A pane at the top of the Inspector, used to nondestructively set the individual regions' playback parameters, including quantization, loop, and fades. These parameters do not alter the audio file. Rather, they affect how the audio regions referencing the audio file are played.

Replace mode An operating state that you can activate in the control bar. In Replace mode, newly recorded content takes the place of the previously recorded content.

ruler The timeline that runs the length of the project, organized into bars, beats, and even finer divisions. It contains the playhead, the cycle, and autopunch areas. It is also displayed at the top of the Tracks area, Piano Roll Editor, Step Editor, and Score Editor.

S

sample accurate Describes editors (such as the Audio File Editor or Tracks area) that display samples or allow you to edit individual samples in an audio region

sample rate The number of times per second an analog audio signal is sampled when converted to digital. When audio comes into an audio interface, analog-to-digital (A/D) converters sample the signal's voltage level. Typical sample rates used in music production are 44.1 kHz (44,100 samples per second) and 48 kHz.

Score Editor A MIDI editor that displays notes in standard Western musical notation

screenset An onscreen layout of windows that you can save. Each screenset retains the position, size, and zoom settings of a layout.

scrubbing Moving the pointer back and forth (in a scrubbing motion) while playing an audio region to locate a specific section

send An output on an audio channel that sends a controlled amount of a channel's sound through a bus to another audio channel strip

SMPTE (Society of Motion Picture and Television Engineers) Refers to both the professional organization, and the synchronization system it developed that divides time into hours, minutes, seconds, frames, and subframes

software instrument The software counterpart to a hardware sampler or synthesizer module, or an acoustic sound source such as a drum kit or guitar. The sounds generated by software instruments are calculated by the computer CPU and played via the audio interface outputs. Often called *soft synths* or *soft samplers*.

solo A way to temporarily allow you to play one or more tracks, events, or regions without playing others that aren't soloed

Solo tool A tool that enables you to independently listen to selected regions (click and hold a region to do so)

standard MIDI file A common file type that almost any MIDI sequencer can read. In Logic Pro, you can export selected MIDI regions as standard MIDI files.

step-input To record notes one step at a time in a MIDI region

synthesizer A hardware or software device used to generate sounds

T

tempo The speed at which a piece of music is played, measured in beats per minute. You can create and edit tempo changes in the Tempo track.

Tempo track A track in which you can view and edit all the tempo changes of a project. The track displays tempo changes as tempo control points and allows you to create a tempo curve between two tempo control points.

Text tool A tool for naming regions in the workspace

time signature Two numerals separated by a slash that appear in the default LCD display in the control bar. The most common time signature is 4/4. The first number denotes the number of beats in a bar, or measure. The second number denotes a unit of time for each beat. For a 4/4 signature, each bar has four beats, and each beat is one quarter note long.

time stretch To change the length of an audio region (and the audio data inside the region) without changing its pitch. You can use Flex editing to time stretch audio regions.

toolbar The toolbar can be opened below the control bar. It contains a number of buttons for key functions. You may freely customize the toolbar to meet your needs.

Tool menus Available in the menu bar of a pane or window, the Tool menus contain tools for editing, zooming, cropping, and otherwise manipulating items in the window.

track A lane in the Tracks area that contains a collection of MIDI or audio regions that can be played. Each track specifies a destination to which the data will go.

Tracks area The main area of the main window; it is made of the Tracks area menu bar, the ruler, the track headers, and the workspace.

track automation Used for programming control changes that are not necessarily tied to a specific region, such as a volume fade or a filter cutoff sweep. The track automation system allows you to quickly find and automate plug-in parameters. It has its own recording modes, which function independently of the other recording features in Logic Pro.

track header In the Tracks area, the header located to the left of a track lane, which can display track name, track color bars, track number, and buttons such as Track Mute and Track Solo

Track inspector A pane located below the Region inspector in the Inspector, used to set track parameters, including Flex mode and Key Limit

Track Stack A collection of tracks that can be collapsed as a group. The main track of a folder stack can control basic volume, mute, and solo functions of the group of tracks, while a summing stack submixes its subtracks onto its main track, allowing you to use audio effect plug-ins to process the submix.

velocity The speed at which a MIDI note is struck. In most instruments, velocity information is used to determine the volume of an individual note.

V

virtual instrument see: software instrument

WAV, WAVE An audio file format primarily used by Windows-compatible computers. In Logic Pro, all recorded and bounced WAV files are in Broadcast Wave Format (BWF).

W

waveform A visual representation of a sound

workspace The primary working space of Logic, where audio and MIDI regions are edited and moved to create a project. The workspace is in the Tracks area, below the ruler, and to the right of the track headers.

Z

zoom An action that enlarges (zooms in on) or reduces (zooms out from) a viewing area in any window

Zoom tool A tool that enables you to zoom in on any part of the display. Pressing Option-Control while selecting a part of the window section enlarges the area.

Index

Differentiate yourself.
Get Apple Certified.

Stand out from the crowd. Differentiate yourself and gain recognition for your expertise by earning Apple Certified Pro status to validate your Logic Pro X skills.

This book prepares you to pass the Apple Certified Pro – Logic Pro X exam, and earn Apple Certified Pro – Logic Pro X status. The exam is available at Apple Authorized Training Centers (AATCs) worldwide. Earning this certification verifies knowledge of Logic Pro X core functionality, including the ability to record, edit, mix and output audio projects with Logic Pro X.

Three Steps to Certification

1 Choose your certification path.
   More info: training.apple.com/certification.

2 All Apple Authorized Training Centers (AATCs) offer all OS X and Pro Apps exams, even if they don't offer the corresponding course. To find the closest AATC, please visit training.apple.com/locations.

3 Register for and take your exam(s).

"Apple certification places you in a unique class of professionals. It not only shows that you care enough about what you do to go the extra mile to get certified, it also demonstrates that you really know your stuff."

— Brian Sheehan, Multimedia Studio Manager,
MFS Investment Management

Reasons to Become an Apple Certified Pro

- **Raise your earning potential.** Studies show that certified professionals can earn more than their non-certified peers.

- **Distinguish yourself from others in your industry.** Proven mastery of an application helps you stand out from the crowd.

- **Display your Apple Certification logo.** Each certification provides a logo to display on business cards, resumes and websites.

- **Publicize your certifications.** Publish your certifications on the Apple Certified Professionals Registry (apple.com//certification/verify) to connect with schools, clients and employers.

Training Options

Apple's comprehensive curriculum addresses your needs, whether you're an IT or creative professional, educator, or student. Hands-on training is available through a worldwide network of Apple Authorized Training Centers (AATCs). Self-paced study is available through the Apple Pro Training Series books, which are also accessible as eBooks via the iBooks app. Video training and video training apps are also available for select titles. Visit training.apple.com to view all your learning options.

televisormusic.com

THE BETA MACHINE

WW.THEBETAMACHINE.COM